WILD
ALASKA

*The Complete Guide to Parks, Preserves,
Wildlife Refuges, & Other Public Lands*

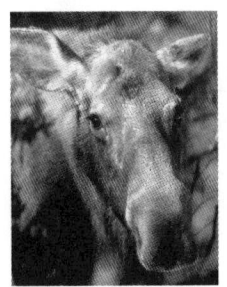

WILD ALASKA

~

The Complete Guide to Parks, Preserves, Wildlife Refuges, & Other Public Lands

Nancy Lange Simmerman

Revised by Tricia Brown

Second Edition

THE
MOUNTAINEERS

Published by
The Mountaineers
1001 SW Klickitat Way, Suite 201
Seattle, WA 98134

First edition (originally titled *Alaska's Parklands: The Complete Guide*): first printing June 1983, revised March 1991. Second edition: first printing May 1999.

Published simultaneously in Great Britain by Cordee, 3a DeMontfort Street, Leicester, England, LE1 7HD

Manufactured in the United States of America

Edited by Christine Clifton-Thornton
Maps by Jacquilyn Weber
Cover design by Jennifer Shontz
Book design and layout by Michelle Taverniti
Cover photograph: *Nooya Lake at Misty Fiords National Monument*, © Nancy Simmerman
Half-title page: *Moose*   USFWS photo
Frontispiece: *Backpacking in Chugach State Park*   ASP photo
Title page: *Dall sheep*   ASP photo

Library of Congress Cataloging-in-Publication Data
Simmerman, Nancy.
   Wild Alaska : the complete guide to parks, preserves, wildlife
refuges, and other public lands / Nancy Lange Simmerman; edited by
Tricia Brown. — 2nd ed.
      p. cm.
   Rev. ed. of: Alaska's parklands, the complete guide. 1991.
   Includes index.
   ISBN 0-89886-583-2
   1. Alaska Guidebooks. 2. Parks—Alaska Guidebooks. 3. Outdoor
recreation—Alaska Guidebooks. 4. Natural history—Alaska
Guidebooks. 5. Historic sites—Alaska Guidebooks. I. Simmerman,
Nancy. Alaska's parklands, the complete guide. II. Title.
   F902.3 .S583 1999
   917.9804'51—dc21
                        99-6429
                          CIP

Contents

MAP LEGEND

═══③═══	Highway or Road, with State Route Number
▬▬▬▬▬	Road Open Only to Vehicles with Permits
==========	Unimproved Road or Tracked-Vehicle Trail
··················	Trail
— · — · ·	Park, Refuge, National Forest, etc. Boundary
— · · — · ·	Political Boundary
▬■▬■▬■▬	Railroad
∿∿∿∿	National Wild River
⌐WW2┬FWA┐	River with White-Water or Flat-Water Rating Between Bars
▨▨▨	Body of Water
•	City or Village
[C]	Access Point
▲	Shelter or Cabin

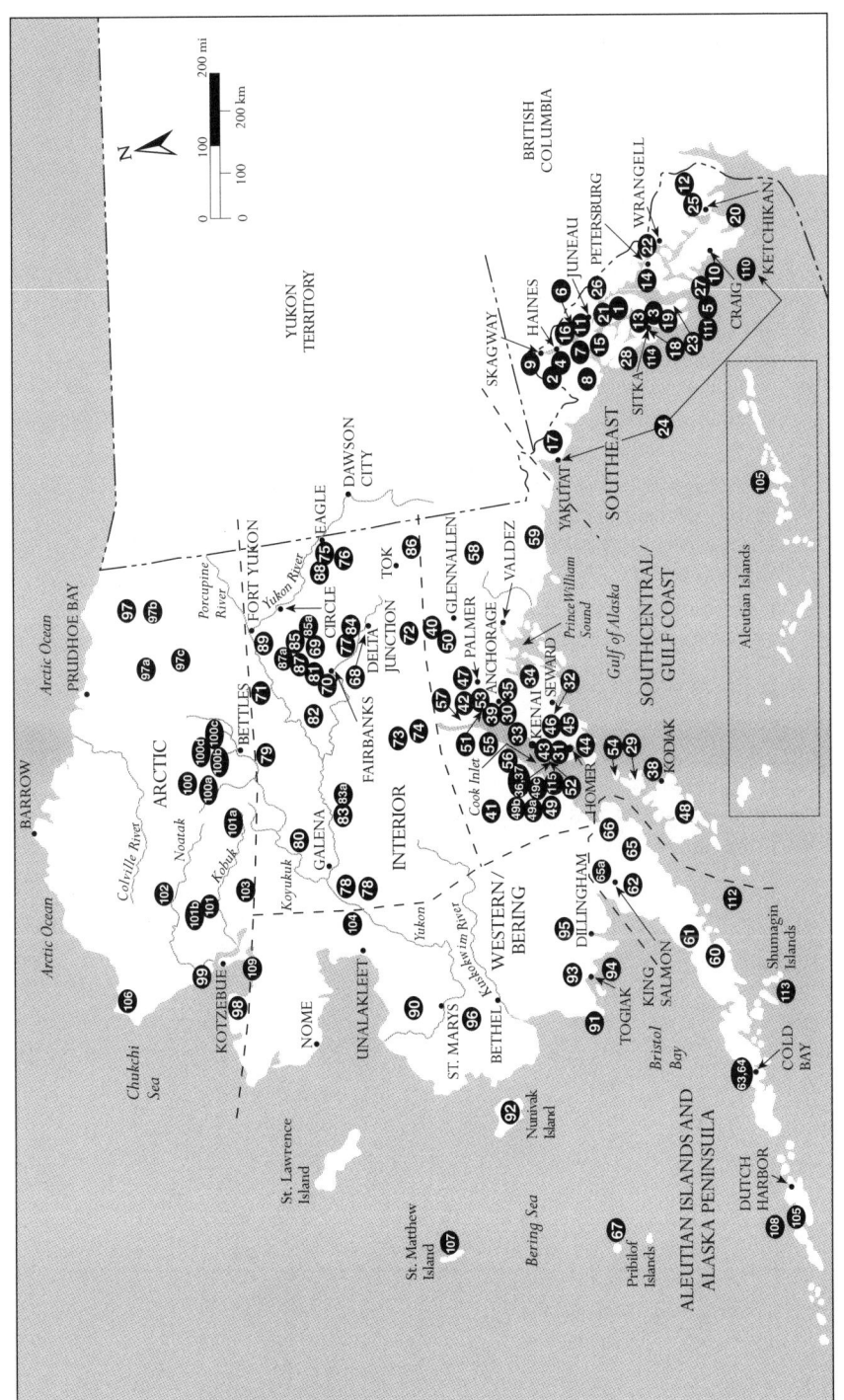

Locations of Alaska's parklands.

Appendix 303

Index 347

A thundering waterfall empties into Terror Bay on Kodiak Island.   USFWS photo

Foreword

In December 1980, some nine years after Congress set the scene by passage of the Alaska Native Claims Settlement Act, it completed action on, and the President signed, the long-debated Alaska National Interest Lands Conservation Act.

The Alaska Lands Act, as most of us call it, profoundly affected the future of Alaska. It set aside over 104 million* acres of the 49th state as parks, refuges, monuments, and wild and scenic river areas. It created over 43 million acres of new parks—designating 32.4 million of those acres as Wilderness. Overall, the act created 13 major additions to the federal national park system and designated 56 million acres of Alaska as Wilderness.

The bill was controversial, and residents of the other 48 states joined Alaskans in a spirited debate over the future of the "Last Frontier." While passage of the bill did not please all Alaskans, it established the "rules of the game," which allowed us to get on with the task of preserving and developing our great expanses.

This book is one of the first of what will likely be many volumes devoted to describing the scenic wonders of the new national conservation areas. It describes the areas' locations, climates, physical descriptions, means of access, available activities, sights to see, and precautions to be taken in what, in many cases, are wild, untrammeled locales.

Now that America has taken steps to preserve the integrity of these areas for eternity, it is only fitting that Americans view the scenic wonders protected inside the boundaries of the conservation areas.

The splendor which is Alaska can be shared by all, not confined as the exclusive domain of the wealthy or learned. This book starts the process of increasing awareness and appreciation of the beauty and solitude preserved in the conservation areas.

This is an important and worthy undertaking—something that will benefit all Alaskans—in fact, all Americans—for decades to come.

Jay Hammond
Governor 1975–1982

*The figure is constantly changing as lands are surveyed, boundaries stabilized, and state and private lands transferred.

Preface to the First Edition

"Will it be Fairbanks or Istanbul?" I threw the two teaching contracts onto the table and stomped into the sweltering Ohio summer. The decision had to be made quickly. College graduation had been the previous week and, with the impatience of youth, I didn't know what to do with the rest of my life.

The problem resolved itself. The contract to teach chemistry and physics in Turkey was for three years, the contract with the chemistry department at the University of Alaska for only one. I wasn't ready to commit myself any more than necessary, so Alaska it was.

In the year of Alaska's statehood, 1959, with a loaded station wagon and a six-week-old puppy for company, I drove north to my future.

With such scenic beauty everywhere, classrooms and laboratories quickly became restrictive, and I turned to outdoor photography for an excuse to roam the mountains and seashores. I crewed on sailboats plying the waters of the Inside Passage and Prince William Sound, kayaked the coast of Katmai National Park, and wandered the Valley of Ten Thousand Smokes. I guided visiting hikers in the Noatak National Preserve, studied animals along the trans-Alaska pipeline, traveled by dogsled in Denali National Park, and skied through the Brooks Range, sleeping in holes in the snow.

Important and far-reaching changes have come to Alaska's wilderness over the years. In the past we could wander, fish, and hunt at will, largely unrestricted. With the transfer of large amounts of land by the state to private individuals and by the federal government to Alaska Natives, and with much land made into parks and refuges, boundaries and regulations proliferated. Longtime Alaskans became perplexed by the new regulations and grumbled about the lack of traditional freedoms, while newcomers faced a complicated wilderness with no signs, boundary markers, or fences to identify rivers, mountain peaks, or private property.

As confused as everyone else, I began to dig for information. I spent innumerable hours talking with land management personnel and reading a six-foot-high stack of reports. Little had been published about a large number of Alaska's wild places. Finally a book about the state's vast and far-ranging public lands began to take shape.

If this book helps you to appreciate this unique state and travel in it, my efforts will have been worthwhile. The likes of Alaska's colorful history, spectacular scenery, and bountiful wildlife cannot be found anywhere else on earth.

N. L. S., Girdwood, 1983

Preface to the Second Edition

My brother-in-law is a gold miner in the Interior who, as it turns out, looks and sounds like a gold miner ought. He has a deep, gravelly voice, a broad back, and, of course, a coppery beard that tends to collect a few crumbs at mealtime. Visitors are fascinated by the sight of a "real" miner and inevitably ask if he's lived in Alaska all his life. He loves the question because he gets to tease them with his response: "Not yet." (As in, I'm not dead yet!)

His answer stands for many who came up around the days of the trans-Alaska pipeline construction, as much of my family did. Looking for jobs, hearing of the adventure, a wave of new pioneers came for a year... and we stayed. I arrived in Alaska one year after the pipeline start-up, in 1978, during a tumultuous period in which President Jimmy Carter was making friends and enemies with the same stroke of his pen. It all had to do with his plan to add millions of acres to the jurisdiction of federal agencies, to protect them as refuges, parks, wilderness areas, monuments, wild rivers, and sanctuaries. In 1980 President Carter made it official when he signed the Alaska National Interest Lands Conservation Act.

The first edition of this book was published in the early years following that move, when land managers, cartographers, biologists, environmentalists, sportsmen, villagers, and the like were scrambling simply to redefine legal use of certain lands, where boundaries existed, what restrictions would be in place, and when. In many instances, people became "citizens" of a park by virtue of having one created around them. They're called "in-holders." Which trails would stand the test of grandfather's rights? Which land manager had jurisdiction when somebody needed quick answers? It was a confusing time that surely no one—no matter on which side of the conservation fence you stood—would want to live through again.

Through these last twenty years, the first edition of *Wild Alaska*, titled *Alaska's Parklands*, has consistently served well, not only as a research tool for travelers and recreationists, but also for hunters, trappers, fishermen, and miners. With this second edition we seek to make it even more useful. This edition includes a reorganization of the state and federal parklands into regional sections, updates on acreage and access, changes in status, and even more information on activities, flora, and fauna.

The importance of researching a place before traveling there cannot be overemphasized. We hope this book will continue to meet that need, whether you're visiting Alaska for the first time or, as I have, you've come to call it home.

T. B., Anchorage, 1999

Acknowledgments

The publication of this book would not have been possible without the valuable assistance of more than 100 staff members associated with the Alaska Department of Fish and Game, the Alaska Division of Parks, the Bureau of Land Management, the National Park Service, the U.S. Fish and Wildlife Service, and the U.S. Forest Service, who helped find obscure information and who read each description for accuracy.

Special thanks are due James C. Allen of the Alaska Department of Environmental Conservation and James A. Wilkerson, M.D., for reviewing the sections on water pollution and treatment; Ron Costello, air taxi operator, for reviewing the section on air taxis; the late Tom Ellis, mountain rescue and emergency medicine instructor, for reviewing the sections on hypothermia, cold-water drowning, and frostbite; Douglas S. Fesler, Alaska Division of Parks, and Edward R. LaChapelle, professor of geophysics and atmospheric sciences, University of Washington, for reviewing the section on avalanches; Louisa Nishitani, fisheries biologist, University of Washington, for reviewing the section on paralytic shellfish poisoning; and James Wise of the Alaska State Climate Center, Environment and Natural Resources Institute, University of Alaska, for his assistance in locating weather records.

Very special thanks are due Betsy Bayes Preis, who helped type the manuscript and unflinchingly met all deadlines, to Alice Copp Smith and Ann Cleeland for their skillful editing of these pages, and to Donna DeShazo for supervising the production of the book.

For assistance with updates in the 1999 edition, additional thanks go to Barbara Mays, U.S. Customs-Anchorage; Claire Holland, ADP-Kodiak; Mark Ross, Alaska Department of Fish and Game-Fairbanks; Lisa Shon Jodwalis, APLIC-Fairbanks; Anna Plager, ADP-Fairbanks; Pete Panarese, ADP-Anchorage; Sean Smith, Tanadgusix Corp.; Chris Smith, APLIC-Anchorage; Roger Delaney and Dan Gullickson, BLM-Fairbanks; Dennis Heikes, ADP-Mat-Su; Fulvia Coster, Recreational Equipment Inc., Anchorage; Jill Fredston of the Alaska Mountain Safety Center, Anchorage; Richard Baranow, Alaska Mountaineering and Hiking, Anchorage; Mike Goodwin, ADP-Glennallen; Brenda Eliason, AMNWR-Homer; Tim Hazelwood, USFS; Brad Hunter, USFS; and Shawn Stephensen, USFWS-Anchorage.

Introduction

Alaska is a big land, with rivers, lakes, and mountains to match. Its portion of the mighty Yukon River winds for 1400 miles (2300 km). Its largest lake, Iliamna, has a surface area of 1000 square miles (2600 square kilometers). It boasts North America's highest peak, 20,320-foot (6194-m) Mount McKinley. Its largest glacier, the Malaspina, is 50 percent larger than the state of Delaware. Its coastline is longer than those of all the other U.S. maritime states put together.

Across a map of this vast state, a bewildering array of national and state parks, monuments, preserves, refuges, forests, and rivers interlock like pieces of an unfinished jigsaw puzzle. This book describes all of these areas, which we'll call "parklands," and provides information about their recreational use, history, geography, wildlife, weather, facilities, and access.

Part I of the book is a guide to getting around in Alaska, from the highway and state ferry systems to accessing the most remote wilderness. There are sections on camping, backpacking, boating, village life in the Bush, Alaska's abundant wild foods, weather, and observing wildlife. Part II consists of individual descriptions of the parklands, illustrated with photos and arranged by region: Southeast, Southcentral/Gulf Coast, Aleutian Islands and Alaska Peninsula, Interior, Western/Bering Sea Coast, Arctic, and Maritime National Wildlife Refuge, and additional areas of interest.

The Appendix contains a list of selected readings, as well as useful information to help you plan your trip: locations of public campgrounds, addresses and phone numbers of land managers, information sources, access and services for each village, uses of each parkland, and booklets you can write for.

If you've never traveled in Alaska before, you'll find it an exciting experience. Basic backpacking skills will stand you in good stead. Beyond these, this book will help you learn about the things unique to Alaska: how to cope with its wildlife, from mosquitoes to bears; how to keep warm in the snow; why many Alaskans think winter is the best season; where you'll find the world's largest concentration of brown (grizzly) bears; which wilderness rivers are seldom visited.

Whether you are a well-traveled Alaskan exploring further afield, a new resident just learning about your adopted state, or a visitor from the Lower 48 or another country experiencing Alaska for the first time, you can use this book to decide where to go and how to get there.

A Note About Safety

Safety is an important concern in all outdoor activities. No guidebook can alert you to every hazard or anticipate the limitations of every reader. Therefore, the descriptions of wilderness areas, roads, trails, routes, and natural features in this book are not representations that a particular place or excursion will be safe for your party. When you follow any of the routes described in this book, you assume responsibility for your own safety. Under normal conditions, such excursions require the usual attention to traffic, road and trail conditions, weather, terrain, the capabilities of your party, and other factors. A trip that is safe in good weather or for a highly conditioned, properly equipped traveler may be completely unsafe for someone else or unsafe under adverse weather conditions. Keeping informed about current conditions and exercising common sense are the keys to a safe, enjoyable outing. —*The Mountaineers*

Bear tracks in the sand   USFS photo

PART I
Travel in Alaska

Getting Around

Automobile Travel. Most of Alaska's parklands are far from the road system or have only minimal road access, but dozens of areas accessible by automobile, including some uncrowded wilderness areas, are described in this book. Relative to its size, Alaska contains very few miles of public highway, and most of them are concentrated near the major population centers. Some roads, however, notably the Dalton Highway, traverse isolated wild lands. Since roads and highways are occasionally closed by break-up (that springtime phenomenon of slush and knee-deep mud), weather conditions, floods, or avalanches, check with the Alaska Department of Transportation or the State Troopers for current information (phone numbers in Information Sources, Appendix).

Although major highways are paved, many of the state's most interesting road miles are not. Good-quality, relatively new tires are recommended for all highways, with an extra spare tire for extensive traveling on gravel back roads. Always carry plenty of fuel, extra engine oil, transmission and brake fluid, extra fan belts, a good jack, a tow chain, a basic tool set, battery jumper cables, road flares, wire, rags, and a flashlight with strong batteries. If you are likely to encounter snow, ice, or low temperatures, be sure your car is protected with adequate antifreeze, lightweight transmission fluid, battery blanket, and proper lubrication. An engine block heater is advisable in deep cold. It warms the engine oil and eases starting. (An electrical plug sticking out of a vehicle grill is evidence of a block heater, and is used to "plug in" a car when it will be parked in below-zero temperatures.) An extension cord is a necessary accessory. Use studded snow tires and carry tire chains, a shovel that can move large quantities of snow, a bag of sand, sawdust, or cat litter for emergency traction, a windshield scraper, sleeping bags or blankets for all passengers, extra warm clothing, matches, a small stove and a saucepan for melting snow, and a supply of high-calorie food that can be eaten cold, such as nuts, cookies, or fruitcake. To start a fire in an emergency without matches, move the automobile's battery a safe distance from the vehicle and touch the ends of the cables together to produce a spark, letting it fall on a gasoline-dampened rag.

Services on Alaska highways are limited and often scattered. Major repairs and parts are not usually available in remote areas and small towns, so have your vehicle thoroughly serviced and checked before beginning a trip. Sanitary dump stations for

17

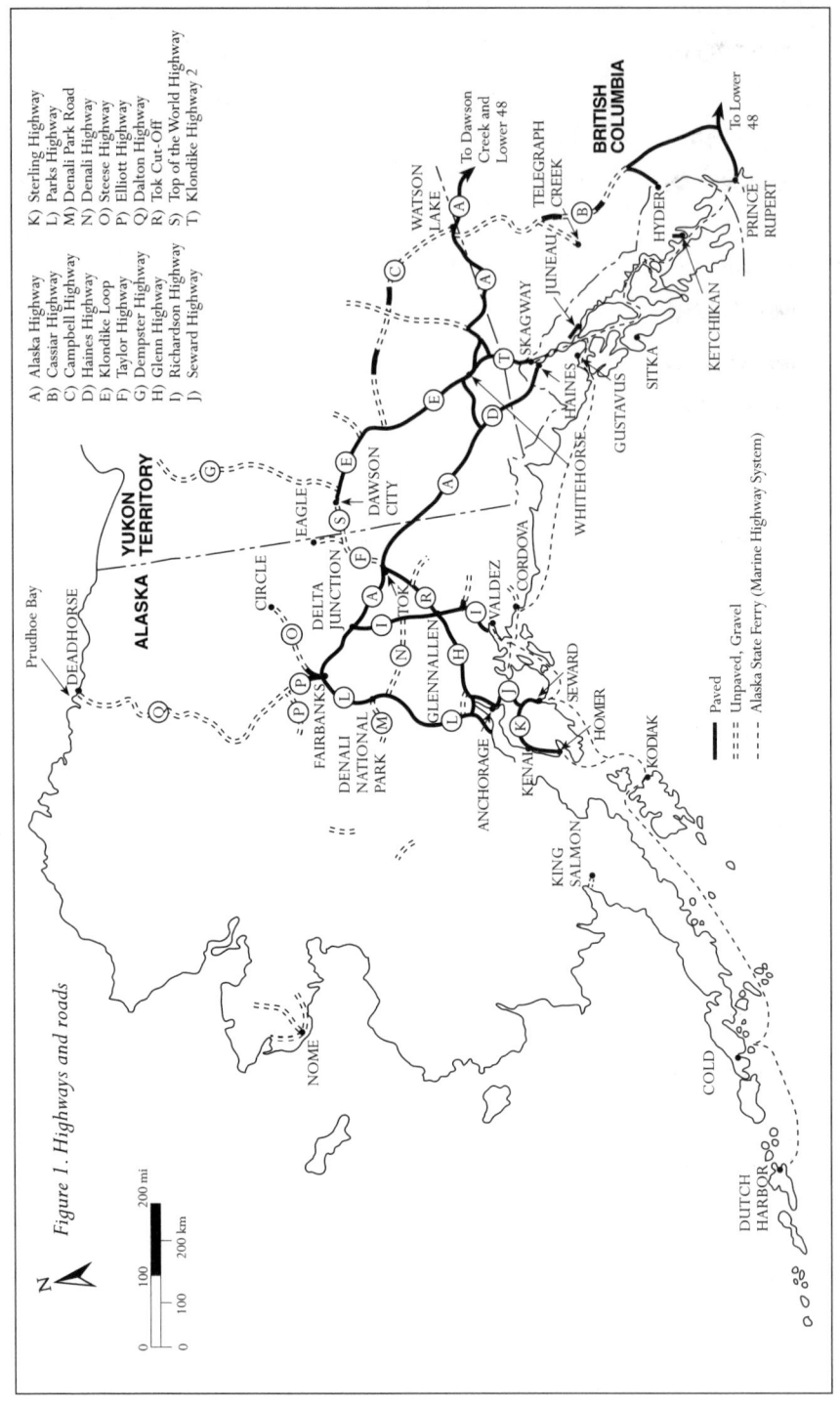

Figure 1. Highwways and roads

A) Alaska Highway
B) Cassiar Highway
C) Campbell Highway
D) Haines Highway
E) Klondike Loop
F) Taylor Highway
G) Dempster Highway
H) Glenn Highway
I) Richardson Highway
J) Seward Highway
K) Sterling Highway
L) Parks Highway
M) Denali Park Road
N) Denali Highway
O) Steese Highway
P) Elliott Highway
Q) Dalton Highway
R) Tok Cut-Off
S) Top of the World Highway
T) Klondike Highway 2

Paved
Unpaved, Gravel
Alaska State Ferry (Marine Highway System)

Biking and camping is a typical summer activity, even on Alaska's limited road system.   ASP photo

recreational vehicles are found in major cities but are virtually nonexistent elsewhere. It is illegal to dump holding tanks at unauthorized locations.

All road travelers should have *The Milepost* (Alaskan Publications, address in Appendix, Information Sources). This mile-by-mile guide, the most comprehensive available, is revised annually.

Rental automobiles are available in most Alaska cities and often in Bush towns and villages. Depending on the season, in many outlying communities, snowmobiles or all-terrain vehicles (ATVs) replace cars. See Table 1 in the Appendix for towns having cars, snowmobiles, or off-road vehicles for rent. Firms in Anchorage, Fairbanks, and Haines rent motorhomes.

Guided Tours and Sightseeing Packages. Many of the parklands can be visited as part of a tour. A wide range of services exist, from luxury cruise ships that ply the Inside Passage to bus tours that travel the Alaska Highway, from posh wilderness lodges to wilderness sailing charters and strenuous backpacking trips. Many guide services will also custom-design a wilderness trip for you. Table 2: Parklands—Access, Special Interests, and Recreational Use, Appendix, shows popular parklands that are visited by commercial tours or guided trips. A list of tour companies, guide services, and wilderness lodges is updated annually in the Alaska Division of Tourism's free publication, "Alaska Vacation Planner." The Division's address and Internet home page is in Information Sources, Appendix; or consult any of the visitors' centers listed there.

Public Transportation. Considering the distances and the logistics involved, Alaska has a fairly good public transportation network of commercial bus lines, ferries, railroads, and airlines. To reach areas not readily accessible by scheduled public transportation, air taxis (Alaska's term for chartered small planes) and charter boats are readily

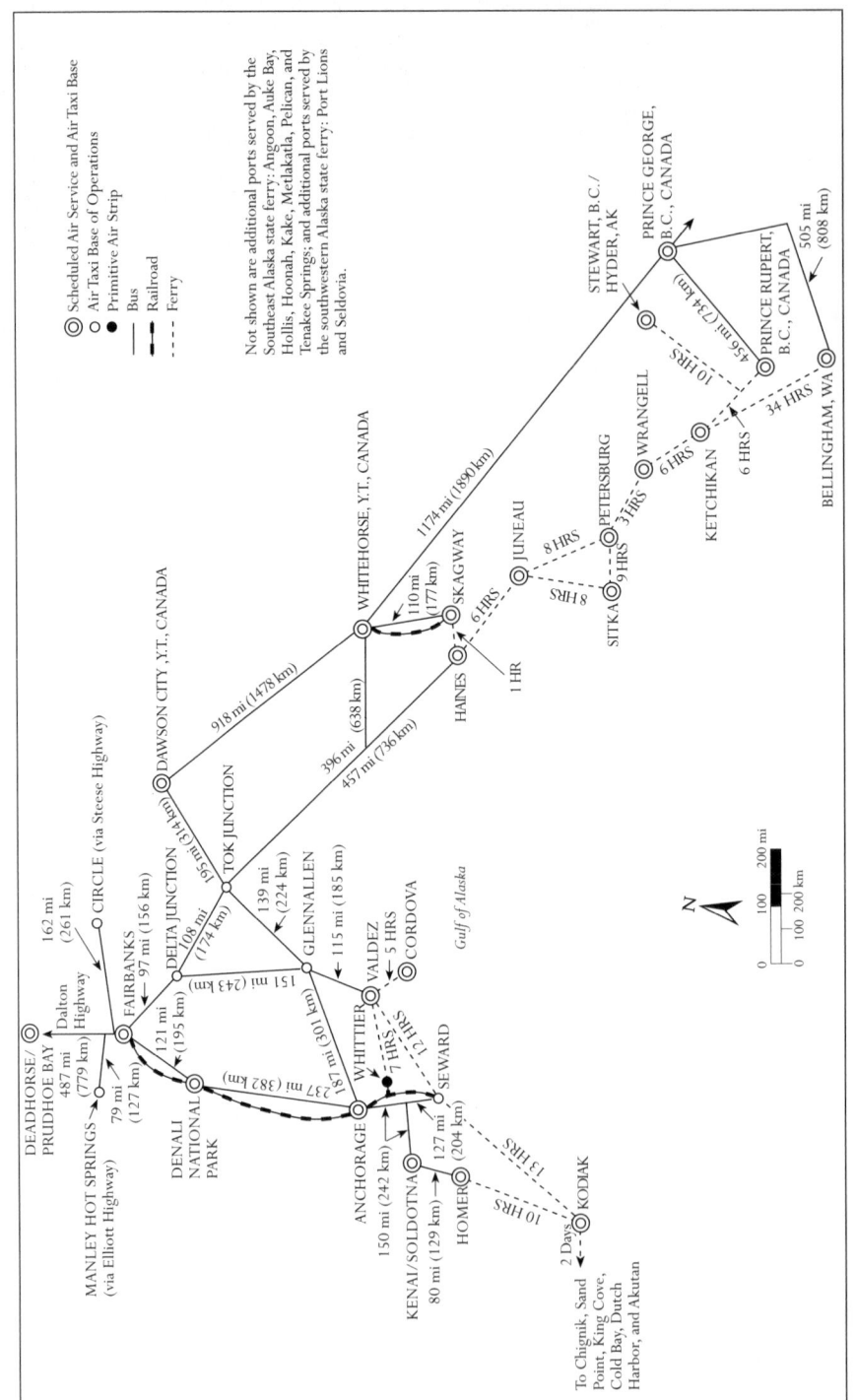

Figure 2. Public transportation

Campers boarding their boat at Glacier Spit   ASP photo by Robert Angell

available. "Alaska Vacation Planner" contains a list of land, air, and water carriers. See Figure 2 for an idea of how all these transportation forms tie together.

Buses. Most major highways, including the Alaska Highway, which officially runs from Dawson Creek, B.C., to Fairbanks, are traveled by commercial bus lines. See Tables 1 and 2, Appendix, for communities and parklands accessible by bus. In Information Sources, the Appendix lists bus lines serving Alaska and the Alaska Highway. Some of the larger communities have local city bus service, and most have taxicabs.

State ferries. The Alaska Marine Highway System (AMHS) consists of two separate units that service Southeast Alaska and Southcentral/Southwest Alaska, which are linked in summer months by monthly sailings of the M/V *Kennicott*, the newest ferry in the state's fleet. The Southeast system serves Panhandle cities and communities from Haines and Skagway south through the Inside Passage to Prince Rupert, British Columbia, and on to Bellingham, Washington; the Southcentral/Southwest system serves Cordova and Valdez west to Kodiak, Cold Bay, and Unalaska/Dutch Harbor.

Most passengers are walk-on, but many board with their cars, recreational vehicles, bicycles, or even kayaks. Any vehicle that may be legally taken on a state highway can be transported on the ferries. A limited number of staterooms are available for overnight travelers, but many passengers choose to sleep in the reclining salon chairs, while others throw sleeping bags on deck at night. Passengers may not sleep in vehicles on the car deck. Reservations are necessary for all travelers and vehicles. The AMHS toll-free number and Internet home page are listed in the Appendix.

Railroads. Two railroads operate in Alaska, the White Pass & Yukon Route in the Southeast, and the Alaska Railroad, which connects the Interior city of Fairbanks with the Southcentral communities of Anchorage, Portage, Whittier, and Seward.

The Alaska Railroad offers express service between Anchorage and Fairbanks, with a stop at Denali National Park. Additionally, tour operators such as Gray Line of Alaska and Princess Tours attach their own specialty railcars to the Alaska Railroad train in the summer months. The railroad also operates daily for trips south from Anchorage to Portage, Whittier, and Seward. Winter service is limited. Check with the Alaska Railroad for schedules and fees. (See Information Sources, Appendix.)

On the Whittier shuttle, also run by the Alaska Railroad, both passengers and vehicles are carried between Portage, on the Seward Highway, and Whittier, a state ferry port and deep-water harbor on Prince William Sound. Until recently, the two communities had no highway link. The shuttle operates daily in the summer and several days a week during the off season. It makes a number of round trips between Portage and Whittier on days of operation, but begins and ends the day in Anchorage for passenger convenience.

Although vehicles with confirmed state ferry reservations are given boarding priority on runs connecting with ferry departures, space is not guaranteed. Travelers are encouraged to take an earlier train and explore Whittier until ferry boarding time.

The White Pass & Yukon Route was built in 1898 to transport gold seekers en route to the Klondike gold fields. Today the railroad carries travelers over historic White Pass and operates summers between Skagway, Alaska, and Fraser, British Columbia. Motorcoach service connects with Whitehorse, Y. T. The White Pass & Yukon Route also operates a shuttle between Lake Bennett and Fraser for Chilkoot Trail hikers, who can hike the trail one way and then catch a train or bus to Skagway or Whitehorse.

Airlines. This is the most efficient way to get around Alaska due to the great distances involved—if the weather permits. Most major cities and towns are served by daily scheduled jetliner service. Nearly all other communities not on the road system have air service at least once a week.

Air Taxis. When the airline's schedule is inconvenient, or when you want to land on a wilderness lake or river bar, a chartered plane is the answer. For the most economical chartering, plan to travel by public transportation or automobile to a settlement that has an air taxi operation as near your destination as possible. Many villages have an agent who can arrange air taxi pickup by radio, but you will probably be charged for all air time accrued by the airplane.

Since travel by air is a way of life in the north, many Alaskans fly their own planes much as most people drive automobiles. Some are excellent and responsible pilots; some are not. If you consider traveling with a non-certified pilot, ask questions *before* you fly. Choose your pilot carefully. A list of certified air taxi operations is available from the Federal Aviation Administration, Flight Standards Division in Anchorage (address in Information Sources, Appendix).

Whenever you plan to fly by air taxi, make reservations by phone or mail as far ahead as possible. Many air taxi operators are booked months in advance during summer and autumn. Without reservations, you may have to wait several days for available time.

Even if you have reservations, be aware that weather conditions along your route may preclude your leaving on schedule. In such a case, the pilot will take you at the first

Flightseers out of Talkeetna land on Mount McKinley's Ruth Glacier.   Tricia Brown photo

break in the weather, but meanwhile he may continue transporting other clients. Arrange your personal schedule and food supply to permit several days' leeway if your pickup is delayed by weather conditions. For added safety and your peace of mind, be sure someone other than the pilot knows where you are going and when you should be back.

Most air taxi operations are quite small, often flying only one or two planes. They land on wheels, floats, skis, or a combination. When you make your reservations, ask to be sure the airplanes have the proper landing gear for your needs. A pilot operating on wheels from his home strip cannot land on a wilderness lake.

White gas and similar camping-stove fuels are not permitted on scheduled commercial airliners but can be carried on air taxi flights. If you travel part of the way by scheduled airline, check on the local availability of your specific fuel when you make air taxi reservations. Most villages have a limited supply of common fuels. Take along your own empty containers to fill from the bulk supply.

If you arrange with a pilot to pick up your party on a certain date, be ready to load at the specified location early in the morning. Better yet, camp there the night before. Air taxi pilots normally have extremely busy schedules and won't wait for you to arrive. If you miss your pickup date, the pilot will return for you later, but at his convenience, and you may be charged for all air travel time involved. Enjoy your pickup day at the specified site—plan to read, write, or take *very short* walks. If weather or mosquito conditions are unpleasant, leave the tent up, but have everything else packed.

During summers in the Arctic, air taxi pilots sometimes work, in full daylight, until midnight or later to take advantage of good flying weather. If your pilot does not arrive on the scheduled day, double-check your calculations to be sure you haven't missed a day, then relax. Weather conditions at his end could prevent his arrival for several days or even a week or more in some areas.

Bush pilots are some of the most colorful and responsible people you'll ever meet. They have incredible logistical problems to contend with just to get fuel, parts, and periodic aircraft check-ups. Don't fret at delays. Once you put yourself in their hands, sit back, relax, and flow with their schedules.

Charter Boats. Most coastal communities have commercial charter boat operations. Where none exist, and in small inland communities along the river systems, an informal charter can often be arranged with a local boat owner. In larger coastal towns, check with the local visitor information bureau (see Information Sources, Appendix) for a Visitor Guide or recommendation for local tour operators.

Off-Road Vehicles. Many Alaskan residents, particularly in remote areas, own four-wheelers, snowmobiles, and other vehicles capable of traveling cross-country. When land-use regulations permit, you can sometimes arrange transportation to a specific area.

If you are considering using your own off-road vehicle (ORV), check the regulations for your entire route. Trail bikes, swamp buggies, snowmobiles, four-wheel-drive vehicles—in short, any motorized vehicles traveling off the road system—are classed as ORVs. Hovercraft are classed as ORVs when on land and as powerboats when on water.

For regulatory purposes, snowmobiles and other vehicles operating on snow are usually treated separately. Since they travel on a snowpack and in winter, they have far less impact on vegetation and wildlife than do off-road vehicles used in summer. Many parklands permit the recreational use of snowmobiles when snowcover is sufficient to protect the vegetation. Due to the snowmobile's conflicts with the wilderness values of skiers, snowshoers, and dog mushers, many parklands have designated certain areas closed to these vehicles and some prohibit their use altogether. However, more pro-tected land is open to them than is closed.

Off-road vehicles used in the summer affect vegetation and wildlife significantly and, for the most part, are not permitted off established roads and trails in parklands.

See Table 2, Appendix, for information on recreational use of off-road vehicles in parklands. Contact the parkland manager for more specific information. The Alaska Department of Fish and Game restricts off-road vehicle crossings of anadromous fish streams. Some areas restrict the use of snowmobiles and off-road vehicles for hunting.

Traveling on a snowmobile or an off-road vehicle? Let someone know where you are going and how long you plan to be gone. Don't go alone—two machines are safer than one. Take plenty of warm clothing, rain gear, maps, a compass, a first-aid kit, matches, signaling flares, and mosquito repellent. Don't forget repair tools and spare parts. And please, use a good muffler; the noise affects both animals and other people using the area.

A little courtesy doesn't hurt, either. Travel beside ski trails and dogsled trails, not on them. Carry out all your garbage; cover any oil or fuel spills. Avoid contaminating streams or ponds, and don't drive over especially sensitive lands where you will leave lasting scars. You will often share the same space with hikers, horseback riders, hunters, fishermen, skiers, snowshoers, and dog mushers. They appreciate your courtesy and consideration.

Snowmobiling on the Chugach State Park trails near Anchorage   ASP photo

Time Zones. For years Alaska was divided into four time zones, resulting in Juneau, the capital, operating on Pacific Standard Time while Anchorage, the business center of the state, was 2 hours later. In an attempt to improve communications between the two cities and the rest of the state, in 1983 Alaska was consolidated into two time zones. Anchorage, Fairbanks, Juneau, and most of the state operate on Alaska Standard Time, 1 hour earlier than Seattle. Only the far Aleutian Islands and St. Lawrence Island are 1 hour earlier than the rest of Alaska.

Maps. Alaska must have been a tough country to explore back in the "old days" before maps were available. The unknown—the incredible distances, the rugged coastline, the endless mountains and swift rivers—would have discouraged most of us. Today we can preview where we are going, thanks to the U.S. Geological Survey and the National Ocean Survey. Their maps are some of the best bargains to be found in these parts. Map-hounds use them for bedtime "reading" or paper the kitchen walls with them, planning next summer's trips while washing dishes.

   Don't set foot in Alaska's backcountry without a good supply of maps or charts— and know how to read them. Small boaters in Alaska should carry USGS maps as well as marine charts, since maps offer more detailed and accurate information about coastal features. For map sources, see Information Sources, Appendix.

If You're New to Alaska...

...or if you're just starting to explore this state in which you've been living, Alaska has treasures to share that you won't find elsewhere. The abundant wildlife, the rich scenery, and the uncrowded wilderness will delight you. But Mother Nature has a few other cards up her sleeve, too. With a little information and some care on your part, even high water, bad weather, and bugs can enrich your Alaskan experience.

Cameras. If you don't bring a camera to Alaska, you'll soon wish you had. The scenery, the animals, and even the people are picturesque.

Most communities have at least one store that carries film in popular sizes and types. Larger cities have camera stores and several have repair shops. But if the shop must order an item for you, expect a wait from two weeks to two months.

You'll need to protect your delicate equipment from some of Alaska's special hazards. Dust can be a severe problem on unpaved roads and on braided glacial riverbeds during windstorms. Backcountry travelers will want plenty of plastic or coated-nylon bags to protect photo gear from rain, during river crossings, or while boating. For the best protection use float bags, or put the camera and lenses into two bags, one inside the other, then roll the package into the middle of your sleeping bag and put the sleeping bag into a waterproof stuff sack or plastic garbage bag.

When you are photographing outdoors in winter, letting the camera reach air temperature is more convenient than trying to keep it warm inside a coat, where it will collect condensation. Before entering a warm building, place the cold camera and lenses in a plastic bag and seal securely. Condensation will form on the bag, not on and in the camera. When the camera reaches room temperature, it can be removed from the bag. Protection from condensation and subsequent rust is particularly important for cameras containing electronic circuitry.

Should disaster strike and your camera end up in the drink, cross your fingers and get busy. If you can, place the camera in fresh water and rush it to a repair shop. Otherwise, first aid goes something like this: If the camera is in fresh water, wind the film back into the cassette and open the camera. If the cassette is wet, put it into the film can and fill with water. (Label the can to warn the processor that the contents are submerged, or they won't appreciate your business.) Your film should be no worse for wear as long as it doesn't dry out.

Leave the camera back open, take off the lens and anything else easily removable, and let the pieces dry in the air or in a warm oven. While the camera is drying, manipulate all its functions until it is totally dry.

If the camera ends up in salt water, rinse it thoroughly in fresh water many times. A slight bit of salt water in the mechanism can do far more harm than lots of fresh water. Either dry the camera as described or keep it totally submerged in fresh water until you can get it to a repair shop. If you should drop a camera or lens into silty glacial water, bury it with a ceremony and tears. The face-powder-fine grit won't rinse out.

Gold Panning. Want to find "color"? Gold panning and other recreational mining is permitted on most public lands and in rivers classified as Wild, but private mining claims do exist within some parklands. Respect "private property" signs and be sure you are not trespassing on someone's unmarked claim. Ask locally for information, or contact the parkland manager.

Legally, holders of mining claims cannot prohibit public travel across their lands. You may not, however, collect rocks or minerals, enter private structures, or interfere with mining operations. Ask permission, if possible, before crossing a claim. For additional information, contact the Land Office of the Bureau of Land Management in Anchorage. (See Land Managers, Appendix.)

For your own safety, remember that old mines and abandoned dredges can be dangerous. Timbers on old dredges are often rotten; mine openings are subject to cave-ins; and mines often contain stagnant air that can kill you.

Firearms. Unless specifically regulated by a parkland, a municipality, or similar authority, rifles, shotguns, and handguns may be carried openly in Alaska. Concealed weapons are illegal without a permit. It is unlawful to shoot from, on, or across a highway or road. Consult specific parkland regulations concerning firearms. One of the following conditions will generally apply: Firearms must be surrendered or made inoperative upon entering the parkland (some national parks and Canada); possession of firearms is permitted, but discharge is prohibited except for self-defense (some state parks); or firearms may be openly carried and used according to safe gun-handling standards and State of Alaska laws. In Canada, handguns are prohibited by law. Contact Canadian customs for more specific information concerning other firearms.

Artifacts and Relics. Many areas of Alaska contain artifacts and relics. The unauthorized collection, theft, or destruction of these cultural resources on federal or state land is prohibited by the Antiquities Act of 1906, the Archaeological Resources Protection Act of 1979, and the Alaska Historic Preservation Act. Since these artifacts and relics, once destroyed, can never be replaced, persons caught violating the acts face heavy fines and possible imprisonment.

If you find an artifact or relic, never pick it up, remove it, or alter it. When the original position of the "find" is lost, much information is destroyed. You can provide a valuable service for Alaska if you make notes about the artifact or relic. Describe your find, make rough sketches or maps, and take photographs. Include any significant features such as hearths, arrowhead caches, and log construction. Describe the location of the find, with latitude and longitude, if possible. Submit all data to the Bureau of Land Management, Alaska State Office Archaeologist in Anchorage, who will enter the information on BLM inventory forms. The information will also be entered in the State of Alaska's centralized data bank for cultural resources.

Icebergs and Glaciers. Mother Nature's ability as a sculptor is at its finest when she carves icebergs. Life-size white, shimmering castles with turrets, delicate spires, and blue walls with windows for peeping through entice people to climb on the bergs, but *don't do it*. Icebergs are floating, even in winter when they seem to be locked in the ice and you can walk right up to them. All the while, however, the submerged portion is being eaten away by water, and when enough is gone, the iceberg is top-heavy. Without warning, it can roll to a new position. If you are standing on the berg or near it

Icebergs float in Glacier Bay.   NPS photo

on lake ice, or floating nearby in a boat, you could be in serious trouble.

Glaciers, too, are "alive." Ice faces frequently crumble or shed large blocks of ice. Summer or winter, keep your distance from walls of ice, whether on land or in a boat. Tidewater glacier faces calve large icebergs and drop others into the water from great heights. The big waves this generates can capsize floating boats and sweep away beached boats or camps placed too near the water.

Travel on glaciers only if you have proper training and equipment. Crevasses are extremely dangerous, and they are often hidden under unstable snow bridges. Some stagnant bodies of glacier ice can be crossed safely, with caution, but stay on bare ice to avoid hidden crevasses and mill holes, the vertical holes by which surface streams enter glaciers.

Tide Flats and Quicksand.
Be cautious when walking on tidelands wherever glacial silt is deposited. Although the fine-grained mud appears firm as you walk on it, if you stand in one spot for a short time your feet can become locked in the dense, sticky silt. If you cannot step out of your boots easily or you don't have a companion to pull you out, you could be held prisoner, a potentially fatal situation if the tide is coming in.

Avoid walking on beaches where water appears to upwell with mud or sand, areas of potential quicksand. If you find yourself sinking, attempt to run lightly out of it. If that doesn't work, drop to the surface and crawl, thus spreading your weight over a greater area. For safety's sake, if you venture onto the mudflats, travel with a companion and watch for bore tides (described in the Boating section).

Biting Insects. While Alaska bird life may rejoice at the abundance of mosquitoes and other biting insects, the human population does not. Modern Alaskans have great admiration for the earlier residents who worked and traveled in clouds of the hungry insects without benefit of modern repellents.

Common throughout the state, mosquitoes are particularly numerous in the Interior, where summers are warm. Coastal areas with wet, cool summers have fewer mosquitoes than inland areas. Early hatches can begin in late May and extend through mid-September. Midsummer through mid-September, other biting insects also appear: no-see-ums, white-socks, black flies, and moose flies. With proper preparation, though, travel and camping can still be pleasant.

Foremost is attitude. Accept the fact that mosquitoes will bite you occasionally, that they'll fall into your food, that you'll need to spend a few minutes each night chasing them out of the tent. Without mosquitoes and eight months of winter, Alaska would be as populated as California.

While camping in the Interior, plan to use a minimum of one 1-ounce (28-g) container of repellent lotion per week for face and hands alone, and carry a can of spray repellent for clothing and tent netting. Choose brands with a high percentage of DEET (diethyl toluamide) as the active ingredient.

The solvent used in most repellents also dissolves many plastics, including the imitation-leather covering on cameras and binoculars. Repellent in stick form is easy to apply to the face and the back of the hands without leaving traces on the fingertips.

If you expect to be in prime mosquito country, spray or soak a vest or overshirt well with the most concentrated form of DEET you can find. Store the garment in a

Glacier walking in the Juneau area   APLIC photo

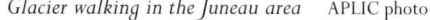

plastic bag when you are not wearing it. Be prepared to button your shirt tightly at the neck, sew shut the slit at the sleeve cuffs, and pull your socks over the outside of your trousers. Ward off bites by wearing clothing made of dense cloth. That's fine for chilly temperatures, but in summer, even in the Brooks Range, temperatures can climb above 90 degrees F (32 degrees C), and insects can keep you from shedding clothes. So try the newest in anti-mosquitowear: Pants and jacket made entirely of mosquito netting that goes over your T-shirt and shorts. And top it off with a mosquito-proof hat (smooth fabrics are best). Many people prefer to use head nets, but in the hot weather of the Interior, these can be extremely uncomfortable.

Be sure your mosquito netting and your tent are in good shape. Carry a strip of Velcro or similar fastener long enough to repair a broken tent zipper. Then relax and enjoy yourself.

Wildlife

One of the great rewards of wandering through Alaska is seeing its abundant animal life. Large portions of the state have been designated as parks, refuges, monuments, and preserves, to protect wildlife populations by preserving habitat. Many of these areas are open to recreational hunting and trapping; almost all are open to recreational fishing. Non-consumptive uses and activities that do not disturb wildlife or habitat are permitted nearly everywhere.

Emperor goose   ASP photo by Robert Angell

For centuries, Native Alaskans have used the meat and skins of wild animals for their very survival. To continue this important cultural heritage and lifestyle, many of the parks and refuges established in 1980 permit the subsistence use of animals and plants by local residents, Native and non-Native. Respect this tradition, and do not tamper with fish wheels, nets, traps, snares, or blinds.

Code of Ethics for the Photographer or Wildlife Observer. All
observers of wildlife have certain responsibilities, a few designated by law, toward the welfare of animals and their habitats. Please observe the following and encourage others to do so as well.

Avoid startling wildlife. Since most wild residents will flee if you surprise them, you'll have more fun and learn more if an animal is unaware of your presence. If an animal sees you but continues about its normal activities unafraid, consider yourself privileged and do not disturb it. If it is upset by your presence, leave the area or move to a more distant observation point.

It is against the law to deliberately feed bears, wolves, foxes, or wolverines, or to deliberately leave out human food or garbage so that it attracts animals. Don't harass, molest, or impede the natural movement of wild animals, including fish. Unless you have a permit from the Alaska Department of Fish and Game, it is against the law to import, release, handle, or capture any live wild animal. If you think an animal has been hurt or abandoned, contact the nearest Alaska Department of Public Safety, Division of Fish and Wildlife Protection office.

Be familiar with the behavior and needs of the animal you are photographing or studying to avoid accidentally damaging it or its environment. If, for example, you tie branches back from the entrance to a den or nest to get a clearer picture, release them before leaving. If the animal is rare or particularly sensitive to disturbance, keep its location secret. Avoid attracting the attention of hunters or trappers through your actions in the field or when setting up blinds for photography.

As of 1998, some 445 species of resident and migratory birds have been identified in Alaska. Coming from as far away as Argentina, Tasmania, Cape Horn, and Antarctica, migratory birds rear their young in Alaska, then fly south in the autumn over glaciers, mountain passes, plains, and endless miles of ocean to their wintering grounds.

The life cycles of millions of migratory birds depend upon the existence of suitable nesting habitats on Alaska's islands, coastal plains, and river valleys. To protect these lands, numerous refuges have been established. Particularly important are the extensive sea-cliff nesting habitats of the Alaska Maritime National Wildlife Refuge and the refuges in the wetlands of the Alaska Peninsula and the Yukon, Kuskokwim, and Kobuk river valleys.

If a bird flushes from its nest as you approach, take a quick look if you wish, then immediately leave the area. The bird should return to the nest quickly. Avoid purposely flushing an adult from its nest during cold, rainy, or extremely hot weather, thus endangering the eggs or young.

Seabirds are particularly sensitive to disturbance by hikers, airplanes, or boats. Both gulls and ravens patrol seabird colonies in search of unattended eggs and chicks. During a panicked departure, an adult can break eggs or kick eggs and chicks from its nest. Larger chicks may run off and get lost.

Horned puffins are among the seabirds found throughout the Aleutian Islands Subunit of the Alaska Maritime National Wildlife Refuge.   USFWS photo

Several species of seabirds nest in burrows dug into the ground. Avoid walking in these burrow areas, since they easily collapse under the weight of a person.

At the seashore, catch or dig only what you will eat. Be careful to collect only seashore life that is abundant. When you turn over a rock, move it gently to prevent crushing nearby animals. Replace the rock as you found it when you are finished looking. If you briefly take specimens from the beach, keep them in cool seawater in an uncrowded aquarium and return them to the proper seashore environment while they are still healthy.

Wherever you are, be familiar with the local regulations concerning collection and removal of plant life.

Sport-Fishing, Hunting, and Trapping. Unless more restrictive sport-fishing, hunting, or trapping regulations are set by a particular parkland, the regulations established by the Alaska Department of Fish and Game apply. Copies of the current sport-fishing, hunting, and trapping regulations are available by mail from the Alaska Department of Fish and Game and from agents in most communities; basic information also is available on the Internet. (See addresses in Land Managers, Appendix.) Some state parks and recreation areas that do not permit the discharge of firearms are open to hunting by other means, such as bow and arrow. Marine mammal hunting is controlled by the federal government; contact the U.S. Fish and Wildlife Service for information.

All residents 16 years of age and older, and all nonresidents regardless of age, must have a valid fishing or hunting license and tags while taking or attempting to take fish or game. Special visitor's sport-fishing licenses are available for 1- and 10-day periods as well as for the standard full year.

In dire emergency, fish or game may be taken without a fishing or hunting license or during a closed season. A "dire emergency" is defined as one in which a person in a remote area, involuntarily without food and without the possibility of obtaining food, would be unable to avoid death or serious and permanent health problems unless the game were taken. All edible portions of the meat must be salvaged and all portions remaining after the emergency has passed must be surrendered to the state.

Ryan Hanley enjoys a fishing outing in Cook Inlet; behind him, Mount Redoubt rises on the distant Alaska Peninsula. Tricia Brown photo

You may also kill animals in defense of life or property if the situation was not brought about by harassment, by an unreasonable invasion of the animal's habitat, or by the improper disposal of garbage or a similar attraction. You must have tried all other practicable means to protect life and property before killing the animal. The carcass becomes the property of the state. You are required to immediately salvage the meat or, if a black bear, wolf, wolverine, or coyote, the hide or, if a brown (grizzly) or polar bear, the hide and skull. The Alaska Department of Fish and Game must be immediately notified of the incident and must receive a written report within 15 days.

Camping

Summer camping in Alaska can be much like camping elsewhere, especially in Alaska parklands that have developed campgrounds with picnic tables, fire pits, water, and toilets. Use a sleeping bag adequate to 20 degrees F (minus 7 degrees C) or wear additional clothing in a lighter bag at low temperatures. Since you will probably encounter warm nights too, a bag with a full-length two-way zipper is practical as it can keep your feet cool or can be opened out and used as a blanket.

In severe conditions, your survival may depend upon the warmth of your bag. Down filling, when wet, provides little insulation. For extended backpacking or for use near freezing and below, synthetic fibers or vapor-barrier bags with fully protected down filling are better choices. Avoid waterproof covers, which invariably cause serious condensation just under the waterproof layer.

Camping with the caribou in the Yukon–Charley Rivers National Preserve   NPS photo by Zoe Leonard

The Matanuska River is a braided, silty stream due to its content of glacial flour from the Matanuska Glacier.   Tricia Brown photo

Alaska ground temperatures are cold, particularly in the northern portion of the state, where you may be sleeping just a few inches above frozen ground. An insulated air mattress or foam pad cuts the ground chill, evident on even the hottest of nights. Never cut boughs from live trees to use as ground cover, especially in northern forests, where vegetation grows so slowly.

Tents should have a sewn-in waterproof floor and well-secured mosquito netting. They should be waterproof or have a rain fly. In the Arctic, a rain fly provides a second important type of protection: Without something to shield the tent from the intense summer midnight sun, the interior of the tent can become unbearably hot, even at 3:00 A.M.

River bars are often the only reasonable places to camp in Alaska. Patches of sand are more pleasant to sleep on than tussock grass, the drainage is excellent, the mosquito populations are smaller, water is nearby, and presence or absence of animal tracks will alert you to the type of neighbors to expect. River bars, too, are the safest place to build campfires, and driftwood usually is handy. High water the next spring will erase the fire scar. Better yet, use your camp stove. Take pride in keeping your campsite and surrounding area clean; leave no trace of your presence except footprints. Be sure to dump waste water and dig your toilet holes at least 200 feet from the river bar. Don't bury toilet paper; pack it out or burn it.

Avoid camping on lichen fields or other fragile vegetation that will not repair itself in one growing season. Wherever you camp, pick a site with good natural drainage. Don't dig a ditch around your shelter—it damages vegetation, leaves a scar that will be visible for many years, and may start serious erosion.

Set up camp near a source of fresh water, but avoid salmon streams during the spawning season. They will contain smelly dead and dying fish, and you'll likely end up with patrolling bears as neighbors. If you see snails in lake water, don't swim. Snails can be host to the parasite that causes "swimmer's itch."

For the most pleasant camping in the wettest areas of Alaska—the coastal rain forests—look for dry ridges or protected beaches with a southern exposure to receive the most sun and best drying conditions. Inviting open spaces in the forest, euphemistically called "meadows," often are covered with soggy, ankle-deep sphagnum moss. Unfortunately, campsites may be difficult to find elsewhere if you are camping along the coast during a period of extreme high tides.

Tidal fluctuations along much of the coastline are large, up to 30 feet (9 m) in some places. Check the tide tables carefully, and note that morning and afternoon tides reach different levels. The lowest ridge of seaweed and other debris on the beach will indicate where the most recent tide has peaked.

Rainy days are a way of life in most coastal areas. Take a large sheet of plastic to hang as a rain and wind shield for cooking, lounging, and storage of gear. Take another sheet of plastic to cover the rain fly of your tent. Good drying-out days may occur only once every week or so, and you won't want to spend a sunny day doing camp maintenance. Take along a handful of large plastic garbage bags, too. You'll find uses for them you never imagined.

Carry matches in waterproof cases or well wrapped in plastic bags. Distribute them throughout your gear to ensure that some will stay dry. A camping stove or fire starter to use with wet wood also makes life more pleasant during long rainy spells.

Setting up camp   NPS photo by Matt Wilson

Wear layers, with polypropylene against your skin to wick away moisture if you heat up. Beyond that, what clothing you bring will depend on your activity level and the season. If you're going to be standing around in a boat in the rain, cover yourself with rubberized rain gear. Hiking and other exercise will call for an outer shell that will breathe, allowing your body heat to escape. Finally, a good pair of rubber boots is more comfortable in coastal rain forests than soggy leather boots.

Many Alaskans look forward to freeze-up, when ice forms on lakes, rivers, and wetlands, and snow blankets the landscape. No longer is surface travel limited to boating on winding rivers or to circuitous footpaths. On a packed ski, sled, or snowmobile trail, the miles slip quickly by. Snow camping can be enjoyable, safe, and quite comfortable. In winter, the layering law is just as important, right down to your socks and gloves. For footwear, it's hard to beat those ridiculous-looking "bunny boots." The oversized, heavy boots are waterproof, and layers of rubber hold trapped air to keep your feet warm. Although the short hours of daylight limit wilderness travel from November through January, by March those skilled in winter travel can enjoy freedoms and scenery unknown to summer travelers.

Anyone living or traveling in snow country should know the basics of winter camping and survival for personal safety. If your automobile stalls on an isolated road at minus 40 degrees F (minus 40 degrees C), or even at 30 degrees F (minus 1 degree C), you might need to know more emergency survival skills than a wilderness traveler equipped with full winter camping gear. Take one of the courses in winter survival and camping taught in many of the larger Alaska communities. Study books on winter wilderness skills, and learn by traveling with skilled companions. Don't travel alone in winter. Avoid inlets and outlets of lakes, where ice is frequently thin and new snow can obscure the danger. Watch for snow bridges or cornices that might collapse, and be alert for avalanche danger.

Before attempting a wilderness trip in winter, practice your skills and try out your equipment close to a heated retreat. The price of poor judgment, poor equipment, or poor planning in the winter can be serious injury, frostbite, hypothermia, or death.

Campfires. Be careful with fires in Alaska, particularly in the Interior. Forest and tundra fires burn hundreds of thousands of acres nearly every summer. In the peaty soil that covers much of the state, fires can burn underground the entire winter, only to blaze again when dry summer weather arrives.

Build campfires only on gravel, sand, or clay, with a water source nearby. Do not build fires on moss or tundra, areas that are underlain by peat. Stay well away from overhanging branches, downed timber, and the root systems of trees.

Burn only downed or dead wood. "Squaw wood," dead small trees and branches easily gathered by hand, often can provide all the wood you'll need, except in treeless coastal areas, where you'll find only large driftwood logs. A collapsible bow saw can cut most firewood. In most parklands, cutting live trees and branches for any purpose is prohibited. A few parks prohibit backcountry campfires, permitting fires only in developed campground fire pits. During extended dry periods, open fires may be banned in other parklands and areas of Alaska as well.

On the treeless Aleutian Islands, on arctic and alpine tundra, and in the Brooks

Range, burnable wood grows so slowly that camping stoves are preferred. Any available downed wood should be saved for emergency use or allowed to return to the soil in its natural cycle.

In the backcountry, wood often is scarce or wet. Gathering wood, building a fire, and cooking over it can be time consuming, unpleasant, and almost impossible in heavy rain, high winds, or a snowstorm—and then the campfire-blackened cooking pots have to be packed. For convenience as well as ecological reasons, more and more backcountry travelers are choosing to carry small lightweight camping stoves that burn white gas, propane, kerosene, or alcohol.

Drinking Water. Many of us have drunk sweet and not-so-sweet wilderness water straight from Alaska's streams and lakes for years without ill effects. Lately, however, an extremely unpleasant illness, caused by the microorganism *Giardia lamblia,* has reached epidemic proportions in Alaska as well as in the Lower 48. The spread of "beaver fever" may be due to increased human and dog traffic in the backcountry. Found in the feces of mammals, *Giardia* cysts are readily transmitted between humans and other animals and, unfortunately for Alaskans, they survive best in cold water. They may be found in any surface water, whether it looks and tastes clean or not; water in and below beaver ponds is particularly suspect.

Giardiasis won't kill you—but you might wish it had. Symptoms are painful and incapacitating, and usually include diarrhea, abdominal cramps, bloating, and loss of appetite and weight. Some victims have lost up to 30 pounds (14 kg) from the illness.

Since symptoms appear 1 to 4 weeks after infestation, many people become ill only after they have returned home. The symptoms can last up to 6 weeks. If giardiasis is not treated it can disappear, only to recur later, and may also be transmitted to others. With proper medication, it can be cured.

Proper sanitation in the wilderness is extremely important. If you are not willing to dispose of your dog's feces as carefully as your own, consider leaving the dog at home. For your safety and that of others, use the following safe disposal methods.

On snow-free terrain: Select a dry spot at least 100 feet (30 m) from any open water. Using a small digging tool, remove a section of tundra or topsoil about 9 inches (23 cm) in diameter. Try to keep the tundra intact so it will continue to grow after you replace it. Dig a hole no deeper than 8 inches (20 cm). The top 6 to 8 inches (15 to 20 cm) of soil contains organisms that decompose organic material, although the process is extremely slow in cold Alaskan soils. After using the hole, fill it with loose soil, replace the tundra mat or topsoil, and press firmly into place. Digging a new hole for each use is better for nature's decomposition system than creating a single large community hole. Pack out or burn used toilet paper.

On snow: Select a spot as far away as possible from any stream, river, or lake. Bury your waste in the snow and pack out or burn all toilet paper. (Snow makes a satisfactory toilet paper substitute.)

On glacier ice: Collect feces in plastic bags and dump the bags into a deep crevasse.

Bathing and dishwashing: Carry waste water in a container to a spot at least 200 feet (60 m) from any water source, where the used water will sink into the soil, not

Fielding Lake cabin is one of dozens available throughout the Alaska State Parks system.
ASP photo by Kathryn Reid

drain directly into a lake, stream, or river. Use biodegradable soap and shampoo. If you wish to swim, first sponge off your grime and mosquito repellent well away from the lake or stream.

Special note to hunters: Bury animal guts left after field-cleaning an animal; they can contain *Giardia*.

Water treatment: To destroy *Giardia* cysts in stream, lake, or snow water, simply boiling the water for 5 minutes is sufficient. If you suspect other contaminating organisms might be present, boil the water for 20 minutes at sea level, longer at higher elevations. Boiling water is often inconvenient, however, and little is known about how well it works at higher elevations. Portable water purifiers often are effective in screening out *Giardia* bacteria and viruses, and some weigh as little as a pound.

Iodine is still a good water purification option, and is the most reliable chemical agent for producing safe drinking water in the wilderness. It's lightweight and inexpensive, but to be effective it needs many minutes to work. A 2-percent tincture of iodine may be used (10 drops per quart/liter), but its strong taste is objectionable to many people. Solutions made from crystalline iodine or potassium iodide are more palatable. (Carrying the crystals themselves is not recommended because of the danger of consumption by small children.) If you add any of the powdered fruit flavorings to the water to mask the iodine taste, be sure that you add it only *after* the required time for purification has elapsed; these flavorings usually contain ascorbic acid, which neutralizes the iodine's effect.

Tetraglycine hydroperiodide tablets are convenient, and highly effective as long as they are fresh. Keep them in a tightly closed container and replace them yearly. One tablet per quart or liter of water is adequate, two if the water is colored by leaching. Allow the water to stand for 10 minutes at 68 degrees F (20 degrees C) or for 20 minutes at 32 degrees to 41 degrees F (0 degrees to 5 degrees C) before drinking.

Bears and Other Large Mammals.

Bears roam freely throughout most of Alaska. If you are going to enjoy yourself, you must learn to camp and travel safely, without fear, but with a healthy respect and appreciation for the bear and its environment. Statistically, your chances of meeting a bear in Alaska are low, and lower still if you learn where and how to travel. Fear of bears is mostly a fear of the unknown. Adventure stories often exaggerate the danger; stories are seldom written about peaceful encounters or the hundreds of thousands of miles traveled in the backcountry without meeting bears.

As a visitor to the wilderness, you have an advantage. You anticipate that bears may be nearby and watch for them. The animals are not expecting you, so if you are alert you can normally avoid a meeting. Bears are not waiting to ambush you—they have far more important things to do with their time and energy. Statistics are no consolation, however, when you and a bear are facing each other. This section is designed to help you avoid problems with bears.

Never forget that bears are unpredictable and can inflict serious injury. In Alaska, a bear may be shot at any time of the year in defense of life or property, but a reasonable effort must have been made to protect life or property by other means. If you decide to use a firearm, shoot to kill; a wounded, angry bear is dangerous.

Three species of bears inhabit Alaska. Black bears occur in most forested areas. (A brown color phase of the black bear is also found, as is a "blue" phase, the glacier bear.) Brown (grizzly) bears, often referred to as "grizzlies" in interior Alaska, are found throughout the entire state except along Alaska's western coast and on islands in the Aleutians and the Bering Sea. Polar bears, which wander the Arctic coast and pack ice in the Arctic Ocean as far south as St. Lawrence Island, are seldom seen.

Wherever you are, study the landscape around you to determine if bears are likely to be present. Black bears prefer heavily wooded areas; brown (grizzly) bears are most often seen on river bars, near timberline, and on the open tundra. When entering a new drainage, especially if you are on foot, find a spot where you have a good view of the countryside and riverbed. With binoculars, "glass" the region carefully for all visible wildlife, looking particularly for bears that might be sleeping or quietly feeding.

Watch, too, for bear signs: fresh tracks, bear trails, scat (droppings), or freshly dug areas. Look for bear tracks in muddy spots and on snow patches. Grizzly claw marks are normally well defined; black bear claw marks less so.

Many sections of Alaska contain so many bears that they create, through usage, well-defined trails. Some are as obvious as well-used human foot trails; others are a series of staggered "footprints," well worn because bears commonly step in the same places on the trail.

Expect to find bear trails along lakeshores, streams, and rivers in which salmon spawn. Trails made by moose, Dall sheep, and mountain goats also are common in the vicinity of natural mineral licks; they may parallel streams in brushy areas and often

A black bear travels along Curry Ridge in Denali State Park.   ASP photo

follow certain topographic features such as ridges or approaches to mountain passes. In country that has few trails maintained by humans, animal trails are a boon to the wilderness traveler, but use them cautiously.

Bears leave massive droppings that may resemble large human feces or merely be large amorphous piles. During berry season, the scats may be blue-black from blueberries or contain numerous whole bright-red high-bush cranberries. A steaming pile indicates a bear not long gone; a pile warm to the touch is only slightly reassuring.

In their search for food, bears, particularly brownies, dig, turning over large areas of tundra while hunting ground squirrels and roots. Although excavations may not be fresh, their frequency gives an idea of how much the area is used by bears at some times of the year.

While traveling in bear country, stay alert and think ahead. Plan your route to avoid blind corners and large areas of brush. Bears are generally considered to have poor vision, but their senses of smell and hearing are excellent. Warn them of your presence in dense brush or forested areas by making noise: talk, sing, rattle rocks in a can, ring bells. Don't whistle, though. You could sound like a ground squirrel or marmot, favorite bear food. Near running water or in the wind, a bear might not hear the noise you make.

If possible, walk with your back to the wind, entering thickets from upwind so your drifting scent will warn of your presence. Then give bears enough time to avoid you. They are just as reluctant to meet you as you are them. At night, use a flashlight.

According to U.S. Forest Service statistics, those traveling alone are at greater risk of a bear mauling. Always travel with one or more companions in bear country. But note that taking your dog is asking for trouble. After attracting the bear's attention, most likely the dog will come running back to you for protection, with an angry bear close on its heels.

Don't approach a bear's food cache. At the first odor of decomposing meat, retreat quietly. A feeding bear will defend a carcass violently once your presence is known. When a bear temporarily leaves a carcass, it normally covers it with leaves, dirt, and branches. The bear is likely to be sleeping nearby. If a bear approaches while you are fishing, leave the area quietly and slowly, donating any fish you have caught for the bear's breakfast.

Avoid approaching a sow bear with cubs. Sows are very protective and will feel your presence as a threat to their young. Curious cubs, seemingly abandoned, probably have an anxious mother nearby who will charge without warning when she discovers you. Whatever the situation, remember that from a bear's point of view, you are an intruder.

For bear-free camping, choose your campsite carefully. Avoid camping in thick brush, on bear trails, or next to water or food sources, especially salmon-spawning streams. If you can camp where climbable trees are available, plan on using them in an emergency.

Cache your food at least 100 yards (90 m) from your tent. Hang food bags from trees, from strong tall willow bushes, or from ropes strung high above the ground between trees. Adult brown (grizzly) bears can easily reach 10 feet (3 m) up a tree, although they normally don't climb. Black bears are excellent tree climbers. Treeless tundra country presents a creative challenge. Consider putting food bags on top of large boulders or in brushy thickets well off any possible trail.

Losing part of your food supply to a bear not only inconveniences you, but also trains the bear to look for other food caches. A growing body of evidence indicates that tying a small net bag containing three or four mothballs on the outside of each cached food bag provides significant additional protection from bears, squirrels, and other interested wildlife if they haven't yet discovered where to find "people" food. The added weight of a few ounces of mothballs per person is worthwhile insurance. A party of four persons on a 2-week trip will use about one-half pound of mothballs. Transport them in a vapor-proof container.

Never sleep in a tent with food or anything carrying food odors. This includes cooking pots, knives, cups, and silverware. And it could include your shirt, if food has spilled on it. Carry a bandanna to use as a napkin, and store it with the cached food at night. Take a few extra minutes after supper to wash your hands and face and brush your teeth. You might want to hang a bag of mothballs on the tent to overpower any remnant food odors on the people inside. The practice of urinating in a perimeter around the camp to "establish territory" has had mixed results. Some bears have been reported to react aggressively to the scent.

Careful food planning will also help minimize bear problems. Never carry peanut butter, smoked fish, or bacon. Wrap hard sausages, cheeses, and similar foods well to contain odors. Spend an extra hour before leaving home to package food properly.

Plan each group meal as a unit, putting the required portions and accessories (paper towels, small piece of scouring pad, after-dinner mints, et cetera) into strong new plastic bags. Label each bag carefully, tie them securely, and put them into a second plastic bag, again tying well. Pack the meals into several sturdy, clean, waterproof cloth bags that, with the mothballs, will be hung from trees. Using a number of food-cache bags reduces the likelihood that your entire food supply might be destroyed. Be sure to count the number of bags cached each night and collect them all in the morning.

Before a trip into bear country, wash your backpack thoroughly. On the trip, cache the pack frame and bag outside the tent in a large plastic garbage bag with some mothballs on top of it.

In bear country, never cook in or near the tent, but plan to cook at least 100 yards (90 m) away. If the local bear population seems large or likely to wander into camp, stop along the trail to cook supper, then travel another hour before camping for the night.

Always keep a clean camp, caching food carefully, disposing of garbage immediately, and keeping utensils washed. Burn all packaging material and leftover food or securely wrap the scraps in a plastic bag and store them with the cached food until garbage can be burned or carried out. Always stir campfire ashes, collecting unburned bits of foil and scorched cans and compressing them in one of the plastic bags. The charred remains will weigh surprisingly little and should be packed out with you. If for some reason you must leave the garbage after burning, bury it.

As more and more people venture into the backcountry, bears learn quickly where to find easy food. If you plan to camp or hike in a heavily used recreation area, ask about the presence of "problem bears"—those that search out campsites and other food sources. Don't endanger the supplies or lives of the next campers by letting bears find food at your campsite and turning them into "problem bears."

"Problem bears" soon become dead bears. Alaska Department of Fish and Game personnel have found that moving a bear to a new environment does not solve the problem. The bear either returns to its original area or continues its destructive habits in its new home. In the Chugach National Forest, "problem bears" are caught in live traps and shot; their hides are sold at state auction and the meat given to charitable institutions. Shooting the bears is preferable to allowing them to maul or kill a human. People who have fed such animals or have allowed them to find food are ultimately responsible for the death of the unfortunate animals.

All bears, like other animals, have a "critical space." By entering into that space either accidentally or intentionally, you are asking for trouble. If you encounter a bear busily picking berries, ripping up the tundra, or fishing, and the bear hasn't seen you, stand quietly until it begins feeding again, then move away inconspicuously, preferably downwind and out of sight.

If the bear has seen you, walk slowly backward, all the while facing the bear. *Do not run;* the bear might feel compelled to give chase. You can't outrun a bear; grizzlies can reach 40 mph (64 kph) for short distances.

If you meet a bear on a trail in the woods, step slowly to the side and out of sight, giving it plenty of room to continue. Avoid putting the bear in a situation in which it might feel cornered. Often, once it can no longer see you, a bear will forget you are nearby.

Most bear charges are bluffs, but if physical contact seems certain, drop to the ground and play dead. Make no noise. Your vital organs are best protected if you lie on your stomach in the fetal position with your hands clasped over the back of your neck.

Like a cat, a bear apparently isn't interested in its victim once it has "killed." Remain motionless until the bear is safely out of sight and sound. Of people injured in bear attacks, 75 percent have survived.

The standard highway flare carried by motorists has also successfully discouraged bears. Both flares and chemical bear sprays are most useful when used within tents, vehicles, and cabins, where the use of firearms is difficult or dangerous. When a party travels with one firearm for the group, the weapon typically accompanies persons leaving camp to fish, hunt, or hike. Chemical bear sprays and flares offer some protection to those left in camp and to those unable or unwilling to use a gun.

Another large mammal deserves a short comment. Moose, found in large numbers throughout Alaska in both wilderness and populated areas, normally coexist peaceably with people. Statistically, the most common danger from moose is an automobile–moose collision, which can severely damage both parties. A cow moose with a calf, however, can be extremely aggressive and may charge without warning. Her protectiveness rivals that of a sow bear with cubs, and her flying hooves can inflict serious injury. Since calves are often hidden in the brush out of sight, treat all moose with distant respect.

Backpacking and Hiking

Whatever your degree of hiking skill and stamina, rewarding trips in Alaska await you. Some of the more accessible parklands have marked trails that can be ends in themselves or serve as accesses to the wilderness beyond. Other parklands are so remote that getting there is an adventure in itself.

Take a few trips on trails suggested in Alaska guidebooks before striking out cross-country. Be competent at hiking, camping, and utilizing survival skills before attempting a wilderness trip. If you are new to hiking or backpacking, read some basic manuals and guidebooks and talk to people who have had extensive experience. Better yet, travel with an experienced person in your party or join one of the many commercial guided wilderness trips. The latter can be as strenuous as you wish, from gentle day hikes and float trips to 3-week wilderness backpacking sojourns, demanding white-water kayaking, or grueling climbs on precipitous mountain peaks.

On tundra and most trails, and when carrying overnight camping gear, most people find that traveling 6 to 10 miles (10 to 16 km) a day on foot is enough. Through brushy, forested, or mountainous country, foot travel can be extremely difficult or relatively easy depending upon the terrain, the density of the ground cover, the difficulty of stream crossings, and whether good animal trails are available. Look for animal trails along lakeshores, streams, or riverbanks, up ridges, approaching mountain passes, or near mineral licks. In many cases, a slightly longer route via animal trails will be faster than bushwhacking through difficult terrain. Allow plenty of time for your trip and extra time for relaxing or exploring from camp.

Study the vegetation as you travel to find out which plant communities are easiest to travel through, and learn to identify them from afar. Then, when you reach a view-point, you can intelligently study the country ahead to choose a route.

Independence Mine, at Hatcher Pass in Southcentral Alaska, is surrounded by trails suitable for families. Tricia Brown photo

Adequate rain gear is essential to prevent hypothermia. Carry rain pants or rain chaps as well as a rain parka or poncho, since vegetation retains water droplets long after rain has quit. Wear sunglasses on snow and glaciers to prevent snowblindness, and carry a small tube of sun block. Don't forget lots of mosquito repellent.

Unless your route takes you over extensive rock or requires technical climbing skills and heavy climbing boots, you'll be more comfortable traveling in medium-weight hiking boots with lug soles. Many wilderness hikers prefer rubber-footed boots with leather uppers, known as "shoe pacs." Whatever your footgear, be sure it is comfortable and gives you adequate foot and ankle support.

If your feet don't get soaked at some point, it's an unusual backpacking trip in Alaska. Rain, stream crossings, soggy tundra, or long sections of tussock grass and bogs will soak even the best-greased leather boot in time. A good pair of gaiters helps, but expect to get wet feet. Take along boot grease and extra socks. Whenever your boots are dry enough, grease them well to protect the leather and to keep it supple. Stiff, dried-out leather can start blisters, even from previously comfortable boots.

Bring a GPS (global positioning system) unit with fresh batteries. But also take along the most detailed topographic maps available for the area you'll be in, and include maps for surrounding areas in the event that you might have to change your route plans. A compass need not be fancy, since most of your navigation will be from topographic maps in large drainages, but always carry one. Know how to allow for magnetic declination, which varies from 27 degrees to 37 degrees east of true north in Alaska. Before taking off on any trip, whether for a few hours or several weeks, leave your route plan and schedule with a responsible person.

One of the delights of traveling the north country in summer is the nearly unlimited daylight. You can determine the amount of daylight for the time of year and the area you'll be in from the graph in the Appendix. Add another hour or two of twilight on either end. If this adds up to 24 hours, you'll have no use for a flashlight, but always carry one at other times, especially on fall and winter trips, even short ones.

Crossing Rivers. If you spend much time wandering the backcountry, you'll be faced with the problem of crossing large streams and rivers. Take your time and plan carefully: Practice crossing rivers in "civilization" before taking off for the wilderness. Alaska Division of Parks or U.S. Forest Service personnel occasionally give 1-day river-crossing seminars.

Alaska has two basic types of rivers and streams: those of glacial origin and those not of glacial origin. (The latter are often called "clearwater," regardless of their color.) The water in streams originating from glaciers is gray and opaque from suspended glacier-ground rock "flour," which can deposit in your clothing, greatly increasing your weight and making it difficult to stay afloat if you fall midstream. The murky water obscures the streambed, making it impossible to gauge the depth visually. Currents generally are swift and the water numbingly cold.

Glacial riverbeds are frequently 0.5 mile (1 km) or more wide, with the river meandering over only a small portion in a many-braided course. Pick a section of the river that has numerous braids; many small streams are easier to cross than one big one. Cross at the top of the islands, where the river splits and flows in shallower riffles.

Water levels are most likely to be lowest in the morning, especially after a cold

Lupines are profuse in midsummer.   APLIC photo

Cathedral Creek in Yukon–Charley Rivers National Preserve   NPS photo by Kurt Menning

night. Levels will be highest when hot sun or heavy rains have accelerated the rate of melting of snowfields and glacier ice. The stream that was a pussycat at breakfast could be a raging lion by suppertime. Plan your route accordingly, or camp and wait for low water rather than risk a dangerous crossing.

Clearwater streams are fed from springs, snowmelt, and rain. The water may be crystal clear, muddy from recent rains, or dark brown from tannin leached from muskeg vegetation. Mountain streams generally flow over rocky or gravel surfaces, but footing is likely to be slippery from algae growing on logs and rocks. Cross where the river is broad, but in an area of shallow riffles.

In the lowlands, small sluggish streams flow through the muskeg in deep channels with nearly vertical banks and few shallows. The streambed often is sticky mud or unconsolidated muck. Crossing can be very difficult, despite the narrow width. Look for a log or rocks to cross on, or a section of swift, shallower water. Larger rivers in the lowlands have typical gravel bars and cut banks, but most of them are too deep to cross by wading unless you can find an area where the river flows over riffles.

Learn to "read" the surface of any river or stream. Drop your pack on the bank and take a 1/2 hour walk up and down the river, studying the water and the terrain. Don't attempt a hasty crossing of a dangerous stream. Avoid crossing at a bend; although the inside may have a gently sloping gravel beach, the current along the outside will be deep and swift, and the bank most likely will be steep and unstable.

On the surface, waves made by the current as it flows over submerged obstacles indicate what is underneath. A large V pointing downstream usually shows that the water is flowing through a deep channel. A V pointing upstream is probably caused by the water splitting around a submerged rock or snag. A hump in the water, known as a standing wave or haystack, indicates a hole in the riverbed just above it. These are also found downstream of large submerged boulders. The turbulence found in large holes can pull a person under. The size and depth of the submerged object determine the amount of surface disturbance: Smaller or deeper obstructions create less surface turbulence.

Never cross a river or stream barefoot. Cold water quickly numbs bare feet, and you won't feel sharp rocks or rolling boulders. An injured foot could create an emergency situation in the wilderness; at the very least, it is an unnecessary and avoidable irritation.

Many hikers carry a pair of lightweight shoes just for stream crossing. Others wear hiking boots for more secure footing but remove their socks, wiping the boots and their feet afterward and then putting their socks back on.

When the route requires frequent wading, you may prefer to wade socks and all, wringing your socks out for long dry sections of the trail. Always have a dry pair of socks tucked away to change into when you make camp. In the morning, if stream crossings are again on the schedule, groan loudly and put on the cold, wet socks—they'll warm up shortly. Wearing two pairs of socks, including lightweight synthetic undersocks, will decrease your chances of getting blisters.

Remove your pants before making crossings that will wet you above the knees. Wear rain pants or chaps to break the cold water, but don't tie the legs at the ankle; if you should fall, they could fill with water and drag you under.

Any stream deeper than a "splash-through" should be crossed with caution. The current will almost always be stronger than you expect. Unfasten backpack chest and waist straps before entering the water so you can immediately release the pack if you fall. You may want to tether the pack to you with a lightweight line that is easily releasable.

Either work your way diagonally downstream, moving with the current, or, facing upstream, shuffle sideways, probing the bottom contour ahead with a long sturdy stick for a "third leg" and keeping your feet pointed directly upstream. When footing is treacherous, cross in pairs, holding hands, each person carrying a probing stick. Only one person should move at a time. If the party includes older children or timid members, interlock arms and grip a large stick horizontally at breast height, with the heaviest or most experienced party member at the upstream end.

When traveling with children, think carefully before undertaking any but the easiest stream crossings. To cross a stream with a young child, tie the youngster to you, either piggyback style or on your chest facing you; never carry the child on your shoulders. Don't carry both the child and your pack at the same time; make two trips.

For very dangerous crossings, use a rope belay from as far upstream as possible, keeping the rope slack at all times. If the person crossing falls, play out the rope fast enough to avoid holding that individual under water. When a number of people must cross and the rope is long enough, rig a fixed line, then belay the last person from the far bank. If the river is too deep to ford safely, change your route.

If you should fall while crossing, immediately get out of your pack. If you are swept downstream, float on your back, feet first so your feet will take the impact of any rocks, until you reach a section of the river that will allow you to work your way to shore.

A typical Interior landscape   Tricia Brown photo

Mountaineering. "The whole state's nothing but mountains!" one visitor exclaimed after arriving in Anchorage by air on a clear day. His observation was not exactly correct, but Alaska does have a lot of mountains. Of the 20 highest in North America, 11 are in Alaska. Nineteen peaks are over 14,000 feet (4300 m).

Climbing the higher peaks in Alaska is far more dangerous and difficult than climbing high peaks in more temperate regions. Most of the routes are on snow and ice, and climbers must often cross extensive glaciers and snowfields. Severe arctic weather conditions prevail at high altitudes. Superior mountaineering skill, stamina and conditioning, sturdy equipment, and the ability to survive long periods of cold and wind are essential. Most attractive climbing areas are extremely remote. A party must be self-sufficient and realize that any rescue attempts might be "too little, too late." Unfortunately, many people have died climbing in Alaska.

Getting to the base of a mountain is often an expedition in itself. Alaska's lack of an extensive road system can require a long wilderness hike over rugged terrain, often with vast swamplands, major rivers to be crossed, and miles of glacial moraine. Most expeditions choose to charter an air taxi, a powerboat, horses, or even dogsleds to reach a convenient starting point.

Denali National Park personnel distribute packets of information intended for mountaineers planning to climb high peaks in the park, but the recommendations apply to climbing any of Alaska's higher mountains. For a listing of mountain and wilderness guide services, consult the current edition of the Alaska Division of Tourism's publication, "Alaska Vacation Planner." The Alaska Association of Mountain and Wilderness Guides sets professional standards for all recreational guides. The Mountaineering Club

The Granite Tors formation in Interior Alaska attracts day climbers.   ASP photo

of Alaska (Anchorage) sponsors climbs and hikes for club members and their guests and can put you in contact with mountaineering clubs in other parts of the state. (Addresses are in Information Sources, Appendix.)

Emergencies. Should an emergency occur along the highway system or in a city or village, telephone the nearest Alaska State Troopers' office. In more isolated locations, many private citizens living in the Bush have two-way radios and will be willing to help contact the proper authority.

Most major communities have hospital facilities. Other communities have well-staffed and -equipped clinics able to treat many serious medical emergencies, while smaller settlements have community health aides, trained and experienced in handling medical problems. Through radio contact with physicians at Alaska's hospitals, the health aide is supported by an extensive medical network and can arrange air evacuation if the situation is critical.

If in the wilderness you are ill, injured, or lost, do not fight the conditions. Conserve your energy and body heat. If you are near a water supply, stay there. You can live for days with only water and warmth. Most large rivers in the state are major transportation routes, summer or winter, so you'll have a better chance of being discovered if you travel or camp near one. Stay calm, plan carefully, and use the resources of the land for your survival. Eskimos and Indians have done it for centuries.

When traveling in remote areas, consider carrying a handheld GPS (global positioning system) unit. A boon to outdoor sports enthusiasts, these personal navigators rely on transmissions from satellites that orbit the earth twice a day. However, to calculate your position, the GPS operates best in open areas so it can receive transmissions from at least three satellites. Also, a GPS is only as good as its batteries, so keep a plentiful supply. Bring along a small two-way radio for emergency use. An alternative is an emergency locator transmitter (ELT), a small radio transmitter designed for emergency use, which when activated sends a distress signal on a frequency monitored by aircraft. However, this transmitter does not allow you to speak to the pilot. Aircraft traffic varies with your location and the season, of course, but a light plane will cruise through the more popular remote drainages at least once every day or two in the summer, generally more often.

To attract the attention of a passing aircraft without using a radio or a locator transmitter is more difficult, but not impossible. Always carry a signal mirror or some item with a flat, shiny surface capable of reflecting the sun, and learn to use it before going into the wilderness. If possible, build a smoky campfire to help the pilot locate you, or lay out a brightly colored tent or tarp.

Other standard signals for help are: three sounds of any kind repeated at intervals; three fires set in a triangle; white smoke produced by laying green branches on a hot fire; black smoke produced by laying rubber or plastic on a hot fire.

To communicate with the pilot of an aircraft once you are spotted, use "SOS," or the following signals adopted in 1982 by the Convention on International Civil Aviation. Make a copy of this page and carry it in your pack.

Cell phones cannot be counted on outside the most populated areas of the state, but inside service areas, they have saved the day for many adventurers who've found themselves sick, injured, or out of time.

Obviously, the best situation is to have no emergencies. That's the sign of a well-planned trip—or luck. Expect the unexpected, travel cautiously, and be as self-sufficient as possible.

Signals

MESSAGE	CODE SYMBOL
Require assistance	V
Require medical assistance	X
No or negative	N
Yes or affirmative	Y
Proceeding in this direction	↑

Figure 3. Ground-to-air visual signal codes for communication with aircraft

Descending the Granite Tors in the Steese National Conservation Area   ASP photo

The U.S. Forest Service's historic vessel, the M/V Chugach, *cruises by South Etolin Wilderness in the Tongass National Forest.*   Patrick McCoy photo

Boating

Float trips down rivers and along the coast are an ideal way to visit Alaska's backcountry. The miles slip by quickly with minimal effect on either you or the land, and you are traveling in a time-honored fashion. The Russian fur traders, in the mid-1700s, arrived by ship; but long before Outsiders bumped into these shores, the original people—the Eskimos, Aleuts, and Indians—floated the rivers and coastal waters in their small but seaworthy craft.

Today the handheld GPS has become a valuable tool for commercial fishermen and pleasure boaters alike, who can program in the coordinates of hot fishing holes, dangerous rocks, and favorite places. But relying entirely on a GPS is unwise. Excellent maps and charts of the state's waters and shorelines are available. Most small boaters prefer to carry USGS maps, the 1:250,000-scale quadrangles for an overview of the route and the surrounding terrain and the 1:63,360-scale for detailed information. Be sure to protect maps well against water and weather. If the area is particularly remote and your party consists of two or more boats, two sets of maps are good insurance. No signposts exist in the wilderness. Contact the manager of the specific wild river or parkland for current information on water levels, hazards, and access.

If your route takes you into Canada at any point, you are entering a foreign country and must clear customs. Contact both the Canadian and U.S. customs for instructions before starting your trip. They understand the logistical problems of crossing the border in wilderness areas and will help find a satisfactory solution to the legal requirements. Addresses are listed in Information Sources, Appendix.

Use clothing and sleeping bags that function well when wet. Rain or drizzle can fall for a week at a time. A thundershower or a capsize can drench your gear unexpectedly, and cool air slows drying time. Keep all equipment dry and in good repair, be able to get out of your craft or your heavy footgear in the event of capsizing, and know how to treat hypothermia and give cardiopulmonary resuscitation (CPR). Whenever capsizing is even a remote possibility, dress warmly regardless of the air temperature. More and more boaters are wearing wet suits to ward off the water's chill, which can range from about 60 degrees F (16 degrees C) to near freezing.

Be particularly cautious on large inland lakes, in coastal fjords (especially in the vicinity of glaciers), and on some mountain-rimmed sections of the Yukon River. Williwaws—sudden violent winds—can strike without warning, building large, breaking waves capable of capsizing small boats. A number of lives have been lost in Skilak Lake on the Kenai Peninsula under such conditions. The waters are extremely cold, producing hypothermia or unconsciousness within a short time. Always wear a life jacket.

River Running. Since access to most rivers in Alaska is by air, collapsible kayaks and inflatable boats are popular. A few air taxi pilots will transport canoes or other rigid craft strapped to the struts of a floatplane, but FAA regulations generally

Rafters enjoy a wet ride down the Nenana River in Denali National Park and Preserve. Tour operators offer trips that range from gentle floats to white-water action.   Tim Fischer / Denali Photo

prohibit transporting passengers at the same time, thus increasing the number of trips required and the expense. Contact the air taxi service well in advance if you plan to use a rigid boat. Such boats are also expensive to ship by airfreight. On the other hand, rental boats are hard to find in Alaska; collapsible boats for rent may not exist. Check with sporting goods stores and rental shops in the larger cities, outfitters, and wilderness lodges.

For safety, always travel with others in two or more boats, preferably three. Small groups are also likely to be more welcome than large ones at small villages en route.

Most boaters average 5 or 6 hours a day of actual travel on the water. The distance covered per day will, of course, depend upon the weather, the speed of the water (rapid in the mountains, much slower in the flatlands), the number of portages or route inspections required, whether you "float" or actively paddle, and the amount of time spent at rest stops, hiking, et cetera. Assume you'll average the following speeds while actually traveling: lakes, 2 mph (3 kph); clearwater rivers, 3 to 4 mph (5 to 6 kph); glacial rivers, 5 to 7 mph (8 to 11 kph).

For both safety and your enjoyment of the trip, allow plenty of time. Figure on at least 1 day for sitting out bad weather, resting, or exploring for every 5 or 6 days of travel.

Alaska waterways are transportation and freight routes today, just as they have been for centuries for Natives, explorers, and prospectors. Log cabins and abandoned villages sit on riverbanks. Many of the cabins are in use today, private retreats on private land; others are relics located on federal land and protected by law. Look at these decaying ruins, fantasize about the people who once lived there, but leave the artifacts intact. Gather your firewood from the forest, not from Alaska's historic structures. The removal or destruction of any historic object on federal or state land is punishable by fine or imprisonment.

Much of the land selected by Alaska Natives under the 1971 Alaska Native Claims Settlement Act lies along rivers and streams. Unless you are sure that the land bordering the river or stream is open to the public, assume it is privately owned, especially in the vicinity of any settlement or village. Ask before you camp.

Do not disturb food or firewood caches. The owner may be depending upon the supplies for survival. Only if your life is truly in danger should you touch the supplies; then replace them as soon as possible or reimburse the owner.

Several Alaska wilderness rivers heavily used by boaters have become unsightly garbage dumps. Be sure to carry out all of your litter, and if you have space in your boat, pack out some of the non-biodegradable garbage you find.

Proper disposal of human waste is a serious problem in Alaska, especially near waterways. Some villages obtain their drinking water directly from rivers and streams. Unless you can find a spring, purify your drinking water, preferably by boiling (see the section on Drinking Water, earlier). Giardiasis has become rampant in Alaska, even in the most remote regions. Help control the problem by being particularly careful with personal hygiene.

Pack all equipment in watertight bags and tie them to the boat. (After a capsize, the boat can normally be found and equipment salvaged, even if the craft is damaged beyond repair, but floating or sunken bags are generally lost for good.) Carry adequate survival equipment, extra paddles, boat-repair materials, a 50- to 100-foot (15- to 30-m) rope, and a first-aid kit. Attach a knife, mosquito repellent, and waterproof matches to your person so they cannot be lost. Always wear a life vest. Wet suits or dry suits are recommended in white water and in silty waters.

Be sure your craft will float even when full of water. If you capsize, stay with the boat and work it to shore to prevent damage to the boat or losing it entirely. In most remote areas, you will be in serious trouble without a boat for transportation. Long distances, rivers to be crossed, and miles of swamp and muskeg make walking out impractical.

If you feel you must abandon your boat, consider your situation before you decide to travel. If you don't know where you are or are not sure of a safe route to your destination, don't travel. Stay with your boat if someone will be looking for you. From the air, searchers are more likely to see a boat than one or two people.

If you decide to abandon the boat, leave the following information in a conspicuous place near or on the boat: when you left, where you are going, your route, your physical condition, and the supplies you are carrying. Make a continuous map of your route as you go, showing enough detail to enable you to retrace your steps if necessary.

River Ratings. River difficulty ratings can change with water levels, depending upon how the water flows over and around obstructions. High water has the added hazard of floating logs, trees, and other debris. Always walk the riverbank to preview any sections that could cause problems.

Be cautious in how you interpret the International Whitewater Scale. Even within the Lower 48 there are some regional differences; a river rated as WW3 on the East Coast might not be classified as WW3 in the Northwest. In the Lower 48 you'd probably be able to walk out to the nearest highway if you should lose your boat. However, in remote wilderness areas of Alaska, the difficulty of rescue adds to the the risk. It's wise to mentally upgrade the river classifications as you plan your trip.

There is some overlap, in terms of difficulty, between the flat-water and white-water classifications. Be sure you understand the differences before attempting these trips.

The following river classification system has been used in this book:

Flat Water

FWA (Class A) Easy. Lakes and standing water or very slow-flowing streams. Tidal currents less than 2 mph (3 kph). Little wind or wave activity expected. Sheltered and accessible location.

FWB (Class B) Moderate. Rivers and streams with currents that can be overcome by backpaddling. Tidal currents 2 to 4 mph (3 to 6 kph). Moderate wind and wave action. Rounding headlands or crossing open bays or channels of 3 to 5 miles (5 to 8 km) probable.

FWC (Class C) More difficult. Rivers, streams, and tidal currents faster than can be overcome easily by backpaddling. Some skill necessary for sharp bends and back eddies in rivers. Landings and launchings require care, some maneuvering skill required. Storm winds and wave action possible. Extended duration of trip or remote wilderness locations.

White Water

WW1 (Class I) Easy. Moving water with small regular waves, riffles, and sand banks. Few or no obstructions.

WW2 (Class II) Medium. Rapids with waves up to 3 feet (1 m) and wide, obvious, clear channels. Some maneuvering is required.

WW3 (Class III) Difficult. Rapids with numerous high, irregular waves capable of swamping an open canoe. A splash cover is necessary. Narrow passages require complex maneuvering. Scouting the route from shore is recommended.

WW4 (Class IV) Very difficult. Rapids with turbulent waters, rocks, and dangerous eddies. Constricted passages require powerful, precise maneuvering, and inspection of the route is mandatory. This water is normally too difficult for experts in open canoes. Boaters in covered canoes and kayaks should be able to Eskimo roll. Crash helmets and positive flotation in the boats are mandatory. For highly skilled boaters.

WW5 (Class V) Extremely difficult. Long violent rapids with rocks, big ledges, a very steep gradient, and other serious obstacles in the route. Scouting the route from shore is required for safety. Rescue could be difficult, and a significant hazard to life exists in event of mishap. The ability to Eskimo roll under adverse conditions is essential. For a team of experts.

WW6 (Class VI) Extraordinarily difficult. Nearly impossible and very dangerous waters; for teams of expert kayakers and rafters only, with experienced rescue teams and equipment on the banks. Cannot be attempted without risk of life.

Much of the land above the 58th parallel is underlain by permafrost (permanently frozen ground). Surface water from spring snowmelt runoff or summer rains cannot percolate through this frozen layer, and runs immediately into the streams. Water levels in small rivers can rise as much as 3 to 4 feet (1 m) in a few hours. Always store your boat well up on the bank, well tied. Conversely, water levels can drop rapidly during dry periods.

Most river and stream channels are given little or no maintenance. In forested areas, sweepers (horizontal low-hanging trees) and logjams are frequent.

Another hazard, an interesting characteristic of the northland with its cold winters, is overflow ice, or *aufeis*. In an area of low gradient, many arctic and subarctic rivers freeze solid, leaving no channel for water coming from upstream. The trapped water breaks through to the surface repeatedly during the winter, forming extensive and deep fields of ice on river floodplains that often last throughout much of the summer. Check the river channel through the ice for a safe passage before running it.

Blue Water

Traveling by small boat on salt water is one of the finest ways to experience Alaska's mountains, forests, and fjords. Before starting a trip, though, ask about local conditions. Many coastal waters have extreme tidal fluctuations, strong currents, uncharted rocks, and frequent high winds and waves. The tidal rise and fall can be extremely large in shallow, narrowing fjords. Upper Cook Inlet, for example, has a maximum daily range of 38.9 feet (11.9 m) during spring tides.

A few bays go nearly dry at low tides. During periods of large tidal fluctuation, the incoming tide in some of these areas can move as a bore—a swift, noisy wall of churning

A kayaker takes advantage of a flat, calm day on Cook Inlet off Clam Gulch.   Tricia Brown photo

water that can capsize small boats. Bore tides are frequent in Turnagain Arm and Knik Arm in the Anchorage area.

Be especially careful in narrow channels where riptides, whirlpools, and standing waves can form. Consult tide tables to determine times of slack water, when you can safely paddle waters that normally have fierce tidal currents. Time your departures to use tidal currents to your advantage, speeding you on your way—a treat in flat-water paddling. Be alert for williwaws; since they tend to recur in the same areas, ask locally for information.

As with river running, always travel in a group with two or more boats. Plan your route so that it parallels shorelines, crossing large bodies of water only during calm seas. Consider a wet suit or dry suit a necessity if you are kayaking or canoeing. An extended dunking in coastal waters, which in summer average 40 degrees to 55 degrees F (4 degrees to 13 degrees C), can be fatal; survival time at 40 degrees F (4 degrees C) with light clothing and a life vest is less than 2 hours.

Rain is a fact of life in coastal Alaska. Expect long periods of fog or low visibility. Avoid major shipping lanes; your small craft probably won't be visible to large vessels, even on sunny days. To increase your chances of being spotted, use brightly colored clothing and boats. (On rainy days, the colors will make you feel better and liven up your photographs as well.)

One of the delights of blue-water boating is watching seals, sea lions, sea otters, and whales. Be cautious, though, when among the large mammals—their actions are unpredictable. The appearance of a killer whale can panic a 2000-pound (900-kg) sea lion into trying to board your small boat.

Give actively feeding whales, too, a wide berth. They normally create no significant danger for the boater, but if a whale surfaces nearby, move slowly out of the area or drift quietly until the animal has moved away. Physical contact with a whale could result in a capsized boat and possibly death to you and your companions. At the very least, you will have disturbed an animal extremely sensitive to your presence.

Power- and sailboat skippers new to northern waters should contact the U.S. Coast Guard and Coast Guard Auxiliary for information about boating in Alaska's waters. Fuel docks are few and far between; the Coast Guard recommends using no more than one-third of your fuel to travel outward and one-third to get back, reserving one-third for emergencies. Always carry a survival suit for each person on board.

No visual weather warnings are displayed by the U.S. Coast Guard in Alaska. Marine weather forecasts are given by radio or telephone only, using the following terms:

Small craft advisory: Sustained weather or sea conditions of more than 2 hours' duration, either present or forecast, which might be hazardous to small boats. Mariners must decide as to the severity of the weather, based upon experience and size and type of boat. Winds of more than 25 knots or hazardous wave conditions are indicated.

Gale warning: Winds from 35 to 50 knots are forecast.

Storm warning: Winds greater than 50 knots are forecast.

Local AM and FM radio stations broadcast marine weather in Anchorage, Bethel, Cordova, Dillingham, Glennallen, Juneau, Ketchikan, Kodiak, Kotzebue, Nome, Seward, Sitka, and Soldotna. Marine and aviation weather is also broadcast weeknights on the "Aviation Weather" program on Alaska's PBS television stations. The National Weather Service gives marine forecasts by telephone in Anchorage, Annette, Cold Bay, Cordova, Juneau, King Salmon, Kodiak, Kotzebue, Nome, Petersburg, Sitka, Valdez, Wrangell, and Yakutat.

The unwritten law of the sea requires that you come to the aid of another mariner in distress. If you see a distress signal, immediately notify the nearest Coast Guard station or other authority by radio (channel 16 on CB; channel 16, 156.8 MHz on VHF marine radio). If you can assist the stricken vessel or its passengers without endangering yourself or your craft, do so. Be sure that your own boat has adequate visual distress signals aboard.

Cold Water. When a person is immersed in cold water, the skin and nearby tissues cool rapidly, but it may take 10 to 15 minutes before the temperature of the heart and brain starts to drop. When the body core temperature reaches 90 degrees F (32 degrees C), unconsciousness occurs; when the core temperature drops to 85 degrees F (29 degrees C), the heart usually fails. Drowning in cold water normally occurs, however, because the victim becomes hypothermic and cannot use his arms and legs.

Survival in cold water depends upon many factors: the temperature of the water, body size, amount of body fat, and the amount of activity in the water. By swimming or treading water, one loses body heat 35 percent faster than by floating quietly. An average person wearing light clothing and a life vest can survive for 2 to 3 hours in 50 degree F (10 degree C) water by remaining still. Alaska's large lakes and coastal waters are generally colder than this. To increase your survival time by conserving body heat, draw your knees up into a fetal position and clasp your arms to your chest; keep your head and neck out of the water. If several people are in the water, huddle closely in a circle.

Water conducts heat from the body many times faster than does air. Since most boats will float even when capsized or swamped, climb onto or into the boat and remain as far out of the water as possible. Always wear an approved life vest; it will keep you afloat even if you are unconscious. The best advice yet is to pack a survival suit with the rest of your essential safety gear.

Whether to swim for shore is a difficult decision. Some good swimmers have been able to swim up to 0.8 mile (1.3 km) in 50-degree F (10-degree C) water before being overcome by hypothermia. Others have not been able to swim 100 yards (90 m). Since distances on the water are deceptive, stay with the boat if there is any chance whatever of rescue. A capsized boat is far easier for a rescuer to see than a person in the water. Swim for shore (wearing your flotation device) *only* if there is no chance of rescue and you are certain you can make it.

Sudden face contact with cold water (below 70 degrees F, 21 degrees C) touches off a primitive response called the mammalian diving reflex. This complex series of body responses shuts off blood circulation to most parts of the body except the heart, lungs, and brain. The oxygen remaining in the blood is transported to the brain, which when cooled requires much less oxygen than usual.

Walruses rest on an ice floe.   APLIC photo

Children and young people are the most frequent drowning victims, but they are also good candidates for resuscitation since they have a more pronounced diving reflex. At the University of Michigan Hospital, two-thirds of the cold-water drowning victims who were successfully resuscitated were three and a half years old or younger. The colder the water and the younger the victim, the better the chance for survival. However, an 18-year-old male who was revived after 38 minutes in icy water, 2 hours of resuscitation, and 13 hours of medical respiratory support sustained no apparent brain damage.

In a cold-water drowning emergency: (1) Immediately clear the air passage and begin mouth-to-mouth rescue breathing and external heart massage. Do not worry about getting water out of the victim's lungs; the body will absorb it quickly. (2) Prevent the victim from losing more body heat but *do not* rewarm the victim. (3) Quickly transport the victim to the nearest medical facility. Continue CPR without interruption until the victim is under the care of competent medical personnel. (4) Do not give up. Cold-water drowning victims appear dead. Their skin is blue and cold to the touch. Their eyes are fixed and dilated, and there is no detectable heartbeat or breathing. In spite of all this, they may still have a good chance of survival.

Beating the Cold and Snow

Although the temperature at Fort Yukon, above the Arctic Circle, has hit 100 degrees F (38 degrees C), Alaska isn't exactly Hawaii. A bit of preparation and know-how will keep the chills away, summer or winter, and allow you to have a fine outdoor experience.

Summer shivers are every bit as real as winter shakes. If your feet are cold, put on a hat or parka hood. By 40 degrees F (4 degrees C), half your body's heat production is lost through an unprotected head. Conserve body heat by staying out of the wind or by wearing windproof clothing; drink warm liquids and eat high-calorie foods. In cold weather, fats are the most efficient body fuel, but at high altitudes carbohydrates are frequently more digestible.

Layer your clothing, beginning with a set of polypropylene long underwear. Next, a layer of fleece, followed by outerwear. What you choose for the top layer depends on the wind, moisture, and your activity level. More activity requires an outer shell that is waterproof and windproof, but will breathe, allowing body heat to disperse. Synthetic underwear and socks will help wick moisture away from the body and keep you warmer. Mittens keep hands warmer than gloves.

Boots should be large enough for a felt insole or for several layers of socks. If your feet are cold, *take off* a layer to permit better blood circulation. Ever wonder why the traditional Eskimo mukluk is soft and roomy like a slipper? For extended periods in severe cold, don't wear leather hiking or ski boots unless you use an insulated cover or overboot. Better yet, wear specialized cold-weather boots. Powder snow around your feet on a clear, windless, sunny day can be 20 degrees F (7 degrees C) colder than the air around your head. Exchanging perspiration-damp socks for dry ones helps to warm the

Chugach State Park offers excellent cross-country skiing.   ASP photo

feet, too. Dry the damp ones next to your body in your sleeping bag at night.

If you're having trouble staying warm, "pre-warm" air by breathing through a scarf or fur ruff or by forming a parka-hood tunnel. At night put a handkerchief over the breathing hole of a drawn-together sleeping bag hood. Inhaling cold air and exhaling warm air causes significant body heat loss.

Avoid exhausting yourself. If you can't see where you are going, don't travel. Prepare a shelter and wait out the darkness or weather.

The Eskimos have known for centuries that snow makes an excellent shelter, and many winter backcountry travelers use snow shelters in preference to tents. If the snow is deep enough, dig a snow cave with a shovel or an automobile hubcap. Since heat rises, make the entrance to the finished cave lower than the cave chamber. Protect the entrance from wind with snow blocks, but don't let it seal shut with blowing snow; maintain adequate ventilation at all times. Enough air normally will pass through most snowpacks, but if the walls and ceiling of your cave become glazed with a light layer of ice from the heat of your occupancy, you could run low on oxygen.

If there is too little snow to construct a cave, dig a trench and cover the top with a tarp. Dead tree branches, grass, or sticks laid on the snow floor of your emergency shelter will keep you off the cold snow itself.

Summer or winter, start your bivouac early, well before daylight fades. If this is your first experience, you may easily spend 2 to 3 hours preparing a shelter and gathering firewood. Try to camp near a water source or plan to melt snow for water. Although snow can safely be eaten for moisture, it will rob the body of valuable heat. By drinking water, even if it is cold, you lose far less body heat.

Be alert to the danger of carbon monoxide when fire is used in poorly ventilated shelters, including tents. Unconsciousness can occur with little warning. Breathe fresh air immediately if you feel pressure at your temples, headache, pounding pulse, drowsiness, or nausea.

Hypothermia. Whenever you and your companions are exposed to windy, cold, or wet weather, watch for the symptoms of hypothermia: uncontrollable and continued fits of shivering; vague, slow, slurred speech; memory lapses and incoherence; fumbling hands; frequent stumbling; and drowsiness. A hypothermic person often is unable to get up after a rest stop and acts exhausted. Since many cases of hypothermia develop from being wet in relatively warm air temperatures, from 30 degrees to 50 degrees F (minus 1 degree to 10 degrees C), or from simply falling into cold water, the danger is easily underestimated.

First aid for hypothermia: Don't let a hypothermic person exercise, walk, or struggle—the activity increases the flow of cold blood from the arms and legs back to the heart. Move the person gently—heartbeat irregularities can result from rough handling. Don't rub or massage any part of the body. Get the person into dry clothes or a warm sleeping bag. If no dry clothing or other covers are available, wring out wet clothes and put them back on, placing the person in rain gear or plastic to slow down heat loss from evaporation and to protect from wind.

Don't give a severely hypothermic person hot liquids to drink. A pharyngeal reflex increases the blood flow to the skin and the extremities, bringing cold blood back to the trunk. If the person is only chilled, drinking hot liquids probably is safe.

Rewarm the victim slowly by applying heat from chemical packs, hot-water containers, or wrapped hot stones to the areas of the body that transfer heat to the body core most efficiently—the groin, the sides of the chest, the head, and the neck. Rewarm cautiously—people have been severely burned from over-enthusiastic warming. While rewarming, insulate the entire body to prevent further heat losses. Less effective, but often the only choice, is to cover the victim entirely with heated clothing and sleeping bags or provide heat with your body, removing your clothing and the victim's and lying skin-to-skin in a sleeping bag. Two warm bodies with the victim between are even better. An open fire can provide heat, too, but guard against "backside" chill by putting a reflector behind the victim. Get medical help as soon as possible. Complications such as pneumonia or heart problems can occur later in severe cases.

Frostbite. Another danger associated with cold weather is frostbite, the damage resulting from freezing body tissues. Hands, feet, face, and ears are the most likely body parts to become frostbitten. Wind chill on exposed flesh speeds freezing; so does direct contact with cold metals and other highly conductive materials. Rather than work bare-handed, for dexterity wear thin thermal gloves when handling cameras or ski bindings or making equipment repairs.

At low air temperatures, with or without wind, check each other's faces and ears frequently for white patches. Make a mental check of yourself to be sure you can feel sensation in every part of your body, and train yourself to snap to alertness when pain or feeling stops.

Anything that reduces the heat-producing capacity of the body (inactivity, fatigue, hypothermia, shock, or low caloric intake) or that robs the body of heat (inadequate or wet clothing, severe cold, wind, or alcohol) contributes to frostbite. An injury, combined with shock, inactivity, and anxiety, sets the stage for serious frostbite. Do not apply traction to arm or leg fractures in cold temperatures; splint the fracture as it lies and watch the victim carefully for signs of frostbite. In such cases, it can develop rapidly and often is severe.

First-aid treatment for frostbite is complicated and must be done correctly to prevent permanent damage to tissues or joints. Before you travel in Alaska in winter, study the procedures for treating frostbite in a good mountaineering first-aid book.

Extremely light frostbite, often called "frost nip," should be treated immediately. Cover a white patch on the face with a warm hand to return the flesh to a rosy glow. Hold frost-nipped fingers or toes (without boots) in a warm armpit. Never rub a frostbitten area with anything, especially snow.

Treat the frostbitten person for hypothermia, and check other areas—particularly ears, hands, wrists, ankles, and feet—for further frostbite. Loosen any tight clothing, but don't ask the person to flex any frozen joints. Get the person to medical help for rewarming as soon as is safely possible.

Begin rewarming the frozen tissue yourself only if the person is in a permanent location and can be completely protected from the cold. If at all possible, don't begin rewarming at high altitudes. The person must not, under any circumstances, use a rewarmed frostbitten part of the body. Walking out on frozen feet will cause far less damage than walking on rewarmed feet.

Avalanches. More than 30 percent of Alaska is subject to avalanche activity for up to 9 months a year. Although most avalanches fall in uninhabited areas without endangering human life or property, in the last half of the twentieth century more than 400 people died in avalanches in the United States.

Anyone living in or visiting Alaska, particularly winter outdoor enthusiasts such as skiers, snowshoers, dog mushers, and snowmobilers, should know about avalanches. So should motorists; the Seward, Richardson, Glenn, and Haines Highways and the Hope Road are a few of the public roads that cross dangerous avalanche paths. Do not rely on state highway precautionary road closures for your safety. Learn to identify hazardous conditions and limit your travel at those times. In summer, mountaineers, hikers, and anyone traveling on snow in the mountains also can face avalanche hazard.

Your best insurance for trouble-free snow-country travel is to educate yourself. Study the publications listed in the Appendix and attend one of the many avalanche education seminars given annually in the state and in the Lower 48. Many sessions are free or have only a nominal fee. Contact the Alaska Division of Parks or the U.S. Forest Service for information. Before starting a winter trip, call the parkland manager or check the statewide avalanche phone advisory listed in Information Sources in the Appendix under Travelers' Current Road and Weather Information.

Make sure that all party members understand avalanche rescue techniques thoroughly. Throughout Alaska, rescue assistance is generally a day or more away, while minutes often mean the difference between survival and death.

All members of a party venturing into hazardous areas should wear avalanche-victim locator beacons (electronic transceivers). Each transceiver, worn like a necklace, is set to transmit continuously. If a companion is buried, searchers switch their units to receive the "beep-beep" signal of the buried beacon, the signal becoming stronger the closer a searcher is to the buried unit. Be sure batteries are strong and fully charged before each trip.

Once the locator beacon has been found, probing with a long stick accurately identifies the exact location of the victim. Some sort of probe should be carried. The standard avalanche probe is a rigid tube about 10 feet (3 m) long, with most models breaking into sections for easy transporting. Ski poles are available that convert into avalanche probes by joining the pole sections after the handles and baskets have been removed.

At least one Alaskan directly owes his life to the locator beacon and to his companions, who efficiently located and uncovered the little box. The victim was encased in hard dense snow, 6 feet (2 m) deep, for 30 minutes before the shovelers freed him. The victim's locator beacon was working, his health was good, and his companions were prepared.

Obviously, each person in the party should carry a shovel. Statistically, a person buried for 30 minutes has a 50 percent chance of being found alive. For burial deeper than 6 feet (2 m), survival is not likely.

The use of avalanche cords has been popular for many years. The cord, a long trailing brightly colored nylon line, is supposed to "float" on the surface of the avalanche, leading rescuers to the victim, but they are unreliable, as often the cord is buried deeper than the victim. Rescue by locator beacon is faster and more effective.

Party members should have training in first aid, especially in cardiopulmonary resuscitation (CPR). Courses are taught frequently in most communities. Five percent of avalanche victims have broken bones; 80 percent of avalanche deaths are caused by suffocation.

If you are caught in an avalanche, fight for your life! Yell immediately to attract attention—let your companions know you are being carried away. If you are on skis or a snowmobile, try to run out of the avalanche to safety. If outrunning it fails, get rid of any equipment such as skis or poles that might pull you under or hurt you. When caught in an avalanche, make a vigorous effort to "swim" in the turbulence. It can help you stay on top of the snow or bring you to the surface. If you have control, try to descend feet first to fend off rocks or trees.

As the snow slows, give an extra kick for the surface. Before the snow stops moving, protect your face with one arm in an attempt to make an air space. With the other, reach for the surface. Your companions will find you more easily if even your fingers show. If you can dig yourself out, do so. Your companions may need help. If you are trapped, stay calm to conserve air and strength. Meditate, relax, avoid panic. Don't shout excessively or struggle. Your rescuers probably won't be able to hear you even if they seem to be standing on your head. If you feel that you might pass out, let it happen. Your body needs less air when you are unconscious.

If a companion is caught in an avalanche and you are not, don't panic. Check first for further avalanche danger. A second slide from a tributary drainage might follow the first. Station an observer in a safe place to watch for further avalanches and establish a safe escape route for all searchers.

Mark the spot where the person was last seen and search downhill, following the flow lines of the avalanche. Work silently, listening for possible cries from the victim. Look particularly wherever snow debris accumulates—in front of trees, on the outside of a turn in the avalanche path, at the foot of the avalanche. Leave any of the victim's possessions in the place where you find them, sticking up in the snow, to help establish the direction the victim was carried. Make probes from whatever is handy—ski poles, tree branches, anything. You are the victim's only hope. Continue probing, digging and marking the searched areas until you have exhausted all possibilities. Search at least 2 hours before giving up. Be sure, however, that you, the survivors, don't endanger your own lives through exhaustion and hypothermia. If the victim is found alive, give CPR immediately if necessary, and treat for shock and hypothermia.

Lest you begin to feel that Alaska presents only challenges beyond the ability of an average person—it isn't so. Few Alaskans have experienced hypothermia, frostbite, or avalanches. Nevertheless, such hazards do exist. If you are out in the backcountry on your own, you should understand them and be prepared.

Villages and the Bush

For decades, to Outsiders, the romance of Alaska has been the cozy snow-laden log cabin and the stilt-legged cache in the forest, snowshoes crossed over the door, smoke curling from the chimney, the northern lights dancing above, and wolves howling in the night air.

Many Alaskans still live in the Bush, but few cabins are as picturesque as those painted on Alaska souvenirs, nor are the people as isolated from society as the early sourdoughs or the nomadic Native Alaskans once were. The heartbeat of rural Alaska today lies primarily within the villages, where schools, supplies, transportation, medical help, and jobs are available. Community events and television received from satellite signals provide entertainment. Most houses are of frame construction, complete with electricity and running water. A snowmobile or four-wheeler sits outside the front door.

You'll find that rural villages of fewer than 400 people have limited services. Most have active community organizations, a church, and perhaps an air taxi operation. Local powerboats might be available for charter. The village store carries basic food and merchandise suited to the local lifestyle, but if a shipment is late, the shelves can be quite empty. Generally, however, fresh fruits and frozen meats are stocked, along with standard canned and packaged foods, and white gas and kerosene. Shopping at village stores can be a pleasant and interesting experience.

In many villages visitors are not frequent; you may be the subject of a lot of curiosity and gossip. Small villages are much like extended families. Enjoy your stay, but be unobtrusive, friendly, and courteous.

Ask before you camp, bathe in the river, or build a fire. You might be tenting in someone's backyard, washing off your accumulated grime upstream from the village

Villagers like those who live in Minto often rely on four-wheelers and snowmobiles (locally called snowmachines or snow-gos) to get around.   Tricia Brown photo

water supply, or burning a private wood supply. Assume that all land in the vicinity of a village is privately owned and you won't be far wrong. Many villages have designated areas for visitors to camp and to use for personal hygiene, so ask. Ask, too, about the village social schedule. You might have arrived in time for a dance or some other special occasion that you may be invited to attend.

Many villages have voted themselves "dry," prohibiting the importation or sale of alcoholic beverages. If your baggage includes alcohol, avoid displaying or consuming it in public until you are aware of local regulations.

A few villages have indicated that they prefer not to have visitors or tourists in their settlements. Please respect their request for privacy and, if your route passes through these villages, be friendly but do not linger. Many Alaskans strongly value their quiet, isolated lifestyle and are justifiably upset when the uninvited world beats a path to their doors.

To appreciate village life, an understanding of the heritage of Alaska's first people is essential. Visit your local or university library for books about Alaska's history and people. A large number of interesting books have been written on the subject, and are available through interlibrary loan if your library does not have them.

The interior of Saints Peter and Paul Church on St. Paul Island. The Russian Orthodox faith has thousands of followers in Alaska, especially in the Bush.   Tricia Brown photo

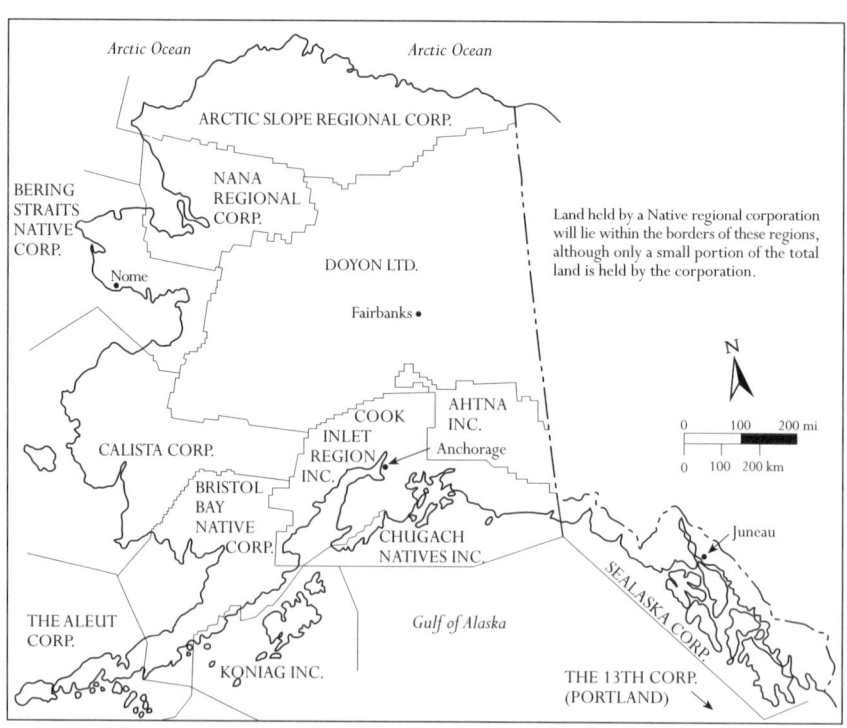

Figure 4. Alaska Native corporation regions (from Anchorage Daily News)

Telephones in the Bush. For years, two-way radios were the standard communication in both isolated households and villages. They are still in use, but the more convenient telephone, using a satellite-bounced signal, now connects almost all Alaska communities. Not every home has a telephone, but every village has at least one community phone at the city hall or tribal government office. To reach an individual or business in a village with a community phone, obtain the village phone number from Directory Assistance and call, either leaving a message or making arrangements to speak directly to the desired person at some time in the future. Many community phones are available for village use only during certain hours. Arrange to be available for a return call from your party at one of the village phone-use times or ask to have your party waiting at the phone for your call. Remember that your party may have to travel a mile or more by foot, boat, snowmobile, or dogsled to reach the telephone. Similarly, the person answering the telephone might have difficulty getting a message to your party.

Private Lands. As a result of the 1971 Alaska Native Claims Settlement Act, one-ninth of Alaska's acreage was transferred to private ownership, most of it in rural areas, some contained within parks and refuges. The national forests, the Yukon Delta, Yukon Flats and Selawik National Wildlife Refuges, and the Wrangell–St. Elias National Preserve contain significant amounts of private acreage, but you can assume that most of the lands and waterways are open to public travel.

Outside parklands, you must assume land is privately held if it is easily accessible from the road system, a village, or a river, or if it contains any type of structure, from a cabin to a fish-drying rack or a permanent campsite. If you wish to cross or camp on private land, ask permission before doing so. Be a courteous guest, protect the vegetation from serious damage, cut no live trees, leave no garbage, and do not hunt.

Before beginning a wilderness trip, contact the appropriate Native corporation (see Figure 4) for information regarding Native land holdings, sending a sketch of your proposed route and a self-addressed stamped envelope. (Addresses are in Information Sources, Appendix.)

The whole concept of public versus private lands throughout the state, and their use, has been a highly controversial issue in Alaska and will continue to be so for some time, so don't be upset by an occasional angry Alaskan. Use all of your diplomatic skills when asking permission for passage on private lands and you'll both be happier.

Land beneath navigable lakes, rivers, and streams is regulated by the state. It is therefore considered public land below mean high water and is open to public travel. (This in no way guarantees public access across private lands to reach the lake, river, or stream.) Those who defined navigability for the Lower 48 many years ago did not foresee the use of floatplanes or the importance of small riverboats, hovercraft, canoes, kayaks, and rafts in Alaska. Nor did they address the use of frozen waterways as transportation corridors—a major use of the river and stream systems in much of Alaska for more than 6 months each year.

For information regarding the status of a specific piece of land, contact the Land Office, Bureau of Land Management (address in Land Managers, Appendix). Because of the continuing transfer of lands from the public domain to private ownership, no current map exists showing land ownership. The BLM coordinates information about all lands within the state, stores it on microfiche, and makes it available to the public.

Wild Foods

To many Alaskans, May and June mean more than spring flowers. Tender young plants lift their leaves toward the warm sun—salads waiting to be gathered. Fish swim the cool stream waters, clams spout on the beaches, and, by August, berry bushes hang heavy with plump fruit. In autumn, hunters stalk the hills for game.

Alaska's bounty awaits you, but be aware of state and parkland restrictions. The harvesting of animal life, including some shellfish, is controlled by the Alaska Department of Fish and Game unless otherwise restricted by parkland regulations. Hunting, fishing, and trapping are discussed in the section about Wildlife.

Plants and Mushrooms. Wild plants and berries for personal use may be gathered on most state and federal lands, although some areas do not permit digging the roots. Be sure you can recognize both poisonous plants and poisonous mushrooms. Check the Suggested Reading list in the Appendix for publications on wild plants.

Paralytic Shellfish Poisoning. At unpredictable times and places, red tides occur along the coast, evidence of dense populations of dinoflagellates, a marine protozoan. Certain species of dinoflagellates can produce potent neurotoxins that can cause death within 2 to 12 hours. Numerous fatalities throughout the history of the Pacific Coast have been attributed to paralytic shellfish poisoning. Not all red tides produce toxin. In Alaska, toxic dinoflagellates rarely form visible red tides; toxic shellfish often occur when the water is not discolored.

Shellfish most likely to concentrate the toxin by consuming the dinoflagellates are clams, mussels, cockles, scallops, rock scallops, and oysters. Crabs, shrimp, and abalone are not known to cause paralytic shellfish poisoning. Most shellfish lose their toxicity within several weeks after exposure, but butter clams can retain the toxin for as long as 2 years. Poisonous shellfish cannot be distinguished by sight, taste, or smell. Isolated pockets of toxic shellfish can occur in an area of nontoxic ones.

Only Alaska's commercial razor clam beaches are monitored for the toxin and bacteria levels on a regular basis by the State of Alaska. If toxin is discovered, an announcement is made through local news media. Monitoring on a few other beaches occurs on an informal, unscheduled basis. Since most of Alaska's clam beaches probably will continue to be unmonitored, treat all clams, mussels, cockles, rock scallops, and oysters as potentially toxic. For current information on toxicity levels, contact the local Alaska Department of Health and Social Services, Division of Public Health, or the Alaska Department of Fish and Game. Remember, however, that the beach that is safe today may be contaminated tomorrow.

Reaction to the toxin may be more severe if the shellfish are consumed with an alcoholic beverage. Some evidence also exists that adaptation to shellfish toxin can occur in people who eat shellfish regularly.

Although some toxin can be removed by discarding the dark digestive gland, gills, the nectar in which the shellfish are cooked, and the siphons of butter clams, there could be enough toxin left in the shellfish to cause illness or even death. The toxin is unaffected by cooking, canning, freezing, pickling, or drying the seafood.

Fireweed light up the roadsides in Southcentral Alaska. APLIC photo

A little clammer gets down to business at Deep Creek on the Kenai Peninsula.
ASP photo by Robert Angell

No antidotes exist for paralytic shellfish poisoning. Swallowing even a small amount of toxic meat or nectar can be fatal. Symptoms of paralytic shellfish poisoning are a tingling or numbness of lips, face, and neck and prickliness in fingers and toes. Headache, dizziness, and nausea may follow. In severe cases, speech becomes incoherent and the victim has a general feeling of weakness and lightness, the pulse is rapid, and breathing is difficult. Death occurs by respiratory paralysis and cardiovascular collapse.

First aid for paralytic shellfish poisoning: Induce vomiting; give a rapid-acting laxative. Treat for shock; use CPR—mouth-to-mouth resuscitation and closed-cardiac massage—if necessary. Do not give alcohol, digitalis, or stimulants. Get the victim to a doctor immediately. If the victim survives longer than 12 hours, chances of recovery are good.

Other types of poisoning can occur from eating shellfish. Those contaminated by raw human sewage can cause nausea, vomiting, diarrhea, and abdominal pain that strike about 10 hours after ingestion and usually subside rapidly. Severe contamination can cause hepatitis, which takes much longer to develop and recover from. Erythematous shellfish poisoning, an allergic reaction to shellfish, produces swelling, itching, and redness affecting the face and neck, and sometimes the whole body.

The Land and the Weather

Bordered on three sides by oceans and on the fourth by continental North America, the landmasses of Alaska are affected by arctic, continental, and maritime air masses. The result is a number of climate patterns, with complex transitions between them. Topography has such a significant effect on weather, climate, and plant life that

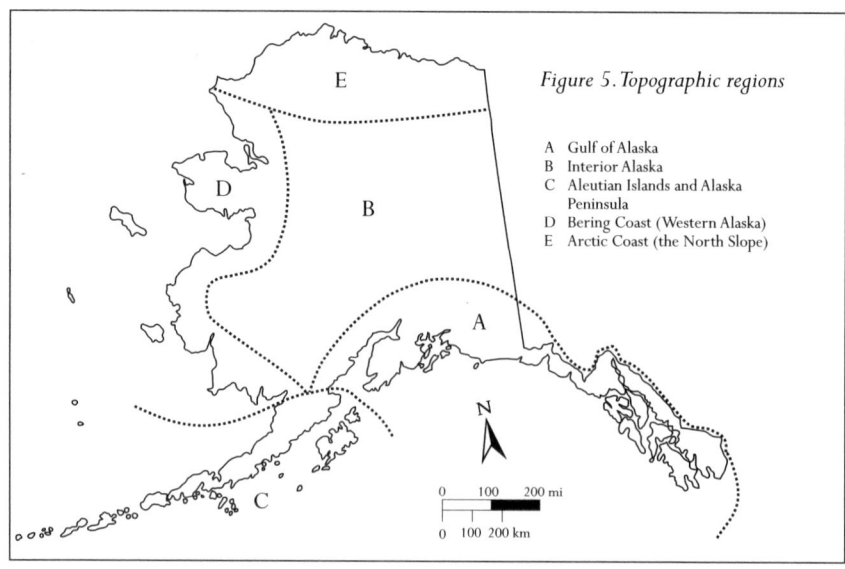

Figure 5. Topographic regions

A Gulf of Alaska
B Interior Alaska
C Aleutian Islands and Alaska
   Peninsula
D Bering Coast (Western Alaska)
E Arctic Coast (the North Slope)

0   100   200 mi
0 100 200 km

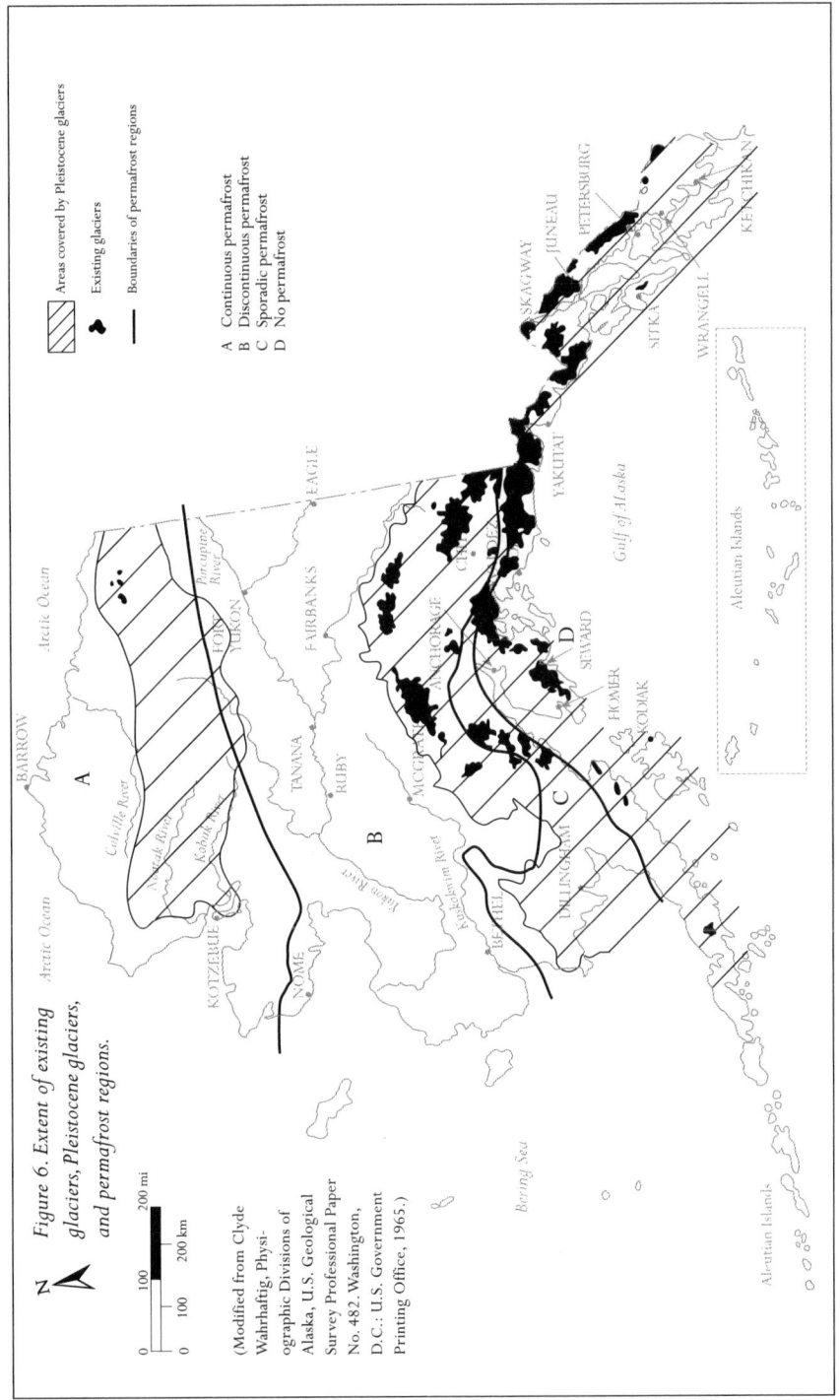

Figure 6. Extent of existing glaciers, Pleistocene glaciers, and permafrost regions.

(Modified from Clyde Wahrhaftig, Physiographic Divisions of Alaska, U.S. Geological Survey Professional Paper No. 482. Washington, D.C.: U.S. Government Printing Office, 1965.)

Areas covered by Pleistocene glaciers

Existing glaciers

Boundaries of permafrost regions

A   Continuous permafrost
B   Discontinuous permafrost
C   Sporadic permafrost
D   No permafrost

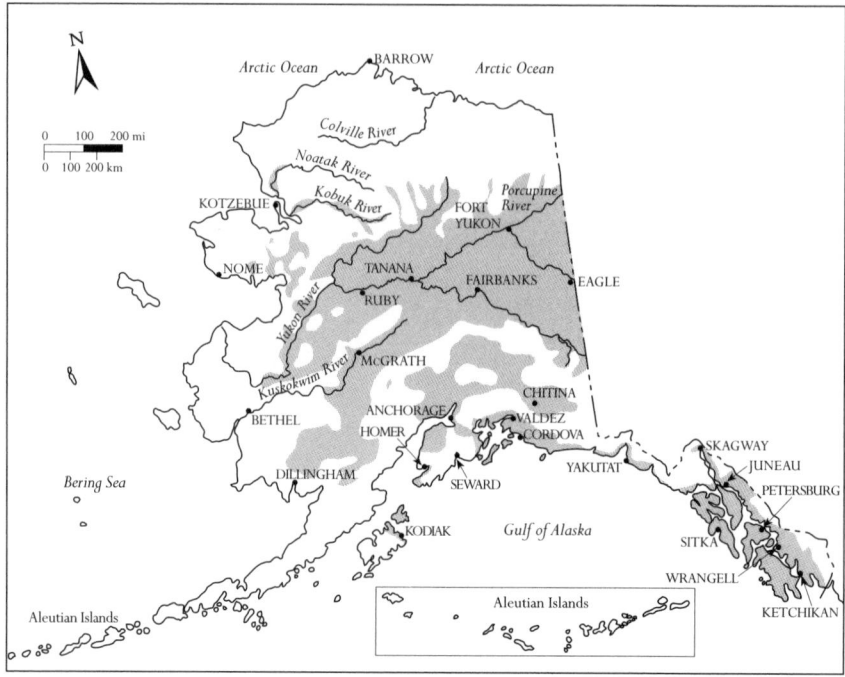

Figure 7. Forested regions   (U.S. Department of the Interior, Fish and Wildlife Service, Circular 211)

climatic and vegetation zones can best be described by major topographic regions (see Figure 5).

Two large mountain belts—the Alaska Range, paralleling the southern coast, and the Brooks Range, in the northern part of the state—separate the lowlands and rolling hills of the Interior from the rest of the state.

North of the Brooks Range, the land slopes gently from the base of the mountains to the Arctic Ocean, forming the North Slope. Along the western Gulf of Alaska, the southwestern extension of the Alaska Range becomes the Aleutian Range and the Aleutian Islands, while along the eastern Gulf Coast, the range becomes the St. Elias Mountains and the Coast Mountains. A spur of the Alaska Range, the Kenai and Chugach Mountains, drops steeply to tidewater along the north Gulf of Alaska coast.

Extensive glaciation has occurred across Alaska. Today, many of its mountainous areas contain massive ice fields and piedmont and valley glaciers, remnants of the latest glacial advance.

Much of Alaska's landmass is underlain by permafrost. Only the Aleutian Islands and the lands adjacent to the Gulf of Alaska do not contain significant amounts of permanently frozen ground (see Figure 6).

The North Slope, western Alaska, the Alaska Peninsula, and the Aleutian Islands are almost entirely treeless. Forests cover only about 30 percent of the state's surface area (see Figure 7). The distribution of many animal species correlates closely with the existence or absence of forests.

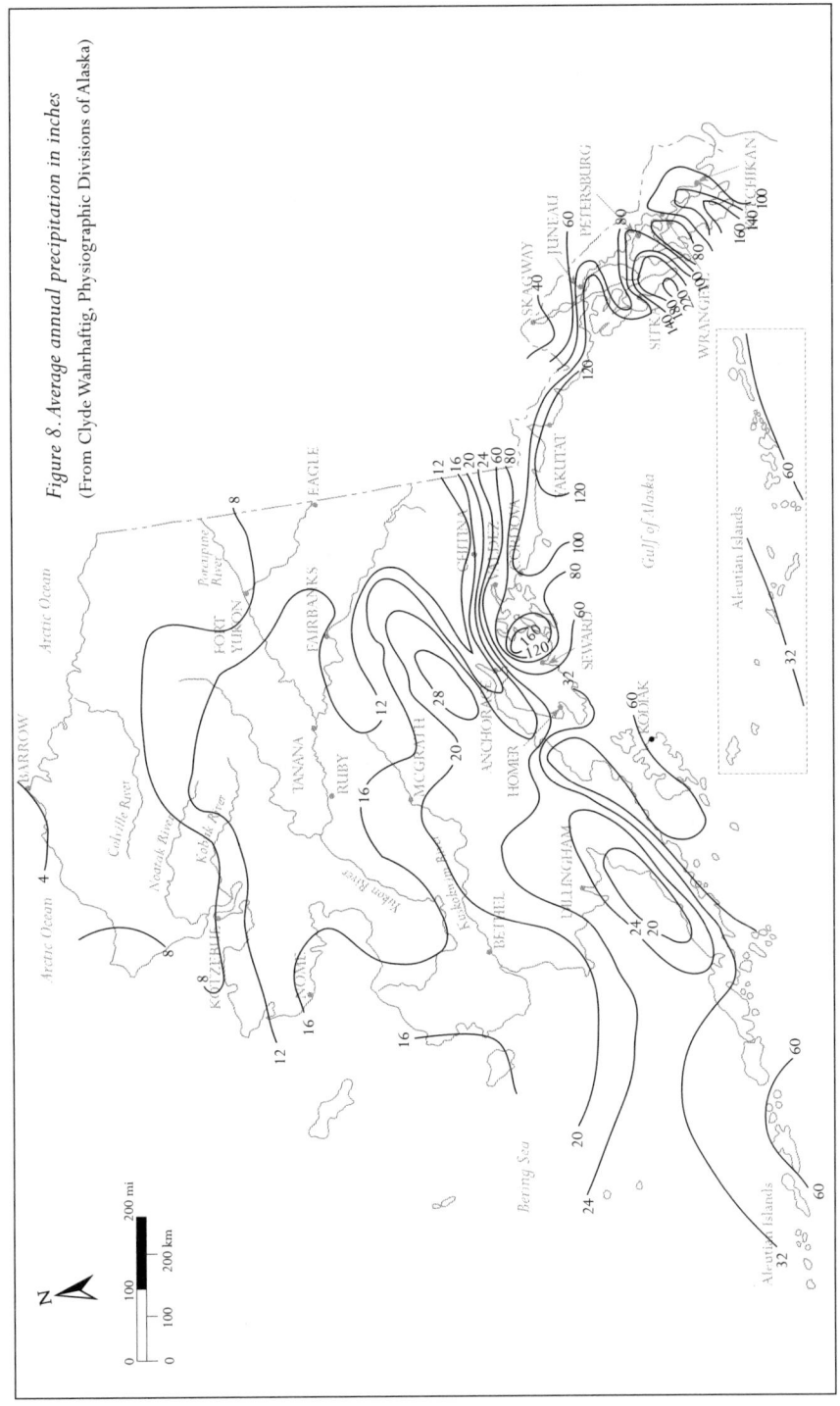

Figure 8. Average annual precipitation in inches
(From Clyde Wahrhaftig, Physiographic Divisions of Alaska)

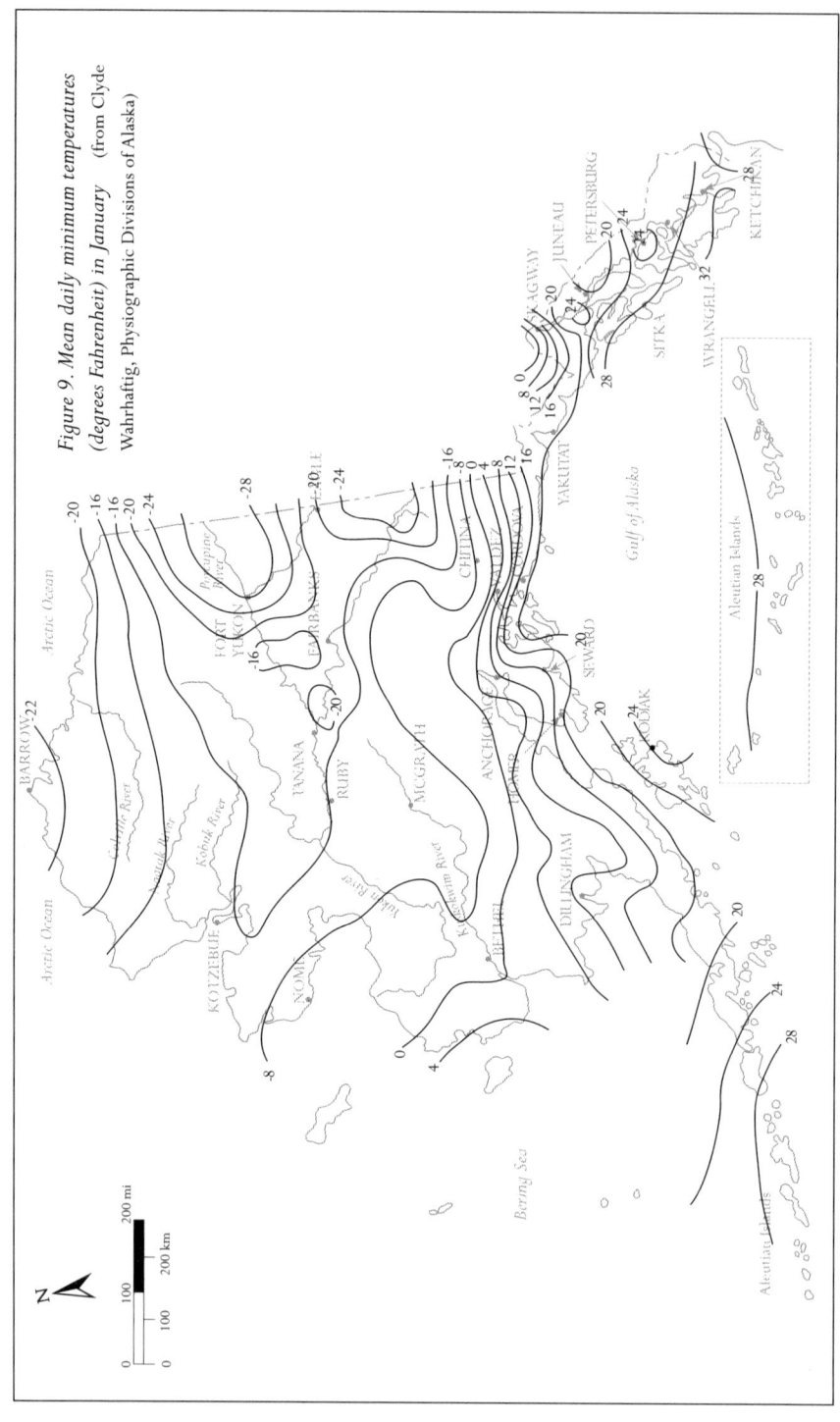

Figure 9. Mean daily minimum temperatures (degrees Fahrenheit) in January (from Clyde Wahrhaftig, Physiographic Divisions of Alaska)

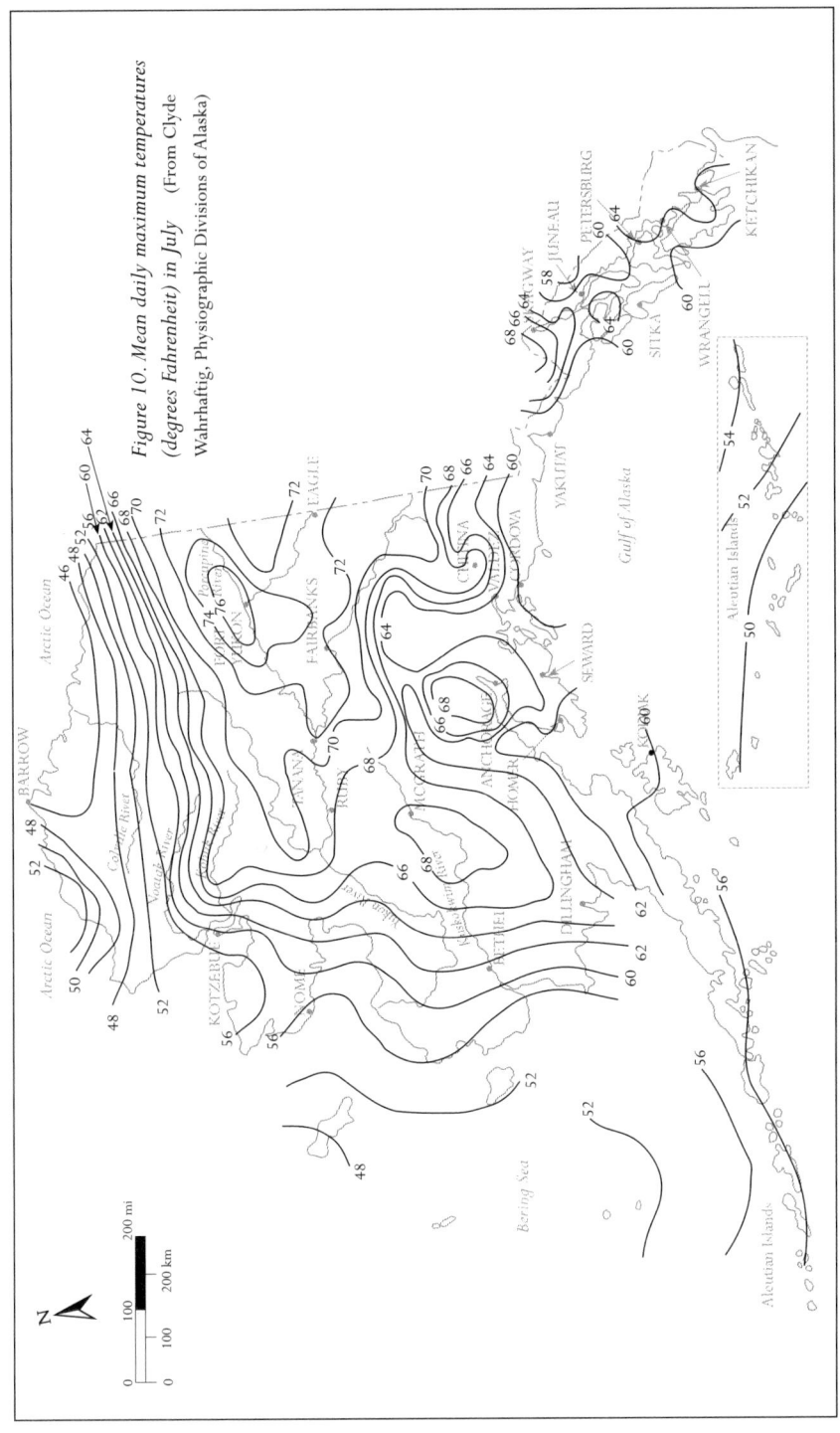

Figure 10. Mean daily maximum temperatures (degrees Fahrenheit) in July (From Clyde Wahrhaftig, Physiographic Divisions of Alaska)

Thirty-three species of trees are native to the state, the fewest number of species found in any of the 50 states. Only 12 species can be classed as large trees—those that reach more than 70 feet (20 m) high. Nine of these species are found only in the coastal forests of southeastern Alaska; Sitka spruce and western hemlock are seen most often in Southeast. Interior Alaska boreal forest (taiga) contains three species of large trees: white spruce, paper birch, and balsam poplar.

Weather Data. Over the years, weather records have been kept for most settlements in Alaska—some sketchily, and for only a few years, some faithfully for decades. Even the most incomplete records are of interest to visitors, since they give some indication of the temperatures and precipitation to be expected for the area.

Because most parklands are some distance from a weather station, study topographic maps and extrapolate, from the Weather Tables in the Appendix, probable temperature and precipitation differences for the area you'll visit. Figures 8, 9, and 10 also will help.

PART II
115 National and State Parklands

About the Parkland Descriptions

The parklands are organized regionally and numbered to make it easy to find them on the overall map. Each parkland description begins with a brief block of at-a-glance information. The text that follows the information block holds more specifics about flora and fauna, weather, recreation ideas, cautions, and directions for access.

Parkland name. The official name at press time is given. Local usage often lags behind official name changes. The two accepted spellings "fjord" and "fiord" have created an unavoidable inconsistency in this book. The National Park Service uses the former spelling, as do we; the U.S. Forest Service uses the latter.

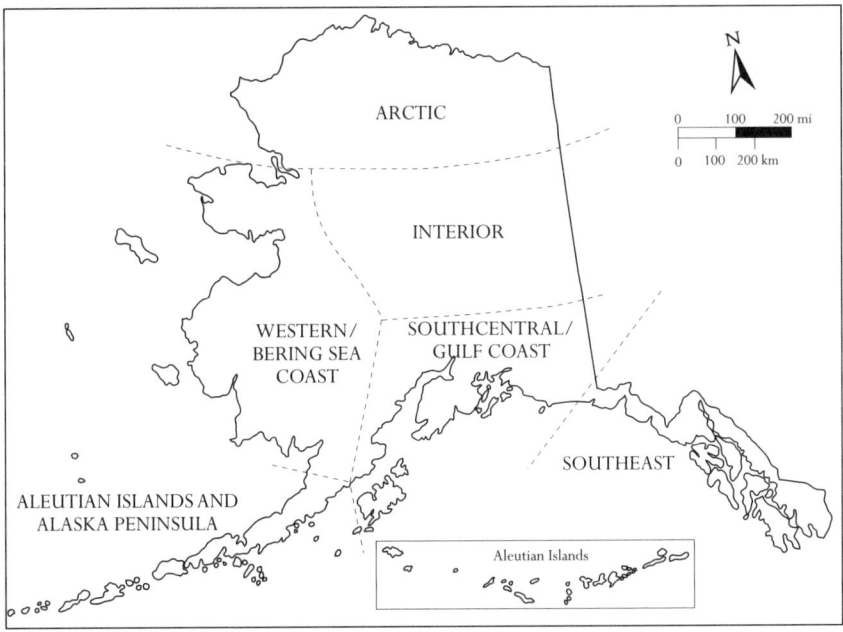

Figure 11. Divisions of the state for locating parklands

Location. The parklands are organized into regional divisions as outlined in Figure 11. A more precise location is given next, referring to a nearby major town, natural feature, or major parkland.

Size. The acreage listed is the best estimate available at press time. Boundaries occasionally are changed through additions, deletions, or land exchanges. In more recently designated parklands, sizes have been estimated until detailed surveys can be made.

High point/low point. Comparison of these figures helps describe the terrain of the parkland, whether it has high or low relief, an alpine or low-elevation environment.

Best time of year. Although some activities can be pursued through the greater part of the year, a few months normally are the most pleasant for a given activity. (Bear in mind, of course, that unusual weather conditions can change everything.) Optimum times for summer travel are indicated by "foot," water travel, by "boat," and winter travel, by "ski."

Daylight. Included is the number of daylight hours for a particular area on June 21 or 22 (summer solstice) and December 21 or 22 (winter solstice). Refer to the chart titled "Hours of Daylight at Sea Level" in the Appendix for more help in determining how many hours of daylight to expect.

Activities. The motto "know before you go" applies here. It's important to understand what activities are permitted in the area you wish to travel. Some parklands are off-limits to hunting, fishing, or other resource extraction; some have limitations on use of off-road vehicles, powerboats, or aircraft. Study the regulations before making travel plans.

USGS maps. Two USGS topographic map scales are most useful for travelers: the 1:250,000 scale, in which 1 inch equals 3.9 miles (1 cm equals 2.5 km), and the 1:63,360 scale, in which 1 inch equals 1 mile (1 cm equals 0.63 km). The maps listed for a parkland are those that most reasonably show the entire unit. To describe the extensive Yukon Delta National Wildlife Refuge requires fourteen 1:250,000-scale maps; most of the refuge is also mapped in the 1:63,360 scale. Tiny Sitka National Historical Park, on the other hand, is best described by Sitka A-4, a 1:63,360-scale map, but the traveler might also wish to refer to the 1:250,000-scale map to understand the relationship of the park to surrounding lands. Canadian maps also are listed for some border areas.

Established. The year in which the area was officially set aside as a protected area is given.

Managed by. Six government agencies—four federal and two state—manage Alaska's public lands. Descriptions of the agencies, addresses, and phone numbers are listed in the Appendix. Parkland descriptions include points of interest and history, wildlife, general recreational information, facilities available, boating information, weather, prominent peaks (not necessarily the highest), cautions, and access information. Parkland regulations given here are current at press time, but are subject to change. Looking over some of the literature available about the parklands is an excellent way to understand more about the land, its significance, and special features. Alaska-oriented publications for suggested reading are included in the Appendix.

SOUTHEAST

Alaska's Panhandle is a geologic jumble of islands and mountainous terrain split by deep-water passages, glaciers, and jagged fjords. Blanketed by rain forest and ice fields, nearly all of the landmass in Alaska's Panhandle is included in the 17-million-acre Tongass National Forest. Timber, fishing, government, and tourism drive the regional economy among small, far-flung communities that are bound to each other through the state-operated ferry system called the Alaska Marine Highway.

Summers are mild, with frequent rains and long periods of overcast skies; winters are also mild, with temperatures usually above or near freezing along the outer coast. Where Gulf of Alaska weather influences prevail, salt water is ice-free in the winter.

Local topography largely determines the amount of precipitation that falls, with the greatest amount on south-facing slopes and coastlines. In general, precipitation is heavy, ranging from 30 inches (76 cm) to an estimated 400 inches (1000 cm) annually. October consistently is the wettest month. Clear days occur most frequently from February through June. Fog can occur anytime during the year, but is most likely in late summer and early winter. Snow often falls wet and heavy, or sometimes initially light and

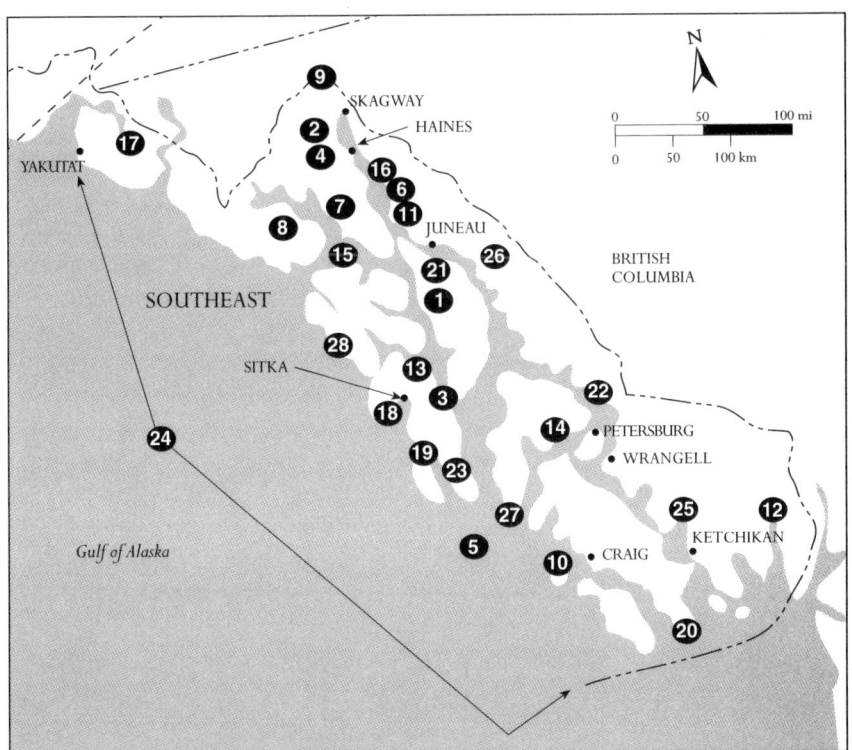

powdery only to turn heavy as temperatures rise. Winds generally are light in protected valleys, but are almost constant and often strong along the coast and at high elevations.

Regional wildlife includes bears, deer, bald eagles, wolves, goats, and small furbearers such as foxes, beavers, and porcupines. Whales, sea otters, seals, sea lions, dolphins, and porpoises may be spotted in coastal waters of the Inside Passage. The water route was made famous during the 1898 Klondike Gold Rush; cruise ships continue to ply the passage seasonally.

Recreationists can travel on many miles of developed trails within the region, and reserve any of the Tongass National Forest's 150 public-use cabins (available for a fee). Other activities on federal and state parklands include skiing, glacier-walking, mountaineering, wildlife photography, boating, fishing, hunting, historical and cultural sightseeing, and more. In the rain forest of Southeast, the key to enjoying the outdoors is dressing for the inevitable: rain.

1 Admiralty Island National Monument, Tongass National Forest

Location: South of Juneau
Size: 957,587 acres (387,530 hectares)
High point: 4650 feet (1420 m)
Low point: Sea level
Best time of year: Foot, June–October; boat, June–October; ski, January–March

Daylight: June 21: 18 hours
   December 22: 6½ hours
Activities: Wildlife-watching, camping, fishing, hunting, canoeing
USGS maps: Juneau, Sitka, Sumdum
Established: 1980
Managed by: U.S. Forest Service

The rugged spine of a partially submerged mountain range, with many bays and inlets, Admiralty Island National Monument has the greatest known concentration of nesting bald eagles in the world, averaging more than one nest per mile (1.6 km) of coastline in Seymour Canal—and one brown (grizzly) bear for every two eagles. Above treeline, rock outcroppings tower over alpine meadows and isolated snowfields. A prominent feature is Eagle Peak, elevation 4650 feet (1417 m).

For centuries, Tlingit Indians have lived and hunted on the island, known to them as *Xootsnoowu,* "the fortress of the bears." And 90 percent of the monument has been designated the Kootznoowoo Wilderness, preserving the old-growth forest as a permanent bear habitat and attracting a growing number of day visitors, who fly in from Juneau for a chance to view bears feeding at Pack Creek.

Admiralty Island was named for the British Admiralty in 1794 by explorer Captain George Vancouver. It contains ruins of more recent occupations by whalers, canneries, and mining operations. The Russian name for the island was *Ostrov Kutsnoi,* which translates as "fear island."

Flora and fauna: Dense spruce–hemlock rain forests rise to about 1500 feet (460 m) on the mountainsides, dotted with muskeg meadows. Trumpeter swans, whistling swans, and other migrating waterfowl stop on the island. Chatham Strait is a major flyway. Watch also for Sitka blacktail deer, beavers and small furbearers, and,

Canoeing below Salt Lake on Admiralty Island   USFS photo

offshore, seals, sea lions, and whales. Humpback whales winter in the canal; sea lions haul out on East Brother and West Brother Islands.

Recreation: The Forest Service maintains 15 public-use recreational cabins (reservations required, fee), 9 Adirondack-style open shelters, and an information office in Angoon. Marked trails include 19 miles (31 km) for hiking and a canoe route with 19 miles (31 km) of water travel and 7 miles (11 km) of portages. Prepare for long periods of rain. Camping in the backcountry is unrestricted; campfires are permitted, but expect wood to be wet. Camp and travel to avoid confrontations with the large numbers of bears. Fishing, hunting, firearms, and fixed-wing aircraft are all permitted; snowmobiles and off-road vehicles are not. Outboard motors of 10 hp or less are permitted on most lakes. Be aware that private lands exist within the monument boundary. Travel gently, without interrupting the personal rhythms and privacy of Angoon residents. Learn about the Tlingit culture before you come.

Water travel: Admiralty Island Canoe Traverse, FWA, Mole Harbor on Seymour Canal to Angoon at Mitchell Bay, with portages, 26 miles (42 km). Swift tidal currents in restricted bays and inlets can make boating hazardous. Plan to travel in these areas during slack water.

Weather and conditions: The maritime climate brings cool, wet, overcast summers and mild, wet, overcast winters. (See the Angoon weather table.) Winds are variable.

Directions/access: The monument is accessible only by boat or floatplane. Nearby Angoon is a port of call for the southeastern Alaska state ferry. Services available in Angoon include air taxis, scheduled air service, and food. Lodging and boat charters are available, but should be scheduled in advance.

2 Alaska Chilkat Bald Eagle Preserve

Location: North of Haines
Size: 44,350 acres (17,740 hectares)
High point: 250 feet (76 m)
Low point: Sea level
Best time of year: Foot, May–October;
  boat, May–October; ski, December–
  March

Daylight: June 21: 18½ hours
  December 22: 6 hours
Activities: Birding, fishing, hiking,
  photography
USGS maps: Skagway B-2, B-3, C-3
Established: 1982; amended 1986
Managed by: Alaska Division of Parks
  and Outdoor Recreation

Between late October and mid-December each year, as many as 3500 bald eagles from Southeast Alaska, British Columbia, the Yukon Territory, and Washington State feed on spawned-out remains of a late chum salmon run in the Chilkat River. Attracting the largest concentration of bald eagles in the world, warm water from the Tsirku (Big Salmon) River tributary keeps a 2-mile (3-km) stretch of the Chilkat River open in the winter, permitting access to the dying salmon after other rivers have frozen. The eagles are easily viewed along the Haines Highway, where they congregate in the trees and on the river bars. Smaller numbers of eagles use the area year-round. Because of the manner in which the eagles perch solemnly in groups on the stately cottonwoods, the area is locally known as the "bald eagle council grounds." Part of the old Dalton Trail, a route to the Klondike gold fields at the turn of the century, passes through the preserve.

Up to 3,500 bald eagles converge each fall at the Chilkat River.   ASP photo

The bald eagle was designated our national emblem in 1782, but long before that the eagle was one of the most important clan totems of the Pacific Northwest Indians.

Flora and fauna: Primarily a braided riverbed, the Chilkat River floodplain supports numerous tall cottonwood trees that provide convenient perches for the eagles. Sitka spruce, western hemlock, and lodgepole pine grow on higher ground. Marine mammals such as harbor seals, Dall porpoises, and sea otters can be seen in nearby inlets and at the mouths of local rivers. Watch for sea lions near tidewater in the Chilkat and Chilkoot Rivers, especially in early May when the eulachon (hooligan) are running.

Recreation: Photographing and observing the eagles are the most popular activities in the preserve, but for your own comfort, avoid standing under perched eagles—their "aim" is excellent. Fishing and hunting are permitted; snowmobiles and off-road vehicles may be used only in designated areas. Preserve facilities include toilets, drinking water, and trails.

Weather and conditions: The maritime climate brings cool, wet, overcast summers and mild, wet, overcast winters. (See the Haines weather table.) Winds are variable and can be strong, with blowing dust on the river bars.

Caution: Harassing or otherwise disturbing the eagles is prohibited by both state and federal laws.

Directions/access: The Haines Highway, from about Mile 8 to Mile 30, runs adjacent to or within the Preserve, making this an easily accessible area. A port of the southeastern Alaska state ferry, Haines also has scheduled bus and air service. Rental cars, stores, restaurants, lodging, and tours to the preserve are available in Haines. Follow the signs for a short drive out to the Southeast Alaska State Fairgrounds and walk through Dalton City, the movie set used in the 1990 Disney film *White Fang*.

3 Baranof Castle Hill State Historic Site

Location: In Sitka
Size: 1 acre (0.4 hectare)
High point/Low point: 50 feet (15 m)
Best time of year: Any time
Daylight: June 21: 18 hours
    December: 7 hours

Activities: Guided or unguided tours
USGS map: Sitka A-4
Established: 1968
Managed by: Alaska Division of Parks
    and Outdoor Recreation

On this hill on October 18, 1867, the American flag was first raised over Alaska during the transfer of the territory from Russian rule. Here, too, in 1959, when Alaska was granted full statehood, the 49-star flag first flew.

Extending their control to Southeast Alaska in 1799, Russian fur traders originally settled at Old Sitka, about 7 miles (11 km) north of this site, but the fort was destroyed in 1802 during a Tlingit Indian attack that sent the Russians into retreat. Two years later, Alexander Baranof, manager of the Russian–American Company and governor of Alaska until 1818, returned and drove the Tlingits from their village nearby. (See Sitka National Historical Park.)

Baranof Castle Hill is where the first American flag flew over Alaska.   Courtesy APLIC

Baranof built a fortified and finely furnished house on this hill in 1804. Seal-oil lamps in the cupola window served as the first lighthouse for mariners in western North America. Baranof, and succeeding Russian governors who built residences on this same hill, controlled an area that stretched from California to Bristol Bay in southwestern Alaska. The site was added to the National Register of Historic Places in 1962.

Interpretive plaques, walkways, and benches invite a leisurely visit. Children will enjoy "protecting" the fort from "sea attack" using the antique cannons.

Flora and fauna: The city lies at the foot of lush mountains blanketed by Sitka spruce and hemlock. From Castle Hill, which commands a magnificent view of Sitka's waterfront, watch for sea mammals—dolphins and porpoises, sea otters, seals, sea lions, and whales.

Weather and conditions: Expect a maritime climate with cool, wet summers and mild, wet winters. (See the Sitka weather table.) Winds generally are light.

Directions/access: You can reach the historic site via stone steps that begin at the corner of Lincoln and Katlian Streets, or from a gentle foot trail behind the hill. The southeastern Alaska state ferry dock is 7 miles (11 km) north of Sitka, on Halibut Point Road. Sightseeing tours, with schedules coordinated to ferry and cruise ship arrivals and departures, stop at the park and other points of interest. Both the ferry terminal and the airport are serviced by local buses. Stores, restaurants, lodging, taxicabs, rental cars, and water and air taxi charters are available in Sitka.

4 Chilkat State Park

Location: South of Haines
Size: 6056 acres (2422 hectares)
High point: 1741 feet (531 m)
Low point: Sea level
Best time of year: Foot, May–October; boat, May–October; ski, December–March
Daylight: June 21: 18 hours

December 22: 6 hours
Activities: Beach-combing, boating, hiking, fishing, picnicking, camping
USGS maps: Skagway A-1, A-2
Established: 1975; amended 1997
Managed by: Alaska Division of Parks and Outdoor Recreation

For years the Chilkat Indians guarded the access to mountain passes into interior Alaska from the Chilkat Peninsula, thus controlling trade between the Russians and the Interior Indians. Early Chilkat Indians dried halibut on what is now known as Battery Point, but after a large group of them died in nearby Lynn Canal, the survivors placed dog-shaped rocks as memorials and abandoned the area. In 1891, the U.S. Coast and Geodetic Survey named it Battery Point because of its resemblance to earthwork fortifications.

The two sections of Chilkat State Park include the former Battery Point State Recreation Area and the entire lower end of the Chilkat Peninsula. The area is tranquil, with spectacular views of Davidson and Rainbow Glaciers across Chilkat Inlet.

Flora and fauna: Hemlock and spruce are the predominant trees in the local forests. Birch, cottonwood, willow, alder, mountain ash, and Douglas maple also may be found. Local berries include highbush cranberries, strawberries, raspberries, and blueberries. Watch for moose, brown (grizzly) bears, black bears, deer, and bald eagles

Hiking Seduction Point Trail in Chilkat State Park   ASP photo by Bill Zack

in the park; whales, seals, and sea otters in Lynn Canal and Chilkat Inlet; and mountain goats on the mountainsides beyond.

Recreation: Chilkat State Park is an excellent destination for families with children and for those who want developed campground facilities. Campfires are permitted in campground fire pits or at established trailside tent sites only. Fifteen campsites are available as well as picnic tables and shelters, toilets, a boat launch, and marked trails. Hunting and snowmobiles are restricted to specific areas; off-road vehicles are not permitted. Do not discharge firearms near campgrounds, roads, or trails.

Weather and conditions: Expect a maritime climate with cool, wet summers and mild, wet winters. (See the Haines weather table.) Winds are generally moderate and constant on exposed headlands.

Caution: Sudden severe winds and waves on Lynn Canal can capsize small boats; there are uncharted rocks.

Directions/access: The two separate sections of Chilkat State Park are reached by two accesses. The developed section is reached via Mud Bay Road, south of Haines 7 miles (11 km). Then take the 2-mile (3-km) side road that leads to the park. Battery Point is reached via a 2.4-mile (3.9-km) trail from the end of Beach Road, about 2 miles (3 km) from downtown Haines. Rental cars, stores, restaurants, and lodging are available in Haines, a highway access point to the southeastern Alaska state ferry system. The town also has scheduled bus and air service.

5 Coronation Island Wilderness, Tongass National Forest

Location: South of Sitka
Size: 19,232 acres (7783 hectares)
High point: 1960 feet (600 m)
Low point: Sea level
Best time of year: April–August
Daylight: June 21: 17½ hours

December 22: 7 hours
Activities: Camping, fishing, hunting
USGS maps: Craig D-7, D-8
Established: 1980
Managed by: U.S. Forest Service

Captain George Vancouver named the island as he sailed past it on September 22, 1793, the anniversary of the coronation of George III of England. The steep, protruding summit of a partially submerged mountain, Coronation Island is covered by a dense spruce–hemlock rain forest. It has windswept beaches, precipitous cliffs, and a few protected coves, all surrounded by rocky shoals. Prominent peaks include Needle Peak, elevation 1960 feet (600 m), and Windy Peak, elevation 1765 feet (538 m).

Flora and fauna: Dominated by stands of spruce and hemlock, Coronation Island is an important seabird nesting and perching area. The island also is used by bald eagles, black bears, Sitka blacktail deer, and wolves. Offshore swim seals, sea lions, sea otters, and whales, with large numbers of harbor seals congregating in the bay near Helm Point.

Recreation: The island is undeveloped. Camping, campfires, fishing, hunting, and firearms are permitted. Since firewood normally is wet and winds strong, camping stoves are recommended.

A killer whale, or orca   ASP photo by Robert Angell

Weather and conditions: In this maritime climate, summers are cool, wet, and overcast; winters mild, wet, and overcast. (See the Sitka weather table.) Winds are constant and moderate to strong, becoming especially severe during autumn storms.

Caution: Prepare for long periods of rain. Prolonged storms can delay scheduled pickup and make boating hazardous. Only experienced boaters should attempt to visit the island.

Directions/access: You can reach the island by floatplane or boat. Air taxis operate from Ketchikan, Petersburg, Sitka, and Wrangell; boat charters are available at most coastal communities. Food and lodging are available at Craig, Ketchikan, Klawock, Petersburg, Sitka, and Wrangell.

6 Eagle Beach State Recreation Area

Location: Northwest of Juneau
Size: 590 acres (236 hectares)
High point: Less than 100 feet (30 meters)
Low point: Sea level
Best time of year: Foot, any time
Daylight: June 21: 18½ hours

December 22: 6 hours
Activities: Hiking, fishing, ski touring, picnicking
USGS map: Juneau
Established: 1996
Managed by: Alaska Division of Parks and Outdoor Recreation

A work in progress that's surrounded by fabulous views, Eagle Beach is a recent addition to the state's parklands. Access is easy from Alaska's capital city, as it lies on the Juneau-area road system.

Most visitors to Eagle Beach enjoy recreational activities along its large tidal beach and river bottom.   ASP photo

Flora and fauna: The park is located in a coastal rain forest of tall conifers. Flowing through the park are Eagle River and Herbert River, both prime habitat for all species of salmon. Wolves, grizzly (brown) bears, beaver, and other furbearers may be found here. Watch for bald eagles, ravens, and sea mammals.

Activities: While campsites have not yet been developed, day and overnight parking (fee) is available in a gravel area. Facilities do include 10 picnic sites, pit toilets, and trails, including groomed ski trails. Amalga Trail leads to Eagle Glacier.

Weather and conditions: The maritime climate is often overcast; summers are cool, winters mild. Winds generally are light in the lowlands, moderate to strong at high elevations. (See the Juneau weather table.)

Directions/access: Scheduled air service to Juneau is available, and car rental can be arranged there. Follow the Glacier Highway north from Juneau to Milepost 29. Groceries, gas, and supplies all can be arranged in Juneau, which is a port of call on the southeastern Alaska state ferry system.

7 Endicott River Wilderness, Tongass National Forest

Location: South of Haines
Size: 98,729 acres (39,954 hectares)
High point: 5805 feet (1769 m)
Low point: 50 feet (15 m)
Best time of year: Foot, May–
    September; boat, May–September
Daylight: June 21: 18½ hours

December 22: 6 hours
Activities: Camping, backpacking,
    fishing, hunting
USGS map: Juneau
Established: 1980
Managed by: U.S. Forest Service

A glacially carved river basin in the Chilkat Range of the St. Elias Mountains, Endicott River Wilderness adjoins the eastern edge of Glacier Bay National Park. The valley heads in snowfields and glaciers. Lower down, there is heavy brush above timberline, changing to rich spruce–hemlock rain forests below. A low pass at the head of the valley leads into Adams Inlet of Glacier Bay National Park. A prominent peak is Mount Young, elevation 5805 feet (1769 m).

Flora and fauna: Typical throughout Southeast, spruce and hemlock trees blanket the lower elevations. Many bald eagles that nest along the banks fish the Endicott River for salmon—as do brown (grizzly) bears and black bears. Moose, wolves, wolverines, and mountain goats are all found in the wilderness.

Recreation: Undeveloped and seldom visited, the scenic rain-forest wilderness can be used for backcountry camping, backpacking, fishing, and hunting. Firearms and

Endicott River in the Endicott River Wilderness   Tim Lydon photo

fixed-wing aircraft landings are permitted. Campfires may be built, but wood generally is wet.

Weather and conditions: The maritime climate often is overcast; summers are cool, winters mild. (See the Haines weather table.) Winds generally are light in the lowlands, moderate to strong at high elevations.

Caution: There are long periods of rain and wind, particularly in the autumn, making camping unpleasant and boating on Lynn Canal hazardous, and that may delay planned pickup. Severe avalanche hazard can exist.

Directions/access: You can reach the wilderness by floatplane or boat, both available for charter in Haines. Small, wheeled planes occasionally land on small river bars. Haines also offers food, lodging, and scheduled air service, and is a port of call for the southeastern Alaska state ferry.

---

8 Glacier Bay National Park, Preserve, and Wilderness

Location: West of Juneau

Size: 6,053,168 acres (2,421,267 hectares)

High point: 15,300 feet (4663 m)

Low point: Sea level

Best time of year: Foot, June–September; boat, May–October; ski (marginal), January–March

Daylight: June 21: 18½ hours

December 22: 6 hours

Activities: Kayaking, day-cruising, hiking, wildlife-watching, photography, river running

USGS maps: Juneau, Mt. Fairweather, Skagway, Yakutat

Established: 1925

Managed by: National Park Service

Massive tidewater glaciers, lofty mountain peaks, ice-sculpted fjords, salt-water beaches, and scoured rock emerging from an ice age—Glacier Bay in the St. Elias Mountains is John Muir country. Some of the glaciers are retreating, some are advancing, and some are holding their own. By walking from the base of a retreating river of ice along its earlier path, you can follow a wonder of nature: the gradual transformation of barren rock into rich coastal forest.

The summit of Mount Fairweather, 15,300 feet (4663 m), stands less than 15 miles (24 m) from tidewater. Nearby, in an indentation of the Gulf of Alaska coast, lies Lituya Bay where, in 1958, a mammoth earthquake triggered a rock and ice slide that crashed into the waters of the bay. The resulting wave scoured timber from the bay's hillsides to a height of 1720 feet (524 m). In addition to Mount Fairweather, other prominent peaks include Mount Quincy Adams, elevation 13,650 feet (4161 m), and Mount Crillon, 12,726 feet (3879 m).

The tidewater glaciers and ice-choked fjords make Glacier Bay one of the most popular destinations for visitors to Alaska. Most cruise ships plying the Inside Passage cruise the bay but do not stop. Park facilities include a lodge, dining room, exhibit area, gift shop, ranger station, fuel dock for boats, a primitive campground, and 7 miles (11 km) of marked trails.

Flora and fauna: The icy, plankton-rich ocean waters are favorite feeding areas for humpback, killer, and other whales, porpoises, sea lions, and seals. In addition to marine mammals, Glacier Bay protects a large bear population, both brown (grizzly) and black. A rare color phase of the black bear, the "blue" glacier bear, occasionally is sighted here. Watch also for moose, wolves, wolverines, Sitka blacktail deer, mountain goats, and bald eagles. The coastline of the Gulf of Alaska is a major migratory bird route. North and South Marble Islands, which contain the largest seabird colonies in the park, are closed to foot traffic during nesting season, from May 1 to September 1. Other bird colonies are similarly protected.

Recreation: Day cruises from nearby Gustavus may include stops for kayakers to disembark. Guided kayaking from the lodge also is available. Backcountry camping and mountaineering are not restricted but, for your own safety, check out and in with the Park Service at Bartlett Cove. Since firewood frequently is wet or unavailable, use a camping stove. The lodge is wheelchair accessible, as is the boardwalk portion of the Forest Loop Trail. Some drainages offer excellent wilderness hiking; other valleys are choked by thick brush or blocked by raging streams. Fishing is permitted, but hunting and the carrying of firearms are permitted only in the preserve.

Weather and conditions: Glacier Bay has a maritime climate, with cool, wet summers and mild, wet winters. Overcast conditions are normal. (See the Glacier Bay weather table.) Winds are variable and calm to strong. At high elevations, severe arctic conditions prevail.

Boat travel: Seeing the park by water is an ideal way to avoid the brush and glacial streams, but be conservative in the icy waters of the fjords, whether in a tiny kayak or a large powerboat. Keep your distance from icebergs and glacier faces. Boating permits are

Some tour operators in Glacier Bay will drop off kayakers.   APLIC photo

required from June 1 through August 31. Check with park rangers regarding restrictions in waters where humpback whales feed. The Alsek River is rated WW2–4 from Haines Junction to Dry Bay, 230 miles (370 km).

Caution: Wherever you travel, prepare for long periods of rain and strong winds—hypothermia is a real danger. Because fog, storms, and winds often affect schedules, plan to bring extra food whether you are traveling on foot or boating.

Directions/access: You can reach the park by air or by water, most often from Juneau. Scheduled air service serves Gustavus. A short bus route connects Gustavus and park headquarters at Bartlett Cove, but the local road system cannot be reached via the contiguous state highway system or from the state ferry. Sightseeing boats leave from Bartlett Cove, Gustavus, and Juneau. The park concessionaire's boat, offering daily trips from Bartlett Cove to Muir Inlet, regularly drops off and picks up backpackers and kayakers. Charter boats are available in Gustavus, Haines, Hoonah, Juneau, and Skagway. Air taxis operate from Gustavus, Haines, Juneau, Skagway, and Yakutat. Food and lodging are found at the Glacier Bay Lodge at Bartlett Cove, and in Gustavus.

9 Klondike Gold Rush National Historical Park

prob brief
Aug 2014

Location: At Skagway and Seattle, Washington

Size: 13,000 acres (5300 hectares)

High point: 3500 feet (1100 m)

Low point: Sea level

Best time of year: Skagway and Seattle, any time; Chilkoot Trail, late June–early September

Daylight: June 21: 18½ hours

December 22: 6 hours

Activities: Historic tours, hiking, flight-seeing, railroad tour

Maps: USGS, Skagway B-1, C-1; Canadian maps (1:50,000 scale), Skagway 104 M/11 East, 104 M/14 East

Established: 1980

Managed by: National Park Service

Four far-flung parks in one, this living memorial to the frenzied Gold Rush of 1898 stretches from Seattle to rugged mountains on the Alaska–Yukon border. Here are the famous town of Skagway, the townsite of Dyea, and the rigorous Chilkoot Trail and White Pass, all of which have been placed on the National Register of Historic Landmarks.

It all started with a note in the *Seattle Post-Intelligencer* on July 17, 1897: "The steamer *Portland*, headed for Seattle out of St. Michael, Alaska, steamed down to Seattle this morning with a ton of gold aboard." In Seattle, where the word "Gold!" reached the outside world and the rush to the Klondike gold fields began, a visitors' center in Pioneer Square now presents interpretive displays, films, and advice.

Up north, Skagway was the end of the line for steamships laden with gold-seekers from Seattle. A boisterous city in its heyday, today Skagway is a viable Alaskan town with many of its original buildings—some with false fronts—and boardwalks, a Gold Rush cemetery, a railroad station, a marina, a museum, a campground, and a National Park Service visitors' center. Walking and bus tours of the historic town are available.

Travel over the strenuous and dangerous Chilkoot Trail all but ceased when the

A century ago, the Gold Rush attracted many thousands to the Klondike gold fields.   APLIC photo

White Pass & Yukon Route was completed in 1900. The historic narrow-gauge railroad hauled passengers, freight, and vehicles between Skagway, Alaska, and Whitehorse in Canada. Today schedules include passage to Fraser and Lake Bennett, B.C., and to Carcross, Yukon Territory. Hikers can climb the Chilkoot Pass and book train passage back. Private railcars, with first-class plush seating, also may be chartered. Check for contact numbers in Information Sources, Appendix.

Klondike Highway 2, nearly 80 years younger than the railroad, also crosses White Pass, paralleling the tracks as it winds up the Skagway River to the 2890-foot (881-m) pass. Canadian customs are near the border 22 miles (35 km) from Skagway; a U.S. customs office is 6 miles (10 km) north of Skagway. The Skagway–Carcross section of highway is not maintained in winter.

The townsite of Dyea, at tidewater 9 miles (14 km) northwest of Skagway, is the beginning of the Chilkoot Trail. Other than Slide Cemetery, the resting place for more than 60 men and women buried in 1898 by an avalanche on the Chilkoot Pass, few relics remain of the busy frontier town. National Park Service facilities include a ranger information station, campground, and parking area.

Recreation: Tour Skagway, book a train ride, or follow the footsteps of the stampeders by hiking over the infamous Chilkoot Trail that traverses Chilkoot Pass in the rugged Coast Mountains. Feel the presence of the '98ers—they labored under similar conditions with a year's supply of grub and equipment, but you'll have the benefit of today's lightweight equipment and freeze-dried food. Write for National Park Service literature (Skagway office) before tackling the pass.

Beginning at Dyea in a coastal rain forest, the trail snakes upward, gradually

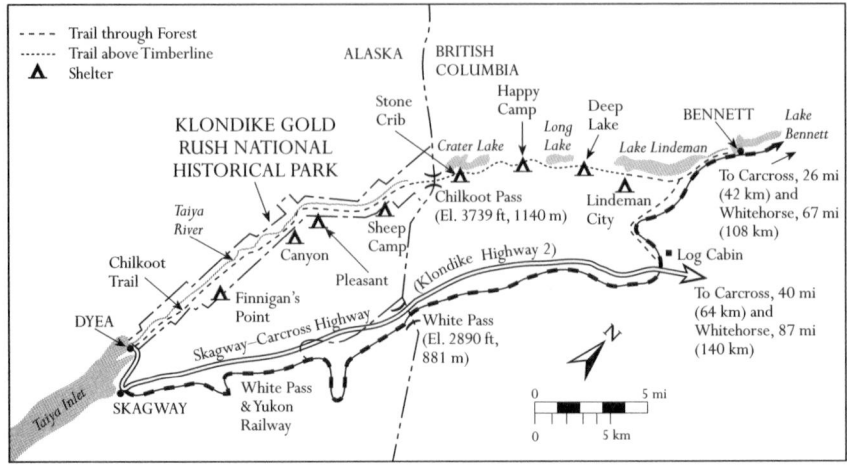

steepening, through a rocky, brushy canyon to the foot of barren Chilkoot Pass. The final ascent to the pass, elevation 3739 feet (1140 m), is extremely steep and filled with unstable boulders—a slope more easily climbed than descended. Allow 3 to 4 days for the 33-mile (53-km) hike.

Trailside facilities include three drying-out log-cabin shelters with woodstoves. Tent shelters and camping are available at Finnigan's Point, Canyon City, Pleasant Camp, Sheep Camp, Stone Crib, Happy Camp, Deep Lake, and Lindeman City. Campfires are permitted only at the designated camping areas; otherwise use a camping stove.

You'll cross into Canada at the summit. Within a few miles the summit snow gives way to spacious meadows of alpine tundra, inviting off-trail exploration. The gentle, pleasant downgrade continues to Lake Lindeman and Lake Bennett, elevation 2153 feet (656 m). Since you'll be crossing the U.S.–Canada border, you must clear customs. Check with the Park Service for current regulations concerning hikers on the Chilkoot Trail.

Buy your railroad ticket before hiking the trail (none are sold at Lake Bennett, nor are there commercial facilities for hikers) and return to Skagway in scenic comfort. Hikers can also board or get off the train at Fraser and Carcross.

To exit via Klondike Highway 2, turn right where the north end of the Chilkoot Trail reaches the railroad and follow the tracks south about 5 miles (8 km) to the highway crossing at Log Cabin, near Kilometer Post 45, 27 miles (43 km) from Skagway. Check the bus schedule or arrange a pickup before starting your hike.

Weather and conditions: In summer the trail is crowded. Weather normally is wet and foggy, but the trip is worth every hardship. (See the Skagway weather table.) The maritime climate changes to a drier, warmer subarctic continental climate in Canada.

Caution: Strong winds at the pass can be dangerous. Driving rain, thick fog, deep mud, and slick rocks are normal, so prepare for them. Hypothermia is a constant danger. Large residual snowfields at the pass persist into late summer; be sure to wear sunglasses if skies are clear to prevent snowblindness, and use extreme caution if the pass is icy. Despite the large numbers of people hiking the trail, conditions are rugged and can be life-threatening. Do not attempt the trip in winter; avalanche hazard can be severe.

The Chilkoot Trail still presents challenges to the modern-day hiker.   APLIC photo

All artifacts in the United States and Canada are protected; do not collect or damage them. Firearms may not legally be taken into Canada; check guns with the Skagway Police Department or the Royal Canadian Mounted Police before the hike. Hunting, horses, and motorized vehicles are prohibited. Dogs must be kept on a leash at all times.

Directions/access: Skagway, Whitehorse, and Carcross are on the highway system and have scheduled bus and train service, food, and lodging; the first two also have campgrounds, scheduled air service, and air taxis. Taxicabs in Skagway can take hikers to the Dyea trailhead. Skagway is a port of call for the southeastern Alaska state ferry.

10 Maurelle Islands Wilderness, Tongass National Forest

Location: South of Sitka
Size: 4937 acres (1998 hectares)
High point: 600 feet (200 m), on
    Anguilla Island
Low point: Sea level
Best time of year: April–August
Daylight: June 21: 17½ hours

December 22: 7 hours
Activities: Salt-water kayaking, camping,
    hiking, photography
USGS maps: Craig C-5, C-6
Established: 1980
Managed by: U.S. Forest Service

An exposed group of about 30 low-relief forested islands, islets, and wave-washed rocks, the Maurelles are surrounded by rocky shoals. With their windswept beaches,

San Lorenzo Island is one of several small islands that make up the Maurelle Islands Wilderness.
USFS photo

rocky shorelines, and rich spruce–hemlock rain forests, the islands make for interesting salt-water kayaking. They were named for the Spanish navigator Don Francisco Antonio Maurelle, who surveyed the region from 1775 to 1779 under the command of Don Juan de la Bodega y Quadra.

Flora and fauna: Spruce and hemlock dominate the forest. Sea otters, seals, sea lions, and whales use the waters. Seabirds nest and perch ashore. On the larger islands you may see black bears, wolves, Sitka blacktail deer, and bald eagles.

Recreation: The islands have no recreational facilities. Camping, campfires, firearms, fixed-wing aircraft, and powerboats are permitted. Carry a camping stove, since wood probably will be wet and winds often are too strong for fire-building. Prepare for long periods of rain and strong winds.

Weather and conditions: Cool, wet, overcast summers and mild, wet, overcast winters are normal for this maritime climate. (See the Sitka weather table.) Winds are constant and often strong, especially during autumn storms.

Caution: Carry extra food, since weather can delay planned pickup. The waters can be hazardous; only experienced boaters should attempt to visit the islands.

Directions/access: The islands are reached by floatplane or boat. Air taxis operate from Ketchikan and Wrangell. Craig and Klawock have boat charters, scheduled air service, food, and lodging.

11 Mendenhall Wetlands State Game Refuge

Location: In Juneau
Size: 3600 acres (1440 hectares)
High point: 10 feet (3 m)
Low point: Sea level
Best time of year: Foot, any time
Daylight: June 21: 18½ hours
    December 22: 6 hours

Activities: Birding, photography, fishing, hunting, boating
USGS map: Juneau B-2
Established: 1976
Managed by: Alaska Department of Fish and Game

In the heart of Juneau, these tidal marshlands and willow thickets are a staging area for migrating waterfowl and shorebirds in the spring (April and May) and fall (September to November). The Mendenhall is well known for large concentrations of Vancouver Canada geese from late winter through spring; you can observe them easily from the road. The refuge also is used by other marsh-associated birds, including bald eagles, short-eared owls, and marsh hawks, and by furbearers, especially river otters and mink. Some year-round resident Vancouver Canada geese and mallards nest in the area.

Harbor seals may be seen near the Mendenhall River or Fritz Cove. Watch for river otter, mink, and short-tailed weasels as well.

Recreation: Other than an interpretive center at Lemon Creek, the refuge is undeveloped. Regularly used by joggers and hikers, it also attracts beach-combers, photographers, fishermen, and waterfowl hunters. Other hunting is prohibited. No aircraft or motorized vehicles (except boats launched outside the refuge) are permitted.

Weather and conditions: Juneau's maritime climate brings cool, wet, overcast summers and mild, wet, overcast winters. (See the Juneau weather table.) Winds are moderate.

Close-up photos of mallard ducks are easy with accessible viewing areas at Mendenhall Wetlands State Game Refuge.   APLIC photo by Glenn Oliver

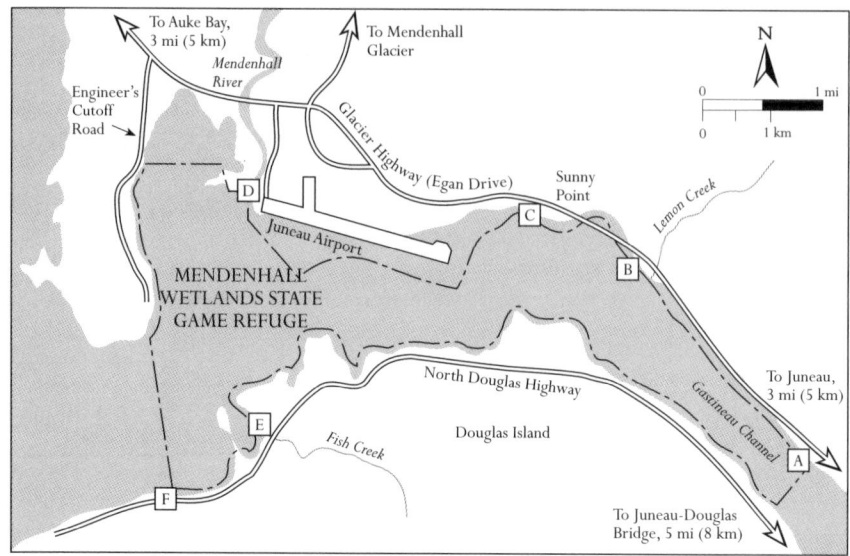

Caution: Use caution when venturing onto the tide flats—windblown high tides can catch the unwary.

Directions/access: The refuge lies beside the Juneau airport and east along Glacier Highway (Egan Drive) from Mile 3 to Mile 10 (measured from the Juneau downtown ferry terminal). The most convenient access points to the refuge's tide flats are at (A) Mile 3 from a parking lot cul-de-sac; (B) Lemon Creek at Mile 6; (C) Sunny Point at Mile 7; and (D) off Berners Avenue at the west end of the Juneau airport. On Douglas Island, the North Douglas Highway parallels the refuge from Mile 4.5 to Mile 9.5. Access is available (E) just before the Fish Creek bridge at Mile 8.5 or at (F) Cove Creek, Mile 9.5.

Rental cars and taxicabs are available at the Juneau airport and in the city of Juneau; scheduled buses travel the Glacier Highway. The southeastern Alaska state ferry calls at either Juneau or Auke Bay, depending upon the particular routing. Stores, restaurants, and lodging are available in Juneau and Auke Bay and along the highway.

aug 20 00

12 Misty Fiords National Monument, Tongass National Forest

Location: East of Ketchikan

Size: 2,294,343 acres (928,491 hectares)

High point: 7499 feet (2286 m)

Low point: Sea level

Best time of year: Foot, May–October; boat, April–October; ski, January–March

Daylight: June 21: 17½ hours

December 22: 7 hours

Activities: Flight/cruise sightseeing, fishing, camping

USGS maps: Bradfield Canal, Ketchikan, Prince Rupert

Established: 1980

Managed by: U.S. Forest Service

Sheer granite walls tower thousands of feet into the clouds above narrow glacier-carved fjords and quiet valleys. The monument lies sandwiched between two impressive fjords, Behm Canal, stretching 117 miles (188 km) long, and Portland Canal, 72 miles (116 km) long. Two spectacular sights are Punchbowl Cove in Rudyerd Bay and New Eddystone Rock, the latter named in 1793 by Captain George Vancouver because of its resemblance to the lighthouse rock off the coast of Cornwall, England. Unusual for Southeast are the periodic lava flows that occur near Blue River. Prominent peaks

The Punch Bowl at Misty Fiords   USFS photo

include Mount John Jay, elevation 7499 feet (2286 m), and Mount Jefferson Coolidge, elevation 7073 feet (2156 m).

Flora and fauna: Although the area is only recently free of major glaciation, vegetation is lush, with dense spruce–hemlock rain forests and inviting muskeg and alpine meadows. Treeline is at about 2000 feet (about 610 m). Wildlife is abundant and varied, with mountain goats, brown (grizzly) bears, black bears, Sitka blacktail deer, wolverines, wolves, red foxes, beavers, mink, marten, river otters, a few moose, and numerous bald eagles. Offshore, watch for seals, sea lions, porpoises, dolphins, and whales.

Recreation: The Forest Service maintains 14 public-use recreational cabins (reservations required, fee), 4 Adirondack-style open shelters, and 23 miles (37 km) of marked trails. Backcountry camping is unrestricted and campfires are permitted, but the wood most likely will be wet. Fishing, hunting, firearms, horses, fixed-wing aircraft, and powerboats are permitted; snowmobiles and off-road vehicles are not.

Weather and conditions: A maritime climate prevails along the coast with cool, wet, overcast summers and mild, wet, overcast winters. (See the Annette Island weather table.) Inland, weather is more continental, with less rainfall. Winds are light to moderate at low elevations, moderate to severe at high elevations.

Caution: Prepare for long periods of rain; prolonged storms can delay planned pickup. In winter, avalanche hazard can be severe. Camp and travel to avoid confrontations with the numerous bears.

Directions/access: You can reach the monument by air or water. Excursion boats from Ketchikan and cruise ships visit the fjords. Charter boats are available at Ketchikan; air taxis are based at Ketchikan and at Stewart, B.C. All three communities have food and lodging. Several wilderness lodges operate within the monument. Scheduled airlines serve Ketchikan and Stewart; Ketchikan is a port of call for the southeastern Alaska state ferry.

13 Old Sitka State Historic Site

Location: North of Sitka	**Activities:** Picnicking, beach-walking,
Size: 51 acres (21 hectares)	fishing, clamming
High point: 50 feet (15 m)	**USGS map:** Sitka A-5
Low point: Sea level	**Established:** 1968
Best time of year: Any time	**Managed by:** Alaska Division of Parks
Daylight: June 21: 18 hours	and Outdoor Recreation
December 22: 7 hours	

Originally established in 1799 by Alexander Baranof, manager of the Russian–American Company, and known as St. Michael the Archangel Redoubt, Old Sitka was the first Russian settlement in Southeast. It eventually consisted of a two-story barracks, warehouses, a bathhouse, a kitchen, an eight-cornered *kashima,* or communal house, for Native workers, a blacksmith shop, and a cattle barn. Baranof would have preferred to build the fort where downtown Sitka now stands, but the area was occupied by Tlingit Indians.

Archaeological sites in the Sitka area yield many exciting finds from the Russian period and earlier. ASP photo

During a Tlingit attack in the spring of 1802, all of the buildings in Old Sitka were burned; most of the men were killed and women and children were taken as hostages. Two years later, Baranof was successful in capturing the site of the Tlingit village to the south, and erected a lavish fortified home on a nearby hill. (See Baranof Castle Hill State Historic Site.)

In 1878, Alaska's first cannery was built on the Old Sitka site, but 4 years later the machinery was moved to the Kasilof River on the Kenai Peninsula. Local students salvaged lumber from the buildings to build the first structure on the Sheldon Jackson College campus in Sitka.

Old Sitka Site was added to the National Register of Historic Landmarks in 1962. Today the site is marked by a Russian Orthodox cross, an interpretive plaque, and a visitors' information center reminiscent of a Russian teahouse. Camping, hunting, use of firearms, snowmobiles, and off-road vehicles are not permitted. The Tongass National Forest Starrigavan Campground is just north of the ferry terminal and the historic site.

Flora and fauna: Old Sitka is located in a coastal rain forest of tall conifers. Watch for bald eagles, ravens, and sea mammals.

Weather and conditions: The maritime climate brings cool, wet summers and mild, wet winters. (See the Sitka weather table.) Winds generally are light, stronger on the beach.

Directions/access: The site is north of the city of Sitka at Mile 6.9 Halibut Point Road, adjacent to the Sitka ferry terminal. Stores, restaurants, lodging, taxicabs, rental cars, scheduled air service, and air and water charters are available in Sitka. Local buses serve the area. Sightseeing tours generally include Old Sitka. Sitka is a port of call for the southeastern Alaska state ferry and most cruise ships.

14 Petersburg Creek-Duncan Salt Chuck Wilderness, Tongass National Forest

Location: West of Petersburg
Size: 46,849 acres (18,740 hectares)
High point: 3577 feet (1090 m)
Low point: Sea level
Best time of year: Foot, May–
September; boat, May–September;
ski, January–March
Daylight: June 21: 18 hours

December 22: 6½ hours
Activities: Picnicking, hiking, fishing,
hunting, camping, boating, ski
touring
USGS maps: Petersburg D-3, D-4, D-5
Established: 1980
Managed by: U.S. Forest Service

Two low U-shaped valleys, richly cloaked in spruce–hemlock rain forest, lie on Kupreanof Island across Wrangell Narrows from Petersburg. With tide flats, a lagoon and a lake, muskeg bogs, and rolling uplands, the wilderness is a popular outdoor recreation area for local residents.

Flora and fauna: Spruce and hemlock dominate the forest. Petersburg Creek, a salmon-spawning stream, attracts black bears; bald eagles perch and nest on tall snags; and Sitka blacktail deer move quietly through the forest. Also found here are wolves, wolverines, and waterfowl, including an occasional swan.

A 6.5-mile national recreation trail leads from the mouth of Petersburg Creek at tidewater to Petersburg Lake. The U.S. Forest Service cabin on the lake is also connected by trail.
USFS photo by R. Romel

Recreation: The U.S. Forest Service maintains two public-use recreational cabins (reservations required, fee), one at Salt Chuck East and one at Petersburg Lake. Backcountry camping is unrestricted and campfires are allowed, but expect the wood to be wet. Use a firepan or a mound fire to minimize the impact.

Petersburg Lake National Recreation Trail, 6.5 miles (10 km) long and wet in places, leads from the tidewater mouth of Petersburg Creek to the lake. The Portage Mountain Trail is a 10-mile (16-km) primitive trail that connects the Petersburg Lake cabin to Portage Bay and the Salt Chuck East cabin. Fishing, hunting, firearms, fixed-wing aircraft, and powerboats are all permitted in the wilderness.

Weather and conditions: Cool, wet, overcast summers and mild, wet, overcast winters are typical of this maritime climate. (See the Petersburg weather table.) Winds are generally light.

Caution: Be cautious on the tide flats—don't get caught by the incoming tide. Boaters planning to enter or leave Duncan Salt Chuck should travel at slack high water to avoid dangerous tidal currents, and watch for shallow submerged rocks in the channel.

Directions/access: The wilderness is reached by boat or floatplane; both are available for charter in Petersburg. Restaurants, lodging, and a wide variety of stores are also found in this charming fishing town. Petersburg has scheduled air service and is a port of call for the southeastern Alaska state ferry.

---

15 Pleasant-Lemesurier-Inian Islands Wilderness, Tongass National Forest

Location: West of Juneau
Size: 23,151 acres (9260 hectares)
High point: 2180 feet (654 m)
Low point: Sea level
Best time of year: Foot, June–
    September; boat, May–October
Daylight: June 21: 18 ½ hours

December 22: 6 hours
Activities: Kayaking, camping, hiking,
    wildlife-watching, photography
USGS maps: Mt. Fairweather A-1, A-2,
    B-1, B-2; Juneau B-1
Managed by: U.S. Forest Service

Comprised of three large islands and a smattering of islets, this wilderness area is a study in topographic diversity and recreational use.

Pleasant Island: A low-profile island covered with old-growth forest and muskeg, Pleasant is the most accessible and visitor-friendly of the three islands. Its beaches allow a safe approach for small boats and kayaks, hiking trails connect the shoreline to small inland lakes, and camping is good in several areas. Located a few miles from Gustavus, the gateway to Glacier Bay National Park, Pleasant Island is a popular destination for picnickers, campers, and kayakers heading to or from the park.

Lemesurier Island: Just west of Pleasant Island, this piece of the wilderness makes a dramatic rise from the sea to 2180 feet (654 m). Unlike Pleasant and the Inian Islands, Lemesurier is not forested; its terrain is subalpine. A small lake on the south side is accessible from the shore, and campers arriving in small boats or kayaks can safely

The view from Pleasant Island looking south toward the village of Hoonah in the Pleasant-Lemesurier-Inian Islands Wilderness   USFS photo by Geno Cisneros

approach several beaches on the north and south shores. Private lands exist on the island's south side. Be respectful of private property.

Inian Islands: Closest to the Pacific Ocean, this grouping of islands are the most hammered by the characteristic outer coast weather, yet their coves traditionally have provided safe harbor for commercial fishing vessels. The half-dozen small islands, with extremely narrow passages between a few, are located between open ocean and Icy Strait. One pass is aptly named the "Laundry Chute," for the swift current moving between islands. Use caution as swells and winds often are unpredictable. Note that the main island includes two small private parcels of land. In the 1920s these islands were used for fox farming.

Flora and fauna: Icy Strait is an excellent place for watching wildlife, particularly marine mammals such as humpback whales, killer whales, sea lions, seals, sea otters, and porpoises. Seabirds and other birds, including murrelets, gulls, terns, and bald eagles, are abundant. On the islands, watch for brown (grizzly) bears, deer, marten, mink, river otters, red squirrels, ptarmigan, and grouse.

Recreation: There are no public facilities on the islands. Campers must pack in and out all of their own gear, supplies, and garbage.

Directions/access: Access is limited to boat, kayak, or floatplane. Scheduled air service and charters are available in Juneau, Gustavus, and Hoonah. All three communities have food, lodging, and accommodations. Juneau and Hoonah are ports of call on the southeastern Alaska state ferry system.

16 Point Bridget State Park

Location: Northwest of Juneau
Size: 2880 acres (1152 hectares)
High point: 800 feet (239 m)
Low point: Sea level
Best time of year: Any time
Daylight: June 21: 18½ hours
    December 22: 6 hours

Activities: Hiking, wildlife-watching, birding, picnicking, photography, skiing, snowshoeing
USGS map: Juneau C-3
Established: 1988
Managed by: Alaska Division of Parks and Outdoor Recreation

In 1988, 14 young people from all over the world came to Point Bridget as part of a volunteer program called Operation Raleigh. The crew spent 4 weeks creating and improving most of the trails that thread through this beautiful parkland of rain forest, meadows, lakes, beachfront, and creeks. Point Bridget truly is a hiker's park, with five groomed trails that offer something for every experience level.

The area is steeped in history, from the time Native Alaskans lived here before contact with Europeans, through the gold rush and into homesteading days.

Flora and fauna: Forested mountains descend into meadows full of fragrant wildflowers such as bog orchid, black lily, and lupine. The rocky beach is a great viewing spot to watch for humpback whales, harbor seals, sea lions, and seabirds, but don't forget to look down, too. Minus tides expose the world of intertidal animals. Small land

The building of Cowee Meadow cabin in Point Bridget State Park was a joint effort among agencies and members of the community.   ASP photo

mammals in this area include porcupines, beavers, and squirrels. Black bears and deer inhabit the forest. Bald eagles are easy to spot in the treetops.

Recreation: Several miles of developed trails skirt the beachfront and wander through the old-growth rain forest of Sitka spruce trees. A public-use cabin, built in the fall of 1992, is available by reservation (fee). Alaska State Parks also has developed an excellent brochure with a map and a detailed description of each trail. (For contact information, see Land Managers, Appendix.)

Motorized vehicles are not allowed in the park. Fires are allowed on beaches, gravel bars, or fire grates provided by the park.

Weather and conditions: The maritime climate brings cool, wet summers and mild, wet winters. (See the Juneau weather table.) Winds generally are light, stronger on the beach.

Directions/access: The Point Bridget State Park trailhead is located north of Juneau at Milepost 39 Glacier Highway. Lodging, groceries, gas, and car rentals are available in Juneau, which is a port of call for the southeastern Alaska state ferry system.

17 Russell Fiord Wilderness, Tongass National Forest

Location: Northwest of Yakutat
Size: 348,701 acres (141,115 hectares)
High point: 7740 feet (2360 m)
Low point: Sea level
Best time of year: Foot, May–September; boat, April–September; ski, January–April

Daylight: June 21: 19 hours
    December 22: 6 hours
Activities: Hiking, fishing, hunting, camping
USGS map: Yakutat
Established: 1980
Managed by: U.S. Forest Service

Densely forested river valleys, tidewater glaciers, a two-armed fjord, alpine meadows, and snowcapped peaks combine to create an area of extraordinary beauty. The wilderness encompasses glacier-carved Russell and Nunatak Fiords and portions of the surrounding rugged, heavily glaciated mountains. The fjord was named for Israel Cook Russell, who explored the Yakutat area and discovered the estuary in 1891.

Of great interest to geologists and biologists is the movement of Hubbard Glacier, north of the wilderness, which in 1986 temporarily closed off the entrance of Russell Fiord to the ocean. Once before, in the 1700s, Hubbard Glacier closed the mouth of Russell Fiord, creating a fresh-water lake that drained from its southern end into the Situk River. In 1986, the glacier dam held for only 6 months until a tremendous volume of water burst through into Disenchantment Bay, creating a spectacular sight.

The Yakutat Tlingit Indians have long used the area for subsistence needs. The Russian fur-traders once hunted here, and the United States fortified the area during World War II.

Flora and fauna: Moose, mountain goats, wolves, brown (grizzly) bears, and black bears are found in the wilderness. Seabirds nest on Haenke Island and Cape

Enchantment, and sea lions haul out on Knight Island. Watch also for Sitka blacktail deer, bald eagles, seals, sea otters, whales, and the rare "blue" glacier bear, a color phase of the black bear. The Gulf of Alaska coastline is a major flyway for migratory birds. The Situk River and Mountain Lake are important spawning waters for all five species of Pacific salmon and for steelhead trout. Fishing is excellent for salmon, trout, and Dolly Varden char. Treeline is about 1500 feet (460 m).

Recreation: Other than one public-use recreational cabin (reservations required, fee) on Situk Lake, the wilderness is undeveloped. However, 6 additional recreational cabins are scattered on the Yakutat Foreland south of the wilderness. A marked hiking trail from Mile 9 Forest Highway 10, east of Yakutat, leads to Situk Lake and the cabin, 7 miles (11 km) away; a brushy bear trail leads another 1.5 miles (2.4 km) to Mountain Lake.

Backcountry camping is unrestricted. Campfires, fishing, hunting, firearms, horses, fixed-wing aircraft, powerboats, and snowmobiles are all permitted.

Weather and conditions: In this maritime climate, expect cool summers and mild winters, with frequent precipitation and overcast. (See the Yakutat weather table.) Winds are moderate, often strong. At high elevations a severe arctic climate prevails.

Caution: Prepare for long periods of rain and strong winds, which can delay planned pickups. Storms are most intense in autumn and winter. Travel and camp to avoid meeting or attracting bears, especially near salmon-spawning streams. Entering Russell Fiord by boat is hazardous due to icebergs from Hubbard Glacier.

Directions/access: You may reach the wilderness by foot, on the Situk Lake trail, or by boat or floatplane from Yakutat. Food, lodging, and scheduled air service are available in Yakutat.

Russell Fiord   USFS photo

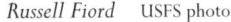

18   Sitka National Historical Park

Location: In Sitka
Size: 107 acres (43 hectares)
High point: 12 feet (4 m)
Low point: Sea level
Best time of year: Any time
Daylight: June 21: 18 hours

December 22: 7 hours
Activities: Picnicking, guided or
    unguided tours, fishing
USGS map: Sitka A-4
Established: 1910
Managed by: National Park Service

Tlingit artist Nathan Jackson carved the Yaadaas Crest Corner Pole in 1980.   NPS photo

A raven sits atop a bear that sits atop a beaver at a bend on a pleasant trail. The stately hemlocks nearby seem to have released their spirits in the form of finely carved Tlingit and Haida totem poles. Watch a new pole being carved and visit the restored Russian Bishop's House, a reminder of colonial Russian America.

In 1802, a Tlingit Indian attack destroyed the first Russian settlement in Southeast, north of the park at Old Sitka. (See Old Sitka State Historic Site.) Most of the Russian and transplanted Aleut men were killed, and the Aleut women and children taken as hostages. Two years later, Alexander Baranof, manager of the fur-trading Russian–American Company, returned with 800 Aleuts, 120 Russians, and four ships to confront the Tlingits on this site. The Battle of Sitka succeeded in forcing the 700 Tlingit warriors and their families to abandon their fort on the Indian River and their homes at Sitka. This was the last major Native act of resistance to white domination in this area. (See also Baranof Castle Hill State Historic Site.)

Recreation: Picnic tables, cooking grills, a shelter, a visitors' center, interpretive programs, and more than 2 miles (3 km) of trails invite a leisurely visit. Fishing is permitted; camping, hunting, and snowmobiles are not. The park grounds are open from 6:00 A.M. to 8:00 P.M. from October 1 to mid-May; the visitors' center is open 5 days a week. Summer hours are 6:00 A.M. to 10:00 P.M., and the visitors' center is open daily.

Weather and conditions: Bordered by Sitka Sound and the Indian River, this flat, wooded peninsula has a maritime climate with cool, wet summers and mild, wet winters. (See the Sitka weather table.) Winds normally are light in the forest.

Directions/access: Only 1 mile (1.6 km) from downtown Sitka, the park is within easy walking distance. Follow Lincoln Street east from the center of town to the park. Food, lodging, rental cars, taxis, and local buses are available. Guided sightseeing tours coordinate with ferry and cruise ship schedules. The southeastern Alaska state ferry dock is 7 miles (11 km) north of Sitka.

19 South Baranof Wilderness, Tongass National Forest

Location: South of Sitka
Size: 319,568 acres (129,325 hectares)
High point: 4528 feet (1380 m)
Low point: Sea level
Best time of year: Foot, May–October; boat, May–October; ski, December–March

Daylight: June 21: 18 hours
December 22: 7 hours
Activities: Camping, hiking, fishing, hunting, salt-water kayaking
USGS map: Port Alexander
Established: 1980
Managed by: U.S. Forest Service

With precipitous mountains, snowfields and hanging glaciers, high mountain lakes, alpine meadows, waterfalls, and long winding fjords, South Baranof Wilderness is a visual delight. Its mountains, the protruding summits of a partially submerged glacier-carved landscape, are cloaked in a dense coastal spruce–hemlock rain forest. Timberline is at about 2000 feet (600 m). A prominent peak is Mount Ada, elevation 4528 feet (1380 m).

The west side of South Baranof Wilderness   USFS photo

The island was named in 1805 for Alexander Andreievich Baranof, the first governor of the Russian–American colonies. Baranof was in charge of building the first headquarters of the fur-trading Russian–American Company at Kodiak in 1792, then later moved it to Sitka.

Flora and fauna: Spruce and hemlock dominate the forest. The abundant wildlife includes mountain goats, Sitka blacktail deer, brown (grizzly) bears, furbearers, bald eagles, and, in the marine waters, sea lions, seals, and whales. An exceptionally high density of sea otters is found in the Necker Islands. The Pacific coast is a major flyway for migrating birds.

Recreation: The U.S. Forest Service maintains three public-use recreational cabins (reservations required, fee), at Avoss Lake, Davidof Lake, and North Plotnikof Lake, as well as several miles of marked hiking trails. Camping, campfires, fishing, hunting, firearms, fixed-wing aircraft, powerboats, and snowmobiles are all permitted.

Weather and conditions: This is a maritime climate in the extreme, with much rain and overcast weather. The area receives some of the greatest precipitation in Southeast. Little Port Walter, south of the wilderness, averages 221 inches (561 cm) a year, while the watershed above Little Port Walter suffers under an estimated 400 inches (1000 cm) a year, making it the wettest location in the state. Summers are cool, winters mild. (See the Little Port Walter weather table.) Precipitation decreases radically to the north, where Sitka, just outside the wilderness, receives 100 inches (250 cm) a year. Winds are variable, but particularly strong off the ocean; during autumn storms they may reach 100 mph (160 kph).

Caution: Firewood will be wet. Camp and travel to avoid confrontations with the island's large bear population. Frequent rainstorms and strong winds can delay planned pickup—bring extra food, good rain gear, and warm clothes. Swift tidal currents in restricted bays and inlets can make boating hazardous. Because the wilderness fronts on the open Pacific Ocean, only experienced boaters should attempt to visit the fjords.

Directions/access: The wilderness is reached by floatplane or charter boat from Sitka, which also has food, stores, lodging, and scheduled air service, and is a port of call for the southeastern Alaska state ferry.

20 South Prince of Wales Wilderness, Tongass National Forest

Location: Southwest of Ketchikan
Size: 90,996 acres (36,825 hectares)
High point: 3580 feet (1091 m)
Low point: Sea level
Best time of year: Foot, May–
    September; boat, May–September
Daylight: June 21: 17½ hours
    December 22: 7 hours

Activities: Camping, hunting, fishing,
    boating, wildlife-watching,
    photography, salt-water kayaking
USGS maps: Craig A-1, A-2; Dixon
    Entrance D-1, D-2, D-3
Established: 1980
Managed by: U.S. Forest Service

An intricate maze of islands, bays, inlets, and lakes, the wilderness sits on the southwestern corner of Prince of Wales Island and takes in the watershed from Brownson Bay in the south to Klakas Inlet in the north. Trees stunted by the full fury of ocean storms sweeping in from Dixon Entrance cling to rocky promontories. The first

Klakas Inlet, Prince of Wales Island   USFS photo

Haida Indian village in Southeast Alaska, now abandoned, was established at Klinkwan in the nineteenth century.

Flora and fauna: The wilderness is an inviting, but remote, low-elevation maritime rain forest, with rolling hills, streams, lakes, muskeg meadows, and tidal lowlands. Wildlife includes Sitka blacktail deer, black bears, wolves, and bald eagles. Numerous migratory waterfowl and seabirds winter in the protected bays. Offshore, watch for seals, sea lions, whales, and, especially in the Barrier Islands, sea otters.

Recreation: The regulations of this undeveloped backcountry wilderness permit camping, campfires, hunting, fishing, firearms, fixed-wing aircraft, and powerboats; off-road vehicles are not permitted.

Weather and conditions: Prepare for long periods of rain and strong winds. Prolonged storms, most intense in autumn and winter, can delay planned pickup. The maritime climate brings cool, wet, overcast summers and mild, wet, overcast winters. (See the Annette Island weather table.)

Caution: Winds are constant, often severe. Swift tidal currents in restricted bays and inlets can make boating hazardous.

Directions/access: You can reach the wilderness by floatplane or boat. Air taxis are based at Ketchikan, charter boats at Hydaburg and Ketchikan. Food is available at Hydaburg, Craig, Ketchikan, and Klawock, all of which have scheduled air service. The last three also have lodging. Southeastern Alaska state ferry service is available between Ketchikan and Hollis, on Prince of Wales Island.

21 Stan Price State Wildlife Sanctuary

Location: Mouth of Pack Creek, Admiralty Island, 30 miles south of Juneau

Size: 610 acres (244 hectares)

High point: 60 feet (18 m)

Low point: Sea level

Best time of year: Foot, June–October; boat, June–October; ski, January–March

Daylight: June 21: 18 hours

December 21: 7 hours

Activities: Wildlife-viewing, photography, fishing

USGS maps: Sitka D-1, D-2

Established: 1990

Managed: Jointly by Alaska Department of Fish and Game's Division of Wildlife Conservation and the U.S. Forest Service

Each summer, this protected habitat attracts about a thousand visitors to Pack Creek, where they can observe brown (grizzly) bears feeding on fish and sedges. The sanctuary is named for the late Stan Price, the "Bear Man of Pack Creek," who made his home here for 40 years.

Peak viewing periods are mid-July through mid-August, when visitors can get close-up views of three or more sows at a time, sometimes with their cubs, feeding on pink and chum salmon returning to the creek. The number of visitors allowed per day is restricted, as are specific viewing times and areas. Sport-fishing is prohibited during bear-viewing season.

Brown (grizzly) bears at Pack Creek are a major attraction at the Stan Price State Wildlife Sanctuary.   USFS photo

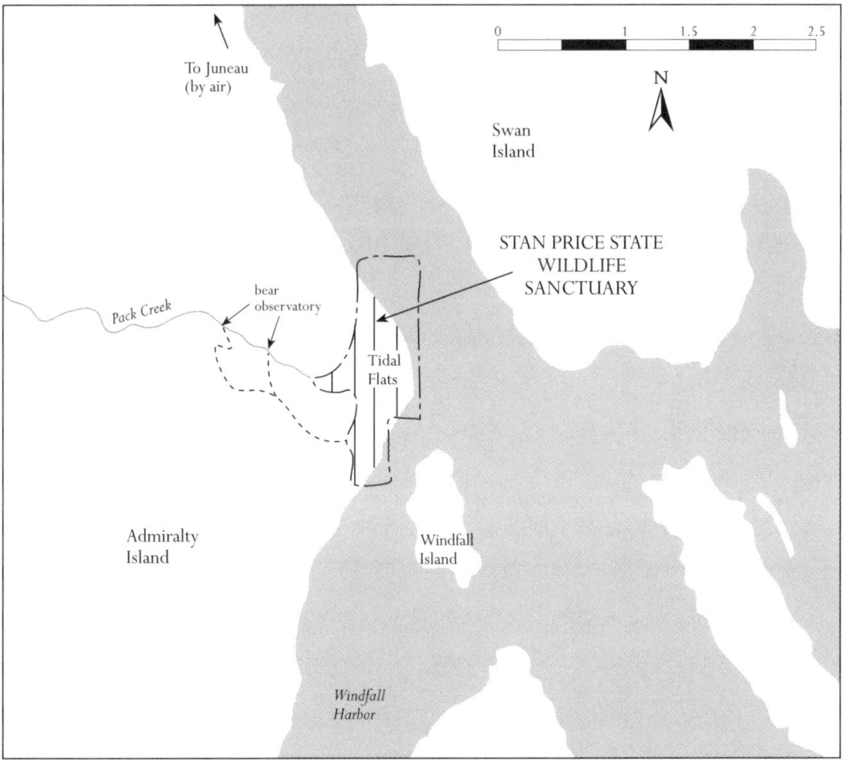

Flora and fauna: With all the bear activity, don't overlook other mammals that visit the sanctuary, such as Sitka blacktail deer, river otter, mink, marten, harbor seals, orcas, and humpback whales. An interesting variety of waterfowl and other migratory birds frequent the mouth of Pack Creek and feed along the shore. Watch for eagles, gulls, white-winged scoters, surf scoters, mergansers, Canada geese, green-winged teal, and harlequin ducks. The tidal areas are marshy and grassy; dense spruce–hemlock rain forests rise to about 1500 feet (460 m) on the mountainsides, dotted with muskeg meadows.

Recreation: The sanctuary is staffed seasonally; however, there are no concession-aires or facilities. Camping is not allowed on Admiralty Island near the sanctuary, but is allowed on Windfall Island, across the channel and reachable by boat.

Directions/access: You must have a permit to visit the sanctuary. Admiralty Island and the sanctuary are accessible only by boat or floatplane. Nearby Angoon is a port of call for the southeastern Alaska state ferry. Services available in Angoon include air taxis, scheduled air service, and food. Lodging and boat charters are available, but should be scheduled in advance.

---

22 Stikine-LeConte Wilderness, Tongass National Forest

Location: East of Petersburg
Size: 448,841 acres (181,640 hectares)
High point: 10,023 feet (3055 m)
Low point: Sea level
Best time of year: Foot, April–September; boat, April–September; ski, January–March
Daylight: June 21: 18 hours

December 22: 6½ hours
Activities: Camping, fishing, hunting, mountaineering, visiting the hot springs, river running
USGS maps: Bradfield Canal, Petersburg, Sumdum
Established: 1980
Managed by: U.S. Forest Service

A wilderness of rugged, heavily glaciated mountains that drop steeply to tidewater, granite spires, ice fields, and glaciers, Stikine–LeConte includes 40-mile- (64-km-) long LeConte Glacier, the southernmost tidewater glacier in North America. The silty, braided Stikine River flows through the Coast Mountains from Canadian uplands, navigable for 158 miles (254 km) from Telegraph Creek, B.C., to tidewater. Prominent peaks include Kates Needle, elevation 19,023 feet (3055 m), and Castle Mountain, elevation 7329 feet (2234 m).

The area has long been occupied by Native peoples, who used the river as a major travel corridor. *Stikine* in the Tlingit Indian language translates as "great river." Joseph LeConte was a professor of geology at the University of California in 1887 when the glacier and bay were named for him.

Flora and fauna: The grasslands, tidal marshes, and sandbars of the Stikine River delta are a major staging ground and nesting area for migratory birds. Dense spruce–hemlock rain forests extend from the coastal flatlands to about 2000 feet (600 m) on the mountain slopes. Stands of cottonwoods forest the valley floors. Along the Stikine River,

The Stikine River flows through Stikine–LeConte Wilderness.   USFS photo

watch for moose, black bears, brown (grizzly) bears, wolves, wolverines, Sitka blacktail deer, and bald eagles. Mountain goats, found in the high country in the summer, use winter ranges nearer tidewater—the Horthe Horn Cliffs north of LeConte Bay, the Wilkes Range, and the slopes of Mount Stinenia. Seals, sea lions, porpoises, dolphins, and whales are found offshore.

Recreation: An area popular with Petersburg and Wrangell residents, the wilderness has a developed picnic site and 12 public-use recreational cabins (reservations required, fee). Two enclosed bathing shelters invite soaking at Chief Shakes Hot Springs on the Stikine River. Backcountry camping, mountaineering, and campfires are unrestricted, but plan for frequent precipitation. Fishing, hunting, firearms, fixed-wing aircraft, and powerboats are all permitted; off-road vehicles are not.

Water travel: Stikine River, WW2–FWB, Telegraph Creek to tidewater, 158 miles (254 km). Where freight boats plied the waters in earlier years, recreational boaters now drift.

Weather and conditions: The maritime climate brings cool, wet, overcast summers and mild, wet, overcast winters. (See the Wrangell weather table.) Significantly less precipitation falls inland. Cold, severe arctic weather prevails at high elevations. Winds are moderate to severe.

Caution: Bears are numerous in lowland areas, especially near salmon-spawning streams. Severe avalanche hazard can exist in the mountains. Thick brush in the lowlands discourages hiking. In LeConte Bay, keep your distance from the glacier face; waves resulting from calving can swamp floating boats and damage beached craft. Floating and rolling icebergs create similar hazards.

Directions/access: The easiest way to reach Telegraph Creek is by air taxi from

Petersburg or Wrangell. Because you cross international borders, you must report to both Canadian and U.S. customs. The wilderness is reached by floatplane or boat. Petersburg and Wrangell have air taxis, charter boats, food, lodging, and scheduled air service, and are ports of call for the southeastern Alaska state ferry. Telegraph Creek, B.C., is also accessible by automobile via a narrow, winding, and steep gravel road that leaves the Cassiar Highway at Dease Lake.

23 Tebenkof Bay Wilderness, Tongass National Forest

Location: On Kuiu Island southwest of Petersburg
Size: 66,839 acres (27,049 hectares)
High point: 3355 feet (1023 m)
Low point: Sea level
Best time of year: Foot, May– September; boat, May–September
Daylight: June 21: 18 hours

December 22: 7 hours
Activities: Camping, fishing, hunting, boating, salt-water kayaking
USGS maps: Petersburg B-6, C-6; Port Alexander B-1, C-1
Established: 1980
Managed by: U.S. Forest Service

An intricate, many-armed bay opening onto Chatham Strait, Tebenkof has long been used by Alaska Natives and local fur farmers. The wilderness includes practically the entire watershed of the bay.

An aerial view of Tebenkof Bay shows the outlet of Dip Lake.   USFS photo by Brad Hunter

Flora and fauna: Rolling uplands of dense rain forest surround the salt-water bay, with muskeg bogs, lakes, and streams; alpine vegetation starts at about 2000 feet (600 m). Watch for Sitka blacktail deer, black bears, wolves, wolverines, bald eagles, and trumpeter swans. Chatham Strait is a major migratory route for waterfowl and seabirds, which use Tebenkof Bay both summer and winter. Seals, sea lions, porpoises, and dolphins use the bay; whales are often spotted in Chatham Strait. Wilderness waters contain cutthroat, rainbow and steelhead trout, Dolly Varden, salmon, crab, shrimp, herring, and halibut. The Troller Islands are the location of one of Southeast Alaska's most important fisheries.

Recreation: The area is undeveloped and camping is unrestricted. To minimize impact, find a campsite where tents and kitchen can be placed on the upper beach above the high tide line but below the tree line. The Petersburg Ranger District offers maps of good campsites on the bay. Campfires are permitted, although firewood probably will be wet. Build fires on the beach gravel, using driftwood. Fishing, hunting, firearms, fixed-wing aircraft, and powerboats are permitted; off-road vehicles are not.

Weather and conditions: Cool, wet, overcast summers and mild, wet, overcast winters are typical of this maritime climate. (See the Sitka weather table.) Winds are variable, often severe during autumn storms.

Caution: Prepare for long periods of rain. Swift tidal currents in restricted bays and inlets and ocean swells can make boating hazardous.

Directions/access: Off the beaten path, the wilderness normally is reached by boat or floatplane. Petersburg and Wrangell have air taxis and, along with Kake, have charter boats, food, lodging, and scheduled air service and are ports of call for the southeastern Alaska state ferry.

---

24 Tongass National Forest

Location: Southeast Alaska

Size: 16,578,000 acres (6,708,900 hectares)

High point: 15,300 feet (4663 m)

Low point: Sea level

Best time of year: Foot, May–September; boat, May–September; ski, January–March

Daylight: June 21: From 17 1/2 hours in the south to 19 hours on the northern boundary
December 22: From 7 1/2 to 6 hours

Activities: Beach-combing, picnicking, hiking, camping, backpacking, boating, diving, river running, ski touring, mountaineering, snowmobiling, fishing, hunting

USGS maps: Atlin, Bradfield Canal, Craig, Dixon Entrance, Juneau, Ketchikan, Mt. Fairweather, Prince Rupert, Port Alexander, Sitka, Skagway, Sumdum, Taku River, Yakutat

Established: 1907; amended 1980

Managed by: U.S. Forest Service

Forested islands, winding steep-walled fjords, towering snowcapped mountains, and massive glaciers—Tongass National Forest covers almost the entire Southeast Alaska panhandle, making it the largest national forest in the United States. Integrally tied to the economy of the local people, the national forest provides timber resources, fish-spawning grounds, wildlife habitat, recreational lands, and tourist attractions. Prominent peaks include Mount Fairweather, elevation 15,300 feet (4663 m); Mount Root, elevation 12,860 feet (3920 m); and Mount Crillon, elevation 12,726 feet (3879 m).

Originally established as the Alexander Archipelago Forest Reserve in 1902, the land became the Tongass National Forest in 1907 and has received numerous additions

The Misty Fiord area. Nearly all of Alaska's Panhandle is included in the 17-million-acre Tongass National Forest.   USFS photo

since. In 1980, specific sections were designated by the Alaska National Interest Lands Conservation Act as National Monuments and Wilderness Areas. These lands are treated separately in this book: Admiralty Island National Monument, Misty Fiords National Monument, and 18 additional wildernesses—Chuck River, Coronation Island, Endicott River, Karta River, Kootznoowoo, Kuiu, Maurelle Islands, Pleasant–Lemesurier–Inian Islands, Petersburg Creek–Duncan Salt Chuck, Russell Fiord, South Baranof, South Etolin Island, South Prince of Wales, Stikine–LeConte, Tebenkof Bay, Tracy Arm–Fords Terror, Warren Island, and West Chichagof–Yakobi.

The lands and waters now within the Tongass National Forest have figured prominently in the history of Alaska, from the arrival of Russian fur traders in 1799 to the transfer of Alaska to the United States in 1867 at Sitka, to the present day of fishermen, loggers, and state legislators.

Flora and fauna: Stands of spruce and hemlock dominate the Southeast rain forest. In a region of varied and abundant wildlife, the most visible animals include bald eagles, black bears, brown (grizzly) bears, coyotes, wolves, red foxes, raccoons, marten, weasels, mink, wolverines, river otters, lynx, Sitka blacktail deer, moose, mountain goats, pikas, snowshoe hares, marmots, red squirrels, northern flying squirrels, beavers, muskrats, and porcupines. In the coastal waters are found sea otters, sea lions, seals, whales, dolphins, and porpoises.

Recreation: The national forest contains about 150 public-use recreational cabins (reservations required, fee), 8 camping shelters, a ski area, 24 picnic areas, 3 boat ramps, and a visitors' center that offers numerous interpretive programs, at Mendenhall Glacier near Juneau. Other facilities include 10 campgrounds (178 units, fee, no reservations) and more than 400 miles (640 km) of marked trails.

Backcountry camping generally is unrestricted, although a few sensitive areas may be closed. Campfires, firearms, sport-fishing and hunting, and fixed-wing aircraft are permitted. Powerboats and snowmobiles may be prohibited in a few environmentally sensitive areas. One of the state's major alpine ski areas, Eaglecrest, is located in the national forest on Douglas Island near Juneau.

Weather and conditions: Weather in the Tongass National Forest is controlled by a maritime climate. Skies generally are overcast; summers are cool, winters mild. Annual precipitation varies from 26 inches (66 cm) at Skagway to more than 220 inches (560 cm) on the south end of Baranof Island. (See the descriptions of individual monuments and wildernesses for specific weather information.)

Water travel: Swift tidal currents in restricted bays and inlets and high winds can make boating hazardous. Check tide tables and enter lagoons and areas of swift tidal currents at slack water.

Rivers and their ratings include Admiralty Island Canoe Traverse, FWA, between Semour Canal and Mitchell Bay, with portages, 26 miles (42 km); Stikine River, WW2–FWB, from Telegraph Creek, B.C., in Canada, to tidewater in the United States, 130 miles (210 km); Situk River, WW1, from Nine Mile Bridge to Situk Landing (Yakutat area), 15 miles (24 km); Alsek River, WW2–4, from Haines Junction to tidewater, with 10 miles (16 km) portage, 140 miles (230 km).

Caution: A large number of bears live in the national forest—camp and travel to avoid confrontations or attracting them. Large sections of private land exist within the national forest boundaries; respect signs and do not enter private structures.

Directions/access: There is no direct land connection with the state or federal highway systems except at Hyder, in Misty Fiords National Monument. Automobiles, trucks, and other vehicles, however, can be taken to all major communities via the southeastern Alaska state ferry system. Ferry ports that connect to the road system include Skagway, Haines, Prince Rupert, B.C., and Bellingham, Washington. Ferries call at Angoon, Haines, Hoonah, Hollis, Juneau, Kake, Ketchikan, Metlakatla, Pelican, Petersburg, Sitka, Skagway, Tenakee, and Wrangell.

Automobiles may be rented at Haines, Hollis, Juneau, Ketchikan, Sitka, and Skagway, while Craig, Hollis, Juneau, Klawock, Metlakatla, Petersburg, Sitka, Skagway, and Wrangell have taxicabs. Scheduled buses serve Haines, Skagway, and Prince Rupert on the contiguous highway system, and local buses run between Juneau, Douglas, and Auke Bay. The White Pass & Yukon Route connects Whitehorse, Y.T., with Skagway.

Scheduled air service stops at Angoon, Annette, Craig, Elfin Cove, Gustavus, Haines, Hoonah, Hydaburg, Juneau, Kake, Ketchikan, Klawock, Pelican, Petersburg, Sitka, Skagway, Stewart, B.C., Wrangell, and Yakutat. Air taxis operate from Angoon, Gustavus, Haines, Juneau, Ketchikan, Metlakatla, Petersburg, Sitka, Skagway, Wrangell, and Yakutat. Charter boats, food, and lodging are found in most communities.

25 Totem Bight State Historical Park

Location: North of Ketchikan
Size: 11 acres (4.4 hectares)
High point: 30 feet (9 m)
Low point: Sea level
Best time of year: Any time
Daylight: June 21: 17½ hours
    December 22: 7½ hours

Activities: Picnicking, walking, wildlife-watching, guided or unguided tours
USGS map: Ketchikan B-6
Established: 1972
Managed by: Alaska Division of Parks and Outdoor Recreation

In the late 1930s, a U.S. Forest Service Civilian Conservation Corps (CCC) program salvaged late nineteenth-century Tlingit and Haida Indian totem poles. Replicas of decaying poles were carved and a clan house was erected. Most of the poles, made of easily worked red cedar, tell a legend or provide a graphic history of an event; they face the sea to greet approaching canoes. The Indians' strong ties with nature are evident in the use of animal symbols; intelligent, bold Raven, creator of the world, frequently stands at the top. Tlingit and Haida clans have sophisticated and highly organized tribal structures, and the totems are among the finest in the Western Hemisphere.

Originally known as Mud Bay, the area was in 1954 given the more euphonious name of Totem Bight, a "bight" being a bay or cove. The site was added to the National Register of Historic Places in 1970.

Recreation: Picnic, walk the beach along Tongass Narrows, fish from shore, and watch for bald eagles, ravens, seals, sea lions, dolphins, porpoises, sea otters, and whales. A 0.25-mile (0.4-km) marked foot trail winds through the totem poles; parking area and

Tlingit totem pole at Totem Bight State Historical Park, just north of Ketchikan   ASP photo

toilets are provided. Hunting, horses, snowmobiles, and camping are not permitted. Several Tongass National Forest campgrounds are nearby.

Weather and conditions: Expect rain. The maritime climate brings cool, wet summers and mild, wet winters. (See the Ketchikan weather table.) Winds normally are light.

Directions/access: Totem Bight is 10 miles (16 km) north of Ketchikan on North Tongass Highway. A port of call for the southeastern Alaska state ferry and many cruise ships, Ketchikan has stores, restaurants, lodging, car rentals, scheduled air service, charter boats, and air taxis. Sightseeing tours are available in Ketchikan.

Aug. 2000

26 Tracy Arm-Fords Terror Wilderness, Tongass National Forest

Location: Southeast of Juneau
Size: 653,179 acres (264,332 hectares)
High point: 8526 feet (2599 m)
Low point: Sea level
Best time of year: Foot, June–October; boat, June–October
Daylight: June 21: 18 hours

December 22: 6½ hours
Activities: Mountaineering, boating, hunting
USGS maps: Sumdum, Taku River
Established: 1980
Managed by: U.S. Forest Service

Sheer rock walls and heavily glaciated mountains surround two narrow, glacier-carved fjords, Tracy Arm and Endicott Arm, each more than 30 miles (48 km) long. At the heads of both fjords are active tidewater glaciers that continually calve icebergs into

A waterfall thunders into Tracy Arm.   USFS photo

salt water. Of the wilderness landmass, 20 percent is covered by ice and snowfields. Among the prominent peaks is an unnamed mountain, elevation 8526 feet (2599 m), and Mount Sumdum, elevation 6666 feet (2032 m).

Fords Terror reportedly was named for the crew member of a naval vessel who, in 1899, rowed into the fjord and was caught in tide rips for 6 terrifying hours. B. F. Tracy was Secretary of the Navy under President Benjamin Harrison from 1889 to 1893.

Flora and fauna: Spruce–hemlock rain forests cover the mountain slopes to about 1500 feet (460 m). Wildlife of the area includes mountain goats, black bears, brown (grizzly) bears, wolves, wolverines, bald eagles, and a few Sitka blacktail deer. Holkham Bay, at the junction of the fjords, is a wintering area for migratory waterfowl and seabirds. In the salt water, watch for seals, sea lions, porpoises, dolphins, and whales.

Recreation: No recreational development is provided, making the area attractive to those looking for uncrowded boating and mountaineering. Camping and campfires are allowed, but level sites are rare due to the steep terrain; firewood is likely to be wet. Fishing is poor. Hunting, firearms, mountaineering, fixed-wing aircraft, and powerboats are all permitted.

Weather and conditions: At low elevations, expect a maritime climate, with cool, wet, overcast summers and mild, wet, overcast winters. (See the Juneau weather table.) High elevations in the Coast Mountains have a severe arctic climate. Winds are variable, frequently extremely strong at high elevations and on exposed headlands.

Caution: Large quantities of floating ice create considerable hazard and frequently prevent boat travel to the heads of the fjords. This is a remote area, not suitable for casual visits. Prolonged storms can delay planned pickup and make boating dangerous. Floating icebergs can roll without warning. Do not approach active glacier faces closely; waves resulting from calving can swamp floating boats and damage beached boats. Severe avalanche conditions can exist in snow-covered areas.

Directions/access: The wilderness is most easily reached by air taxi or charter boat, both available in Juneau and Petersburg. Both cities have a wide variety of stores, restaurants, and lodging, and are served by scheduled airlines and the southeastern Alaska state ferry. Neither is accessible from the contiguous highway system.

---

27 Warren Island Wilderness, Tongass National Forest

Location: South of Sitka

Size: 11,181 acres (4525 hectares)

High point: 2329 feet (710 m)

Low point: Sea level

Best time of year: April–August

Daylight: June 21: 17½ hours

December 22: 7 hours

Activities: Camping, fishing, hunting

USGS map: Craig D-6

Established: 1980

Managed by: U.S. Forest Service

An exposed island fronting on the Pacific Ocean, Warren Island was discovered in 1793 by Captain Joseph Whidbey; Captain George Vancouver later named it in honor of Sir John Borlase Warren, a rear admiral in the British Navy, later ambassador to Russia.

The coastline of Warren Island   USFS photo

Prominent peaks include Warren Peak, elevation 2329 feet (710 m), and Bald Peak, elevation 2212 feet (674 m).

Flora and fauna: Richly forested, with rocky shorelines, sea cliffs, and rocky shoals, the island is a seabird nesting and perching area. Sea otters, sea lions, seals, and whales use the waters; Sitka blacktail deer, black bears, wolves, and bald eagles are found on shore.

Recreation: Undeveloped, the island offers primitive camping, fishing, and hunting, but prepare for long periods of rain and strong winds. Often inaccessible due to winds and seas, the island has a few protected coves on the leeward side. Carry a camping stove, since wood in this rain forest is normally wet.

Weather and conditions: The maritime climate brings overcast skies and rain year-round, with cool summers and mild winters. (See the Sitka weather table.) Winds, prevailing from the southeast, are constant and often extremely strong, especially during autumn storms.

Caution: Prolonged storms can delay planned air or water pickup and make boating hazardous. Only experienced boaters should attempt to visit the island.

Directions/access: You may reach the island by floatplane or boat. Air taxis operate from Ketchikan, Petersburg, Sitka, and Wrangell. The nearest communities that have scheduled air service, Craig and Klawock, also have charter boats, food, and lodging.

28 West Chichagof-Yakobi Wilderness, Tongass National Forest

Location: Northwest of Sitka
Size: 264,747 acres (107,140 hectares)
High point: 3613 feet (1101 m)
Low point: Sea level
Best time of year: Foot, May–October; boat, May–October; ski, December– March

Daylight: June 21: 18 hours
December 22: 6½ hours
Activities: Camping, fishing, hiking, hunting, boating, kayaking
USGS maps: Mt. Fairweather, Sitka
Established: 1980
Managed by: U.S. Forest Service

A mountainous island wilderness with a rugged 65-mile (105-km) coastline fronting on the Pacific Ocean, West Chichagof–Yakobi also includes many exposed offshore islands, islets, and rocks. Intricate bays, lagoons, tidal meadows, and estuaries offer well-protected anchorages. The area, rich in wildlife, has long been occupied by Tlingit Indians. The islands also contain mineral wealth: Mines on Chichagof Island have produced almost a million ounces of gold. Prominent peaks include Apex Mountain, elevation 3613 feet (1101 m); E1 Nido, elevation 3358 feet (1024 m); and Mount Lydonia, elevation 3262 feet (994 m).

Yakobi Island was named in 1804 for Russian general Ivan Yakobi. Admiral Vasili Yakov Chichagov explored Arctic regions in 1765 and 1766; the island was named for him in 1805.

Flora and fauna: Along the outer coast, savannas spread invitingly among open spruce forests. Timberline is at about 1500 feet (460 m). Wildlife is varied and abundant,

Kimsham Cove to Granite Island, part of the West Chichagof–Yakobi Wilderness   USFS photo

including Sitka blacktail deer, brown (grizzly) bears, furbearers, seals, sea lions, porpoises, and dolphins. The waters south of Herbert Graves Island support a large population of sea otters. The Pacific coasts of Chichagof and Yakobi Islands lie along a major migratory waterfowl and seabird route. The Fish and Wildlife Service has reestablished sea otters at Surge and Khaz Bays.

Recreation: The Forest Service maintains 4 public-use recreational cabins (reservations required, fee) and several miles of marked trails. Backcountry camping is unrestricted and campfires are permitted, but expect the wood to be wet. Fishing, hunting, firearms, fixed-wing aircraft, and powerboats are permitted; off-road vehicles are not.

Weather and conditions: A maritime climate brings summers that are cool, wet, and overcast, and winters that are mild, wet, and overcast. (See the Sitka weather table.) Winds are constant, severe during autumn storms.

Caution: Travel and camp to avoid disturbing the numerous bears, particularly along streams draining into Peril Strait. Hypothermia is a constant danger; prepare for long periods of rain and strong winds. Swift tidal currents in restricted bays and inlets can make boating hazardous.

Directions/access: You can reach the wilderness by boat or floatplane. Air taxis are based at Sitka, charter boats at Sitka and sometimes at Pelican. Both Sitka and Pelican have food and scheduled air service and are ports of call for the southeastern Alaska state ferry. Lodging is available in Sitka.

SOUTHCENTRAL/GULF COAST

The most densely populated and developed portion of the state lies in Southcentral Alaska. About half of Alaska's population lives in the Anchorage area; however, with a statewide population of only 622,000, it's hardly elbow to elbow. The Alaska Range and the Gulf Coast are strongly influenced by air masses that flow from the Gulf of Alaska. Summers are mild, with frequent rains and long periods of overcast. Winters are mild, too, with temperatures above or near freezing along the outer coast, becoming colder in protected interior regions south of the Alaska Range. Salt-water ports along the Gulf of Alaska are ice-free in the winter. Long summer days accompany short twilight nights in June and July.

Southcentral residents love to recreate, and it's easy to get into the wilderness from the city. Anchorage lies on the road system and the Alaska Railroad route, and serves as an important base for small aircraft travel. Chugach State Park and outstanding day hikes are a few minutes' drive away. The Kenai Peninsula attracts sportsmen seeking world-class fishing. Anchorage's Lake Hood is the busiest floatplane base in the nation and remote fly-in parklands are a short flight away. Wrangell–St. Elias National Park is the place for a rugged backcountry experience. And the nation's biggest bears await on Kodiak Island.

The coastal communities on Prince William Sound are small and inviting. Fishing, oil, and tourism drive their economies. Each town offers stores, accommodations, and arrangements for getting into the backcountry.

Local topography largely determines the amount of precipitation that falls in a given area, with the greatest amount on south-facing slopes and coastlines. In general, precipitation is heavy, ranging from 30 inches (76 cm) to an estimated 400 inches (1000 cm) annually. October consistently is the wettest month. Clear days occur most frequently from February through June. Fog occurs the entire year, but is most likely in late summer and early winter. Snow often falls wet and heavy, or sometimes initially light and powdery only to turn heavy as temperatures rise. Winds generally are light in protected valleys, but almost constant and often strong along the coast and at high elevations.

Dense coniferous forests occur in coastal areas of high precipitation from the Gulf of Alaska to Kodiak Island. Boreal forests cover the drier regions of the Kenai Peninsula and northern Cook Inlet. The topography generally is steep and mountainous; timberline ranges from 2000 to 3000 feet (300 to 900 m). Much of western Kodiak Island is covered by thick brush; the eastern portion of the island and Afognak Island contain coastal rain forest.

Extensive alder thickets crowd the mountainsides from sea level to alpine tundra meadows, filling forest openings not occupied by bogs and choking most avalanche paths, streambeds, and riverbanks. Ferns and spiny devil's club grow among the alders.

Muskeg, a ground cover of thick sphagnum moss, sedges, rushes, low shrubs, and fruticose lichens, forms where drainage is poor in flat areas, in depressions, and on

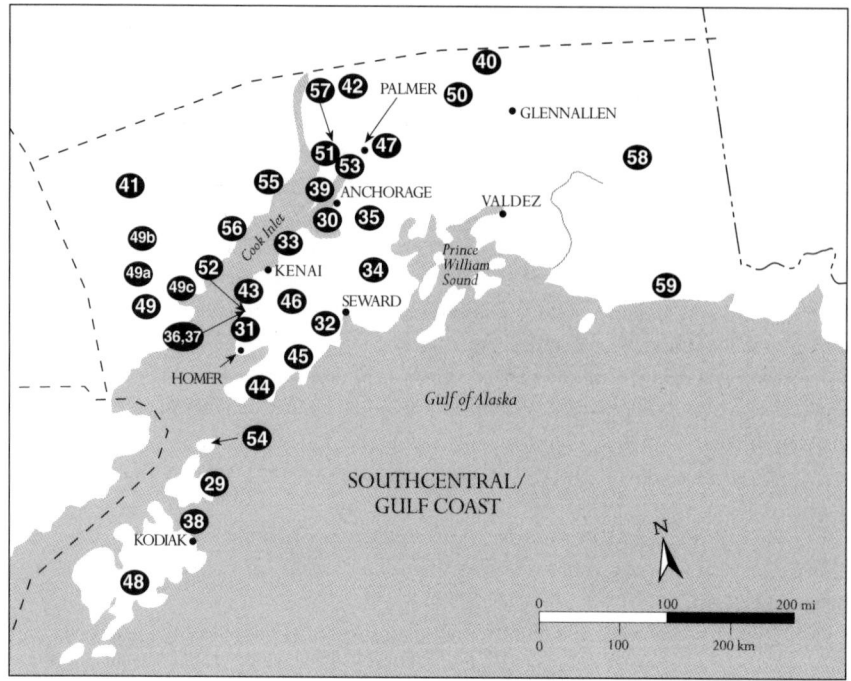

slopes with abundant water. Beneath its surface a thick layer of peat has built up, and ponds frequently lie terraced in the peat.

On mountain slopes and ridges above timberline not covered by permanent snowfields or glaciers, and wherever winter snows linger late into the spring, alpine tundra, a tenacious, low mat of herbaceous and shrubby plants, is found.

29 Afognak Island State Park

Location: North of Kodiak
Size: 48,750 acres (19 500 hectares)
High point: 1928 feet (578.4 m)
Low point: Sea level
Best time of year: Foot, May–August; boat, May–August; ski (marginal), January–March
Daylight: June 21: 18 hours

December 22: 6½ hours
Activities: Fishing, hunting, boating, hiking, salt-water kayaking
USGS maps: Afognak A-1, B-1, B-2, A-0, B-0
Established: 1994
Managed by: Alaska Division of Parks and Outdoor Recreation

The ruffled edges of Afognak Island's northeast coast are an attractive playground, particularly for experienced kayakers who long to explore its coves and bays. A single, undeveloped park made up of two areas separated by Tonki Bay, this region is remote and ruggedly beautiful.

A single lakeside public-use cabin at Pillar Lake is available by reservation for a fee. It's about 20 minutes from the city of Kodiak by floatplane. Nearby Edge Mountain, elevation 1928 feet (578.4 m), is the prominent peak on Tonki Cape Peninsula.

Flora and fauna: The dense coastal spruce forest reaches to about 700 feet (210 m) in elevation. The waters off Afognak are rich with marine mammals such as sea lions, porpoises, sea otters, seals, and whales; seabird populations likewise are exceptional. Land mammals include the Kodiak brown bear and Sitka blacktail deer.

Recreation: For those who want to combine hiking and fishing, take the 3-hour wilderness hike from Pillar Lake to the lake south of Big Tonki Bay, with access to steelhead and salmon. Dolly Varden and rainbow trout may be found in Pillar Lake. High precipitation is a given; dress for wet conditions.

Weather and conditions: The weather is unpredictable and can deteriorate rapidly. Rough seas and high winds are frequent in open waters. Inner bays are more protected, but beware of the dangers of hypothermia. Rainfall during summer months averages 4 to 6 inches a month; ambient temperatures range from 40 degrees to 65 degrees F (5 degrees to 17 degrees C).

Caution: Pillar Lake sometimes freezes as early as November 1. To access the public-use cabin, you may need to secure a wheeled plane to land on the Izhut Bay beach behind the cabin.

Directions/access: North of Kodiak city, the park is accessible by water but more easily by air. Commercial flights are available to Kodiak city from Anchorage or Homer; from Kodiak, air charters offer floatplane service. Groceries and other necessities may be purchased in Anchorage, Kodiak, or Homer. Kodiak and Homer are ports of call on the southcentral/southwestern Alaska state ferry system.

Hiking near Pillar Lake in Afognak Island State Park   ASP photo

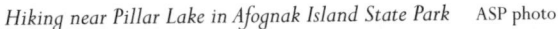

30 Anchorage Coastal Wildlife Refuge

Location: Anchorage coastal areas from Point Woronzof south to Potter Creek
Size: 33,800 acres (13,520 hectares)
High point: 15 feet (5 m)
Low point: Sea level
Best time of year: Foot, April–October; ski, January–March
Daylight: June 21: 19½ hours
December 22: 5½ hours

Activities: Wildlife-viewing, hunting, photography, walking
USGS maps: Anchorage A-8; Tyonek A-1
Established: 1988; originally established in 1971 as Potter Point State Game Refuge
Managed by: Alaska Department of Fish and Game

Anchorage's backyard refuge contains Potter Marsh, a popular bird-watching area along the Seward Highway south of town that includes a boardwalk over a portion of the wetlands. Not so well known are the tide flats and forested strip of Turnagain Arm coastline that lie across the highway northwest of Potter Marsh and continue north and east to Point Woronzof. The point, on the Knik Arm side of Anchorage, is a popular place for taking in the sunset.

Flora and fauna: The coast is dominated by mudflats that are flooded with every high tide. Transitional zones include grassy marshes that provide food and cover for the waterfowl. During the spring migration in late April and early May, binocular-draped visitors line the Potter Marsh boardwalk, glassing for pintails, widgeon, mallards, green-

Birding at Potter Marsh, part of the Anchorage Coastal Wildlife Refuge ASP photo by Robert Angell

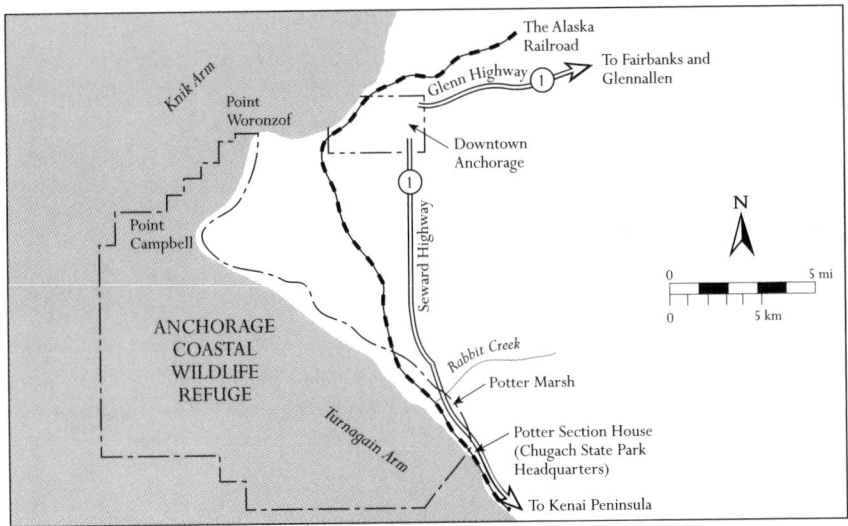

winged teal, lesser Canada geese, and whistling swans. More than 130 species of birds have been identified here. Illustrating the term "gaggle of geese," Canada geese nest within sight of the highway and rear their downy young to the fascination of just about everyone. Horned grebes, red-necked grebes, arctic terns, sandhill cranes, and numerous ducks and gulls also nest in the marsh. Watch, too, for moose, coyotes, snowshoe hares, beavers, mink, and muskrats. Salmon spawn in Rabbit Creek.

Recreation: The Anchorage Coastal Wildlife Refuge was established in part to protect waterfowl and enhance their habitat. Stay off the highway shoulders and do not feed the waterfowl. To avoid disturbing nesting waterfowl, fishing in Rabbit Creek is prohibited. The area between the New Seward Highway and the Old Seward Highway is closed to hunting. Some types of hunting are permitted in other parts of the refuge in certain winter months. Since regulations are subject to change, check with the Alaska Department of Fish and Game Wildlife Conservation Division before hunting. Only shotguns may be used. Motorized vehicles require permits; snowmobiles are not allowed. Hovercraft and motorized hang-gliders require a written permit. A public state outdoor rifle range is on the west side of the Seward Highway. Some private lands exist within the refuge.

Weather and conditions: Summers are cool and frequently overcast, and winters cold and overcast, typical of a subarctic maritime climate. (See the Anchorage weather table.) Winds are moderate, occasionally strong.

Caution: Walking on the tidal flats is not recommended; unvegetated areas can contain spots of quicksand-like silt and incoming tide may leave you stranded and in danger of death by hypothermia or drowning.

Directions/access: The Anchorage Coastal Wildlife Refuge is one of the most accessible refuges managed by the Alaska Department of Fish and Game. Rental cars and taxicabs are available in Anchorage; scheduled buses travel the Seward Highway. The Alaska Railroad, en route from Anchorage to Whittier, parallels the highway through the refuge but does not stop.

The Tony Knowles Coastal Trail, while not included in refuge lands, parallels Cook Inlet for several miles, allowing joggers, walkers, bikers, and skiers excellent views of the coast while they exercise. Downtown Anchorage access is at the west end of Second Avenue.

31 Anchor River State Recreation Area

Location: North of Homer
Size: 213 acres (85 hectares)
High point: 200 feet (60 m)
Low point: Sea level
Best time of year: June–September
Daylight: June 21: 19 hours

December 21: 6 hours
Activities: Camping, fishing, picnicking
USGS map: Seldovia D-5
Managed by: Alaska Division of Parks and Outdoor Recreation

The Anchor River State Recreation Area is as far west as you can go on the U.S. highway system. Legend says that Captain James Cook named this river when he lost an anchor near its mouth. Descriptions of the land and its Native inhabitants are recorded in Cook's 1778 journals. The Kenaitze tribe of Athabascan Indians once lived in a village near the river mouth, where they found plentiful fish and game.

Flora and fauna: The river wends through a coastal forest of birch and spruce, creating a habitat that supports large fish and wildlife populations, particularly salmon and moose. King, silver, and pink salmon runs are staggered throughout the summer

Fishing along the Anchor River   ASP photo by Robert Angell

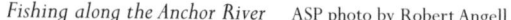

months. Steelhead and Dolly Varden also are sought-after sportfish. Watch also for black bears, brown (grizzly) bears, wolves, wolverines, beavers, and bald eagles.

Recreation: The five campground names—Silverking, Cohoe, Steelhead, Slidehole, and Halibut—hint at why most people come to the Anchor River: fishing, fishing, and more fishing. Each campground has a dozen or so tent sites, a couple dozen parking sites for campers, and additional parking for day use. Facilities include toilets, picnic tables, and drinking water. Campground bulletin boards include posted information about good fishing holes, emergency closures, and bear warnings.

Alaska Department of Fish and Game regulations are subject to change based on numbers of fish, so call the fishing hotline for the latest information, at (907) 235-6930 in Homer or (907) 262-2737 in Soldotna. ATVs may be used on salt-water beaches only. Fire grates are provided; use only dead and downed wood.

Weather and conditions: The lower Kenai Peninsula can experience sunny summer days into the high 70s, yet if a storm moves in, it can drop 20 degrees F within hours. Periods of chilly rain and wind are common. Plan to dress in layers, and bring rain gear.

Directions/access: From Mile 157 Sterling Highway, take the Beach Access Road to any of the five campgrounds. Groceries, gas, and supplies may be purchased in Soldotna, Homer, or any number of roadside businesses.

32 Caines Head State Recreation Area

Location: South of Seward
Size: 6250 acres (2500 hectares)
High point: 3380 feet (1030 m)
Low point: Sea level
Best time of year: Foot, May–September; boat, May–September; ski, February–April
Daylight: June 21: 19 hours December 22: 6 hours

Activities: Primitive camping, wildlife-watching, photography, hiking, beach-combing
USGS maps: Blying Sound D-7; Seward A-7
Established: 1971; amended 1975
Managed by: Alaska Division of Parks and Outdoor Recreation

In the waters of Resurrection Bay, pilings of an old military dock stand as quiet sentinels. An old road about 2 miles (3 km) long, overgrown by alders, climbs from tidewater to an exposed point on the towering shale cliffs of Caines Head. Here cling bunkers and other remnants of Fort McGilvray, part of Alaska's World War II coastal defense system.

Recreation: The recreation area appeals to boaters who enjoy primitive camping, hiking, and beach-combing. Camping is unrestricted; campfires, fishing, and hunting are permitted. Facilities include 4 campsites, picnic shelters, and trails.

Flora and fauna: The terrain is steep, with numerous creeks and ponds dotting the dense coastal forest. Watch the ocean for sea mammals—dolphins, porpoises, seals, sea lions, sea otters, and whales. On land expect moose, black bears, brown (grizzly) bears, mountain goats, wolves, and bald eagles.

Weather and conditions: The maritime climate brings cool, wet, overcast summers and mild, wet, overcast winters. (See the Seward weather table.) Winds are moderate, frequently strong.

Caution: Be cautious on Resurrection Bay; its waters can be treacherous during periods of high winds, and strong tidal currents can make landing difficult.

Directions/access: Fast access to Caines Head is by boat or floatplane. Another option is to drive to the end of Lowell Point Road, south of Seward, to a trailhead parking area. A 4.5-mile (7-km) beach trail, exposed only at low tide, leads to Caines Head. Air taxis, charter boats, stores, restaurants, and lodging are available in Seward, 6 miles (10 km) from the recreation area.

War memorial at Caines Head   ASP photo by Robert Angell

A picnic at Captain Cook State Recreation Area on the Kenai Peninsula   ASP photo by Mike Lee

33 Captain Cook State Recreation Area

Location: North of the city of Kenai
Size: 2900 acres (1160 hectares)
High point: 125 feet (38 m)
Low point: Sea level
Best time of year: Foot, May–October; boat, May–October; ski, February–April
Daylight: June 21: 19 ½ hours

December 22: 5 ½ hours
Activities: Camping, boating, picnicking, hiking, fishing, swimming, snowmobiling, skiing
USGS map: Kenai D-3
Established: 1969
Managed by: Alaska Division of Parks and Outdoor Recreation

In 1778 English explorer Captain James Cook sailed into Cook Inlet, searching unsuccessfully for a "Northwest Passage" through North America. According to his log, he sent a boat ashore to bury a marker at Point Possession northeast of here, claiming the land for King George III, although the marker has never been found.

Flora and fauna: In this area of gently rolling wooded knolls and lakes, watch for moose, black bears, brown (grizzly) bears, beaver, wolves, coyotes, red foxes, porcupines, bald eagles, and migratory waterfowl. Whales travel the waters of Cook Inlet.

Recreation: Captain Cook State Recreation Area is a developed, but uncrowded, park on the shores of Cook Inlet, an excellent destination for families with children, especially Discovery Campground, one of 7 sites within the recreation area. Facilities include picnic shelters, 2 campgrounds (65 units), and many picnic areas, including a remote boat-in picnic site on Stormy Lake, water, toilets, and a boat launch on Stormy Lake. A cross-country ski trail, 2 miles (3 km) long, starts at Bishop Creek Campground. Discovery Campground also has developed trails. Backcountry camping is permitted.

Build campfires in campground fire pits only; use a camping stove elsewhere. Picnicking, beach-combing, hiking, boating, fishing, swimming, snowmobiling, ski touring, and ice fishing are popular activities. Powerboats are permitted; horses, fixed-wing aircraft, snowmobiles, and off-road vehicles are not. The discharge of firearms is prohibited.

Weather and conditions: Expect cool, overcast summers and cold, overcast winters. The maritime climate is strongly influenced by continental land masses that bring in subarctic winter cold. (See the Kenai weather table.) Winds are constant and moderate along the beaches of Cook Inlet, lighter inland.

Caution: Swimming and boating are not recommended in Cook Inlet; the incoming tide can be swift and dangerous. Drive with care on the salt-water beaches; the sand frequently is too soft to support standard tires.

Directions/access: Various entrances to the recreation area can be found along Kenai Spur Road, from Mile 36 to Mile 39. The recreation area is about 25 miles (40 km) north of the city of Kenai, which has car rentals, taxicabs, scheduled bus and air service from Anchorage, stores, restaurants, and lodging. The recreation area is also the terminus of the Swanson River Canoe Trail (see Kenai National Wildlife Refuge).

54 Chugach National Forest

Location: Southeast of Anchorage

Size: 5,940,000 acres (2,404,000 hectares)

High point: 13,176 feet (4016 m)

Low point: Sea level

Best time of year: Foot, May–October; boat, May–October; ski, January–March

Daylight: June 21: 19½ hours

December 22: 5½ hours

Activities: Hiking, camping, rafting, birding, photography, hunting, fishing, salt-water boating and kayaking

USGS maps: Anchorage, Bering Glacier, Blying Sound, Cordova, Middleton Island, Seward, Valdez

Established: 1907

Managed by: U.S. Forest Service

A magnificent area of forests, mountains, glaciers, lakes, rivers, fjords, and seashores, Chugach National Forest includes 41-mile- (66-km-) long Columbia Glacier and the Sargent Icefield. Prince William Sound, a large island-protected sea with fjords and tidewater glaciers, is surrounded by high, heavily glaciated mountains. Along the western boundary, on the Kenai Peninsula, the Seward Highway winds through once-glaciated mountains and beside large lakes. Prominent peaks include Mount Marcus Baker, elevation 13,176 feet (4016 m); Mount Valhalla, elevation 12,135 feet (3699 m); and Mount Witherspoon, elevation 12,012 feet (3661 m).

The region had long been occupied by Chugach Eskimos and Eyak Indians when Captain James Cook explored Prince William Sound and Turnagain Arm in 1778. A gold rush began to the Kenai Peninsula in 1888; later, copper mines were established on Latouche Island and at Ellamar in Prince William Sound. Canneries and salteries scattered throughout the Sound processed the abundant fish harvest, and fur farmers raised blue foxes on small islands. By 1930, major mining activity had ceased; in the 1960s the last of the remote canneries shut down. Today the Sound is fished commercially for halibut, salmon, herring, and herring roe. Tankers carrying North Slope oil from Valdez travel through eastern Prince William Sound en route to the Lower 48.

The epicenter of the destructive 1964 earthquake (9.2 on the Richter scale) was near Miner's Lake, west of Columbia Glacier. Land to the west sank up to 8 feet (2.4 m), while land to the southeast rose as much as 35 feet (11 m).

Flora and fauna: Dense conifer forests rise to about 1000 feet (300 m). Higher, a band of nearly impenetrable brush finally yields to alpine tundra. Wildlife is abundant in the national forest and in the waters of Prince William Sound. Moose are particularly abundant on the Kenai Peninsula, north of Turnagain Arm and on the Copper River delta. The bountiful delta, nesting grounds and staging area for more than 2 million migratory waterfowl and 40 million shorebirds, was made a Critical Habitat Area within the national forest in 1978. Dall sheep are found primarily in the mountains on the western side of the national forest, while mountain goats range over most of the forest's uplands. Caribou have been reestablished on the Kenai Peninsula, with a small band in the vicinity of Resurrection Creek and American Pass. Sitka blacktail deer are found primarily on Montague and Hinchenbrook Islands. Other wildlife includes brown (grizzly) bears, black bears, wolves, wolverines, coyotes, beavers, red foxes, snowshoe hares, lynx, marmots, marten, mink, muskrats, river otters, porcupines, pikas, arctic ground squirrels, red squirrels, bald eagles, and about 250 other species of birds. Offshore, in Prince William Sound, watch for seals, sea lions, sea otters, dolphins, porpoises, and whales.

Recreation: The entire national forest is a popular recreation area for both Alaska residents and visitors. Most people stay near the road system for picnicking, berry-picking, and camping. Mount Alyeska, Alaska's largest ski resort and a popular tourist attraction, is located at Girdwood, southeast of Anchorage. Much-photographed Portage Glacier and Portage Lake, with a visitors' center and interpretive programs, lie at the head of Turnagain Arm. A concessionaire operates 1-hour cruises to the face of Portage Glacier on the M/V *Ptarmigan*, a double-hulled vessel that was designed and constructed for cruising among icebergs.

The national forest maintains 16 campgrounds (433 units, fee), 42 public-use recreational cabins (reservations are first-come, first-served, fee; call toll-free (877) 444-6777), 9 boat ramps, and almost 200 miles (320 km) of marked trails. Backcountry camping is unrestricted. Campfires in campgrounds are permitted in existing fire pits

Gold panning in the Chugach National Forest   USFS photo

only; in the backcountry, fires are permitted except during periods of extreme fire danger. Firewood may be cut for personal use from dead or downed trees only, 200 feet (60 m) or more from main roads, campgrounds, or trails. Gold panning on public lands is permitted, but use of other recreational mining equipment may be restricted.

Popular off-road activities include hiking and backpacking, river running, beach-combing, and ski touring. The national forest is also extensively used for fishing, hunting, and snowmobiling, and, to a lesser extent, for horseback riding, powerboating, and off-road vehicle travel, all of which are subject to restricted periods or places of use. During the red salmon runs of July and August, the Russian River is the most intensively used fishery in the state, with fishermen standing elbow to elbow. Firearms are permitted, but may not be used near campgrounds, roads, or trails. Fixed-wing aircraft are permitted by the Forest Service, although State of Alaska and FAA restrictions may be in effect.

Water travel: Alaganik Slough, FWA–B, Mile 22.3 Copper River Highway bridge to the boat ramp at the end of the 3-mile (5-km) side road from Mile 17 Copper River Highway, 4.5 miles (7 km). Strong winds or adverse tidal conditions can prevent your return to the boat ramp from downstream. Granite Creek/East Fork, WW1–2, Mile 65.5 Seward Highway (Bertha Creek Campground) to Mile 60 Seward Highway (just below the Silvertip Highway Maintenance Camp), 9 miles (14 km). Beyond this point are WW3–5 rapids. East Fork/Sixmile River, WW2–5, Mile 60 Seward Highway to Sunrise, 11 miles (18 m). Upper Kenai River, WW1–2, Mile 47.8 Sterling Highway (at the Kenai River bridge) to Mile 0.2 Skilak Lake Loop Road (Jean Creek Campground), 15 miles (24 m). Portage Creek, WW1, outlet of Portage Lake to Mile 79 Seward Highway, 6 miles (10 km). The waters of the rivers and lakes of the national forest and Prince William Sound are extremely cold; wet suits and adequate flotation equipment are mandatory.

Weather and conditions: Two climate patterns prevail in the national forest. Inland, Kenai Peninsula has cool, often overcast summers; winters are crisp and cold. (See the Moose Pass weather table.) Winds are light to moderate. Prince William Sound, on the other hand, has a typical maritime climate, with cool, wet summers and mild, wet winters. (See the North Dutch Group weather table.) The Sound stays ice-free all winter except where bays receive large amounts of fresh water from rivers and streams. Winds are light to moderate, with severe storms in autumn.

Caution: Since large numbers of bears live in the national forest, travel and camp to avoid contact with them. Severe avalanche hazard can exist in winter and spring; fatalities have occurred. And last, but extremely important: Do not climb on icebergs or approach glacier faces at any time, winter or summer.

Within eastern Prince William Sound are lands selected by Natives under the Alaska Native Claims Settlement Act of 1971. Ask for permission at the Cordova office or the office of the Chugach Alaska Corp., (907) 563-8866, in Anchorage before camping or hunting in their areas. Numerous private landholdings and mining claims exist elsewhere within the national forest; respect private property and do not enter buildings or disturb claim markers and equipment.

Directions/access: The western portion of the national forest on the Kenai Peninsula is easily accessible by automobile via the Seward and Sterling Highways. Automobiles can be rented in Anchorage and Seward, while scheduled buses travel both highways. Sightseeing tours from Anchorage regularly visit Mount Alyeska and Portage Glacier. The Alaska Railroad makes daily runs in the summer from Anchorage to Portage and Whittier, with a less frequent schedule in winter. The summer schedule also includes daily service to Seward.

The Prince William Sound region has two highway portals: the Richardson Highway to Valdez, and the vehicle-carrying Alaska Railroad from Portage to Whittier. At press time, however, construction was underway to connect Portage and Whittier by road as well. The southcentral Alaska state ferry connects the ports of Cordova, Valdez, Whittier, and Seward. The Alaska Marine Highway System also offers monthly cruises on the M/V *Kennicott*, the newest oceangoing vessel in the system, connecting the Southeast route and the Southcentral/Southwest route. From Cordova, the Copper River Highway leads through the delta to the river, but is not connected to the state highway system. Automobiles can be rented in Seward, Valdez, and Cordova. Sightseeing tours and cruise boats travel in summer between Whittier and Valdez, with a stop to view Columbia Glacier.

Scheduled air service is available between Anchorage, Cordova, and Valdez; air taxis are based at Anchorage, Cooper Landing, Cordova, Moose Pass, Seward, and Valdez. Sailboats may be chartered in Seward, Valdez, and Whittier, while powerboat charters operate from Cooper Landing, Cordova, Seward, Valdez, and Whittier. All communities have stores and restaurants, and lodging is available at roadside motels, wilderness lodges, Cooper Landing, Cordova, Girdwood/Alyeska, Moose Pass, Seward, Valdez, and Whittier.

35 Chugach State Park

Location: East of Anchorage
Size: 502,450 acres (200,980 hectares)
High point: 8005 feet (2440 m)
Low point: Sea level
Best time of year: Foot, June–October; boat, June–October; ski, February–April
Daylight: June 21: 19½ hours December 22: 5½ hours

Activities: Hiking, picnicking, camping, fishing, hunting, boating, mountaineering, snowmobiling, skiing, wildlife-watching, river running
USGS maps: Anchorage, Seward
Established: 1970; amended 1987
Managed by: Alaska Division of Parks and Outdoor Recreation

An impressive glaciated landscape of forested and alpine valleys, sharp ridges, lakes, meadows, and craggy summits, Chugach State Park presses against the Municipality of Anchorage to create a stunning backdrop for the city. In the eastern section of the park, the pastoral beauty gives way to a wild white symphony of snaking glaciers, perennial snows, and shining peaks. Prominent peaks include Bashful Peak, elevation 8005 feet (2440 m); Baleful Peak, elevation 7900 feet (2400 m); and Bellicose Peak, elevation 7640 feet (2329 m).

Turnagain Arm, a fjord along the southern boundary of the park, has one of the highest tidal variations in the world, approaching 40 feet (12 m). Tidal bores, turbulent incoming tides with a breaking wave in the lead, are frequently seen from the Seward Highway.

Flora and fauna: Tree line is at about 2000 feet (600 m); some areas have a band of dense brush above the trees before giving way to alpine tundra. Wildlife includes moose, black bears, brown (grizzly) bears, mountain goats, Dall sheep, wolves, wolverines, coyotes, red foxes, porcupines, hawks, and bald eagles. In May, when the smelt (hooligan) migrate through Turnagain Arm to their river spawning areas, white beluga whales and eagles come in to feed on the tasty fish.

Recreation: A popular recreation area at Anchorage's doorstep, Chugach State Park has room for picnickers, hikers, campers, backpackers, rock climbers, mountaineers, boaters, river runners, hang gliders, ski tourers, dog mushers, snowmobilers, fishermen, and hunters. Firearms, hunting, horses, aircraft landings, powerboats, snowmobiles, and all-terrain vehicles are permitted in specific areas only.

Highway waysides, picnic areas and shelters, campgrounds (147 units), and a nature center at Mile 12 Eagle River Road are some of the facilities. Park rangers schedule programs about wilderness survival and avalanche awareness as well as interpretive lectures and guided hikes. The park contains 160 miles (256 km) of marked hiking trails,

Backcountry camping in Chugach State Park   ASP photo

50 miles (80 km) of marked ski trails, and 25 miles (40 km) of marked snowmobile trails. Backcountry camping is unrestricted, but groups must be no larger than 20. In summer, campfires may be built only in campground fire pits; use camping stoves elsewhere.

Water travel: Upper Eagle River, WW1–3, from Mile 9 Eagle River Road to Eagle River Campground area, 13 miles (21 km). Below the campground, Eagle River becomes severely turbulent—for experts only.

Weather and conditions: Although the park's climate is transitional between subarctic maritime and continental, local topography and elevation largely determine its weather. In general, summers are mild, winters can be either mild or cold. (See the Anchorage weather table.) The maritime influence increases from west to east, causing cooler summers, warmer winters, and increased precipitation in the eastern section. Anchorage averages 15 inches (38 cm) of precipitation a year, while Girdwood/Alyeska, only 30 miles (50 km) away, receives 70 inches (180 cm). Winds generally are light in the valleys, frequently severe in the mountains.

Caution: Hikers should practice crossing glacial streams before attempting Eagle River. Boaters on Eklutna Lake need to watch for sudden strong winds that can capsize small boats. Quicksand-like mud makes the tide flats of Turnagain Arm unsafe. Many cliffs and peaks contain "rotten" rock unsafe for climbing. In winter, spring, and early summer, avalanche danger can be severe throughout the park.

Directions/access: Chugach State Park has many road access points from the Seward Highway, the Hillside area of Anchorage, and the Glenn Highway. Contact park personnel for a brochure and map. Rental cars, taxicabs, and air taxis are available in Anchorage. The Anchorage municipal "People Mover" bus has routes to the Hillside area;

intercity buses travel the Seward and Glenn Highways. Lodging, stores, and restaurants are found in Anchorage, Bird Creek, Eagle River, Eklutna, Girdwood/Alyeska, Indian, and Peters Creek.

36 Clam Gulch State Recreation Area

Location: South of Soldotna
Size: 494.75 acres (198 hectares)
High point: 387 feet (116 m)
Low point: Sea level
Best time of year: June–September
Daylight: June 21: 19 hours
December 21: 6 hours

Activities: Camping, clam-digging, beach-combing, observing commercial fishing
USGS map: Kenai A-4
Established: 1967; amended 1981
Managed by: Alaska Division of Parks and Outdoor Recreation

An easy-to-miss sign near a gravel road off the Sterling Highway marks the way to one of the most accessible clam-digging beaches in Alaska. And with it comes a bonus: From atop the bluff near the Clam Gulch campground there's a fabulous panoramic view across Cook Inlet to three active volcanoes on the Alaska Peninsula—Mount Spurr, Mount Redoubt, and Mount Iliamna. In the distance, drift-net fishing boats work the waters of the inlet; closer to shore, the gray water is dotted with bright buoys and aluminum skiffs of local set-net fish sites. When the scene is silhouetted against the pink-orange wash of a late summer sky, it's as if you've stepped into a painting.

Flora and fauna: Razorneck clams, eagles, moose, gulls, small birds, and mammals can be seen here. There are wildflowers such as fireweed, lupine, Jacob's ladder, and wild geranium, and the prickly rose grows along the edges of the coastal forest.

Recreation: Facilities include campsites (116), with paved parking for RVs and a grassy area for tent camping and picnics. A fee is charged, and a maximum stay of 15 days applies. Fresh water, a picnic shelter, fire grates, trash dumpsters, and pit toilets are on site. Two productive salmon and steelhead streams—the Kasilof and Ninilchik Rivers—flow within a few miles of the campground. Charter-fishing packages can be arranged through local lodges; horseback riding also is available.

A weather-protected bulletin board offers informational updates on clamming conditions and tides, and bear warnings. A strong run of red salmon begins around July 4, and surf-fishing during high tide should bring success below the campground. The rest of the beach is accessible for clam-digging during any minus tide, but minus 2 feet or less is best. Consult your tide book for times. An Alaska sport-fishing license is required for anyone over 16 years old. Each person is limited to 60 clams per day, and must keep all clams that they dig. Consult current regulations of the Alaska Department of Fish and Game for salmon catch limits.

Weather and conditions: Expect the extremes. Clam Gulch can experience sunny summer days into the high 70s, yet if a storm moves in, it can drop 20 degrees F within hours. Periods of chilly rain and wind are common. Plan to dress in layers, and

A set-netter's skiff is tied off in Cook Inlet. In the distance stands Mount Redoubt.   Tricia Brown photo

cover it all with rain gear. Clam diggers should be waterproofed from head to toe. Bring a clam shovel, a bucket, and a sharp knife.

Caution: At the base of the bluffs along the beach are the seasonal camps of set-net fishing permit holders; respect their property and activity. Since the beach is their main thoroughfare, do not be tempted to drive down unless you have a four-wheel-drive vehicle. You'll only block the way as you wait for a tow.

Directions/access: From Anchorage, take the Seward Highway south to the Sterling Highway turn-off. Follow the Sterling Highway to Mile 117.5, about 20 miles south of Soldotna. From Homer, drive north 55 miles. The campground pullout is 0.5 mile off the main road. Wooden stairs provide beach access for explorers. Use four-wheel-drive vehicles to access the beach following the steep, single-lane rocky road alongside Clam Creek.

---

37 Deep Creek State Recreation Area

Location: North of Homer, on the western coast of the Kenai Peninsula
Size: 155 acres (62 hectares)
High point: 200 feet (60 m)
Low point: Sea level
Best time of year: Foot, May–September; boat, April–October
Daylight: June 21: 19 hours

December 21: 6 hours
Activities: Camping, fishing, clamming, picnicking, photography, wildlife-watching
USGS map: Kenai A-5
Managed by: Alaska Division of Parks and Outdoor Recreation

Among Southcentral Alaska anglers, the Deep Creek beach launch is a favorite place to launch a salt-water fishing adventure. Successful fishermen return from a trip out on

Stream fishing at Deep Creek. Salt-water anglers can access deep water for great halibut fishing off the nearby beach.   ASP photo by Robert Angell

Cook Inlet with door-sized halibut and king salmon weighing 50-plus pounds. The river itself supports healthy runs of king and silver salmon as well as Dolly Varden. What the campground lacks in development, it makes up in the view. From here the view across Cook Inlet encompasses a row of spectacular volcanoes: Mounts Augustine, Iliamna, Redoubt, and Spurr.

Flora and fauna: Located on the western side of the Sterling Highway, the beach at the mouth of Deep Creek is rugged: rocks, gravel, and sand. Seams of coal are visible in the high cliffs behind the beach. Nearby wetlands attract waterfowl. In spring, sandhill cranes and other shorebirds rest and feed in the salt-water marsh as part of their annual migration. Offshore, watch for whales, seals, and otters. Bald eagles may be seen year-round.

Recreation: Facilities include 300-plus undeveloped campsites, which are often full on summer weekends, toilets, a sheltered picnic area, and fresh drinking water. A boat ramp on the river makes Cook Inlet accessible at high tides. For launching from the beach at any time, a private launch service uses tractors to tow boats in and out of the surf. Clamming is good at minus tides. A sport-fishing license is required for all fishing and clamming. Be familiar with Alaska Department of Fish and Game regulations before you go.

Weather and conditions: Winters are mild, with temperatures ranging from 14 degrees to 27 degrees F (minus 10 degrees to minus 3 degrees C); in summer, expect temperatures in the range of 45 degrees to 65 degrees F (7 degrees to 18 degrees C). As in any Cook Inlet coastal area, wind and rain are commonplace in summer. Dress in layers and bring rain gear. Clammers should be suited up from head to foot.

Caution: Boat-launch users should keep an eye on the clock so they can return on a high tide. The U.S. Coast Guard makes frequent checks to ensure boaters meet minimum safety regulations, as weather and tides can change rapidly.

Directions/access: The park is located at Mile 137 Sterling Highway, just 2 miles south of the Ninilchik State Recreation Area. Roadside businesses offer groceries, gas, supplies, food, and lodging. Charter fishing in fresh or salt water also is available.

38 Fort Abercrombie State Historical Park

Location: Near Kodiak on Kodiak Island
Size: 183 acres (74 hectares)
High point: 100 feet (30 m)
Low point: Sea level
Best time of year: Foot, May–October;
  boat, May–October; ski, January–
  March
Daylight: June 21: 18 hours

December 22: 6½ hours
Activities: Camping, fishing, swimming,
  canoeing, hiking, beach-combing
USGS map: Kodiak D-2
Established: 1969
Managed by: Alaska Division of Parks
  and Outdoor Recreation

An observation post on this forested cliff overlooking Narrow Strait and the Gulf of Alaska was manned 24 hours a day after the attack on Pearl Harbor in December 1941. Following Japanese attacks on Attu, Kiska, and Unalaska in the western Aleutian Islands, the post was fortified and renamed for Lt. Col. William R. Abercrombie, who was instrumental in U.S. Army explorations of Alaska in the late nineteenth century. From

Fort Abercrombie State Historical Park is perched atop a rocky promontory on Kodiak Island.
ASP photo

1942 to 1944, as many as 200 men were stationed here; the fort appears to have been abandoned after 1944. The site was placed on the National Register of Historic Places in 1970. Today the gun mounts and bunkers sit quietly in the wind.

Flora and fauna: Keep an eye open in the rain forest for Sitka blacktail deer, red foxes, snowshoe hares, red squirrels, and weasels (ermine). Salmonberries are ripe by August. Watch the ocean for porpoises, dolphins, sea otters, seals, sea lions, and whales.

Recreation: The park has a campground (13 units, some of them walk-in sites) set in tall Sitka spruce trees, a visitors' center, and a 3-mile (5-km) marked trail. Campfires are permitted only in campground fire pits. Wood is likely to be wet. Keep children away from the sea cliffs. At Lake Gertrude, swim, fish, and canoe; beach-comb along the coast. Hunting, use of firearms, horses, powerboats, snowmobiles, and off-road vehicles are prohibited.

Weather and conditions: Expect rain. Kodiak Island's maritime climate is wet, with cool summers and mild winters. (See the Kodiak weather table.) Winds generally are light in the forest, gusty on exposed headlands.

Directions/access: To reach the park, follow Rezanoff Road from downtown Kodiak 3.9 miles (6.3 km) to a sign for the park. A short side road leads to the right. Rental cars, restaurants, and lodging are available in Kodiak. A port of call for the southwestern Alaska state ferry, Kodiak also has scheduled air service.

39 Goose Bay State Game Refuge

Location: North of Anchorage
Size: 11,000 acres (4400 hectares)
High point: 250 feet (76 m)
Low point: Sea level
Best time of year: Foot, April–October; boat, April–October; ski, January–March
Daylight: June 21: 19½ hours

December 22: 5½ hours
Activities: Camping, birding, fishing, hunting, photography
USGS map: Anchorage B-6
Established: 1975
Managed by: Alaska Department of Fish and Game

Only 12 miles (19 km) by air from downtown Anchorage, Goose Bay State Game Refuge is of special interest to waterfowl lovers. It includes the marshlands and mud flats

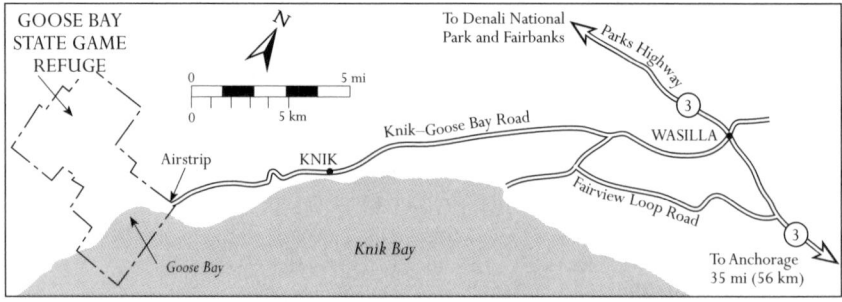

of lower Goose Creek and the surrounding lowlands. Canada geese, pintails, green-winged teal, and mallards are the most common species that nest here and use the area as a resting ground during spring and fall migrations.

Recreation: Bird-watchers and photographers are the chief visitors during late April and early May, while waterfowl hunters appear in September and October. The scattered hunting shacks, in existence before the establishment of the refuge, are private property and should not be disturbed. Undeveloped for recreational use, the refuge sports a usable abandoned airstrip at the southern end of the Knik–Goose Bay Road. Camping on public land for up to 14 days is unrestricted; campfires are permitted, but little wood is available. Firearms, horses, powerboats, off-road vehicles, snowmobiles, and fixed-wing aircraft landings are all permitted.

Weather and conditions: Located at tidewater, the refuge has a subarctic maritime climate. (See the Anchorage weather table.) Winds generally are moderate to strong.

Caution: Incoming tides can be swift, with frequent large tidal bores. Tide flat mud is soft and treacherous.

Directions/access: The refuge is most easily reached by air taxi from Anchorage, Eagle River, Palmer, or Wasilla, or by automobile via the mostly paved Knik–Goose Bay Road from Wasilla, a distance of 22 miles (35 km). The nearest stores, restaurants, and lodging are in Wasilla.

40 Gulkana National Wild and Scenic River

Location: Eastern Alaska, north of Glennallen

River rating: Main river and Middle Fork, WW4–FWA; West Fork, WW2–FWA

Popular trip lengths: 35 to 119 miles (56 to 191 km)

Best time of year: August–September

Annual high water: June

Daylight: June 21: 20 hours December 22: 5 hours

USGS maps: Paxson Lake to Sourdough: Gulkana D-4, C-4; Middle Fork to Sourdough via Tangle Lakes: Mt. Hayes A-5; Gulkana D-5, D-4, C-4; West Fork to Sourdough: Gulkana D-6, C-6, C-5, C-4; Sourdough to Gulkana: C-4, B-4, B-3

Designated as Wild River: 1980

Managed by: Bureau of Land Management (above Sourdough)

Flowing southward through the forested foothills of the Alaska Range, the Gulkana is a heavily traveled, moderately difficult white-water river with three floatable branches. Most boaters begin at Paxson Lake, easily accessible by automobile. There are two sets of rapids, WW3 for 3 miles (5 km) below Paxson Lake and the Canyon Rapids, with a 0.25-mi (0.40-km) portage, then WW3–4 for 8 miles (13 km) around boulders and logs. The remainder of the river to Sourdough, where the trans-Alaska oil pipeline crosses overhead, is WW1–2. From Sourdough to the village of Gulkana, the river is WW2, with a short stretch of WW3. From Paxson Lake access to Sourdough is 45 miles

Wolves are among the wildlife that may be seen in the Gulkana region.   ASP photo by Robert Angell

(72 km) and to Gulkana, another 35 miles (56 km). Below Sourdough, the river flows through Native lands of Ahtna, Inc.

The Middle Fork begins at Dickey Lake, accessible by portages from Tangle Lakes, which have a highway access. The longest portage is 1.3 miles (2.1 km). The upper river is shallow, swift, and rocky, requiring frequent lining; sweepers and logjams can be a problem until the Middle Fork joins the main Gulkana below Paxson Lake. From Tangle Lake to Sourdough is 84 miles (135 km).

The West Fork is a relaxed meandering stream, but watch for sweepers and logjams. From the headwaters to Sourdough is about 100 miles (160 km).

Flora and fauna: Wildlife is typical of the boreal forest: moose, black bears, brown (grizzly) bears, wolves, wolverines, coyotes, red foxes, lynx, and beavers. Caribou, during their spring and fall migrations, cross the river between Paxson and Glennallen. Approach eagles' nests no closer than 300 feet (90 m). Red salmon spawn in the headwaters; rainbow trout, whitefish, and grayling also are found.

Recreation: Above Sourdough, camping is unrestricted and campfires are permitted, but boaters are encouraged to use camping stoves to reduce the impact on the forests. Cache food high in trees at night to avoid attracting bears. Expect large populations of mosquitoes and other biting insects from June through August. Fishing, hunting, firearms, fixed-wing aircraft, and powerboats are all permitted on public lands.

Weather and conditions: The climate is subarctic continental mountain; summers are cool, often drizzly, and overcast. (See the Denali National Park weather table.) Winds normally are light.

Directions/access: Access to Paxson Lake, elevation 2553 feet (778 m), is at

Paxson Lake Campground, Mile 175 Richardson Highway. Up the lake 4 miles (6 km),
automobiles can drive to the water's edge at a state wayside. The Sourdough access,
elevation 1900 feet (580 m), is at BLM's Sourdough Creek Campground (60 campsites)
at Mile 147 Richardson Highway. The Gulkana public take-out, elevation 1400 feet (330
m), is on Native land on the west (right) bank near the bridge, Mile 127 Richardson
Highway. The boat ramp on the east bank is a commercial facility.

Middle Fork access starts at the Tangle River Campground, elevation 3000 feet (900
m), Mile 22 Denali Highway, or you can take an air taxi to Dickey Lake, elevation 2870
feet (875 m). To reach the West Fork, fly to Dickey Lake or Tangle Lakes, elevation 2700
feet (820 m), at the headwaters.

Scheduled buses travel the Richardson Highway; air taxis operate from Gakona,
Glennallen, and Paxson. Food and lodging are readily available at roadside businesses and
at Gakona, Glennallen, and Paxson. The historic Sourdough Roadhouse was destroyed by
fire in 1992.

41 Iditarod National Historic Trail

Location: Southcentral, Central, and
Western Alaska, from Seward to
Nome
National Historic Trail System: 2264
miles (3645 km)
High point: 3400 feet (1000 m)
Low point: Sea level
Best time of year: Foot, June–
September (Seward–Anchorage area);
winter travel, February–March
Activities: Hiking, skiing, dog mushing,
snowmobiling
USGS maps: (East to west) Seward,
Anchorage, Tyonek, Talkeetna, Lime
Hills, McGrath, Medfra, Iditarod,
Ophir, Ruby, Nulato, Unalakleet,
Norton Bay, Solomon, Nome
**Established as National Historic
Trail:** 1978
Managed by: Alaska Division of Parks
and Outdoor Recreation and Bureau
of Land Management

Although portions of the Iditarod route have been used for centuries by Eskimos
and Athabascan Indians, it was thousands of Outsiders, attracted by gold strikes at the
turn of the century, who created a major winter trail network connecting Seward and
Nome. The first substantial gold strike, on the north shore of the Kenai Peninsula in
1889, attracted large numbers of prospectors who soon stamped out trails in the valleys.
Ten years later, the famous gold-bearing sands of Nome's beaches started another
stampede.

With land and waters locked in snow and ice for 8 months of the year, an alternative to summer river travel was necessary, and the winter trail was born. Eventually the
trail took the name of the active Iditarod mining district. The southern portion of the
trail, near Seward, was first marked about 1890; the remainder was surveyed and
marked after 1907.

Soon roadhouses sprang up, spaced about 20 miles (30 km) apart along the trail—
about the distance that could be traveled in a winter's day by dogsled. From 1914 to

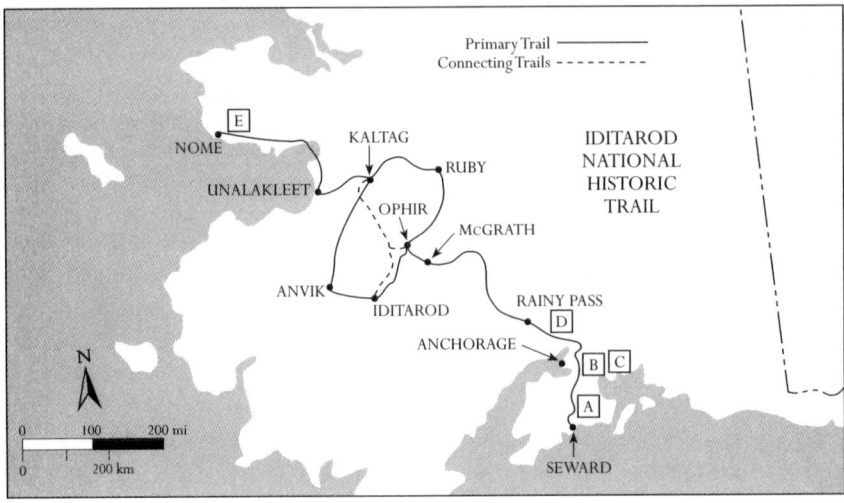

1921, the trail also was used by mushers who contracted to carry the U.S. mail. The Iditarod had a final surge of glory in the winter of 1924–25, when a relay of 20 dog mushers rushed serum from Nenana to diphtheria-stricken Nome, 674 miles (1085 km), in a record 127½ hours. After 1925, when air travel reached Alaska, freighting and extensive travel over the trail nearly ceased.

Recreation: Of this trail network, 2264 miles (3645 km) have been designated as a National Historic Trail. The primary route from Seward to Nome is 938 miles (1510 km) long. Since much of the route winds west of Anchorage through uninhabited river valleys, vast wetlands, and coastal flatlands, winter travel is the most appropriate. Some sections of the trail, not yet included in the national trail system, cross private lands or mining claims. Trail easements exist in most of these areas, but travelers and campers must remain on the easements. Campfires generally are permitted on public lands, but are specifically prohibited in Chugach State Park. Severe avalanche hazard exists along mountainous portions of the trail. Prepare carefully for winter travel; temperatures can drop well below minus 40 degrees F (minus 40 degrees C) between Anchorage and Nome. (Since the trail crosses several climatic regions, refer to the descriptions of nearby parklands and the weather tables for weather information.)

A few small sections of the trail south of Anchorage are popular summer hiking trails. Much of the remainder of the southern part of the historic route is part of the state highway system. Villagers along the northern half use the trail for winter travel between villages.

A major segment of the trail, with a length officially designated as 1049 miles (1688 km), has been used since 1973 for the annual Iditarod Trail Sled Dog Race from Anchorage to Nome. The mushers vie for $450,000 in prize money, with the first-place musher receiving $50,000. The record time stands at 9 days, 2 hours, 42 minutes, and 19 seconds, set by Doug Swingley in 1995.

Directions/access: Marked portions of the Iditarod Trail accessible from the road system are: (A) Johnson Pass Trail, Chugach National Forest, a 21-mile (34-km) hiking

Mushers in the annual Iditarod Trail Sled Dog Race follow many of the connecting trails in the historic trail system. Tricia Brown photo

trail with trailheads at Mile 32.5 and Mile 63.8 Seward Highway. (B) Crow Pass/Eagle River Trail, Chugach National Forest and Chugach State Park, a 20-mile (32-km) hiking trail with trailheads at Mile 5.5 Crow Pass Road (from Girdwood) and Mile 12 Eagle River Road (from Eagle River). The U.S. Forest Service maintains a public-use recreational cabin at Crow Pass (reservations required, fee). The Eagle River Nature Center is at the Eagle River trailhead. (C) Indian Pass/Ship Creek Trail, Chugach State Park, a 21-mile (34-km) hiking or ski-touring trail with trailheads accessible from Mile 103 Seward Highway (a 1-mile [2-km] side road leads north to the trailhead) and Mile 5

Glenn Highway (follow the Arctic Valley Ski Bowl Road 6 miles [10 km] to the trailhead). (D) Knik/Finger Lake Trail, a 100-mile (160-km) dog-mushing or ski-touring trail starting from Mile 13.5 Knik–Goose Bay Road (from Wasilla). The Nome to Council Road (E) parallels the Iditarod Trail for 33 miles (53 km) between Nome and Solomon.

42 Independence Mine State Historical Park

Location: Northwest of Palmer
Size: 272 acres (110 hectares)
High point: 3400 feet (1000 m)
Low point: 3200 feet (980 m)
Best time of year: Foot, June–
    September; ski, October–April
Daylight: June 21: 20 hours

December 22: 5 hours
Activities: Hiking, berry-picking, gold-
    panning, skiing, visiting historic sites
USGS map: Anchorage D-7
Established: 1979
Managed by: Alaska Division of Parks
    and Outdoor Recreation

Weather-bleached frame buildings stand ghost-like on the foggy tundra, surrounded by the craggy Talkeetna Mountains; at the mine shafts, high on perpendicular cliffs, more buildings cling to imperceptible niches. Originally staked in 1907 by the Alaska Gold Quartz Mining Company, the claims, known as the Independence Mines, were transferred to the Alaska-Pacific Consolidated Mining Company in 1933. From then to 1943, they yielded more than 10,300 pounds (4670 kg) of gold, making them the second-largest lode-gold producer in Alaska (the Alaska-Juneau Gold Mining Company was larger). Wartime priorities closed the mines during World War II, and later attempts to reopen them failed. The mine buildings were placed on the National Register of Historic Places in 1974.

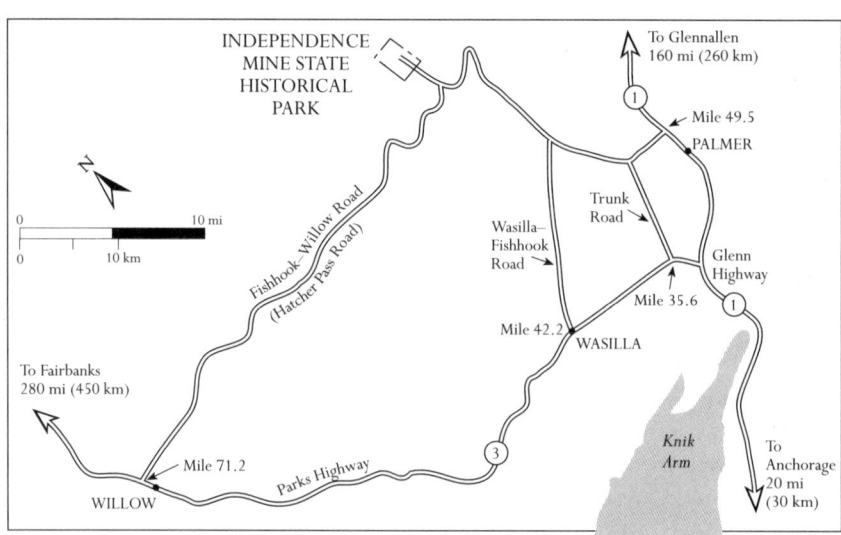

The buildings of the Independence Mine are slowly undergoing renovation.   ASP photo

Flora and fauna: Tundra wildflowers are at their best in late June and early July. Wildlife is rather sparse, but watch for marmots, mountain goats and Dall sheep, brown (grizzly) bears, caribou, wolves, and wolverines.

Recreation: Entirely above tree line and sitting in a bowl-shaped valley at the headwaters of Fishhook Creek, the Independence Mine area is renowned for having the earliest and lightest accessible powder snow in the area, attracting cross-country skiers from all over Southcentral. (Caution: Avalanches can occur.) Although the park occupies only a small area, the entire valley is popular with summer visitors for picnicking, berry-picking, hiking, and hang gliding.

Facilities include a visitors' center and museum. Until restoration is complete, visitors are not permitted to wander within certain buildings. Camping is permitted, although campfires are not; use a camping stove. Hunting, horses, snowmobiles, and off-road vehicles are prohibited. Numerous mining claims and private lands exist in the area, so ask before picking up rocks or panning for gold; obey "No Trespassing" signs. The visitors' center will loan gold pans and offer directions so you can try your hand at panning.

Weather and conditions: Astride the transition from a subarctic maritime to a subarctic continental climate, the mine area has cool, frequently overcast summers and cold, clear winters. (See the Anchorage weather table.) Winds normally are light.

Directions/access: The park is accessible by automobile from the Fishhook–Willow Road (Hatcher Pass Road), which can be reached from four state highway points: (1) Mile 49.5 Glenn Highway, intersection with the Fishhook–Willow Road, 1 mile (2 km) north of Palmer; the park is 18 miles (29 km) away. (2) Mile 35.6 Parks

Highway, intersection with Trunk Road, 0.3 mile (0.5 km) north of the junction of the Parks and Glenn Highways. Follow Trunk Road 6.6 miles (10.6 km) to its intersection with Fishhook–Willow Road. (3) Mile 42.2 Parks Highway, intersection with Wasilla–Fishhook Road (Wasilla's Main Street). Follow it north 10.5 miles (17 km) to the Fishhook–Willow Road. (4) Mile 71.2 Parks Highway at Willow, intersection with the west end of the Fishhook–Willow Road (Hatcher Pass Road); the park is about 32 miles (51 km) away. Not maintained in winter, the road over Hatcher Pass from Willow normally is plowed for only the first 17 miles (27 km). By mid-June, the full length is open. The other accesses are open year-round.

Rental cars are available in Anchorage; groceries, gas, restaurants, and lodging are found at roadside businesses along the highways and in Palmer, Wasilla, and Willow. One or two lodges operate near Independence Mine.

43 Johnson Lake State Recreation Area

Location: South of Soldotna

Size: 332 acres (133 hectares)

High point: 200 feet (60 m)

Low point: 150 feet (45 m)

Best time of year: Foot, May–
September; boat, May–September;
ski, December–March

Daylight: June 21: 19 hours

December 21: 6 hours

Activities: Camping, fishing, hunting,
swimming, nonmotorized boating,
picnicking

USGS map: Kenai B-4

Established: 1967; amended 1974, 1986

Managed by: Alaska Division of Parks
and Outdoor Recreation

State recreation areas on the Kenai Peninsula developed as the road system did, created as pullouts or waysides along the Sterling Highway by the Department of Transportation. Beautiful Johnson Lake has long been a favorite destination for locals and more recently has been discovered by visitors.

Flora and fauna: Set in a boreal forest of spruce and aspen, the habitat supports dwarf dogwood, fireweed, and lupine, among other wildflowers. An old beaver house on the lake is likely abandoned. Moose pass through the recreation area often and occasionally caribou or a black bear are spotted nearby.

Recreation: Facilities include a campground (50 units) in a 5-day use area, fire pits, tables, toilets, and drinking water. Just outside the park on the roadside is a day-use area for picnickers. A boat launch allows access for canoes, kayaks, and other nonmotorized watercraft. An informational bulletin board holds important information about permitted uses of the area. There are no marked trails, but an undeveloped trail does follow the lakeside. The Alaska Department of Fish and Game stocks the lake with rainbow trout. Be familiar with regulations before beginning your fishing trip.

Weather and conditions: Winters are mild, with temperatures ranging from 14 degrees to 27 degrees F (minus 10 degrees to minus 3 degrees C); in summer, expect temperatures in the range of 45 degrees to 65 degrees F (7 degrees to 18 degrees C).

Directions/access: The western portion of the Kenai Peninsula is easily

A family prepares to launch a canoe trip on Johnson Lake.   ASP photo

accessible by automobile via the Seward and Sterling Highways. The recreation area is located between Soldotna and Homer. At Mile 110 Sterling Highway, turn south to Tustumena Lake Road, then turn east. Automobiles can be rented in Anchorage. Scheduled air service is available to Soldotna and Homer; air taxis may be arranged in Anchorage, Soldotna, or Homer. Groceries, gas, and supplies are available at all three communities or at any number of roadside businesses.

44 Kachemak Bay State Park and Wilderness Park

Location: Southern tip of the Kenai Peninsula

Size: 380,000 acres (152,000 hectares)

High point: 4233 feet (1290 m)

Low point: Sea level

Best time of year: Foot, May–October; boat, April–October; ski, February–March

Daylight: June 21: 18 ½ hours December 22: 6 hours

Activities: Wildlife-watching, boating, hiking, beach-combing, ski touring

USGS map: Seldovia

Established: 1970; amended 1989

Managed by: Alaska Division of Parks and Outdoor Recreation

With noisy seabird and seal rookeries, spawning streams, and important salt-water nurseries, this park protects a wide variety of wildlife habitats. Precipitous peaks, immense glaciers, and the Harding Icefield make for spectacular scenery. Nearly 24,000

Hikers pause for a photo at Kachemak Bay on the Kenai Peninsula.   ASP photo by Robert Angell

acres (9600 hectares) were added to the park in 1989 using funds from the *Exxon Valdez* oil spill settlement.

The region appears to have been occupied by Eskimos in the eighth century B.C. In 1778, Captain James Cook explored Kachemak Bay; in 1795, Russians established a sawmill here. The community of Halibut Cove, center of a thriving fishing industry from 1911 to 1928, is today home for some of Alaska's finest artists and craftspersons.

Flora and fauna: In the rugged maritime mountain range, the densely forested slopes extend to about 1000 feet (300 m); brush continues to 2500 feet (800 m). Watch for moose, black bears, brown (grizzly) bears, mountain goats, wolves, bald eagles, seabirds, dolphins, porpoises, seals, sea lions, and whales. Avoid disturbing the seabird and seal rookeries.

Recreation: Five public-use cabins are available with reservations (fee). Other development includes primitive campsites (22 units) with pit toilets and a network of about 80 miles (48 km) of marked trail. (Maps are available at the park office.) Beachcomb, hike to the glaciers, climb the mountains, or ski tour—this is some of the finest wilderness available in Southcentral. Backcountry camping is unrestricted; campfires are permitted. Avoid trespassing on the numerous private landholdings scattered along the Kachemak Bay shoreline. Fishing and hunting are permitted; snowmobiles, all-terrain bicycles, and off-road vehicles are not. Horses are allowed on a designated trail. A few areas are open to fixed-wing aircraft and powerboats.

Weather and conditions: Weather is controlled by the maritime climate; expect cool, overcast summers and mild, overcast winters. (See the Homer weather table.) Winds are light to moderate at low elevations, often strong on the peaks. Williwaws can occur in Sadie Cove and Tutka Bay. Expect tidal fluctuations of up to 28 feet (8.5 m). Much of the mountainous area is subject to avalanches.

Caution: Use caution crossing Kachemak Bay in small boats; winds can build large waves in a short time.

Directions/access: Air taxis, water taxis, and excursion boats transport visitors to the park from Homer and Seldovia. Popular access points are: Glacier Spit; Halibut Cove, from which a 2-mile (3-km) trail leads to Grewingk Glacier; Sadie Cove; Tutka Bay; and a road from Seldovia to Rocky Bay on the Gulf of Alaska coast via Jakolof Bay. Jakolof Bay has a public dock. Both Homer and Seldovia have stores, restaurants, and lodging. A number of attractive wilderness lodges lie within or near the park.

45 Kenai Fjords National Park

June 2012 and Aug 2014

Location: Southwest of Seward
Size: 587,000 acres (238,000 hectares)
High point: 6340 feet (1932 m)
Low point: Sea level
Best time of year: Foot, mid-June–August; boat, late April–early August; ski, February–April
Daylight: June 21: 19 hours

December 22: 6 hours
Activities: Sightseeing cruises, wildlife-watching, camping, fishing, boating, salt-water kayaking
USGS maps: Blying Sound, Kenai, Seldovia, Seward
Established: 1980
Managed by: National Park Service

Boasting snowy peaks with glaciers grinding to the sea, steep-walled fjords, and the massive Harding Icefield, the Kenai Fjords is one of Alaska's most scenic—and treacherous—parklands. The Kenai Mountains, pressed toward the ocean by tectonic forces,

From the water or the air, the Kenai Fjords are some of the most beautiful country in Southcentral Alaska.   APLIC photo

front on the stormy Gulf of Alaska. Many of the park's glaciers are rapidly retreating.

Flora and fauna: Starting at one of the glaciers, follow the colonization of plant life on the barren moraine, from the first tenuous lichens near the ice masses to the full climactic richness of the stately coastal forests.

Mountain goats feed on the crags. In the lowlands roam moose, black bears, coyotes, wolverines, and red foxes. Brown (grizzly) bears are found in the Resurrection River valley and on hillsides bordering Resurrection Bay. Bald eagles are widespread, while tufted puffins, horned puffins, kittiwakes, murres, and auklets nest abundantly in Aialik and Harris Bays. Harbor seals congregate at the heads of most fjords, while sea lions breed on offshore islands. Watch the coastal waters for sea otters and whales.

Recreation: Camping and campfires are permitted throughout. Expect wet weather and strong winds, especially along the coast; hypothermia is a constant danger. Hiking, except in the Resurrection River valley, is difficult because of the steep terrain; mountaineering is unrestricted. Boaters will find few beaches or well-protected bays. Fishing, firearms, horses, powerboats, fixed-wing aircraft, and snowmobiles are all permitted; hunting and off-road vehicles are not.

Weather and conditions: The maritime climate brings cool, wet summers and mild, wet winters. (See the Seward weather table.) Winds are light in protected areas, moderate to strong on exposed headlands, ridges, and peaks. Extensive storm systems isolate the fjords after late August.

Caution: In winter, heavy snows or rain often produce severe avalanche hazard. The fjords themselves are hazardous; all front on the unpredictable Gulf of Alaska and have strong tidal currents, poorly charted bays, and uncharted rocks. Only experienced boaters should attempt to visit these waters. If you depend on an air taxi or charter boat, weather and high seas can delay your pickup for days or even weeks.

Directions/access: The park is accessible from an 8-mile (13-km) road up the Resurrection River valley from Mile 3 Seward Highway. A bridge over the river provides access to Exit Glacier and the nearby ranger station.

An hour or two of flightseeing from Seward or Homer or a daylong charter cruise are the most popular ways to view the outer coast. The southwestern Alaska state ferry between Seward and Kodiak provides views of the park but does not stop. Stores, restaurants, and modern lodgings are available in Seward and Homer.

46 Kenai National Wildlife Refuge and Wilderness

Location: Kenai Peninsula
Size: 1,906,214 acres (762,485 hectares)
High point: 6612 feet (2015 m)
Low point: Sea level
Best time of year: Foot, May–October; boat, June–September; ski, February–April
Daylight: June 21: 19 hours
December 22: 6 hours

Activities: Picnicking, berry-picking, fishing, hunting, hiking, backpacking, camping, boating, river running, . ski touring, snowmobiling, mountaineering
USGS maps: Kenai, Seldovia, Seward
Established: 1941
Managed by: U.S. Fish and Wildlife Service

Covering a long, broad swath of the western Kenai Peninsula, the refuge originally was known as the Kenai National Moose Range. Its name was changed in 1980, when 240,000 acres (97,100 hectares) of land were added; 1,350,000 acres (546,300 hectares) of the combined lands were designated as Wilderness. The highest peak within the refuge is Truuli Peak, elevation 6612 feet (2015 m), in the heavily glaciated backbone of the Kenai Mountains along the southeastern boundary of the refuge; here, too, is the massive Harding Icefield. The Swanson River area oil wells were the first to supply oil in Alaska in commercial quantities.

Flora and fauna: A vast system of mountains, forests, rolling hills, wetlands, rivers, streams, and lakes supports several large fish and wildlife populations, particularly salmon and moose. Large wildfires in the refuge, particularly those that occurred in 1947 and 1969, have been beneficial for the moose, since the new growth of willow, aspen, and birch appeals to their taste. Moose are most likely to be seen along the road system in winter and spring, when snow drives them to the lowlands. Alaska Department of Fish and Game surveys showed that in 1995 there were 16,312 trumpeter swans in the Pacific Coast population, 99 percent of them in Alaska. Many pairs nest in the refuge. Watch also for Dall sheep, mountain goats, caribou, black bears, brown (grizzly) bears, wolves, wolverines, beavers, bald eagles, loons, ptarmigan, and grouse.

Recreation: A popular recreation area for Cook Inlet area residents and visitors, Kenai offers picnicking, berry-picking, fishing, hunting, hiking, backpacking, camping, boating, river running, ski touring, snowmobiling, and mountaineering. Particularly popular are the Swan Lake and Swanson River canoe routes, chains of more than 40 lakes, two rivers, and numerous wetlands in the northern part of the refuge; these are gentle waters for novice boaters. Horses are permitted throughout; off-road vehicles are prohibited. Use of powerboats, snowmobiles, and aircraft is restricted in some areas.

Facilities include 15 picnic sites, 80 campsites, 8 boat ramps, a visitors' center in

A cow and calf feed along the Sterling Highway. The Kenai National Wildlife Refuge is heavily populated by moose.   Tricia Brown photo

Soldotna, interpretive displays, more than 250 miles (300 km) of walking trails, and 100 miles (160 km) of canoe trails. Additional camping space is available at commercial roadside campgrounds; backcountry camping is unrestricted. Campfires are permitted except when forest fire danger is high.

Water travel: Kenai River, WW3–FWA, from Kenai Lake to the city of Kenai, 90 miles (145 km); Swan Lake Canoe Route, FWA, numerous routes up to 60 miles (97 km) long; Swanson River Canoe Route, FWA, numerous routes up to 80 miles (129 km) long. On Skilak and Tustumena Lakes, boaters should stay near shore; several lives have been lost in the large waves and white water generated by sudden violent winds.

Weather and conditions: Weather patterns in the refuge are typical of a subarctic maritime climate: cool summers and frequent overcast skies near the coast and mountains, warmer and sunnier inland on the rolling hills. Winters are cold, especially inland. (See the Kenai weather table.) Winds generally are light in the mountain valleys (but with the possibility of williwaws) and moderate to strong near the coast and on mountain peaks.

Caution: In mountainous regions, winter travelers may encounter severe avalanche hazard.

Directions/access: The paved Sterling Highway, from Mile 54.7 to Mile 76, about 120 miles (190 km) from Anchorage, runs through the heart of the refuge. Major side roads, mostly unpaved, are: Skilak Lake Loop Road, 18 miles (29 km); Swanson River and Swanson Lake Roads, a total of 35 miles (56 km); Kenai Spur Road (see Captain Cook State Recreation Area); Tustumena Lake Road, from the Kasilof area, 6 miles (10 km) long. Scheduled buses travel the Sterling Highway from Anchorage to Soldotna and Kenai; scheduled air service is available to Homer, Kenai, and Soldotna. Air taxis are based at Cooper Landing, Homer, Kenai, Seward, and Soldotna; charter boats at Homer, Soldotna, and Sterling. A small passenger ferry, primarily used by sport fishermen, crosses the Kenai River from Mile 55 Sterling Highway to the mouth of the Russian River. Rental cars are available in Anchorage and Kenai; restaurants and lodging are found at numerous roadside businesses and in Homer, Kenai, Soldotna, and Sterling.

---

47 Kepler-Bradley Lakes State Recreation Area

Location: Northwest of Palmer
Size: 346 acres (138 hectares)
High point: 150 feet (45 m)
Low point: 85 feet (25.5 m)
Best time of year: Foot, May–October; boat, June–October; ski, January–March
Daylight: June 21: 19½ hours

December 22: 5½ hours
Activities: Picnicking, fishing, boating, hiking, ski touring, snowshoeing, ice fishing
USGS map: Anchorage C-6
Established: 1981
Managed by: Alaska Division of Parks and Outdoor Recreation

The advance and retreat of a glacier some 8,000 to 10,500 years ago created the ridges and lakes that make up this lightly developed day-use area. For families and

The chill of late August paints the trees surrounding Kepler-Bradley Lakes.   Tricia Brown photo

fishermen, picnickers and Frisbee-throwers, Kepler–Bradley is a beautiful place to recreate.

Unlike its name implies, Kepler–Bradley Lakes State Recreation Area is made up of not just two lakes, but several, including Matanuska Lake, Sliver Lake, Long Lake, Klaire Lake, Victor Lake, Irene Lake, Canoe Lake, and No-name Lake.

Flora and fauna: Watch for moose, beavers, hawks, owls, and migrating water-fowl. Arctic and common loons nest here. The area is forested with birch, spruce, and aspen.

Recreation: The state recreation area is developed for day use only. No overnight camping is allowed; however, state and private campgrounds may be found nearby. Facilities include picnic areas, toilets, drinking water, fishing platform, informational bulletin boards, and several miles of marked trails (some are wheelchair accessible). All-terrain vehicles are not permitted. Fires are allowed in fire pits only.

While gas-powered motors are not permitted on the lakes, boaters may use electric motors. Walk-in boat launches are accessible for most of the lakes. Anglers enjoy excellent fishing in the recreation area, thanks to the stocking program by the Alaska Department of Fish and Game. Rainbow trout and grayling may be found in Kepler, Bradley, and Canoe Lakes; rainbows are in Long, Sliver, and Irene Lakes; and silver salmon are in Victor Lake. Familiarize yourself with Alaska Department of Fish and Game fishing regulations before making a fishing trip.

Weather and conditions: Summers are cool and frequently overcast, and winters cold and overcast, typical of a subarctic maritime climate. (See the Anchorage weather table.) Winds are moderate, occasionally strong.

Caution: Much of the lakefront property is private, especially on Irene and Canoe Lakes. Also, please do not disturb nesting birds.

Directions/access: The recreation area is located west of Palmer at Mile 36.4 Glenn Highway. Those driving from Anchorage should take the Glenn Highway north. The entrance is just over a mile past the turnoff for the Parks Highway. A second entry point is just east of Mile 38. Turn north on Colleen Street, left on Bradley Lake Street, right on Green Jade Place, left on Kilarney Drive, and follow the road to more day parking and access to Canoe, Irene, and Long Lakes. Restaurants, lodging, groceries, gas, and supplies may be found in Anchorage, Eagle River, Wasilla, Palmer, and any number of roadside businesses.

48 Kodiak National Wildlife Refuge

Location: Portions of Kodiak, Afognak, and Uganik Islands
Size: 1,878,015 acres (751,206 hectares)
High point: 4470 feet (1362 m)
Low point: Sea level
Best time of year: Foot, May–August; boat, May–August; ski (marginal), January–March
Daylight: June 21: 18 hours

December 22: 6½ hours
Activities: Fishing, hunting, beach-combing, boating
USGS maps: Afognak, Kaguyak, Karluk, Kodiak, Trinity Islands
Established: 1941
Managed by: U.S. Fish and Wildlife Service

Protecting one of the chief strongholds of the Alaska brown (grizzly) bear, the refuge is a spine of once-glaciated mountains and rolling tundra uplands. Steep-walled fjords create 800 miles (1300 km) of coastline. An estimated 2700 bears—one of the world's highest densities—fed by abundant spawning salmon, inhabit the refuge. The brown (grizzly) bear is the largest living terrestrial carnivore, with males weighing up to 1200 pounds (540 kg) and females to 700 pounds (300 kg).

Flora and fauna: The Afognak part of the refuge is forested with Sitka spruce; most of the western section is treeless, except for large cottonwoods in the valleys, and covered by thick grasses and brush. Other wildlife found in the refuge includes bald eagles, Sitka blacktail deer, feral reindeer, mountain goats, red foxes, river otters, ptarmigan, and colonies of tufted puffins and cormorants; numerous waterfowl winter in the refuge. The Afognak Island section of the refuge contains introduced Roosevelt elk. Watch the ocean and bays for seals, sea lions, sea otters, and whales.

Recreation: Most visitors come to the refuge to fish, hunt, beach-comb, or boat. Cross-country hiking can be extremely difficult due to thick brush. Any trails on the island were created by the bears, who regard them and the salmon streams as their property; be careful where and how you hike and camp. Horses, powerboats, and floatplanes are permitted; off-road vehicles are not. In this windy, rainy area, hypothermia is a constant danger. Since scheduled air or water pickup can be delayed, carry extra food. Expect large populations of mosquitoes and other biting insects from June through September.

Wild irises thrive in Kodiak's coastal wetlands. USFWS photo

Camping is unrestricted and campfires are permitted, but wood may be wet or scarce. Refuge facilities consist of a visitors' center near Kodiak city and 7 public-use recreational cabins, all accessible by floatplane; 3 are also accessible by oceangoing boats. Cabin reservations are selected by lottery from applications received prior to each of the four drawing dates. Contact the refuge manager for information. Cabins not reserved during the drawing are available on a first-come, first-served basis. Respect private lands within the refuge boundaries.

Water travel: Karluk River, FWB, from Karluk Lake to Karluk Village, 25 miles (40 km).

Weather and conditions: The maritime climate brings cool, wet summers and mild, wet winters. Expect intense autumn storms with prolonged rain. (See the Kodiak weather table.) Rainfall varies greatly, dependent upon topography, with the northwestern coast receiving half the precipitation of the southeastern coast and Kodiak. Winds are constant and moderate, generally severe during storms. Prominent peaks include Koniag Peak, elevation 4470 feet (1362 m), and Mount Glottof, elevation 4405 feet (1343 m).

Directions/access: The only practical means of access to the refuge is by air taxi from Kodiak or Larsen Bay or by charter boat from Kodiak, both expensive. Mail planes with limited passenger space service Akhiok, Alitak, Amook, Karluk, Larsen Bay, Old Harbor, and Olga Bay, but access into the refuge overland is impractical. Lodging may be available at commercial hunting lodges (reservations required). Kodiak, a port of call for the southwestern Alaska state ferry, has charter boats, stores, restaurants, lodging, rental cars, and taxicabs. Frequent scheduled airline service connects Kodiak with Anchorage and Seattle.

49 Lake Clark National Park and Preserve

Location: West of Cook Inlet
Size: 3,655,000 acres (1,479,000 hectares)
High point: 10,197 feet (3108 m)
Low point: Sea level
Best time of year: Foot, June–September; boat, June–September; ski, February–April

Daylight: June 21: 19½ hours
 December 21: 5½ hours
Activities: Backpacking, river running, fishing, lake kayaking
USGS maps: Iliamna, Kenai, Lake Clark, Lime Hills, Seldovia, Tyonek
Established: 1978
Managed by: National Park Service

Turquoise lakes, glaciers, steaming volcanoes, precipitous granite spires, thundering waterfalls, and wave-washed seashores are all here. A rugged wilderness not yet well known, the Lake Clark area holds some of Alaska's finest scenery. The Tlikakila River flows through a major earth fault that runs through the area. The park's two spectacular volcanoes, Iliamna, elevation 10,016 feet (3053 m), and Redoubt, elevation 10,197 feet (3108 m), are easily seen from Anchorage and the Kenai Peninsula. Redoubt Volcano erupted in December 1989 and again in August 1990, spewing ash over the Anchorage area. Originally established as a national monument, the area became a park in 1980, with 2,470,000 acres (1,000,000 hectares) designated as Wilderness.

Flora and fauna: Moist coastal forests beside Cook Inlet give way inland to alpine tundra and mountain-rimmed lakes, all rich with wildlife. Moose roam throughout, as

Beautiful Lake Clark is the state's second-largest lake.   APLIC photo

do brown (grizzly) bears, black bears, wolves, wolverines, and red foxes. Dall sheep live on many of the peaks. The mobile Mulchatna caribou herd, numbering 200,000, may be found primarily in the western uplands of the preserve. The only known inland seal population in the United States is in Lake Iliamna, lying just outside the boundary but formed from headwaters within the park. This watershed is one of the most important producers of red salmon in the world.

Recreation: The lakes and numerous rivers, including three designated National Wild Rivers—the Chilikadrotna, the Mulchatna, and the Tlikakila—attract boaters and fishermen. Backpackers and mountaineers appreciate the uncrowded wilderness and varied terrain. Winter travelers should be aware of severe avalanche hazard in many areas.

Other than a ranger station at the settlement of Port Alsworth on Lake Clark, there are no Park Service visitor facilities. Camping is unrestricted; campfires, fishing, firearms, powerboats, fixed-wing aircraft, and snowmobiles are permitted. Hunting is permitted in the preserve but not in the park.

Water travel: Travel the park's lakes cautiously—dangerous large waves and strong winds can develop swiftly.

49a *Chilikadrotna National Wild River.* Rated WW3–FWB, the Chilikadrotna is managed by the National Park Service. It was designated a Wild River in 1980. Annual high water is June and August; best time of year to visit is between June and September.

Flowing down the west side of the Alaska Range through gentle upland forests of spruce, birch, and aspen, the Chilikadrotna is a swift, twisting, narrow river, most suitable for rafts or kayaks; canoeists attempting it should be very experienced. A popular trip length is 70 to 200 miles (110 to 320 km). Although only the first 10 miles (16 km) from its source in Twin Lakes is designated as Wild River, the remainder to its confluence with the Mulchatna is *de facto* wilderness. Combine the Chilikadrotna with the Mulchatna and the Nushagak (see the Mulchatna National Wild River description below) for a float trip of about 200 miles (320 km) to New Stuyahok.

Expect a series of WW2–3 rapids the first 5 miles (8 km) below Twin Lakes and again about 5 miles (8 km) below Little Mulchatna River. Numerous sweepers overhang the river after the first 8 miles (13 km). Be alert for logjams.

To reach the river, take an air taxi to Twin Lakes, elevation 1979 feet (603 m). End the trip by taking an air taxi from the Dummy Creek area of the Mulchatna, elevation 600 feet (200 m), or continue to New Stuyahok on the Nushagak River, elevation 100 feet (30 m). New Stuyahok has scheduled air service and a general store. Air taxis are available from Anchorage, Dillingham, Homer, Iliamna, Kenai, and Port Alsworth.

49b *Mulchatna National Wild River.* Managed by the National Park Service, the Mulchatna was designated a Wild River in 1980. It is rated WW3–FWC. Annual high water is June and August; the best time to visit is June through September.

From jewel-like Turquoise Lake nestled at the base of Telaquana Mountain, the Mulchatna flows through the rolling Bonanza Hills in a challenging, shallow, rocky channel, more suitable for rafts and kayaks than canoes. West of the Bonanza Hills, about 20 miles (30 km) below Turquoise Lake, the valley broadens; here the river trip is a gentle float through forests of spruce, birch, and aspen. From here on, watch for sweepers and logjams. Expect a stretch of fast white water above Bonanza Creek; a portage is possible. After winding through low hills, the river floodplain widens to wetlands and joins the lowlands of the Nushagak. From Turquoise Lake to New Stuyahok on the Nushagak is about 230 miles (370 km). Although only the upper 24 miles (39 km) are designated as Wild River, the watershed remains wild. Private lands border the river in the vicinity of New Stuyahok.

Reach the river by air taxi to either Turquoise Lake, elevation 2504 feet (763 m), or the small lakes below the Bonanza Hills, elevation 1200 feet (370 m). Floatplanes can land on the river at Dummy Creek, elevation 600 feet (200 m), or at the Koktuli River, elevation 300 feet (90 m), or boaters can continue to New Stuyahok, elevation 100 feet (30 m), and return by scheduled air service. Lodging, meals, groceries, and gas are available in the village. Air taxis are available from Anchorage, Dillingham, Homer, Iliamna, Kenai, and Port Alsworth.

49c Tlikakila National Wild River. Rated WW 1–4, the Tlikakila

was designated a Wild River in 1980 and is managed by the National Park Service. Annual high water is July and August; the best time to visit is July through September.

A small glacier-fed river flowing through the deep narrow valley of a major earth fault, the Tlikakila is surrounded by rugged snowcapped peaks, glaciers, waterfalls, and sheer rock cliffs. From its alpine headwaters at Summit Lake in the heart of the Chigmit Mountains to its mouth at turquoise Lake Clark, boaters float through some of the most impressive scenery in Alaska.

Summit Lake, in Lake Clark Pass where glaciers from all sides almost meet on the valley floor, is the portal to excellent hiking terrain. When you run the Tlikakila, take a few extra days to explore this country.

From Summit Lake, the river drops through a densely forested valley with thick underbrush. Gravel bars of the North Fork invite foot travel, but don't plan extensive hiking from the lower river. Just below the confluence with the North Fork, a short section of WW 3–4 rapids can be portaged on the left bank. At high water levels, other WW 3–4 rapids appear in the next 3 miles (5 km). The entire 50-mile (80-km) length is designated as Wild River. A ranger station at Port Alsworth on Lake Clark lies 23 miles (37 km) down the lake from the river's mouth.

To reach the river, take a floatplane to Summit Lake, elevation 1000 feet (300 m). A short portage from the lake to floatable water is necessary. After running the river, take an air taxi from the river's mouth at Lake Clark, elevation 245 feet (75 m), or paddle to Port Alsworth. Air taxis are based at Port Alsworth, Anchorage, Homer, and Kenai. Lodging and meals are available at wilderness lodges in the Lake Clark area; reservations generally are required.

Other rivers: Necons–Stony Rivers, WW2–FWB, from Two Lakes to Stony River village, 150 miles (140 km); Newhalen River, WW1–5, from Sixmile Lake to Newhalen (portage possible), 25 miles (40 km); Telaquana River and Stony River, WW3–FWB, from Telaquana Lake to Stony River village, 150 miles (240 km).

Weather and conditions: Expect cool summers in the mountains and, with the proximity to salt water, mild winters with frequent overcast skies. (See the Port Alsworth weather table.) Winds generally are light to moderate

Caution: Travel and camp to avoid meeting or attracting bears.

Directions/access: Access to the park and preserve is normally by air taxi from Anchorage, Kenai, or Iliamna. Frequent, but unscheduled, air service connects Anchorage and Port Alsworth. The only nearby bed-and-board services are at wilderness lodges within and near the park and preserve; reservations generally are required.

---

50 Lake Louise State Recreation Area

Location: Northwest of Glennallen

Size: 425 acres (170 hectares)

High point: 2362 feet (709 m)

Low point: 2500 feet (750 m)

Best time of year: Foot, May–September; boat, June–September; ski, February–April (low elevations)

Daylight: June 21: 19½ hours

December 22: 5½ hours

Activities: Camping, fishing, hunting, boating, ski touring, snowmobiling

USGS map: Gulkana B-6, B-5, A-5

Established: 1974; amended 1999

Managed by: Alaska Division of Parks and Outdoor Recreation

"Ike was here." If President Dwight D. Eisenhower were given to graffiti, he might have scratched those words on a tree. He really did visit this place, according to interpretive plaques posted along the self-guided nature walk in the park. During the years following World War II, Lake Louise was something of a recreation destination for the military. At this retreat, soldiers could relax and go boating and fishing in some of the most beautiful scenery in the state.

It's just as beautiful 50 years later, and only a bit more civilized. Although there are 3 crumbling cabins, they're not recommended for overnight guests. Still, there are plenty of opportunities for R&R.

Flora and fauna: Not far beneath the surface of the soil, the ground is riddled with permafrost, and only trees with shallow root systems survive. Willow scrub and black spruce are a telltale sign of permafrost. Big trees are rare in this mixed taiga environment. Caribou and moose are frequently sighted.

An unusual feature in this park is the presence of a cormorant rookery on a small island offshore—this on an inland lake. Other bird life includes trumpeter swans and various migratory waterfowl that use the small bays and coves for summer nesting.

Grayling, lake trout, and burbot may be found in the lake; however, check with Alaska Department of Fish and Game regulations before you wet a line.

Recreation: Along with the 0.5 mile of groomed trail, some of which is wheelchair

Lake Louise State Recreation Area is a popular destination for Glenn Highway travelers.
ASP photo by Mike Goodwin

accessible, the park features 65 campsites, fresh drinking water, toilets, fire pits, a picnic shelter, and plenty of tables. You'll find a boat launch, too, with a warning that it's somewhat shallow here.

Power watercraft are allowed on the lake. Fishing and hunting are permitted according to Alaska Department of Fish and Game regulations. In winter, snowmobiling and ski touring are popular activities, and sightings of moose and caribou are more frequent, especially along the access road.

Weather and conditions: The subarctic continental climate brings warm, dry summers and cold, dry, severe winters at these low elevations. Winds generally are light.

Caution: Much of the shoreline is private land. Be respectful with your wake and hours of operating power watercraft on the lake.

Directions/access: From Palmer or Glennallen, drive to Milepost 160 Glenn Highway and turn north at Lake Louise Road, a good secondary gravel road. Follow it for 18 miles to its dead-end in the park. Gas, groceries, and supplies are available in Palmer, Glennallen, or any number of roadside businesses. Private lodges on the lake can provide lodging, mooring, and fishing packages. There is a floatplane base and landing strip at Lake Louise.

51 Nancy Lake State Recreation Area

Location: West of Wasilla
Size: 22,600 acres (9040 hectares)
High point: 375 feet (114 m)
Low point: 116 feet (35 m)
Best time of year: Foot, May–October; boat, June–October; ski, January– March
Daylight: June 21: 19 ½ hours
December 22: 5 ½ hours

Activities: Picnicking, swimming, fishing, boating, hiking, berry-picking, cross-country skiing, snowshoeing, dog mushing, snowmobiling, ice fishing
USGS maps: Anchorage C-8; Tyonek C-1
Established: 1966; amended 1970
Managed by: Alaska Division of Parks and Outdoor Recreation

Nancy Lake State Recreation Area is an excellent, lightly developed playground for families who enjoy water sports and gentle hiking terrain. Now richly forested and studded with more than 130 lakes, the area was once the bed of a giant glacier that scoured out Cook Inlet as it flowed from the Alaska Range south into the Gulf of Alaska.

After the glacier's retreat, plants and animals returned and the Tanaina Indians established a subsistence culture at Indian Bay on Nancy Lake. Today, the lake's clear waters provide some of the finest recreation in the Cook Inlet area. Amid gently rolling hills known as drumlins, the forests, marshes, streams, and lakes are home for numerous animals, birds, and fish.

Flora and fauna: Watch for moose, black bears, brown (grizzly) bears, beavers, lynx, coyotes, wolves, hawks, owls, and migrating waterfowl. Red-necked grebes nest here, as do arctic and common loons; sandhill cranes greet spring with their courtship dances en route to nesting grounds. The area is forested with birch, spruce, and aspen. In August, blooming fireweed add spectacular purple to roadside wild growth.

Recreation: Portions of the recreation area are closed to snowmobiles and powerboats; horses, off-road vehicles, and aircraft landings are not permitted. Hunting is allowed, but firearms may not be used. Thirteen public-use cabins are available within the recreation area for a fee. You can make reservations through the Public Lands Information Center in Anchorage or any area office of Alaska State Parks (see Information Sources and Land Managers, Appendix). Other facilities include picnic tables, boat ramps, water, toilets, a campground (99 units), and 27 primitive campsites on the canoe trails. Thirty additional developed campsites are accessible from the Parks Highway at Nancy Lake Wayside just outside the recreation area. Campfires are restricted to campground fireplaces; use camping stoves elsewhere. Backcountry camping is permitted. Black bears are common—do not leave food or garbage where it might attract them. Swimmers may contract swimmer's itch in the warmer lakes. Marked trails: 11 miles (18 km) for hikers and 10 miles (16 km) maintained for cross-country skiers. Private lands exist within the recreation area boundaries; respect signs and do not disturb buildings.

Water travel: Nancy Lake State Recreation Area canoe lake route, FWA with portages, 16 miles (26 km); Little Susitna River, FWB, from Little Susitna River bridge, Mile 57 Parks Highway, to the portage trail into Nancy Lake SRA canoe trail system, 25

Nancy Lake's Bald Lake cabin is one of several that are available for a fee. Reservations are required. ASP photo

miles (40 km). Do not destroy or change beaver dams; they maintain critical water levels in the lakes.

Weather and conditions: The subarctic maritime climate is influenced by continental land masses; summers are warm and sunny, winters dry and cold. (See the Talkeetna weather table.) Winds normally are light.

Directions/access: The recreation area lies 67 miles (108 km) north of Anchorage at Mile 67.2 Parks Highway, between Wasilla and Willow. Automobiles can be rented in Anchorage. Scheduled buses serve the Parks Highway. Stores, restaurants, and lodging are available along the road and at Wasilla.

52 Ninilchik State Recreation Area

Location: Kenai Peninsula, north of Homer

Size: 97 acres (39 hectares)

High point: 50 feet (15 m)

Low point: Sea level

Best time of year: June–September

Daylight: June 21: 19 hours
December 21: 6 hours

Activities: Camping, fishing, clamming, picnicking, photography, wildlife-watching

USGS map: Kenai A-5

Established: 1968; amended 1975, 1980

Managed by: Alaska Division of Parks and Outdoor Recreation

In one of the most picturesque settings in Southcentral Alaska, the recreation area straddles the Sterling Highway on the western coast of the Kenai Peninsula. Camping at

Ninilchik may mean finding an RV site in the forested campground east of the highway, or turning west to camp on the bluff. A third option is setting up a tent below the bluff on the Cook Inlet beachfront. Anglers can head for the Ninilchik River; clam diggers must wait for minus tides and find their rewards in the excellent clamming adjacent to the beach campgrounds.

With a name that harkens back to Alaska's Russian period, the nearby village of Ninilchik was founded in the mid-1800s by the large extended family of Grigorii and Mavra Kvasnikoff. In a mingling of Russian and Native Alaskan cultures, the early-day residents subsisted on trapping, hunting, fishing, gardening, and gold-panning. Today the village numbers nearly 650 people and the local economy is mostly based on commercial fishing.

A beautiful Russian Orthodox church that overlooks Cook Inlet, the Holy Transfiguration of Our Lord Chapel, is on the National Register of Historic Places. A footpath leads from the village to the small church at the top of the hill, or you can drive to it on Coal Road. Fringed by a lavish growth of wildflowers in summer, the church is a popular subject for photographers. Visitors are urged to respect its continued use as a place of worship by local believers.

Flora and fauna: The forested area is dominated by stands of spruce and birch. Local wildlife includes moose, bald eagles, squirrels, ravens, and magpies. Offshore, watch for whales, seals, and otters. The Ninilchik River supports healthy runs of king and silver salmon, and Dolly Varden. Halibut may be found in the waters of Cook Inlet. Razor clams thrive in the tidal zone at the southern half of the beach camping area.

Recreation: In all, the campground areas include 56 developed sites, and more

Surf fishing at Ninilchik State Recreation Area   ASP photo by Robert Angell

than 100 undeveloped campsites on the beach. Facilities at Ninilchik View and Ninilchik Campgrounds include toilets, drinking water, picnic shelters, and short trails that lead to the river or to stairs connecting the bluff and the beach. A pay station is in operation at each entrance. At the bottom of the Ninilchik Beach Access Road you'll find day-use parking and a boat ramp for access to Cook Inlet during high tides. Consult a tide book for minus tides and excellent razor clamming.

Weather and conditions: Winters are mild, with temperatures ranging from 14 degrees to 27 degrees F (minus 10 degrees to minus 3 degrees C); in summer, expect temperatures in the range of 45 degrees to 65 degrees F (7 degrees to 18 degrees C). As in any Cook Inlet coastal area, wind and rain are commonplace in summer. Dress in layers and bring rain gear. Clammers should be suited up from head to foot.

Directions/access: Drive from Soldotna or Homer to 135 Mile Sterling Highway, then turn west on the Ninilchik Beach Access Road. Ninilchik has a state-owned gravel airstrip. Homer has an airport, harbor, and access to the southwestern Alaska state ferry system. Restaurants, groceries, supplies, and gas are available at any number of roadside businesses. Lodging and fishing charters are available in Ninilchik.

53 Palmer Hay Flats State Game Refuge

Location: Southwest of Palmer
Size: 28,164 acres (11,266 hectares)
High point: 150 feet (46 m)
Low point: Sea level
Best time of year: Foot, April–October; boat, April–October; ski, January–March
Daylight: June 21: 19½ hours
December 22: 5½ hours
Activities: Waterfowl viewing, photography, hunting
USGS maps: Anchorage, B-7, C-7
Established: 1975; amended 1985
Managed by: Alaska Department of Fish and Game

In this popular area, you can see more than 80 species of birds, including thousands of whistling and trumpeter swans as well as large populations of migratory and nesting Canada geese, pintails, and mallards. Consisting entirely of tidal grasslands and mudflats in the Matanuska and Knik river deltas, the refuge is "rubber boot country."

Recreation: The spring migration occurs in late April and early May; the fall migration occurs in September and October, when hunting is permitted. Camping for up to 14 days is allowed in this undeveloped refuge, although few dry sites are available. Campfires, firearms, horses, and snowmobiles are permitted. Landings of fixed-wing aircraft are prohibited from April 1 to November 9. Off-road vehicles with limited weights are allowed on trails after freeze-up. The Knik and Matanuska Rivers, and Knik Arm, are open year-round to motorized boats; restrictions exist for powerboats on Rabbit Slough.

Weather and conditions: Expect cool, overcast summers and cold, overcast winters in this subarctic maritime climate. (See the Anchorage weather table.) Winds are normally moderate to strong, frequently blowing dust.

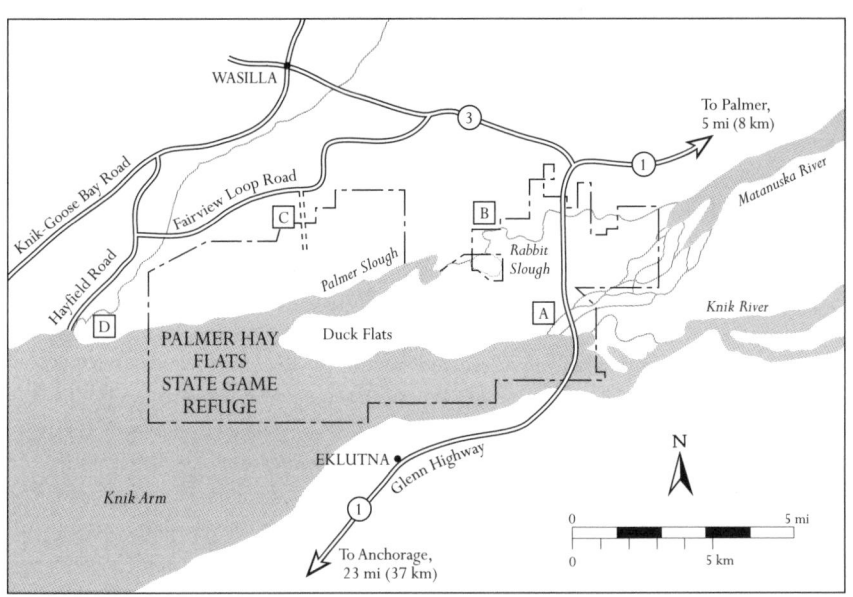

The Palmer Hay Flats off the Glenn Highway between Anchorage and Palmer   Tricia Brown photo

Caution: Swift incoming tides can strand unwary visitors. Sections of tide flats contain spots of quicksand-like mud. Be alert, and always travel with a companion.

Directions/access: The refuge is accessible (A) by boat from the Knik River Bridge, Mile 31 Glenn Highway; (B) by floating Rabbit Slough, Mile 33 Glenn Highway (part of the route crosses private property); (C) from Mile 6 Fairview Loop Road, where a side road leads south to the Hay Flats; or (D) from Hayfield Road, which leaves Fairview Loop Road at about Mile 9.4. Rental cars are available in Anchorage; scheduled buses between Anchorage and Palmer or Fairbanks travel the Glenn Highway. Meals and lodging are found at roadside businesses throughout the general area and in Anchorage, Eagle River, Palmer, and Wasilla.

54 Shuyak Island State Park

Location: North of Kodiak
Size: 49,740 acres (19,896 hectares)
High point: 472 feet (141.6 m)
Low point: Sea level
Best time of year: Foot, May–August; boat, May–August; ski (marginal), January–March
Daylight: June 21: 18 hours

December 22: 6½ hours
Activities: Kayaking, camping, fishing, hiking, wildlife-viewing, photography
USGS maps: Afognak C-1, 2, 3, B-2
Established: 1984; amended 1997
Managed by: Alaska Division of Parks and Outdoor Recreation

At 12 miles long and 11 miles wide, Shuyak Island, north of Kodiak Island, contains more sheltered interior waterways than anywhere else in the Kodiak Archipelago, making it an especially attractive destination for kayakers.

Flora and fauna: Only one species of tree—Sitka spruce—grows in this part of the coastal forest system. Resident game includes a limited number of Kodiak brown (grizzly) bears and Sitka blacktail deer. Watch the water for whales, sea lions, Dall porpoises, and harbor seals. Seabirds are everywhere on land and water. Among them are puffins, black oystercatchers, cormorants, common and red-throated loons, mergansers, harlequin ducks, and bald eagles. Anglers will find healthy runs of sockeye, pink, and coho salmon, as well as Dolly Varden, rainbow trout, and halibut.

Recreation: The maze of sheltered bays, channels, and other waterways creates a kayaking paradise. Park officials recommend using folding kayaks as transporting a rigid kayak can be expensive. Four public-use cabins are available for a fee, with reservations. Deer hunting and sport-fishing are other popular ways to enjoy Shuyak. Consult Alaska Department of Fish and Game guidelines before arranging your trip. There are a few trails; more are under development.

Weather and conditions: The weather is unpredictable and can deteriorate rapidly. Rough seas and high winds are frequent in open waters. Inner bays are more protected, but beware of the dangers of hypothermia. Rainfall during summer months averages 4 to 6 inches a month; ambient temperatures range from 40 degrees to 65 degrees F (5 degrees to 17 degrees C).

Portage to Western Inlet in Shuyak Island State Park   ASP photo by Claire Holland

Directions/access: Fifty-four air miles north of Kodiak city, Shuyak Island is accessible only by water or air. Commercial flights are available to Kodiak city; air charters offer floatplane service from Kodiak or Homer. Groceries and other necessities may be purchased in Anchorage, Kodiak, and Homer.

---

55 Susitna Flats State Game Refuge

Location: Northwest of Anchorage
Size: 301,400 acres (120,560 hectares)
High point: 600 feet (200 m)
Low point: Sea level
Best time of year: Foot, April–October; boat, April–October; ski, January– March

Daylight: June 21: 19½ hours
    December 22: 5½ hours
Activities: Birding, photography, hunting
USGS map: Tyonek
Established: 1976; amended 1984, 1986
Managed by: Alaska Department of Fish and Game

The extensive wetlands and rolling low hills of the Susitna River delta are prime resting grounds for migrating waterfowl and excellent nesting terrain. Of particular interest are the large populations of Thule white-fronted geese, Canada geese, arctic loons, widgeons, and green-winged teal. Trumpeter swans nest in the uplands.

Recreation: The best time for watching migrating birds is late April and early May. Numerous hunters use the area in September. Camping and campfires are permitted, but

Wildlife photographers appreciate the healthy numbers of Canada geese that migrate seasonally at Susitna Flats State Game Refuge. APLIC photo by Glenn Oliver

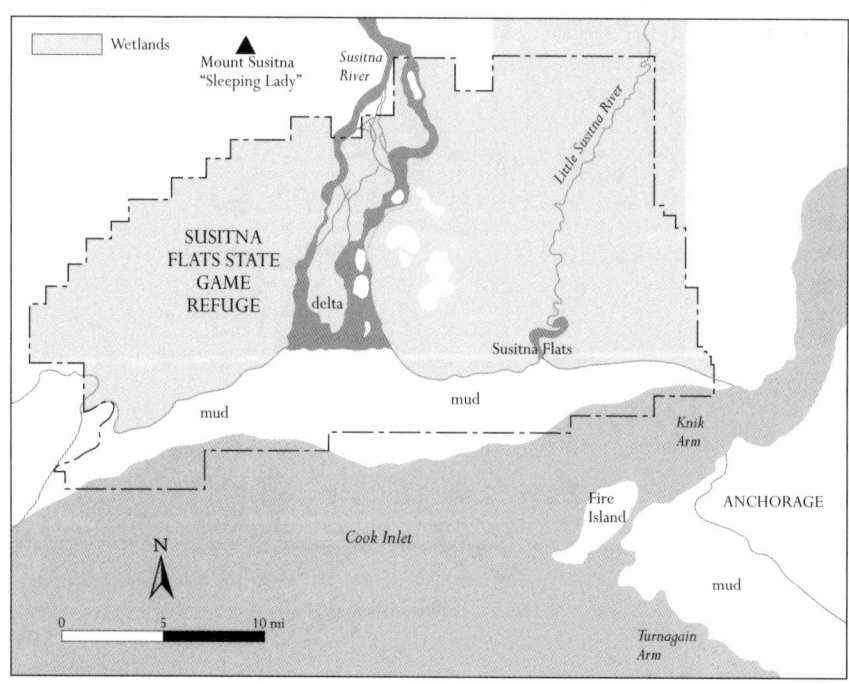

dry land and wood are scarce in the tidal grasslands. Boat launching and camping are available at the Little Susitna River Public Use Facility, Mile 18 Knik–Goose Bay Road. Hunting cabins, built before the establishment of the refuge, are private property and should not be disturbed. Firearms, fishing, horses, powerboats, snowmobiles, off-road vehicles, and fixed-wing aircraft are allowed by special area permit from Alaska Department of Fish and Game. To avoid disturbing nesting waterfowl, airplanes must maintain a minimum altitude of 500 feet (150 m) over the refuge except when landing or taking off between April 1 and October 31.

Weather and conditions: Expect cool, overcast summers and cold, overcast winters in this subarctic maritime climate. (See the Anchorage weather table.) Winds are moderate, often strong.

Caution: Tide flats contain treacherous areas of "bottomless" soft silt. Incoming tides can be swift and strand the unwary.

Directions/access: Although the refuge is only 4 miles (6 km) across Knik Arm from Anchorage International Airport, consider it remote and do not visit it without full survival equipment. Access is available by snowmobile, small plane, or boat. In winter, snowmobiles can follow the trail from Knik–Goose Bay Road out of Wasilla. Air taxis, stores, restaurants, and lodging are available in Anchorage, Chugiak, Eagle River, Palmer, and Wasilla.

56 Trading Bay State Game Refuge

Location: Southwest of Anchorage
Size: 162,700 acres (65,080 hectares)
High point: 650 feet (200 m)
Low point: Sea level
Best time of year: Foot, April–October; boat, April–October; ski, January–March

Daylight: June 21: 19½ hours
December 22: 5½ hours
Activities: Birding, photography, hunting
USGS maps: Kenai, Tyonek
Established: 1976; amended 1986
Managed by: Alaska Department of Fish and Game

Located at the mouth of the Chakachatna and McArthur Rivers, the refuge protects prime waterfowl habitat on the shores of Cook Inlet.

Flora and fauna: Of special interest are large numbers of migrating snow geese, Pacific white-fronted geese, and cackling Canada geese during late April and early May. Watch also for moose, black bears, brown (grizzly) bears, and wolves. The terrain consists of tidelands, salt-grass flats, river delta wetlands, and rolling lowlands.

Spring waterfowl migration begins in late April, fall migration in September, when numerous hunters use the area. Camping for up to 14 consecutive days is permitted, as are campfires, but dry land and wood are scarce in the tidal grasslands. There is no public recreational development. Private recreational cabins should be not disturbed. Firearms, horses, powerboats, snowmobiles, and fixed-wing aircraft are permitted. Special restrictions exist for use of motorized vehicles and off-road vehicles. To avoid disturbing nesting waterfowl, airplanes should maintain a minimum altitude of 500 feet (150 m)

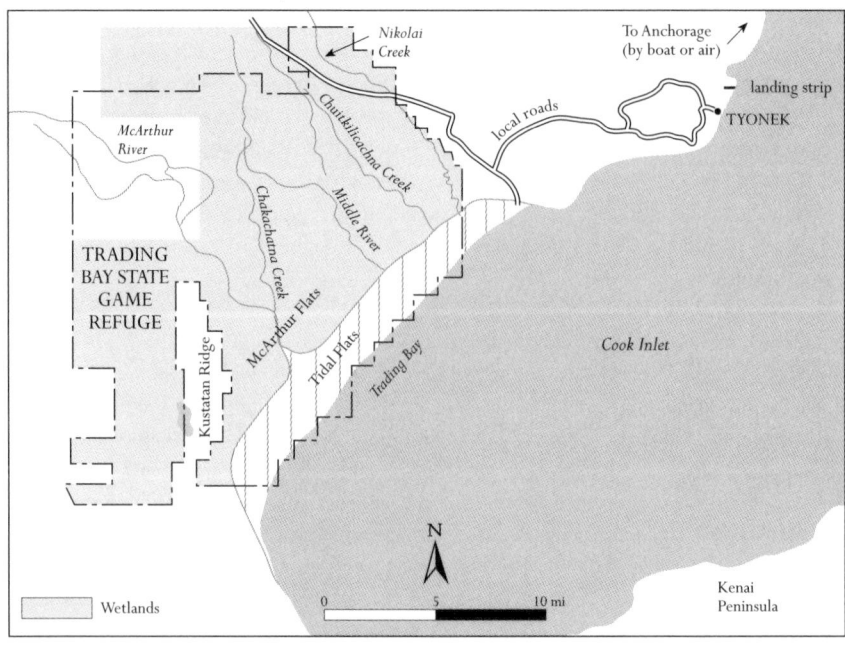

Trading Bay is a prime habitat for snow geese.   USFWS photo

over the refuge, except when landing or taking off. Tide flats contain treacherous areas of "bottomless" soft silt. Incoming tides can be swift, stranding the unwary.

Weather and conditions: Summers are cool and frequently overcast, and winters cold and overcast, typical of a subarctic maritime climate. (See the Anchorage weather table.) Winds are moderate, often strong.

Directions/access: A remote area at the foot of the scenic snow- and glacier-covered Chigmit Mountains, the refuge is rarely visited by anyone other than hunters. It is most easily accessible by air. Air taxis are available at Anchorage, Kenai, and Tyonek. Tyonek, Anchorage, and Kenai have food; the latter two have lodging as well.

57 Willow Creek State Recreation Area

Location: North of Wasilla

Size: 2,953 acres (1181 hectares)

High point: 200 feet (60 m)

Low point: 50 feet (15 m)

Best time of year: Foot, May–September; boat, June–September; ski, November–April

Daylight: June 21: 19 ½ hours

December 22: 5 ½ hours

Activities: Camping, fishing, boating, hiking, picnicking, ski touring, dog mushing

USGS map: Tyonek D-1

Established: 1987

Managed by: Alaska Divison of Parks and Outdoor Recreation

Willow Creek is a family-oriented campground, where children play noisily into the bright summer nights and anglers tromp back from the river with garbage bags of salmon slung over their shoulders. The fishing here is remarkable. Even before 1987, when the Matanuska–Susitna Borough completed the gravel road to the mouth of the creek, people slogged across a bog and hiked cross-country in their hip waders to reach the place. The state played catch-up in the early 1990s, building a campground, grooming trails, and making improvements all around.

Summer visitors will find day-use parking for 150 vehicles, a roomy campground, informational bulletin boards, and a campground host to help with questions or problems.

The borough road is not plowed in the winter, so access is limited to any number of dog-mushing trails and snowmobile trails that crisscross the region. Check at the Willow Community Center on the Parks Highway for maps and information on winter trails.

Flora and fauna: This gentle terrain is richly forested with birch, spruce, and willow. Watch for moose, black bears, brown (grizzly) bears, beavers, lynx, coyotes, wolves, hawks, and owls.

Recreation: Willow Creek is known throughout Southcentral Alaska for its king and silver salmon fishing, attracting so many anglers that some refer to this as one of the state's "combat" fishing zones. It's true that fishermen often stand elbow to elbow in their quest for the big fish, but it's also true that those who are willing to endure the crowds do catch fish. It's a good place to teach a youngster to fish, but only if you have patient fishing neighbors. Facilities include 139 campsites, toilets, drinking water, and 0.5 mile of wheelchair-accessible trails that lead to the fishery. The mouth of the Willow,

"Combat" fishing at Willow Creek State Recreation Area   ASP photo by Robert Angell

where it flows into the Susitna River, also is a take-out for rafters who put in at the bridge on the Parks Highway.

Powerboats are allowed on Willow Creek, but there is no boat launch within the recreation area.

Directions/access: Drive north from Anchorage on the Parks Highway to Mile 70.8 and take the gravel access road, Willow Creek Parkway, to its dead end at the park. Charter fishing packages out of Anchorage include air service to Willow. Supplies and groceries are available in Anchorage and Wasilla. Roadside restaurants and smaller stores may be found along the Parks Highway.

58 Wrangell-St. Elias National Park and Preserve

Location: East of Glennallen and Valdez
Size: 12,400,000 acres (5,020,000 hectares)
High point: 18,008 feet (5489 m)
Low point: Sea level
Best time of year: Foot, May–September; boat, June–September; ski, February–April (low elevations)
Daylight: June 21: 19½ hours

December 22: 5½ hours
Activities: Wilderness backpacking, mountaineering, river running, beach-combing, ski touring
USGS maps: Bering Glacier, Cordova, Gulkana, Icy Bay, McCarthy, Mt. St. Elias, Nabesna, Valdez, Yakutat
Established: 1980
Managed by: National Park Service

Alaska's most extensive and rugged glaciated wilderness, Wrangell–St. Elias is country you write home about. Some of North America's highest peaks are here, topped by regal Mount St. Elias. The massive Bagley Icefield, 90 miles (140 km) long, is reportedly 4000 feet (1200 m) thick. The spectacular Malaspina Glacier, a piedmont glacier, is almost 50 percent larger than the state of Delaware. Through every valley, turbulent braided rivers carry their loads of glacial silt to the lowlands. Of the total, 8,700,000 acres (3,520,000 hectares) is designated as Wilderness. The southeastern section of the park adjoins Canada's similarly rugged Kluane National Park, with its peaks, ice fields, and glaciers, which contains Mount Logan, second-highest peak in North America.

The sighting of Mount St. Elias by Vitus Bering on July 16, 1741, is the first record of northwestern America in Russian archives. Bering named Cape St. Elias on Kayak Island on the day of that saint, July 20, and the name was later applied to the mountain. The peak was first climbed in 1897.

To the south, the mountain slopes spill massive spreading piedmont glaciers nearly to tidewater in the Gulf of Alaska. The Chitina River bisects the range. Prominent peaks in the park are: Mount St. Elias, elevation 18,008 feet (5402 m); Mount Bona, elevation 16,421 feet (4926 m); Mount Blackburn, elevation 16,390 feet (4917 m); Mount Sanford, elevation 16,237 feet (4871 m); Mount Wrangell, elevation 14,163 feet (4249 m); Mount Drum, elevation 12,010 feet (3603 m).

The geology of the region is diverse and fascinating. Its mineral wealth attracted attention when the Kennecott Copper Company was formed in the early 1900s to mine the rich copper deposits high in the Chitina River drainage above the Kennicott Glacier. A railroad was built from Cordova to the mines—an exciting story immortalized in Rex Beach's novel *The Iron Trail*. After the mines closed in 1938, Kennecott and nearby

Historic Kennecott Mine is within Wrangell–St. Elias National Park.   APLIC photo

Most of the park is inaccessible due to its heavily mountainous terrain.   APLIC photo

McCarthy became ghost towns. Today the mine buildings are visitor attractions; in 1998, ownership was transferred from private parties to the federal government.

Flora and fauna: From a backbone of heavily glaciated volcanoes and peaks, the terrain drops to tundra and boreal-forested uplands in the north. The park and preserve contain a diversity of wildlife habitats. While Dall sheep stay mostly on mountainsides inland, mountain goats are attracted to the coastal mountains with their deeper winter snow cover. Caribou roam on the rolling uplands of the north to western plateaus. Bison, introduced in the Copper River drainage, frequently can be seen near Chitina. Moose, black bears, brown (grizzly) bears, wolves, wolverines, beavers, coyotes, red foxes, and marmots are common throughout the forests and tundra lands.

Recreation: Wrangell–St. Elias offers excellent wilderness backpacking, mountaineering, river running, beach-combing, and ski touring. Several historic horsepacking trails cross the park, but dangerous large braided rivers prevent following them all the way on foot. Air taxis can provide access to remote portions. Administrative offices and a visitors' center are at Mile 105.5 Old Richardson Highway, Copper Center, while ranger stations are located at Chitina (seasonally), Slana, and Yakutat. Camping and campfires are permitted on public lands. Please respect the numerous private lands within the boundaries and do not use old structures for firewood. Fishing generally is permitted, as are firearms, horses, fixed-wing aircraft, powerboats, and snowmobiles; off-road vehicles are not. Sport hunting is permitted in the preserve but not in the park. Expect large populations of mosquitoes and other biting insects in the lowlands in summer months. Do not venture onto glaciers without experience and proper equipment. In winter and after summer snows, avalanche hazard can be severe in the mountains.

Water travel: Chitina River, WW2–FWC, McCarthy to Chitina, 60 miles (100

km); Copper River, WW2–FWB, Slana to Copper River Highway near Cordova, 250 miles (400 km); Nabesna River, WW2–FWA, Nabesna to Northway, 66 miles (110 km).

Weather and conditions: Inland, the subarctic continental climate brings warm, dry summers and cold, dry, severe winters at low elevations; expect precipitation in the mountains any time of year. Lowland winds generally are light. (See the McCarthy weather table.) Along the coast, a mild maritime climate prevails, with cool, wet summers and mild, wet winters; winds are moderate. At high elevations, expect a cold, severe arctic climate with frequent storms and high winds.

When the weather is clear, the views of the volcanic peaks Sanford, Wrangell, and Drum are spectacular from the Richardson, Glenn, and Edgerton Highways.

Caution: In this undeveloped park with extremely remote areas, only those experienced and prepared should undertake backcountry travel.

Directions/access: Although no visitor facilities have as yet been developed, two primitive gravel roads penetrate the preserve. One, 52 miles (84 km) long, leads from the Glenn Highway (Tok Cutoff) at Slana to long-standing mining interests in the northern preserve. The other, 63 miles (101 km) long, begins at Chitina on the Edgerton Highway and follows the reworked bed of the historic Copper River and Northwestern Railroad leading to the Kennecott mines, but stops short at the Kennicott River. A footbridge replaced the small hand-operated tramway that once was the only transportation across the raging waters, still 5 miles (8 km) from Kennecott.

The remainder of the park and preserve primarily are accessible by air taxi, with operations based at Cordova, Gulkana, Glennallen, Northway, Valdez, and Yakutat. Scheduled air service is available to Cordova and Yakutat; McCarthy's mail plane, leaving from the Gulkana Airport, often can carry a passenger or two. Food and lodging are available at roadside restaurants and motels and at wilderness lodges (reservations required) within the parkland and at Chitina (sometimes), Copper Center, Gakona, Glennallen, McCarthy, and Yakutat.

---

59 Yakataga State Game Refuge

Location: Southeast of Cordova, along the Gulf Coast
Size: 82,300 acres (32,920 hectares)
High point: 110 feet (33 m)
Low point: Sea level
Best time of year: Foot, May–September; boat, May–August
Daylight: June 21: 18½ hours

December 22: 6 hours
Activities: Commercial, sport, and subsistence fishing; hunting, wildlife-viewing, photography
USGS maps: Bering Glacier, Icy Bay
Established: 1990
Managed by: Alaska Department of Fish and Game

An important region for hunters and fishermen from Yakutat and Cordova, this region is rich in coho, sockeye, and pink salmon, as well as wild game such as moose, mountain goats, brown (grizzly) bears, wolves, and other furbearers. Commercial set-net sites may be found at the mouths of every major river in the Tsiu/Tsivat river system

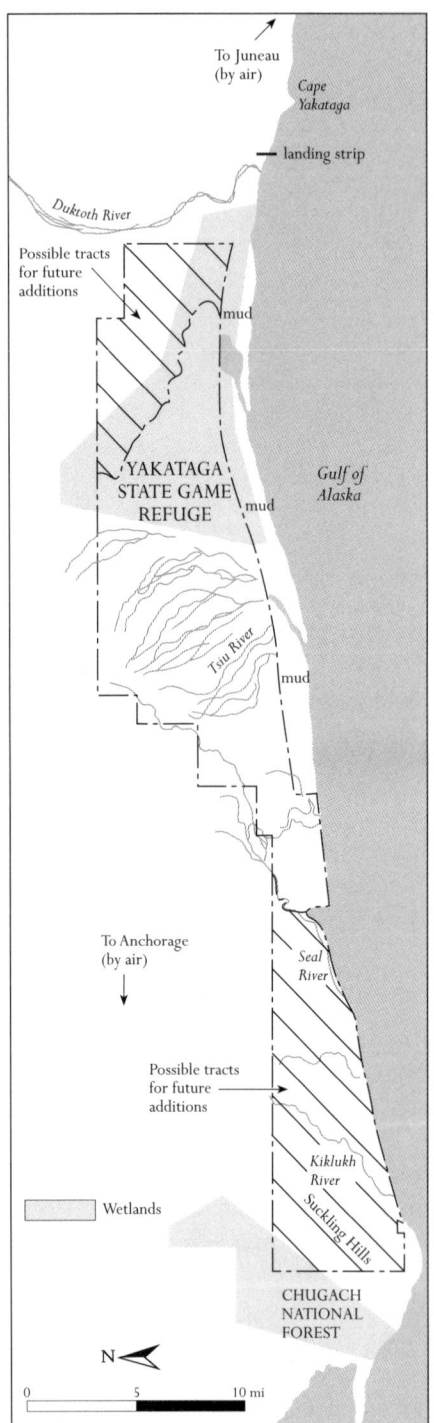

Bald eagles are frequently sighted at Yakataga. ASP photo by Robert Angell

as well as the Seal, Kaliakh, and Chiuki Rivers. The Tsiu River is especially popular for coho sport-fishing.

Flora and fauna: Located on a major flyway for migrating waterfowl, the refuge is used heavily each spring and fall as millions of birds stop to rest and feed. Look for high densities of trumpeter swans, some of which overwinter here. Hundreds of bald eagles spend their winters in this region, too.

Recreation: The refuge is undeveloped for public use, and certain restrictions apply to avoid disturbing the wildlife or damaging the habitat during sensitive periods.

Weather and conditions: As is typical of a maritime climate, the area experiences frequent overcast skies, with cool, wet summers and mild, wet winters. (See the Yakutat weather table.) Winds normally are moderate to strong. Dress in layers.

Directions/access: Located along the stormy north coast of the Gulf of Alaska, the lowlands of the refuge are accessible primarily by boat or plane. The southcentral Alaska state ferry docks at Cordova. Air taxis and guides may be arranged in Cordova or Yakutat.

ALEUTIAN ISLANDS AND ALASKA PENINSULA

The Alaska Peninsula, the Aleutian Islands, and the islands of the Bering Sea are under a strong maritime influence and rarely receive whole days of sunshine. Clouds, fog, heavy precipitation, high winds, an annual temperature range of 30 degrees to 55 degrees F (minus 1 degree to 13 degrees C) and high humidities make this one of the most uncomfortable regions in the world. In the Aleutians, for example, expect cloudiness 90 percent of the time in the summer, 50 percent of the time in the winter. During the summer months, cloud-ceiling heights are below 1000 feet (300 m) about 50 percent of the time. Seas are ice-free year-round.

Steep pressure gradients between the air masses of the Bering Sea and the North Pacific cause frequent gale-force winds and williwaws (sudden strong winds created by mountain topography) with gusts of over 70 knots (36 m per second).

This region is almost treeless. Vegetation primarily is cottongrass tussocks, with occasional low, dense heath shrubs and meadows of tall grasses.

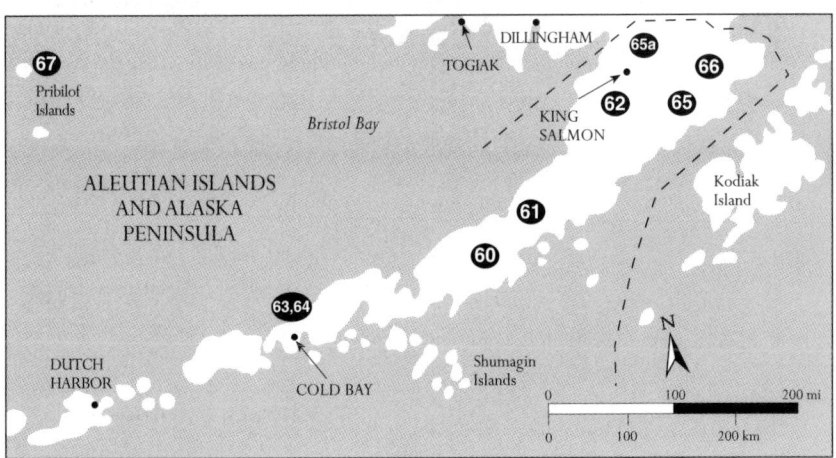

60 Alaska Peninsula National Wildlife Refuge

Location: On the Alaska Peninsula
Size: 3,500,085 acres (1,400,034 hectares)
High point: 8905 feet (2714 m)
Low point: Sea level
Best time of year: Foot, May–September; boat, May–August
Daylight: June 21: 18 hours December 22: 7 hours

Activities: Wildlife-watching, fishing, hunting, beach-combing, backpacking, mountaineering
USGS maps: Chignik, Cold Bay, False Pass, Port Moller, Stepovak Bay, Sutwik Islands, Ugashik
Established: 1980
Managed by: U.S. Fish and Wildlife Service

The Alaska Peninsula lies along a major flyway for migrating waterfowl. ASP photo

In this exceptionally scenic area a long chain of active volcanoes rises from sea level, connected by treeless lowlands, rolling tundra-covered hills, grasslands, lakes, rivers, and a long, varied Pacific Ocean coastline. Pavlof Volcano, one of the most active in the world, has erupted at least 30 times in the past 200 years.

Flora and fauna: Rich in animal life, the refuge contains major populations of brown (grizzly) bears, caribou, moose, bald eagles, migratory waterfowl, and salmon as well as wolves, wolverines, peregrine falcons, seabirds, sea otters, seals, and sea lions. Many of the bears den on volcano slopes.

Recreation: Wildlife observation, fishing, hunting, beach-combing, backpacking, and mountaineering attract most visitors to the refuge. No recreational facilities have been developed, although a few commercial fishing and hunting lodges (reservations required) are on private lands within the refuge boundaries. Camping is unrestricted on public lands. Respect private property and ask permission before camping or trespassing. Campfires are permitted in the refuge; the beaches have large quantities of driftwood, but plan to use a camping stove inland. Travel cautiously and avoid attracting the numerous bears when you camp. Mosquitoes and other biting insects may be a problem from June through mid-September; carry head nets and plenty of repellent. Horses, powerboats (except airboats), snowmobiles, and aircraft landings are all permitted; aircraft must operate at altitudes and in flight paths that will not disturb wildlife.

Weather and conditions: Expect cool, wet summers and mild, wet winters along the Pacific coast, colder winters and less rain all year inland and along Bristol Bay. (See the Cold Bay weather table.) The area experiences strong winds, long periods of

188

rain, and frequent storms. Hypothermia is a constant danger. Since weather often delays planned air or water travel, carry extra food. Prominent peaks in the refuge are Pavlof Volcano, elevation 8905 feet (2714 m), and Mount Veniaminof, elevation 8225 feet (2507 m).

Directions/access: Access to the refuge is by air or water. Cold Bay, King Cove, King Salmon, Port Heiden, and Sand Point have scheduled airline service; the first three towns also have air taxi services. The southwestern Alaska state ferry docks at Chignik, Cold Bay, King Cove, and Sand Point on a limited schedule. Boat charters are available in most communities, sometimes on an informal basis, but caution is advised; frequent strong winds, fog, and storms make boating hazardous. Cold Bay, King Salmon, and Sand Point provide limited stores, restaurants, and lodging.

61 Aniakchak National Monument and Preserve

Location: On the Alaska Peninsula
Size: 586,000 acres (237,000 hectares)
High point: 4400 feet (1300 m)
Low point: Sea level
Best time of year: Foot, June–September; boat, June–September
Activities: Rafting, hiking, photography

Daylight: June 21: 18 hours
    December 22: 6½ hours.
USGS maps: Bristol Bay, Chignik, Sutwik Island, Ugashik
Established: 1978
Managed by: National Park Service

A massive, rugged, active volcano that rises starkly from lush coastal beaches and grasslands, Aniakchak contains one of the largest calderas in the world, 6 miles (10 km) in diameter. It holds the turquoise waters of Surprise Lake as well as cinder cones, lava plugs, and hot springs. Aniakchak last erupted in 1931, in a large explosion that spewed ash over a large area of Alaska. If the weather is clear, both the Pacific Ocean and the Bering Sea can be seen from the rim of the caldera.

Flora and fauna: The area is treeless, with rolling grasslands on the Pacific coast, moist tundra on the Bristol Bay drainage, and brushy stream banks in the lowlands. Watch for brown (grizzly) bears, moose, caribou, bald eagles, red foxes, and, offshore, seals, sea lions, sea otters, and whales.

Weather and conditions: Only the strong, fit, and well-prepared should undertake a visit to this scenic and exciting volcano. The weather on Aniakchak is severe; life-threatening conditions can develop rapidly. Extremely violent winds in the caldera, particularly near "The Gates," can shred tents and prevent air rescue. To retreat to the Meshik River, 20 miles (32 km) to the west, requires a climb of 1000 vertical feet (300 m) to the caldera rim, then a 2400-vertical-foot (730-m) descent to sea level through wetlands and brush—a superhuman undertaking in stormy weather. In contrast to the southeast side of the mountain, where annual precipitation is 128 inches (325 cm) a year, the northwest side has only 15 inches (38 cm) a year. Temperatures on the southeast side range from 60 degrees to 20 degrees F (16 degrees to minus 7 degrees C), while temperatures on the northwest side can range from 80 degrees to minus 30 degrees F

The Aniakchak Caldera is evidence of historical volcanic activity in this region.   USFS photo

(27 degrees to minus 34 degrees C). Cloud cover at 1500 feet (500 m) on the mountain is normal. Winds average 15 to 20 mph (24 to 32 kph) with storm gusts over 100 mph (160 kph).

Recreation: In this undeveloped area, camping is unrestricted. Carry a camping stove; firewood is scarce away from the beaches. A public-use cabin is available at Aniakchak Bay accessible by boat or floatplane (high tide arrival is best). No user fee or reservation is required. Just call the King Salmon office at (907) 246-3305 for first-come, first-served availability. Rough seas, fog, or storms often delay pickup, so take extra food. Sport hunting is permitted in the preserve, but not in the monument. Fishing, firearms, powerboats, and fixed-wing aircraft are permitted throughout; snowmobiles are limited to months with adequate snow cover.

61a *Aniakchak National Wild River.* This river is rated WW1–4.

A popular trip length is 32 miles (52 km); best months to float it are June through September. The challenging Aniakchak River drains Surprise Lake, passing turbulently through "The Gates," a 2000-foot- (600-m-) deep canyon eroded through the caldera rim, to empty into the Pacific Ocean at Aniakchak Bay, a distance of 32 miles (52 km). Rafts are recommended for the turbulent river. To reach the headwaters at Surprise Lake, elevation 1055 feet (322 m), take an air taxi from King Salmon and arrange for a pickup from Aniakchak Bay at sea level.

Caution: Prepare for long periods of cold, rainy, windy weather—hypothermia is a constant danger in this maritime climate where summers are cold and wet, and winters mild and wet. (See the Cold Bay weather table.)

Directions/access: Both King Salmon and Port Heiden have scheduled airline service and food; modern lodging is available at King Salmon.

---

62 Becharof National Wildlife Refuge and Wilderness

Location: South of King Salmon
Size: 1,200,017 acres (486,007 hectares)
High point: 4835 feet (1474 m)
Low point: Sea level
Best time of year: Foot, June–September; boat, June–September; ski, February–April
Daylight: June 21: 18½ hours

December 22: 6½ hours
Activities: Photography, wildlife-viewing, hunting, fishing
USGS maps: Karluk, Mt. Katmai, Naknek, Ugashik
Established: 1978
Managed by: U.S. Fish and Wildlife Service

The refuge, of which 400,000 acres (160,000 hectares) were designated as Wilderness in 1980, encompasses virtually the entire watershed surrounding Becharof Lake. Becharof is the second-largest lake in Alaska; only Iliamna Lake is larger. A prominent peak is Mount Peulik, elevation 4835 feet (1474 m).

Flora and fauna: In one of Alaska's finest brown (grizzly) bear habitats, as many as

Becharof National Wildlife Refuge and Wilderness is located on the Alaska Peninsula.
USFWS photo by Joe Keller

300 bears congregate in the eastern portion of the refuge when the abundant red salmon spawn. A large bear may weigh 1400 pounds (640 kg) and stand 10 feet (3 m) tall. This area of the Alaska Peninsula is a major spawning ground for the important Bristol Bay salmon fishery.

The rolling tundra-covered hills and lake-dotted wetlands provide excellent habitat for caribou, moose, and waterfowl. Numerous bald eagles, nesting on sea cliffs, patrol for carrion and seabirds. Also found in the refuge are wolves, wolverines, beavers, red foxes, tundra hares, snowshoe hares, muskrats, and river otters. Along the seashore, watch for sea otters, seals, sea lions, and whales.

Recreation: Wildlife is the major attraction of the refuge, bringing photographers, wildlife observers, big-game hunters, and fishermen. Powerboats, snowmobiles, and fixed-wing aircraft landings are permitted. Boaters on Becharof Lake should stay near shore; without warning, violent winds can whip the lake surface to white water with large waves. The refuge visitors' center is adjacent to the airport in King Salmon. Backcountry campers are invited to stop by for directions and information; bear-proof storage cannisters are available there for a modest fee. Firewood is scarce in this treeless wilderness; plan to use a camping stove. Prepare for long periods of wind and rain.

Water travel: King Salmon River, WW1, from the largest lake at the headwaters of Gertrude Creek to Egegik, 70 miles (110 km). (Note that another King Salmon River is located southwest of Becharof Lake, draining into Ugashik Bay.)

Weather and conditions: The refuge has a maritime climate, with cool, wet summers, mild, wet winters, and frequent overcast skies. (See the King Salmon weather table.) Winds normally are strong. Heavy storms lasting several days, generally accompanied by violent winds, can restrict air travel. Carry extra food in case your air taxi pickup is delayed.

Directions/access: The refuge is most easily reached via air taxi from King Salmon, which has stores, restaurants, and lodging. Scheduled air service lands at King Salmon.

63 Izembek National Wildlife Refuge and Wilderness

Location: On the Alaska Peninsula
Size: 303,094 acres (121,238 hectares)
High point: 5784 feet (1763 m)
Low point: Sea level
Best time of year: Foot, May–September; boat, May–September; ski, January–March
Daylight: June 21: 17½ hours

December 22: 7 hours
Activities: Camping, fishing, hunting, wildlife-watching, photography
USGS map: Cold Bay
Established: 1960
Managed by: U.S. Fish and Wildlife Service

The lagoon was named for Karl Izembek, surgeon aboard the Russian sloop *Moller.* Russian ships wintered in nearby Bechevin Bay in the early 1800s, and their encampment site is still visible inside Hook Bay. Residents trapped furbearers extensively in the area until World War II, when the military moved into the area; quonset huts and scattered

Emperor geese are among the migratory birds that nest at Izembek National Wildlife Refuge and Wilderness. APLIC photo

fuel barrels now rust in the sea air. Prominent peaks include Frosty Peak, elevation 5784 feet (1763 m); Mount Dutton, elevation 4834 feet (1473 m); and Aghileen Pinnacles, elevation 4800 feet (1500 m).

Flora and fauna: Hugging the north shore of the tip of the Alaska Peninsula, the largest eelgrass beds in the world supply food for nearly the entire North American population of migrating black brant. From mid-April until about May 20 and again from August to early November, these geese, up to 200,000 strong, feed in the refuge on the way to and from their northern nesting grounds. Large concentrations of other water-fowl and shorebirds also use the large salt-water lagoons, notably emperor geese, Taverner's Canada geese, cackling Canada geese, bald eagles, pintails, mallards, oldsquaws, harlequin ducks, and rock sandpipers, as well as a nonmigratory population of about 600 whistling swans. Steller's eiders are the most abundant wintering duck.

Harbor seals search the lagoons, brown (grizzly) bears patrol the beaches and streams for spawning salmon, and caribou roam the treeless uplands. Watch also for wolves, wolverines, red foxes, land otters, porcupines, and arctic hares. Offshore, look for sea otters, porpoises, sea lions, and whales, especially gray whales.

Recreation: Camping and campfires are unrestricted. Driftwood is available on beaches, but use camping stoves inland. Camp and travel to avoid the many brown (grizzly) bears. Fishing, hunting, and horses are permitted. Snowmobiles and any other vehicles are restricted to designated roads. Aircraft may land only below mean high tide, which is outside the refuge boundary. Motorboats are allowed on the refuge, but jetboats are not.

Weather and conditions: In this area of rolling tundra-covered hills rising on the northeast to the spectacular volcanic Aghileen Pinnacles, a subarctic maritime climate prevails, with cool, overcast summers, and cold, dry, severe winters. (See the Cold Bay weather table.) Winds are constant and moderate to strong, with frequent storms or fog often delaying air travel. Violent wind squalls can make the lagoons treacherous for small boats.

Directions/access: Refuge headquarters are in the nearby town of Cold Bay. A 10-mile (16-km) road from town provides access to Izembek Lagoon; travel to other parts of the refuge is limited to foot and boat. Both Cold Bay and King Cove have scheduled air service and are visited on a limited schedule by the southwestern Alaska state ferry. A store, a restaurant, lodging, and one air taxi are available in Cold Bay.

64 Izembek State Game Refuge

Location: On the Alaska Peninsula
Size: 181,440 acres (72,576 hectares)
High point: Less than 50 feet (15 m)
Low point: Sea level
Best time of year: Foot, May–
   September; boat, May–September;
   ski, January–March
Daylight: June 21: 17½ hours

December 22: 7 hours
Activities: Wildlife-viewing, birding,
   hunting, fishing, photography
USGS map: Cold Bay
Established: 1960
Managed by: Alaska Department of Fish
   and Game

Adjacent to the Izembek National Wildlife Refuge, the state game refuge supports one of the largest eelgrass beds in the world and has gained worldwide recognition with the designation of "Wetland of International Importance." Each year millions of waterfowl and shorebirds stop to rest and feed here on their way to and from nesting grounds in the north.

Flora and fauna: The refuge is a major staging area for most of the world's population of black brant, emperor geese, and Steller's eiders. Other waterfowl number in the thousands, such as northern pintails, mallards, oldsquaws, scoters, and Taverner's and cackling Canada geese. Shorebirds are most dense in the fall as they feed during low tide periods. Bald eagles also are a common sight.

Brown (grizzly) bears feed along the shores of Izembek Lagoon or go streamside fishing for salmon. Other furbearers include wolverine, mink, river otters, wolves, red fox, and caribou. Watch for sea otters in the lagoon and harbor seals on the outer beaches of the barrier islands.

The lagoon is rich in Pacific herring, walleye pollack, greenling, sculpin, Pacific sand lance, cod, capelin, and smelt, as well as halibut and flounder. Five species of salmon pass through the lagoon on their way to spawning streams.

Recreation: Wheeled aircraft may land on unimproved beaches by permit. There are no public-use facilities. Violent wind squalls can make the lagoon treacherous for small boats. Check with the Alaska Department of Fish and Game in Anchorage or the Izembek National Wildlife Refuge office in Cold Bay for current restrictions on off-road vehicles.

A wintery day at Izembek State Game Refuge   USFWS photo

Weather and conditions: A subarctic maritime climate prevails, with cool, overcast summers and cold, dry, severe winters. (See the Cold Bay weather table.) Winds are constant and moderate to strong, with frequent storms or fog often delaying air travel.

Directions/access: Izembek Lagoon can be accessed by boat or by road from the community of Cold Bay. A 10-mile (16-km) road from town provides access to the lagoon; travel to other parts of the refuge is limited to foot and boat. Both Cold Bay and King Cove have scheduled air service and are visited on a limited schedule by the southwestern Alaska state ferry. A store, a restaurant, lodging, and one air taxi are available in Cold Bay.

65 Katmai National Park and Preserve

Location: Northwest of Kodiak Island

Size: 3,955,000 acres (1,601,000 hectares)

High point: 7606 feet (2318 m)

Low point: Sea level

Best time of year: Foot, June–September; boat, June–September; ski (marginal), February–April

Daylight: June 21: 18½ hours

December 22: 6 hours

Activities: Backcountry camping, hiking, photography, wildlife-viewing, hunting, fishing, kayaking, river running

USGS maps: Afognak, Iliamna, Karluk, Mt. Katmai, Naknek

Established: 1918

Managed by: National Park Service

Katmai is a land of contrasts: the "moonscape" barrens of the volcanically formed Valley of Ten Thousand Smokes, dense forests with lakes and streams where brown

While sport-fishing continues to be a major attraction at Katmai, more visitors arrive with hopes of viewing the brown (grizzly) bears feeding at Brooks Falls. APLIC photo

(grizzly) bears fish for salmon, Pacific Ocean shores where eagles soar, spacious rolling tundra lands, and snowcapped summits of steaming volcanoes. In recent years, this parkland has evolved into a world-class bear-viewing destination.

In June 1912, Mount Katmai volcano and nearby Novarupta erupted in an incandescent lava flow, burying an entire 20-mile- (32-km-) long valley under ash and pumice. After Mount Katmai collapsed, forming a caldera, a glacier formed within—the only glacier in the world whose date of origin is known.

Archaeological excavations indicate that the area has been occupied by Native cultures for at least 4500 years. Originally established as a national monument, Katmai has received additional lands four times. In 1980, some 3,473,000 acres (1,405,000 hectares) of its land were designated as Wilderness. Prominent peaks include Mount Denison, elevation 7606 feet (2318 m); Mount Griggs (Knife Peak), elevation 7600 feet (2300 m); Mount Mageik, elevation 7250 feet (2210 m); and Mount Katmai, elevation 6715 feet (2047 m).

Flora and fauna: The largest sanctuary for brown (grizzly) bears in the United States, Katmai owes its fame to the major red salmon runs in the Naknek River drainage that attract the bears. Most of the bears weigh from 400 to 800 pounds (180 to 360 kg). Excellent sport-fishing for salmon, rainbow trout, lake trout, northern pike, and grayling in the rivers and lakes attracts fishermen from all over the world. The rich forest and tundra lands abound in moose, caribou, red foxes, wolves, wolverines, lynx, river otters, mink, marten, beavers, migratory waterfowl, and shorebirds. Bald eagles nest throughout—near lakes and streams inland and on rock spires along the Pacific coast—while offshore swim seals, sea lions, sea otters, and whales.

Recreation: Facilities are concentrated on the lakes west of the Aleutian Range. Concessionaire-operated Brooks Camp includes a lodge, a dining room, and 16 cabins. The camp also offers a convenience store, guide-operated boats, and rentals of canoes and fishing gear. In addition, at Brooks Camp is a National Park Service visitors' center, a ranger station, interpretive programs, and a campground (60-person limit) with cooking shelters, fire pits, and caches for food storage.

Wherever salmon are found, bears create well-traveled trails parallel to rivers and lakeshores. An elevated platform at Brooks Falls allows for bear-viewing on the river's south shore. A second bear-viewing platform may be found along the lower river.

Van tours to the Valley of Ten Thousand Smokes visitors' center leave the Brooks Camp area daily (fee). Essentially a roadless wilderness, the park offers good hiking on volcanic tuff in the Valley of Ten Thousand Smokes; no trails are needed. A 6-mile (10-km) marked trail climbs Dumpling Mountain near Brooks Camp.

Backcountry camping and mountaineering in the park and preserve are unrestricted, although backcountry use permits are required (available from the Brooks Camp ranger station or the King Salmon headquarters). No wood is available in the Valley of Ten Thousand Smokes; since wood in forests may be wet, carry a camping stove. Hunting, firearms, and off-road vehicles are not permitted within the park; powerboats, fixed-wing aircraft, and snowmobiles are zoned. In the preserve, hunting is permitted.

Water travel: Kayaking and canoeing are popular sports on the inland lakes and rivers and on the scenic Pacific coast bays. Stay near shore on the large lakes; sudden winds can whip lake surfaces to white water. Bay of Islands lake trip: FWA, from Brooks Camp to the Bay of Islands in Naknek Lake and return, 40 miles (64 km). "Savonoski Loop": WW2–FWA, from Brooks Camp to Grosvenor Lake, down Savonoski River and return to Brooks Camp on Naknek Lake, 72 miles (116 km) with a 1-mile (1.6-km) portage.

65a *Alagnak National Wild River.* From Kukaklek Lake, the

Alagnak is rated WW3–FWC; from Nonvianuk Lake, WW1–FWC. A popular trip length is 60 to 70 miles (100 to 110 km). High-water months are June and August; the best time to visit is June through September. The Alagnak was designated a Wild River in 1980 and it is managed by the National Park Service. Contact the Park Service at King Salmon, Brooks Camp, or Nonvianuk for the required backcountry use permit.

From the northwestern corner of Katmai National Preserve, the Alagnak flows through gently rolling hills to the wetlands of Kvichak Bay. Scattered stands of spruce dot the open tundra.

The river heads in two separate lakes. From Kukaklek Lake, it flows in white water through a canyon within which dangerous WW3 rapids appear without warning around a blind corner. The rapids are particularly hazardous at high water, and the steep canyon walls do not permit portaging. From Nonvianuk (Nanwhyenak) Lake, the river takes a gentler gradient without serious obstacles. The current on the lower part of the river is affected by ocean tides. From Kukaklek Lake to Hailersville is about 70 miles (110 km); from Nonvianuk Lake to Hailersville, about 60 miles (100 km). (Hailersville, abandoned, exists in name only.)

To reach the river, take a floatplane to either Kukaklek Lake, elevation 800 feet (240 m), or Nonvianuk Lake, elevation 631 feet (192 km). Leave the river by air taxi from the lower Alagnak or the Hailersville area, elevation 50 feet (15 m).

Weather and conditions: The maritime climate brings cool, rainy summers with warmer, somewhat drier weather inland. Winters are mild and wet near the coast, cooler and drier inland. (See the King Salmon weather table.) Winds are frequently strong, with heavy storms lasting several days accompanied by violent winds; anticipate delays if you travel by air taxi.

Directions/access: Most common access to Katmai is by air from King Salmon, which has daily scheduled air service from Anchorage. Frequent amphibious flights connect to Brooks Camp. Air taxis based at Naknek, King Salmon, and Kodiak can give scenic tours or transport visitors to drop-off points throughout the park. Naknek and King Salmon are connected by road, and a gravel road connects King Salmon with Lake Camp, on Naknek Lake just inside the western boundary at the head of Naknek River. Neither road is connected with the contiguous state highway system. King Salmon and Naknek both provide food and lodging. Several small fishing lodges on private lands within the preserve also provide accommodations and transportation (reservations required).

66 McNeil River State Game Refuge and Sanctuary

Location: Southwest of Homer
Size: 254,200 acres (101,680 hectares)
High point: 4672 feet (1424 m)
Low point: Sea level
Best time of year: Foot, May–October; boat, April–October; ski, February–March
Daylight: June 21: 18½ hours
December 22: 6 hours

Activities: Wildlife-viewing, photography, fishing in the sanctuary and refuge; hunting and trapping within the refuge only
USGS maps: Iliamna, Afognak, Mount Katmai
Established: 1967; amended 1993
Managed by: Alaska Department of Fish and Game

A mecca for wildlife photographers, the sanctuary was established to protect the numbers of brown (grizzly) bears that congregate at McNeil River Falls in July and August to fish for migrating salmon. From 60 to 100 bears at a time may be at the falls or sleeping nearby. In June, another 25 or so can be seen on nearby Mikfik Creek. Before visitor restrictions were put into effect, the crush of competing photographers caused the bears to leave the falls temporarily. With fewer visitors, restricted to a permanent viewing "cave" (a shallow depression in a gravel bank about 150 feet [46 m] from the main fishing area), the bears tolerate the intrusion and continue their normal activities. The state game refuge, to the north, provides important habitat and a protective buffer for the bears.

Flora and fauna: The terrain of the sanctuary consists of tide flats, shrubby lowlands of the McNeil River valley, and nearby tundra-covered uplands. As well as a

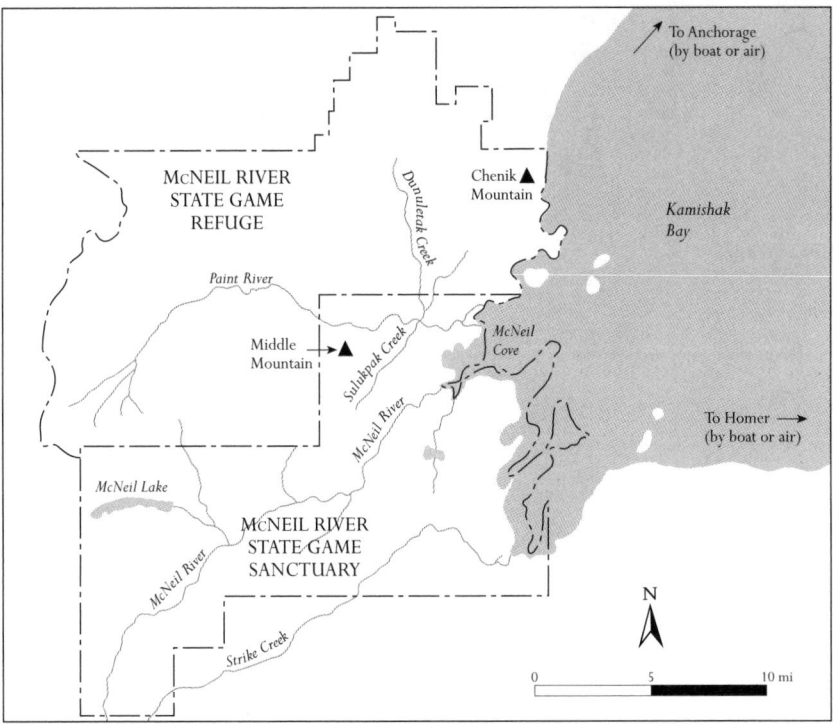

healthy population of brown (grizzly) bears, look for spawning salmon, small furbearers, and bald eagles.

Recreation: There are no developed public-use facilities in the refuge. Check current Alaska Department of Fish and Game regulations for rules on hunting, fishing, and trapping within the refuge.

At a rate of ten per day, permits to visit McNeil River Falls each summer are issued by a system administered by the Alaska Department of Fish and Game Wildlife Conservation Division office in Anchorage. The cost of a permit for Alaska residents is $150 for 4 days of viewing; nonresidents pay $350. It costs $25 per person to enter the lottery for a permit.

Visitors to the falls must remain within the designated area and behave quietly and unobtrusively. Additional restrictions may be put into effect at any time. Firearms are permitted for self-protection, but are not necessary; armed Alaska Department of Fish and Game personnel accompany visitors each day. Visitors are required to sign a liability waiver, but there have been no cases of human injury from bears at McNeil River and no bears have been destroyed since the permit system was initiated.

Weather and conditions: In this maritime climate, expect cool, overcast summers and mild, overcast winters. (See the Homer weather table.) Winds generally are moderate, often severe.

Directions/access: Access to the sanctuary and refuge is by floatplane, large-tired beach-landing aircraft, or boat. Most visitors arrive by air taxi, timing the arrival to

A brown (grizzly) bear waits in his favorite fishing hole on McNeil River as migrating salmon make their way upstream.   ASP photo by Dan Rosenberg

coincide with high tide. Since fog, storms, or high winds often delay scheduled pickup, pack extra food. The Alaska Department of Fish and Game distributes a list of licensed air carriers that fly to McNeil River; include a self-addressed stamped envelope. Air taxis, stores, restaurants, and lodging are available in Anchorage, Homer, Kenai, King Salmon, and Soldotna.

67 Pribilof Islands

Location: In the Bering Sea north of the Aleutian Islands

Size: St. Paul Island, 28,160 acres (11,400 hectares); St. George Island, 22,000 acres (8900 hectares)

High point: St. Paul Island, 590 feet (180 m); St. George Island, 946 feet (288 m)

Low point: Sea level

Best time of year: June–August

Daylight: June 21: 18 hours
December 22: 7 hours

Activities: Seal viewing, cultural tours, birding, photography

USGS map: Pribilof Islands

Managed by: Municipalities of St. George and St. Paul, Tanadgusix and Tanaq Corporations, and U.S. Fish and Wildlife Service, National Marine Fisheries Service

One million fur seals and thousands of colorful seabirds, including puffins, are commonly seen on these beautiful and remote islands. The hauling-out ground for great numbers of fur seals, sea otters, sea lions, and walrus, the Pribilof Islands were discovered in 1786 by Russian fur traders who exterminated the sea otter population and slaughtered large numbers of the fur seals for their valuable furs. The Pribilof Aleut people suffered under Russian rule and, later, under U.S. rule as well, not gaining full rights of citizenship until 1966.

Sitting isolated and treeless in the stormy Bering Sea, St. Paul and St. George Islands have villages of the same names, home to a thousand people. With a population of 800 people, St. Paul is the largest Aleut community in the world.

Flora and fauna: The northern fur seal herd, about a million animals, is managed by the National Marine Fisheries Service, U.S. Department of Commerce, and the local tribal leaders, with a subsistence harvest each July. Portions of St. Paul and St. George Islands and all of nearby tiny Walrus and Otter Islands are in the Alaska Maritime National Wildlife Refuge.

Seabirds nest on all four islands. While St. Paul has much greater numbers of seals, St. George contains by far the largest populations of seabirds, including thick-billed murres; least, crested, and parakeet auklets; and red-legged kittiwakes—a total of more than 2,500,000 birds. Large numbers of reindeer graze on the islands' grasses. Watch also for arctic foxes.

Recreation: Guided tours of the rookeries and island cultural tours are available. Viewing blinds are provided at the rookeries. Camping on St. Paul and St. George Islands is limited to designated backcountry areas.

Weather and conditions: The islands' weather normally is foggy and overcast; summers are cool, winters are cold in this subarctic maritime climate. (See the St. Paul weather table.) Winds generally are strong with frequent storms. Prepare for rain and strong winds.

Directions/access: Visitors to St. Paul most often arrive on a package tour out of Anchorage that includes air fare, a bus tour of the island, and lodging at the island's three-story hotel (see Pribilof Islands in Key to Addresses of Described Parklands, Appendix).

The beaches of the Pribilof Islands are important breeding grounds for northern fur seals.
ASP photo by Robert Angell

ꞮNTERIOR

The large area of plains, hills, and low mountains lying between the Brooks Range and the Alaska Range experiences sunny, sometimes hot summers from late May to late August. Winters are long and cold; occasional "chinooks" (warm southerly winds) can bring above-freezing temperatures, but at other times, temperatures can drop to minus 50 degrees F (minus 51 degrees C).

Precipitation is greater than on the North Slope, but is still considered light, 12 to 20 inches (30 to 50 cm) a year. In summer, rain may fall either as periods of drizzle or as heavy showers, often accompanied by thunder and lightning. The greatest number of clear days occurs in winter, although in populated areas ice fog—formed when moisture in the air crystallizes and remains suspended as fine ice particles—blocks the sun for weeks at a time. Winds generally are light.

The long summer days of May, June, and July end in a brief colorful twilight nominally designated as "night." Winter days are short, with an hour or two of twilight before darkness falls and before sunrise.

Boreal forest, or taiga, grows in this area of light precipitation and extreme climatic conditions. On north-facing slopes and moist lowlands, particularly in areas underlain by an impervious permafrost layer, a slow-growing scrawny black spruce forest with a thick moss ground cover usually forms. Trees 2 inches (5 cm) in diameter can be over 100 years old.

In swales and flat areas too wet for tree growth, there are bogs of sphagnum

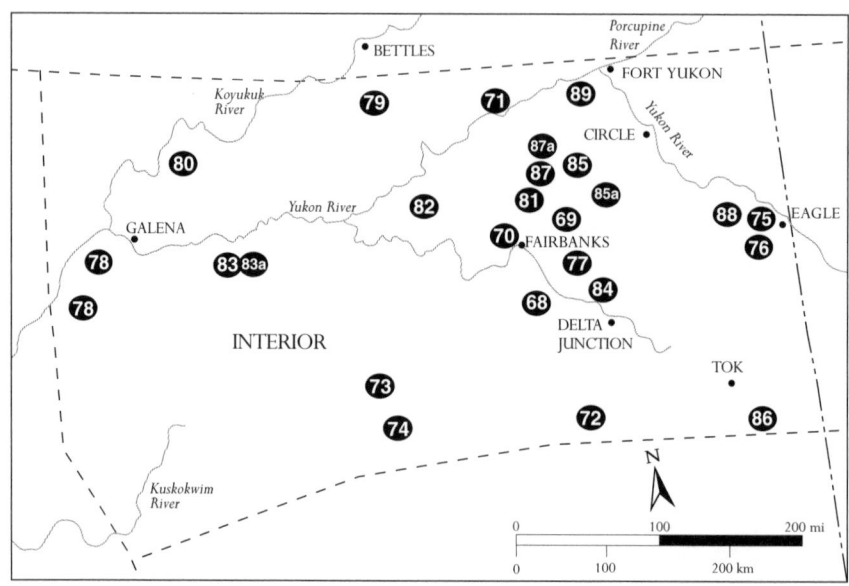

mosses, grasses, and sedges. Most bogs occur where old river terraces, flood and outwash plains, old river deltas, sloughs, and ponds have filled with vegetation.

Willow and alder thickets are found near tree line, often dense, sometimes growing open and well spaced on alpine tundra. Alders predominate in the wetter areas. On newly formed alluvial deposits on braided river floodplains, willow thickets dominate.

68 Big Delta State Historical Park

Location: Near Delta Junction
Size: 10 acres (4 hectares)
High point/Low point: 995 feet
(303 m)
Best time of year: Foot, May–October;
boat, June–September; ski, February
Daylight: June 21: 21½ hours

December 22: 4½ hours
Activities: Tour museum displays; walk
the grounds
USGS map: Big Delta A-4
Established: 1977
Managed by: Alaska Division of Parks
and Outdoor Recreation

After the Tanana Valley gold strike in 1902, a spur to Fairbanks was added to the Valdez-to-Eagle trail. The new route, now part of the Richardson Highway, was a primary access to interior Alaska. Roadhouses grew up along the trail, providing food and shelter for travelers and acting as freight destinations for nearby residents. One roadhouse—larger than most and the ultimate in functional design and construction—began operating in 1909 on the southern bank of the Tanana River; a government toll ferry worked nearby. About 1918, Swedish-born Erika "Rika" Wallen began working at the roadhouse until, in 1925, she reportedly was deeded the property by owner John Hajdukovich in lieu of back wages. That year Rika became the first postmistress of the new Big Delta post office, operated in the east wing of the roadhouse, a position she held for many years. At the time of her death in 1969, at the age of 93, she lived in a nearby cabin. The roadhouse closed in 1947.

Flora and fauna: Watch for animals typical of the river floodplain—moose, black bears, snowshoe hares, river otters, and beavers. Fishing is permitted in the river; the park is closed to hunting, use of firearms, horses, snowmobiles, and off-road vehicles.

Recreation: Rika's Roadhouse, now restored and the centerpiece of the 10-acre historical park, was placed on the National Register of Historic Places in 1976. Also at the park are the Delta Historical Society Museum and a station for the Washington–Alaska Military Cable and Telegraph System, also known as WAMCATS. Tour guides lead groups through the park and grounds; a concessionaire operates a gift shop and serves meals in the Packhouse Pavilion.

Overnight parking for two dozen recreational vehicles is available on site with sanitary dump station facilities. Just 7½ miles away, 22 more campsites are available at the Delta State Recreation Site, located at Mile 267 Richardson Highway.

Weather and conditions: The subarctic continental climate brings warm, dry summers and cold, dry, severe winters. (See the Fairbanks weather table.) Winds are light. Expect large populations of mosquitoes during June and July.

This archival photo depicts the roadhouse at Big Delta, which was built in 1928. Later it was called Rika's Roadhouse, named for the proprietress. A. Sundstedt photo courtesy ASP

Directions/access: The park is open May 16 to September 15, 7 days a week, from 8:00 A.M. to 7:00 P.M. It is accessible by automobile or scheduled bus (Fairbanks–Delta Junction route) from Mile 275 Richardson Highway, 9 miles (14 km) northwest of Delta Junction. A short side road (signed "Rekas Road") leads north to the roadhouse. More stores, restaurants, and lodging are available in Delta Junction and Fairbanks. Automobiles may be rented in Fairbanks.

69 Chena River State Recreation Area

Location: East of Fairbanks
Size: 252,800 acres (101,120 hectares)
High point: 4421 feet (1348 m)
Low point: 700 feet (210 m)
Best time of year: Foot, May–October; boat, May–September; ski, February–April
Daylight: June 21: 22 hours December 22: 3 ½ hours

Activities: Hiking, rock-climbing, horseback riding, fishing, hunting, river running, ski touring, dog mushing, snowmobiling
USGS maps: Big Delta D-5, D-6; Circle A-5, A-6
Established: 1967; amended 1975
Managed by: Alaska Division of Parks and Outdoor Recreation

A section of the Chena River floodplain, with its sloughs, marshes, and the surrounding rolling hills, forms the Chena River State Recreation Area. Float the river as it winds through the forests of spruce, aspen, and birch; or climb to the Granite Tors, large vertical outcroppings of quartz diorite and granite on the hills south of the Chena River, some standing 200 feet (60 m) high.

Flora and fauna: Wildlife is typical of interior Alaska—moose, black bears, brown (grizzly) bears, caribou, wolves, wolverines, coyotes, red foxes, beavers, river otters, porcupines, grouse, ptarmigan, hawks, and golden eagles. Stands of spruce and birch along with scrub willow and aspen may be found throughout the recreation area. Look for fat blueberries in August, especially in the marshy areas.

Recreation: The easily accessible recreation area is popular with Fairbanks residents and equipped with campgrounds, picnic areas, toilets, and 35 miles (56 km) of marked trails. Camping and campfires are permitted in the backcountry. Sections are closed to horses and snowmobiles.

Weather and conditions: Expect warm, dry summers with occasional thundershowers and some cool, rainy days in this subarctic continental climate; winters are cold, dry, and severe. (See the Fairbanks weather table.) Winds generally are light, but may be strong on hilltops. The terrain primarily is rolling boreal-forested uplands with alpine tundra above 2800 feet (850 m). Prominent peak: Chena Dome, elevation 4421 feet (1348 m).

Water travel: Chena River, WW1–FWB, from Mile 39.6 Chena Hot Springs Road to Fairbanks, 70 miles (113 km). This is one of the finest canoe rivers in the Fairbanks area, but watch for sweepers and logjams.

Directions/access: The recreation area is accessible by automobile from Mile 26 through Mile 53 Chena Hot Springs Road, which bisects the park. Restaurants and lodging are available within the park, at Chena Hot Springs (Mile 58), and in Fairbanks, 30 miles (50 km) away. Fairbanks also has auto rentals.

A fisherman tries his luck from a gravel bar in the Chena River.   ASP photo

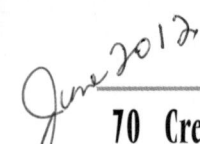

70 Creamer's Field Migratory Waterfowl Refuge

Location: In Fairbanks
Size: 1770 acres (708 hectares)
High point: 500 feet (150 m)
Low point: 450 feet (140 m)
Best time of year: Foot, April–October;
    ski, December–March
Daylight: June 21: 22 hours
    December 22: 3½ hours

Activities: Birding, hiking, touring
    Farmhouse Visitor Center, ski
    touring, dog mushing, skijoring
USGS map: Fairbanks D-2
Established: 1968
Managed by: Alaska Department of Fish
    and Game

Creamer's Dairy, once the nation's northernmost milk producer, is situated on a major waterfowl migration route. In 1903 C. T. Hinckley began a dairy farm in the Alaska wilderness; 25 years later he sold it to Charlie and Anna Creamer. With its grazing cows and rippling hayfields, Creamer's farm brought a touch of nostalgia to Alaskans transplanted from the Lower 48. The fallow hayfields emerging from winter snows attracted thousands of hungry traveling birds and numerous resident bird-watchers.

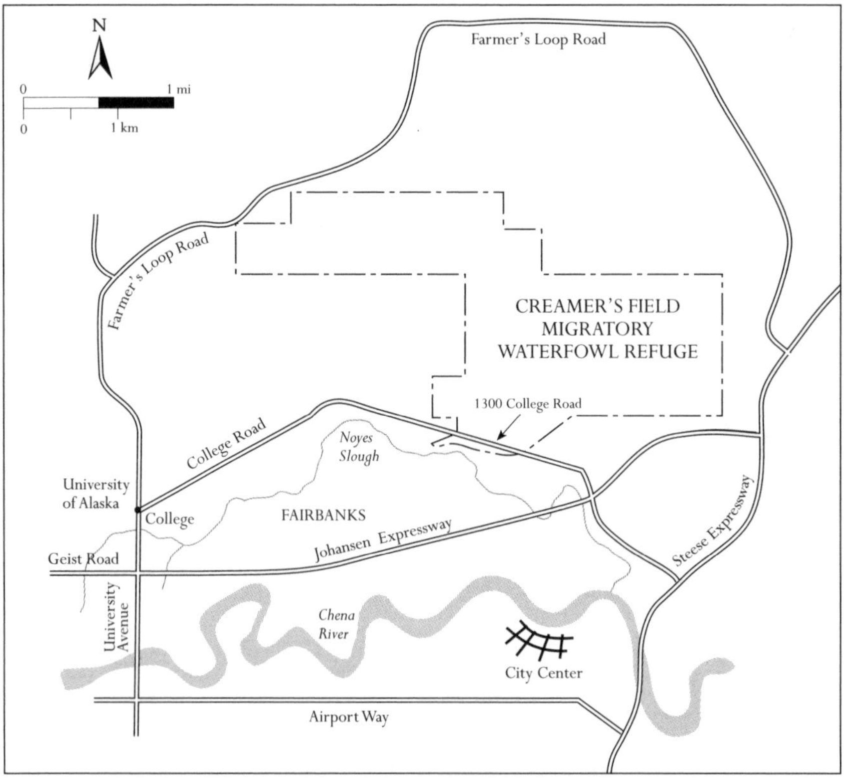

N

0   1 mi
0   1 km

Farmer's Loop Road

Farmer's Loop Road

CREAMER'S FIELD
MIGRATORY
WATERFOWL REFUGE

1300 College Road

College Road

Noyes
Slough

University
of Alaska

College

FAIRBANKS

Johansen Expressway

Steese Expressway

Geist Road

University
Avenue

Chena
River

City Center

Airport Way

Creamer's Field is the site of a historic dairy in Fairbanks.   ADF&G photo by Herb Melcior

When the Creamers retired from farming in 1967, Fairbanks area residents thwarted efforts to turn the fields into housing subdivisions, leading to the establishment of a wildlife observation and environmental education area. The original farmhouse and dairy buildings were admitted to the National Register of Historic Places in 1977.

Flora and fauna: Waterfowl populations—including sandhill cranes, Canada geese, and a variety of ducks—are greatest from late April through May and again in August. The east field is closed to entry during the spring migration period. Wild iris, wild calla lillies, dwarf dogwood, and wild roses are among the wildflowers than can be spotted along the nature trails that lead through birch and spruce stands to bogs and tussock meadows. Watch for voles, foxes, snowshoe hares, and moose. Other resident birds include alder flycatchers, Lincoln sparrows, and orange-crowned warblers.

Recreation: The farmhouse was restored in 1991 and now serves as a visitors' center and interpretive site. Staff members lead nature walks and the Alaska Bird Observatory conducts bird-banding demonstrations. Instructors teach hunter safety and bowhunter courses on the refuge.

With interpretive signs, observation platforms, and a variety of nature trails, the refuge is open to visitors year-round. Camping is not permitted. Frequent winter sights are dog mushers, cross-country skiers, and snowmobilers. Sections are open to hunting and trapping; moose may be taken with bows.

The buildings of Creamer's Dairy provide a historic and photogenic background to a long-standing Fairbanks wildlife attraction. Don't miss this charming refuge.

Weather and conditions: Fairbanks, with its subarctic continental climate, enjoys warm, dry summers and endures cold, dry, severe winters. (See the Fairbanks weather table.) Winds normally are light.

Directions/access: Creamer's Field is located at 1300 College Road, between the Fairbanks city center and the University of Alaska. Rental cars and taxicabs are available in Fairbanks; city buses travel College Road and stop at the refuge. Stores, restaurants, and lodging are available in Fairbanks.

71 Dalton Highway

Location: Central and Northcentral Alaska, between Livengood and Deadhorse/Prudhoe Bay
Length: 414 miles
High point: 7610 feet (2320 m)
Low point: 300 feet (90 km)
Best time of year: Automobile, May–September; foot, mid-May–September
Daylight: Depending upon latitude, June 21: 22 to 24 hours December 22: 3½ to 0 hours

Activities: Camping, hiking, wildlife-watching, river running
USGS maps: (South to north) Livengood, Tanana, Bettles (Evansville), Wiseman, Chandalar, Philip Smith Mountains, Sagavanirktok
Established: 1971 as Trans-Alaska Pipeline Utility Corridor
Managed by: Bureau of Land Management and Alaska Department of Natural Resources

The Dalton Highway, originally known as the "North Slope Haul Road," penetrates a scenic, hitherto-roadless wilderness as it parallels the trans-Alaska oil pipeline across the Yukon River and north to Prudhoe Bay on the Arctic Ocean. Traversing the broad, scenic valleys of the Yukon, Koyukuk, and Dietrich Rivers and crossing the crest of the Brooks Range to the North Slope, the corridor protects wildlife habitat and allows low-impact public recreation. BLM manages the road from Mile 0 (where the Elliott Highway turns westward) to Mile 301. From there north to Happy Valley, the road is under state jurisdiction. Portions of the largely unpaved road were covered with a new experimental surface in 1998.

The road passes the historic town of Wiseman, on the Middle Fork of the Koyukuk River south of the Brooks Range. Its heyday was about 1910 during the gold rush, but Wiseman today is a quiet village of 19 people who like their privacy. Numerous private landholdings and mining claims are in the vicinity of Wiseman. With the exception of the Wiseman Trading Post, all buildings are private property; do not trespass. Fuel is not available at Wiseman, but is at nearby Coldfoot.

Prominent peaks include Table Mountain, elevation 6425 feet (1958 m); Snowden Mountain, elevation 6400 feet (2000 m); Sukapak Mountain, elevation 4200 feet (1300 m); and Slope Mountain, elevation 4010 feet (1222 m).

Flora and fauna: Boreal forests line river valleys south of the Brooks Range, with trees giving way to tundra on many summits and ridges. From the crest of the Brooks Range north is arctic tundra. Wildlife is abundant by northern standards. Watch for moose, black bears, brown (grizzly) bears, caribou, Dall sheep, wolves, wolverines, lynx, coyotes, red foxes, snowshoe hares, marmots, porcupines, red squirrels, northern

The trans-Alaska pipeline parallels the Dalton Highway, which used to be called the North Slope Haul Road. USFWS photo

flying squirrels, arctic ground squirrels, raptors, migratory waterfowl, and other birds. Feeding wild animals is a state offense punishable by fine, imprisonment, or both. Guard against curious bears—they can be dangerous.

Recreation: The Dalton Highway is a remote gravel road, with gas, tire repair, wrecker service, emergency communications, food, and toilets at the Yukon River bridge and Coldfoot. A public boat launch is on the north bank of the river at the bridge. The road was only recently opened to the public and will undoubtedly have additional services in the future. Stop only at turnouts, drive with headlights on at all times, and carry adequate food, water, fuel, and extra spare tires.

The pipeline corridor provides excellent recreational opportunities for hiking, rock-climbing, wildlife observation, and river running. Camping is not generally restricted, but designated areas are suggested. Do not camp on the pipeline right of way. Campfires, fishing, hunting, firearms, horses, fixed-wing aircraft landings, powerboats, and snowmobiles are all permitted; unauthorized use of off-road vehicles is not permitted.

Water travel (listed south to north): Hess Creek, WW1–FWB, from Mile 24 Dalton Highway to Rampart, 70 miles (110 km); Yukon River, FWC, from Mile 56 Dalton Highway; Kanuti River, WW1–FWB, from Mile 107 Dalton Highway to Hughes, 240 miles (390 km); Fish Creek, WW2, from Mile 115 Dalton Highway to Allakaket, 120 miles (190 km); Jim River, WW2, from Mile 141 Dalton Highway to Allakaket, 140 miles (230 km); Koyukuk River, South Fork, WW1–2, from Mile 156 Dalton Highway to Allakaket, 140 miles (230 km); Koyukuk River, Middle Fork, WW1, from Mile 207 Dalton Highway to Bettles (Evansville), 120 miles (190 km); Ivishak National Wild

River, WW1–FWC, see description No. 97a, Arctic National Wildlife Refuge and Wilderness.

Weather and conditions: South of the Brooks Range, the subarctic continental climate brings warm, dry summers, with cooler temperatures and more rain in the mountains. Winters are cold, dry, and severe. (See the Wiseman weather table.) Winds generally are light. North of the Brooks Range, the summers are cool and drier. (See the Galbraith weather table.) Winds on the open tundra are moderate to light.

Caution: Clouds of dust and flying rocks from large tractor-trailers traveling at high speeds make this a hazardous road for the family car. For your safety and comfort, contact the Alaska State Troopers or the Alaska Department of Transportation in Fairbanks for current conditions before driving the road.

Directions/access: Scheduled air service lands at Allakaket, Bettles (Evansville), Deadhorse, and Wiseman; air taxis operate from Bettles (Evansville). Food is available at Bettles (Evansville), Coldfoot, Deadhorse, Livengood, and the Yukon River crossing. Lodging can be obtained at Bettles (Evansville), Coldfoot, Deadhorse, and the Yukon River crossing.

---

72 Delta National Wild, Scenic, and Recreational River

Location: Eastern Alaska, south of Delta Junction
River rating: WW1–3 with WW5 rapids (portage possible)
Popular trip length: 35 miles (56 km)
Best time of year: June–September
Annual high water: June
Daylight: June 21: 21½ hours

December 22: 4½ hours
USGS maps: Mt. Hayes A-4, B-4 (WW5 and beyond), C-4, D-4; Big Delta A-4
Designated as Wild and Scenic River: 1980
Managed by: Bureau of Land Management

Flowing north literally through the snowcapped Alaska Range, the Delta is an anomaly in the world of mountain rivers. Rising in the tranquil alpine Tangle Lakes in the southern foothills, it meanders cold and clear. Entering the range, it picks up icy, gray, silty water from four major glaciers and myriad smaller ones. Becoming braided and violent in the heart of the mountains, it is suitable only for expert boaters below Mile 212.5 Richardson Highway.

Soon the river flows past the chaotic moraine of Black Rapids Glacier (more easily viewed from the highway). In 1937, the 20-mile- (30-km-) long glacier surged more than 4 miles (6 km), advancing up to 200 feet (60 m) a day, stopping just short of the highway and historic Black Rapids Roadhouse. Beyond the glacier, the river becomes more gentle again.

A popular recreational river, the Delta is accessible from the highway system. From Tangle Lakes to the first take-out is 35 miles (56 km) and to Delta Junction another 55 miles (89 km).

Two miles (3 km) below Tangle Lakes, waterfalls mark the river's crossing of the

Denali Fault, one of the longest fault zones in Alaska, which extends westward through the summit of Mount McKinley. A 0.25-mile (0.4-km) two-section portage follows a well-defined trail. Below the falls, 2 miles (3 km) of WW3 can be run along the left side or lined from the right bank. Requiring skillful handling around rocks, this section takes its toll of canoes each year. WW2 continues to the first highway contact. Beyond the take-out, the next 30 miles (50 km) should be run only by experienced boaters in rafts or kayaks.

Flora and fauna: Wildlife includes moose, caribou, brown (grizzly) bears, black bears, coyotes, red foxes, wolves, wolverines, lynx, and beavers. Watch for bison (introduced in the 1950s) along the lower river. Approach no closer than 300 feet (90 m) to eagles' nests.

Recreation: Camping is unrestricted and campfires are allowed. Since wood may be scarce on the upper river, use a camping stove. The lower riverbanks are forested. Fishing, hunting, firearms, fixed-wing aircraft, and powerboats are all permitted. Expect mosquitoes and other biting insects in summer.

Weather and conditions: In this subarctic continental mountain climate, summers are cool, moist, and often overcast. (See Denali National Park weather table.) Winds are moderate to strong.

Directions/access: The headwaters of the river are at Round Tangle Lake, elevation 2791 feet (851 m), accessible from the Tangle Lakes Campground, Mile 22 Denali Highway. The first take-out, elevation 2600 feet (800 m), is at Mile 212.5 Richardson Highway, where the river parallels the road. Below Black Rapids Glacier, an

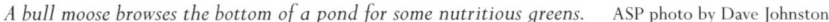

A bull moose browses the bottom of a pond for some nutritious greens.   ASP photo by Dave Johnston

access, elevation 2200 feet (670 m), is at Mile 229 Richardson Highway, near Onemile Creek. You can also leave the river at Delta Junction, elevation 1100 feet (340 m).

Scheduled buses travel the Richardson Highway. Food and lodging are available at roadside businesses, Delta Junction, and Paxson.

73 Denali National Park and Preserve

Location: North of Anchorage
Size: 6,000,000 acres (2,430,000 hectares)
High point: 20,320 feet (6194 m)
Low point: 525 feet (160 m)
Best time of year: Foot, June–September; boat, June–September; ski, February–April
Daylight: June 21: 21½ hours December 22: 4½ hours
Activities: Mountaineering, camping, hiking, wildlife-viewing, photography, bus touring, dog mushing, ski touring,

flightseeing, canoeing, river running
Maps: USGS, Healy, Kantishna River, Mt. McKinley, Talkeetna
Special maps: USGS, Mount McKinley National Park (the original park on one map for convenience); Bradford Washburn, "A Map of Mount McKinley, Alaska" (the mountain and its immediate vicinity in excellent detail)
Established: 1917
Managed by: National Park Service

With towering granite spires and snowy summits lost in the clouds, Denali National Park and Preserve straddles a 160-mile-long (260-km) section of the Alaska Range. Dominating the skyline, Mount McKinley is North America's highest mountain.

The long-standing name "Mount McKinley National Park" was changed in 1980. Most Alaskans prefer "Denali"—the Athabascan Indian name for the mountain, meaning "the high one." At the same time the name was changed, an additional 3,756,000 acres (1,520,000 hectares) were added to include, finally, the southern flanks of the Alaska Range, with its immense glaciers draining from the McKinley–Foraker massif, and the spectacular Cathedral Spires to the southwest. Except for a strip of land containing the Park Road, the original park was designated as Wilderness and retains the original management restrictions.

Mount McKinley towers at 20,320 feet (6194 m); Mount Foraker, known by local Indians as *Menlale* ("Denali's Wife"), is 17,395 feet (5302 m). Other prominent peaks include Mount Hunter, elevation 14,580 feet (4444 m); Mount Silverthrone, elevation 13,220 feet (4029 m); Mount Crosson, elevation 12,775 feet (3894 m); Mount Carpe, elevation 12,550 feet (3825 m); and Mount Huntington, elevation 12,240 feet (3731 m).

Flora and fauna: Boreal-forested flatlands and the rolling Kantishna Hills to the north complete the habitat protection for caribou, moose, bears, and wolves of the park.

Long famous for its abundant and visible large mammals, Denali National Park is on the "must-see" list of visitors to Alaska. Paralleling the Alaska Range and traversing rolling open tundra, the Park Road provides ideal viewing for wide-eyed wildlife

Mount McKinley, or Denali as it it's known locally, is North America's tallest peak.   NPS photo

enthusiasts. Watch wolves stalk caribou and see brown (grizzly) bears feed from a moose carcass or scratch their backs on road signs.

Recreation: The open tundra of the park seems to have been created for the foot traveler—no trails are needed along the mountain streams and over the rolling hills. Marked trails are found primarily in the forest areas at park headquarters, the visitors' center, and near Wonder Lake. Backpacking, hiking, and camping are so popular that the National Park Service has had to develop a quota system for backcountry use to protect the fragile tundra and provide an uncrowded wilderness experience for each user. Permits for backcountry travel are available 1 day in advance at the visitors' center in the summer months and at park headquarters during the winter months. Between May and September, you may reserve a seat on a camper bus (fee) that takes campers and their gear to remote tenting campgrounds. No permits are required for day hikers. Park Service personnel encourage backcountry users to consider trips in the north and south additions and in nearby Denali State Park.

With the increase in off-road foot travelers comes a serious problem: Grizzlies can become "park bears," animals that search out visitors and their campsites, hoping for tasty handouts. Bear-resistant storage cannisters are loaned to backcountry permit-holders and are available for purchase. Camp and travel carefully, and check with the Park Service before traveling anywhere on foot, to avoid the territories of "problem bears." In the wilderness, campfires are permitted in campground fire pits only; use camping stoves in the backcountry. In the remainder of the park and in the preserve, campfires are permitted.

Read about crossing rivers before trying your first one; park rivers are swift, braided glacial streams. Prepare for mosquitoes in June and July. Fishing is permitted throughout; hunting is allowed only in the preserve. Park regulations prohibit pets, firearms, horses, fixed-wing aircraft, powerboats, and snowmobiles in the wilderness, but all except snowmobiles are permitted in the remainder of the park and in the preserve. Check with the National Park Service for snowmobile regulations, which were under discussion at press time. Nonmotorized uses of the wilderness in winter are encouraged, particularly ski touring and dog mushing. Registration with the National Park Service is required for climbing on Mount McKinley or Mount Foraker.

Visitors' facilities include 8 campgrounds (250 units, some reserved; some first-come basis; check at the visitors' center). Campgrounds are open from May to September, except the Riley Creek Campground, just inside the park entrance, which is open year-round with limited facilities in winter. Park Headquarters is open year-round at Mile 3.4 of the Park Road. Facilities include a visitors' center and gift shop, hotel, dining room, bar, telephone, post office, service station, grocery store, railroad depot, and an airstrip. Interpretive programs are given daily in the summer.

For a fee, shuttle buses travel the Park Road regularly during daylight hours, connecting the visitors' center with stops at Polychrome Pass, Eielson Visitor Center, Wonder Lake, and Kantishna. The bus ride can be up to 12 hours round-trip. Popular with hikers, photographers, and animal watchers, the buses can be left or boarded at any point along the Park Road. In spring, as snow clearing permits, private vehicles are permitted as far as Mile 30, the Teklanika Campground, until the Thursday before Memorial Day weekend. Each fall, an annual lottery determines who will be allowed to drive the length of the park during a 4-day period in September. Contact the park for details on applying. See Land Managers, Appendix.

Discovery hikes are conducted out of the Denali National Park visitors' center.   ASP photo

River travel: Kantishna River, FWA, from Lake Minchumina to Manley Hot Springs on the Tanana River, 250 miles (400 km); Nenana River, WW1–5, from the Denali Highway to Healy, 40 miles (60 km); Wonder Lake, FWA, hand-powered or sailboats only.

Weather and conditions: Summer weather can be cool, often with long periods of overcast or drizzle, despite the park's Interior location. Temperatures in winter are cold with little precipitation, but warmer with more snow south of the Alaska Range. (See the Denali National Park weather table.) Winds generally are light in the lowlands, often severe on mountain peaks.

Directions/access: For automobile travelers, the park entrance is at Mile 237 Parks Highway, 237 miles (381 km) north of Anchorage. The area is also served by scheduled buses between Anchorage and Fairbanks, the Alaska Railroad, and scheduled air service. Air taxis operate from Denali National Park, Cantwell, and Talkeetna. The Park Road winds 87 miles (140 km) through the park and continues a short distance to a dead-end in the Kantishna area of the north addition. The area south of the Alaska Range is most accessible by air taxi from Talkeetna or by foot from the end of the Petersville Road, an unimproved 33-mile (53-km) homestead and mining access road leaving Mile 115 Parks Highway at Trapper Creek. Inquire locally about the condition of the road. Food and lodging are available at numerous roadside businesses and at Denali National Park, Healy, Cantwell, and Talkeetna.

---

74 Denali State Park

Location: North of Anchorage
Size: 325,460 acres (130,184 hectares)
High point: 4558 feet (1389 m)
Low point: 500 feet (150 m)
Best time of year: Foot, June–September; boat, June–September; ski, February–April
Daylight: June 21: 19½ hours
December 22: 5½ hours

Activities: Hiking, camping, boating, swimming, picnicking, photography, wildlife-watching, flightseeing, mountain biking, river running
USGS maps: Talkeetna, Talkeetna Mountains
Established: 1970; amended 1976
Managed by: Alaska Division of Parks and Outdoor Recreation

Straddling the Parks Highway, the southern foothills of the Alaska Range provide panoramic views of Mount McKinley, 35 miles (56 km) away, Mount Hunter, Mount Silverthrone, the Moose's Tooth, Tokosha Spires, and Ruth, Buckskin, and Eldridge Glaciers. Ruth Glacier Overlook, Mile 135 Parks Highway, is just 5 miles (8 km) from the glacier's terminus. The view of Mount McKinley and the Alaska Range from Curry Ridge was a popular goal for passengers on the early Alaska Railroad, when Curry was a regular overnight stop on the 2-day trip between Anchorage and Fairbanks. Sydney Laurence, renowned pioneer Alaskan artist, frequently painted Mount McKinley from a vantagepoint in the Peters Hills, at the western end of the park.

Flora and fauna: Watch for moose, black bears, brown (grizzly) bears, Dall sheep,

The view from Spink Lake Ridge in Denali State Park   ASP photo

caribou, red foxes, coyotes, wolves, wolverines, lynx, golden eagles, bald eagles, and peregrine falcons. Boreal forest covers rolling hills and lowlands. Fireweed and other wildflowers add spectacular color at roadside as well as in the backcountry.

Recreation: In this relatively undeveloped park, popular activities are photography, picnicking, swimming, hiking, camping, boating on Byers Lake, fishing, river running, ski touring, and wilderness travel. Hunting is permitted, but discharge of a weapon may not occur within 0.5 mile of a developed facility, 0.25 mile of the Parks Highway, or 0.5 mile of the trail around Byers Lake. Fixed-wing aircraft and powerboats are restricted to specific areas. Registered snowmobiles are permitted after snow cover is adequate to protect vegetation. Horses are permitted in the park except on developed trails and on South Curry Ridge. Off-road vehicles are not permitted.

In summer months, a small visitors' information center is open 7 days a week at the Alaska Veterans Memorial, Mile 147.1 Parks Highway. Camping facilities include campgrounds at Byers Lake (66 units), Lower Troublesome Creek (20 units), and Denali View North (23 units). Other park facilities include informational exhibits, highway rest areas, picnic sites, drinking water, and wheelchair-accessible toilets. Campfires are permitted in campground fire pits only; use a camping stove elsewhere. Backcountry camping is unrestricted. A total of 37 miles (59 km) of marked trails includes the route from the Byers Lake Campground to Curry Ridge and on to Troublesome Creek. It connects to another trail that climbs from the highway along Little Coal Creek to timberline on Kesugi Ridge at the northern end of the park. Trailhead access for the 3.1-mile (5-km) Ermine Hill Trail, which leads to the Kesugi Ridge Trail, may be found at Mile 156.3 Parks Highway. Once above timberline, about 2000 feet (600 m) elevation, hiking is easy on the alpine tundra. Numerous small lakes dot the landscape.

Water travel: Chulitna River, WW3–FWC, from Mile 194.5 Parks Highway to Talkeetna, 98 miles (158 km).

Weather and conditions: Although the park's weather is moderated by its proximity to the ocean, many features of a subarctic continental climate prevail. Summer weather is typical of mountainous areas—often cool, with frequent overcast; winters are cold and brisk. (See the Talkeetna weather table.)

Directions/access: Paralleling the Chulitna River, the paved George Parks Highway, from Mile 132 to Mile 170, runs north–south through the park, making it one of the most accessible parks in Alaska. Scheduled bus service and sightseeing tours travel the highway daily in summer; rental cars are available in Anchorage and Fairbanks. Several private tour operators also offer pickup and drop-off services to the park.

East of the highway, on the other side of Curry and Kesugi Ridges, the Alaska Railroad, from Mile 243.5 to Mile 279, winds along the edge of the park boundary. Whistle stops, in which passengers can hail the train to embark or disembark anywhere along the route, occasionally are permitted north of Talkeetna. Disembark on the western side of the Susitna River, just past Gold Creek. The western extent of the park, in the Peters Hills, is reached from the Petersville Road, which leaves Mile 115 Parks Highway at Trapper Creek. Inquire locally about the current condition of the gravel road. Air taxi service is available in Talkeetna. Restaurants and lodging can be found at numerous roadside businesses near the park and at Talkeetna and Cantwell.

---

75 Fort Egbert National Historic Site

Location: Eagle, east of Fairbanks
Size: 40 acres (16 hectares)
High point: 900 feet (270 m)
Low point: 862 feet (259 m)
Best time of year: Foot, June–
    September; boat (Yukon River,
    June–August; Charley River,
    June–September); ski,
    February–April

Daylight: June 21: 22 hours
    December 22: 3 ½ hours
Activities: Guided and self-guided
    historical tours, camping, picnicking,
    photography
USGS map: Eagle
Established: 1975
Managed by: Bureau of Land
    Management

The charming, historic town of Eagle lies along the Yukon River in Alaska's Interior, established in the late 1800s next to one of the first trading posts in the area. In the fall of 1898, the gold mining community numbered 1700 in more than 500 cabins and tents. The Secretary of War established a military reservation that year, which included the town, until a civil government was established. Later the camp was named for the late Brigadier Gen. Harry C. Egbert. Here was the seat of a federal court district over which Judge James Wickersham presided. Later, when mining activity dwindled, the seat was moved to Fairbanks. By 1911, Fort Egbert was abandoned. The Army Signal Corps remained and operated a telegraph and wireless station until around 1925.

The town was nominated for the National Register of Historic Places in 1970.

Eagle is a historic gold-mining town along the Yukon River.   BLM photo

Today the historic district includes the town and the fort, which is managed by BLM. The agency began restoring the fort in 1975 with help from state, federal, and local groups. Most of the original 46 buildings at Fort Egbert are gone today. Those that remain have been carefully stabilized and restored. Among the surviving buildings are the water wagon shed, the granary, the quartermaster storehouse (the oldest surviving structure, dating to 1899), the quartermaster stables, and the sled dog kennels.

Alaska Senator Ted Stevens, a prime mover in preserving the fort, gave the keynote address at Fort Egbert's dedication in August 1980.

A prominent nearby peak is Eagle Peak, elevation 2247 feet (674 m).

Flora and fauna: Typical of growth on soil underlain with permafrost, trees with shallow root systems, such as black spruce, are common. Well-drained soils support willow, aspen, and birch trees. Moose, black bears, beaver, muskrat, hares, wolves, and lynx inhabit the area. The Yukon River supports healthy runs of salmon.

Recreation: The BLM operates a campground near the fort. Walk the grounds of the fort with its interpretive exhibits and photo displays, or wander through the historic town. The courtroom of Judge James Wickersham has been restored in the Courthouse Museum, and the U.S. Customs Museum is an interesting stop. A church near the riverfront dates from 1901. A public boat launch and Yukon River tour boat landing are upriver on the Village Road. The commercially operated riverboat plies the river between Eagle and Dawson City, Yukon Territory. Canoes may be rented in Eagle.

The town remains a popular jumping-off point for Yukon River boaters and travelers headed downriver to Yukon–Charley Rivers National Preserve (see description No. 88). The National Park Service maintains its headquarters here for the preserve.

Weather and conditions: Snow closes the Taylor Highway between October and April. Eagle, with its subarctic continental climate, enjoys warm, dry summers and endures cold, dry, severe winters. (See the Fairbanks weather table.) Winds normally are light.

Caution: Local Athabascan Indians practice a subsistence lifestyle. Be respectful of their privacy and property.

Directions/access: Eagle lies near the Alaska–Canada border on the Taylor Highway, a gravel-surfaced road that is not maintained for winter driving. From Tok, on the Alaska Highway, Eagle is 172 miles (275 km) northeast. Scheduled air service and air taxi service is available from Fairbanks; air taxis also operate out of Circle, Delta Junction, and Tok. Summer visitors may purchase groceries and gas in Chicken or Eagle.

76 Fortymile National Wild, Scenic, and Recreational River

Location: Eastern Alaska, northwest of Tok

River rating: WW1–2 with WW3–5 rapids (line or portage)

Popular trip lengths: 70 to 170 miles (110 to 270 km)

Best time of year: May–September

Annual high water: May

Daylight: June 21: 21½ hours December 22: 4 hours

Maps: USGS, from West/Dennison forks to O'Brien Creek, Tanacross D-3, D-2; Eagle A-2, B-2, B-1. From Middle Fork to O'Brien Creek, Eagle B-5, B-4, B-3, B-2, A-2, B-1. From O'Brien Creek to Eagle (USGS maps), Eagle B-1, A-1; [Canadian maps (1:50,000 scale), Dawson quad] 116 C/7, 116 C/8, 116 C/9, 116 C/10; (USGS maps) Eagle C-1, D-1.

Designated as Wild, Scenic, and Recreational River: 1980

Managed by: Bureau of Land Management

With clear sparkling rapids, quiet pools, forested riverbanks, and white marble bluffs, the Fortymile River flows through gentle, rounded mountains to join the Yukon River. It was named, in 1886, because it was 40 miles (64 km) downstream from the Hudson's Bay post Fort Reliance. Placer and hydraulic gold mining began in the Fortymile country in 1886, 10 years before the Klondike strike in Canada, and it continues today. Mammoth gold dredges that once operated on the Walker and South Forks stand among the fireweed as ghostly relics of the industry of an earlier day.

The river has numerous access points from the gravel-surfaced Taylor Highway as it winds over the Tanana–Yukon uplands to Eagle. The West, Dennison, and Mosquito Forks are mainly WW1, with some WW2–3 rapids that present no serious obstacles. The Middle Fork, although primarily WW1 with WW2 rapids, has dangerous WW3 at "The Chute," which can be lined on the right bank. A short distance farther, WW5 rapids at "The Kink" must be portaged. Below O'Brien Creek, WW3 "Deadman Riffles" can cause trouble for canoes. Across the Canadian border, the canyon contains a two-part WW4 rapids, separated by calm water. It can be lined; use the north bank at times of high water. Watch for sweepers anywhere.

Rock ptarmigan in its winter plumage. The birds' coloring changes with the season so they remain camouflaged. APLIC photo

Distances to O'Brien Creek are: on the South Fork from Mile 49 Taylor Highway, 69 miles (111 km), and from Ketchumstuk on Mosquito Fork, 79 miles (127 km). On the Middle Fork from Joseph to O'Brien Creek is 88 miles (142 km). From O'Brien Creek to Eagle via the Yukon River is about 100 miles (160 km).

Flora and fauna: Watch for wildlife typical of the boreal forest—moose, black bears, brown (grizzly) bears, wolves, wolverines, coyotes, red foxes, lynx, porcupines, grouse, ptarmigan, grayling, northern pike, and sheefish. The Fortymile caribou herd migrates through the area.

Recreation: Due to heavy use of the river by recreational miners, camping along the river for more than 10 days requires a special permit. Rainstorms upriver can raise the water level rapidly; choose campsites carefully and tie boats at night. Campfires are permitted, but build them on river gravel. In 1966, forests of the Middle and Dennison Forks burned. Fishing, hunting, firearms, fixed-wing aircraft, and powerboats are all permitted. Sporting weapons may be taken into Canada, but handguns are prohibited. Expect hungry mosquitoes and other insects in summer months.

Weather and conditions: The Fortymile country has pleasant, warm, dry summers, but prepare for periods of rain and thundershowers in this subarctic continental climate. (See the Eagle weather table.) Winds normally are light.

Caution: The Fortymile flows through many mining claims and other private lands. Do not trespass or enter privately owned structures. Removal of any artifact or object of historic value from federal or state land is prohibited and subject to prosecution.

Directions/access: Access to the West and Dennison Forks is at Mile 49 Taylor Highway, at the West Fork bridge, elevation 1850 feet (564 m), floatable at high water only. Other accesses are at Chicken, Mile 66, elevation 1550 feet (472 m), and at the South Fork bridge, Mile 75, elevation 1500 feet (460 m). Many people pull out at O'Brien Creek, Mile 112, elevation 1300 feet (400 m); land on the right bank immediately below the bridge, where an access road leads to the highway. To float the Middle

Fork, take an air taxi to the airstrip at Joseph, elevation 2300 feet (700 m). Just before the river enters the Yukon, it touches the highway system again at Clinton Creek in Canada, elevation 900 feet (300 m) (no services available), or you may continue on the Yukon to Eagle, Alaska, elevation 900 feet (300 m), Mile 161 Taylor Highway and the end of the road. Air taxis, food, and lodging are available at Eagle and Tok. Eagle also has scheduled air service.

If you travel into Canada, you are required to clear customs. Contact Canadian customs at Dawson City or Whitehorse before starting the float trip. (Addresses and phone numbers are in the Appendix.) Officials are aware of the inconvenience this causes for river travelers and make the legal requirements as painless as possible. You may clear Canadian customs in person at Little Gold Creek Station at the Alaska–Yukon border on Alaska Route 5/Yukon Highway 9, 44 miles (71 km) from Chicken. Upon reentry into the United States, you must clear customs at Eagle.

77 Harding Lake State Recreation Area

Location: Southeast of Fairbanks
Size: 169 acres (68 hectares)
High point/Low point: 720 feet (220 m)
Best time of year: Foot, May–October; boat, June–September; ski, February–April
Daylight: June 21: 21½ hours
December 22: 4½ hours
Activities: Swimming, fishing, ice fishing, hiking, cross-country skiing, snowshoeing, boating
USGS map: Big Delta B-6
Established: 1980
Managed by: Alaska Division of Parks and Outdoor Recreation

A large lake surrounded by rolling hills of spruce, birch, and aspen, Harding is one of the few large Interior lakes accessible from the road system. The highly developed recreation area is excellent for families with small children. The water level in the lake has dropped significantly, creating a shoreline with a very shallow gradient. Deep water is at least 0.25 mile (0.4 km) from the water's edge, so the warm lake waters are a safe place for family play.

Flora and fauna: Numerous birds nest along the shores and in the surrounding boreal forest. Watch for muskrats in the lake and for forest animals—moose, black bears, red foxes, snowshoe hares, lynx, porcupines, grouse, flying squirrels, and red squirrels.

Recreation: Harding Lake has 35 picnic sites, shelters, a boat ramp, drinking water, toilets, and an RV waste dump. Horseshoes, volleyballs, nets, and baseballs can be checked out at the ranger station. Camping is permitted only in the campground (105 units) and at a walk-in campsite; campfires are restricted to campground fire pits. Snowmobiles (when there is sufficient snow cover) and powerboats are permitted; hunting, trapping, firearms, horses, off-road vehicles, and aircraft are prohibited.

Weather and conditions: The warm, dry summers of the subarctic continental climate make this a popular playground for Fairbanks and Delta Junction residents. Winters are cold, dry, and severe. (See the Fairbanks weather table.) Winds normally are light.

Fairbanks area residents find Harding Lake a popular spot for swimming and picnics.
ASP photo by Michel Lee

Caution: Since this is interior Alaska, expect large populations of mosquitoes and other biting insects in June and July. As the lake waters warm, swimmers may contract "swimmer's itch."

Directions/access: The recreation area, 42 miles (68 km) southeast of Fairbanks, is reached from Mile 321.4 Richardson Highway, between Fairbanks and Delta Junction, by a 1.4-mile (2.3-km) side road leading from the highway. (Don't be confused by Harding Lake Road, an access to summer homes near Mile 320.) Scheduled buses travel between Fairbanks and Delta Junction; automobiles can be rented in Fairbanks. Roadside businesses provide food and lodging, as do Fairbanks and Delta Junction.

78 Innoko National Wildlife Refuge and Wilderness

Location: East of Unalakleet
Size: 3,850,160 acres (1,540,064 hectares)
High point: 1330 feet (400 m)
Low point: 50 feet (15 m)
Best time of year: Foot, June–September; boat, June–September; ski, March–April
Daylight: June 21: 24 hours
December 22: 0 hours with about
6 hours of twilight
Activities: Birding, camping, hunting, fishing, boating, snowmobiling, photography
USGS maps: Holy Cross, Iditarod, Nulato, Ophir, Unalakleet
Established: 1980
Managed by: U.S. Fish and Wildlife Service

Lying in two parts along the east bank of the Yukon River, the refuge is 80 percent wetlands, with muskeg, islands of black spruce, lakes, and meandering rivers and streams. Rolling hills border the river. In the southeastern corner of the refuge, 1,240,000 acres (502,000 hectares) are designated as Wilderness.

Russian fur traders set up a post at Nulato in 1838, but long before that, local Indians traded fine beaver pelts with coastal Eskimos. Yukon River salmon continue to be a staple food for both humans and dogs.

Flora and fauna: The lands, transitional between the open tundra of western Alaska and the boreal forest of interior Alaska, are used by locals for subsistence food and supplies. A major nesting area for waterfowl, the refuge harbors more than 380,000 ducks and 65,000 geese each summer; of the 338 species of birds found in Alaska, 140 can be found in the refuge. Most abundant species are pintails, widgeon, scaup, white-fronted geese, and Canada geese. In addition to the 20,000 beavers, other furbearers thrive in this wet refuge, as do moose and black bear. Found here also are caribou and brown (grizzly) bears. So are large numbers of another choice Alaskan wildlife species—mosquitoes.

Recreation: The refuge is roadless and undeveloped. Camping is unrestricted on public lands, although dry campsites may be difficult to find; campfires are permitted. Numerous private lands exist within the boundaries—do not disturb buildings, fish camps, or equipment. Hunting, fishing, powerboats, snowmobiles, and fixed-wing aircraft landings are permitted.

Water travel: Yukon River, FWB within the refuge; Innoko River, FWB within the refuge.

Weather and conditions: Expect warm, dry summers and cold, dry, severe winters in this subarctic continental climate. (See the Galena weather table.) Winds are normally light.

Directions/access: Access to the refuge is by air taxi from Galena or Grayling or by charter boat, available informally at most villages in the area. Scheduled air service is available to Anvik, Galena, Grayling, Kaltag, Koyukuk, and Nulato, all of which have general stores. Galena has lodging; Koyukuk and Nulato prefer not to have tourists.

A wintery scene in Innoko National Wildlife Refuge, with black spruce trees that are stunted by permafrost-rich soil. USFWS photo by Jo Goldmann

79 Kanuti National Wildlife Refuge

Location: South of Bettles (Evansville)
Size: 1,430,002 acres (572,001 hectares)
High point: 3536 feet (1078 m)
Low point: 350 feet (110 m)
Best time of year: Foot, June–
September; boat, June–September;
ski, March–April
Daylight: June 21: 24 hours

December 22: 2½ hours
Activities: Camping, river running,
birding, photography
USGS map: Bettles (Evansville)
Established: 1980
Managed by: U.S. Fish and Wildlife
Service

Rafters float through Kanuti Canyon. USFWS photo

In a refuge on the rolling, partly forested plain of the Kanuti and Koyukuk Rivers, the lakes, ponds, and marshes provide nesting habitats for large populations of migratory waterfowl. Sithylemenkat Lake, in the southeastern corner of the refuge, is thought by some scientists to be an ancient meteorite crater.

Flora and fauna: Alaska's greatest nesting density of white-fronted geese is found here. On the river terraces roam moose, black bears, brown (grizzly) bears, coyotes, red foxes, lynx, wolves, and wolverines. Beavers, marten, mink, and muskrats live in the wetlands. The Western Arctic caribou herd comes into the area in the winter.

Recreation: Camping and campfires are permitted in this undeveloped, roadless refuge. Fishing is permitted throughout; hunting, powerboats, snowmobiles, and fixed-wing aircraft are subject to certain restrictions; off-road vehicles are not permitted. The area is extensively used by locals for subsistence hunting and fishing; respect private lands and equipment within the refuge. Expect large populations of mosquitoes and other biting insects in summer.

Water travel: Jim River, WW2, from the Dalton Highway to Allakaket, 130 miles (210 km); Kanuti River, WW1–FWB, from the Dalton Highway to Hughes, 240 miles (390 km); South Fork of the Koyukuk River, WW1 through the refuge; Fish Creek, WW2, from the Dalton Highway to Allakaket, 130 miles (210 km).

Weather and conditions: The refuge has a subarctic continental climate with warm, dry summers and cold, dry, severe winters. (See the Bettles weather table.) Winds are normally light.

Directions/access: The refuge can be reached by foot, air, or boat. Skirting the eastern boundary, from Mile 123 to Mile 135, the Dalton Highway crosses several rivers that flow west through the refuge. Scheduled air service is available to Allakaket, Bettles (Evansville), and Hughes; air taxis are based at Bettles (Evansville). Both Allakaket and Bettles (Evansville) have general stores; the latter has a lodge.

80 Koyukuk National Wildlife Refuge and Wilderness

Location: North of Galena

Size: 3,550,000 acres (1,420,000 hectares)

High point: 3200 feet (980 m)

Low point: 125 feet (38 m)

Best time of year: Foot, June–September; boat, June–September; ski, March–April

Daylight: June 21: 24 hours

December 22: 3 hours

Activities: Camping, fishing, hunting, river running, snowmobiling

USGS maps: Hughes, Kateel, Melozitna, Nulato, Shungnak

Established: 1980

Managed by: U.S. Fish and Wildlife Service

A classic river floodplain with oxbow lakes and scroll meanders surrounding the village of Huslia, the refuge area is of great importance to the local people. Because it was not covered by glaciers in the last Ice Age, the region is thought to have been a refuge for humans and wildlife, who have used the area ever since.

The sight of sand dunes in the subarctic comes as a surprise to many travelers.   USFWS photo

Flora and fauna: Primarily wetlands, with sloughs, lakes, muskeg, and boreal-forested lowlands, the river basin is surrounded by high rolling hills along the refuge boundaries. Tree line is at about 3000 feet (900 m). The unexpected Nogahabara Sand Dunes lie west of Huslia in a 400,000-acre (162,000-hectare) wilderness.

The refuge includes prime habitat for large populations of moose, furbearers, particularly beavers, and nesting waterfowl, primarily pintails, mallards, green-winged teal, widgeons, canvasbacks, scaups, scoters, white-fronted geese, and Canada geese. The Koyukuk River basin appears to be the northwestern nesting limit of the trumpeter swan. Watch also for black bears, brown (grizzly) bears, coyotes, red foxes, lynx, wolves, and wolverines. Portions of the Western Arctic caribou herd winter here.

Recreation: The area is remote and roadless, with no recreational development. Camping and campfires are permitted on public lands. Numerous private lands exist within the refuge, particularly along navigable streams. The people of the area do not encourage tourists and other visitors; please respect their property and privacy. Fishing is permitted; with certain restrictions, so are hunting, powerboats, snowmobiles, and fixed-wing aircraft. Expect large populations of mosquitoes and other biting insects during summer months.

Water travel: Koyukuk River, FWA within the refuge.

Weather and conditions: In this subarctic continental climate, summers are warm and dry, winters are cold, dry, and severe. (See the Galena weather table.) Winds normally are light.

Directions/access: Access to the refuge is by air or boat. Galena, Hughes, Huslia, and Koyukuk have scheduled air service and general stores; Galena has lodging and air taxis.

81 Lower Chatanika River State Recreation Area

Location: Elliott Highway, north of Fairbanks

Size: 571 acres (228 hectares)

High point: 1500 feet (450 m)

Low point: 500 feet (135 m)

Best time of year: Foot, May–October; boat, May–September; ski, February–April

Daylight: June 20: 22 hours December 22: 3 hours

Activities: Hiking, fishing, camping, picnicking, boating

USGS map: Livengood A-2

Managed by: Alaska Division of Parks and Outdoor Recreation

In the days of the Fairbanks area gold rush, nearly a century ago, Olnes was a bustling commerce center for the thousand people who lived in the hills around the Chatanika River. As of the mid-1990s, the historic site had a year-round population of one. Today all that remains of the original settlement are house pits that may be seen in a large clearing next to the Chatanika River and west of Olnes Pond.

The pond was created by the builders of the trans-Alaska pipeline, who needed gravel for bedding material for the pipeline and access roads.

Flora and fauna: Stands of paper birch and white spruce grow along the riverbank and floodplain. Black spruce is the dominant species of tree in this region, a telltale sign that only a tree with a shallow root system can survive on this permafrost-riddled soil. Below the organic mat, perennially frozen soil begins at 13 to 23 inches down. The recreation area provides habitat for beaver, moose, red squirrel, hares, red

The Lower Chatanika River dressed in its fall foliage   Tricia Brown photo

fox, porcupine, and black bear. Songbirds, waterfowl, raptors, and shorebirds all may be found in the area, including bald eagles, Canada geese, chickadees, ravens, ducks, golden eagles, gulls, kingfishers, loons, sandpipers, sparrows, and terns. Arctic grayling, burbot, king and chum salmon, whitefish, and northern pike may be found in the Chatanika River. Olnes Pond is stocked annually with arctic grayling and rainbow trout by the Alaska Department of Fish and Game.

Recreation: Since the park is only 20 miles from Fairbanks, it's a popular destination for a day trip. For overnight visitors, 2 campgrounds lie within the recreation area, with just 0.5 mile between them. The Olnes Pond facilities include 15 campsites, picnic areas, toilets, and a fresh-water pump. At the Whitefish campground, there are 11 campsites, picnic areas, toilets, drinking water, a covered picnic shelter, and a boat ramp (fee). Both campgrounds include wheelchair access. Check Alaska Department of Fish and Game sport-fishing regulations before fishing in the pond or river. River access is possible at many points along the river and from a trail at Olnes Pond. Hunting and trapping is permitted in some areas of the park. The use of motorized watercraft is not allowed on the pond.

Weather and conditions: Fairbanks area summers are mild, dry, and often sunny, with high temperatures in the range of 70 degrees to 80 degrees F (21 degrees to 27 degrees C). Winds are light. August is the wettest month. Interior winters can be harsh, with temperatures lingering at minus 40 degrees F (minus 40 degrees C). (See the Fairbanks weather table.)

Caution: Swimming in Olnes Pond may result in "swimmer's itch." Watch the campground bulletin board for informational notices on symptoms and preventive measures.

Directions/access: From Fairbanks, drive north on the Steese Highway to Fox, then proceed north on the Elliott Highway, to Mile 10.5 for the Olnes Pond Campground, or Mile 11 for the Whitefish Campground. Fairbanks and Fox have lodging, gas, and groceries.

82 Minto Flats State Game Refuge

Location: West of Fairbanks
Size: 497,800 acres (199,120 hectares)
High point: 294 feet (88 m)
Low point: 317 feet (95 m)
Best time of year: Foot, May–October; boat, May–September; ski, February–March
Daylight: June 21: 22 hours
December 22: 3½ hours

Activities: Camping, boating, fishing, hunting, snowmobiling, dog mushing, berry-picking
USGS map: Livengood A-5, A-4; Fairbanks D-4, D-5, D-6
Established: 1988
Managed by: Alaska Department of Fish and Game

A vast complex of rivers, sloughs, shallow lakes, and other wetlands, Minto Flats is famous for the number and variety of waterfowl that breed there. To local Athabascan

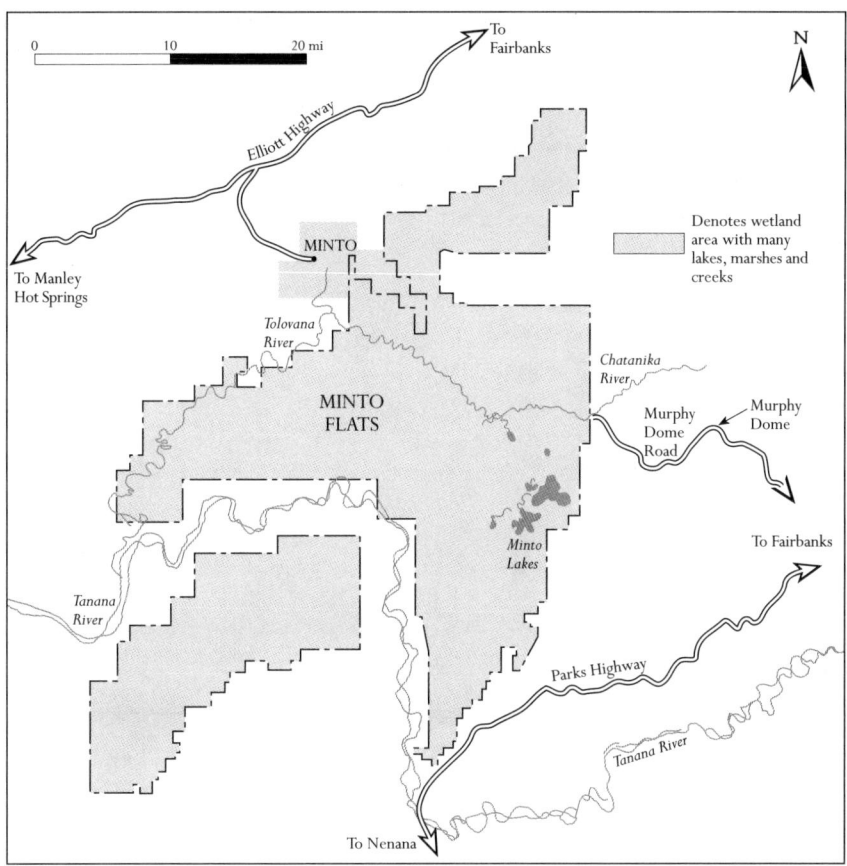

Natives, the flats represent their means of subsistence—a habitat for birds, furbearers, big game, and fish. Evidence of prehistoric settlements exists here on whitefish- and salmon-bearing streams. To sportsmen, especially waterfowl hunters, the region is a dream come true. The breeding population averages 213 ducks per square mile; the trumpeter swan breeding population is one of the largest in North America.

Flora and fauna: Due to the presence of permafrost in the soil, black spruce forests are common. Stands of willow and birch trees are found in the upland forest. Sedge tussocks, mosses, and shrubs grow on level terrain. Fire and flooding have created a diversity of habitats across the region. These naturally occurring events help recycle nutrients and increase young plant life, which is favorable for some animals. Furbearers include wolves, coyotes, red foxes, lynx, wolverines, river otters, marten, weasels, mink, beavers, and muskrats. The flats support high numbers of moose.

The wetlands are important nesting and staging areas for large numbers of migratory birds, especially dabbling ducks, trumpeter swans, sandhill cranes, and geese.

Recreation: There are no developed public-use facilities, including no campgrounds or picnic areas. Campers must be self-sufficient. This is one of the best waterfowl

Trumpeter swans represent a large number of the migratory birds that rest and feed at Minto Flats.   ASP photo

hunting habitats in the state, especially along the Big Minto Lakes. Big-game hunting is mostly for moose and black bears. Among anglers, Minto Flats is respected for its large northern pike. Other fish include whitefish, arctic grayling, burbot, and least cisco. Chinook and chum salmon find their way to spawning areas in the Chatanika and other Tolovana River tributaries. Sport-fishing for pike is a relatively new trend.

Weather and conditions: Interior Alaska, with its subarctic continental climate, enjoys warm, dry summers and endures cold, dry, severe winters. (See the Fairbanks weather table.) Winds normally are light.

Caution: The subsistence lifestyle is important to the Minto villagers. Do not disturb any gear or activity. Ask before you camp on or cross Native land.

Directions/access: The area is accessible from Fairbanks, Minto, and Nenana by boat, horse, aircraft, dog team, snowmobile, and off-road vehicle. Road access is available from an extension of Murphy Dome Road on the east and the Minto village access road on the north. Water access is from the boat launch on the Chatanika River at the end of the Murphy Dome Road extension, the Tolovana River at Minto village, and via the Tanana River. Lodging is available in Fairbanks, Nenana, or Minto. All three communities have scheduled air service. Air taxis or charters may be arranged in Fairbanks.

83 Nowitna National Wildlife Refuge

Location: East of Galena
Size: 1,560,000 acres (642,000 hectares)
High point: 2341 feet (714 m)
Low point: 135 feet (41 m)
Best time of year: Foot, June–
September; boat, June–September;
ski, March–April
Daylight: June 21: 22 hours
December 22: 3½ hours
Activities: Camping, fishing, boating,
snowmobiling
USGS maps: Kantishna, Medfra,
Melozitna, Ruby
Established: 1980
Managed by: U.S. Fish and Wildlife
Service

An interior Alaska "solar basin," the refuge contains forested lowlands and excellent wetland habitat for waterfowl and furbearers. The Nowitna National Wild River, an important sheefish spawning stream, flows broad, clear, and deep, into the Yukon River.

Flora and fauna: The rolling hills in the southeastern portion of the refuge drop to lake-dotted wetlands in the Yukon River floodplain, a boreal-forested lowland. A quarter of a million waterfowl each fall leave the refuge, most to follow the Central Flyway to the Lower 48, although many canvasbacks travel to the Atlantic Coast, and pintails and widgeons go to California. As many as 200 trumpeter swans, the largest waterfowl in North America, nest in the refuge. Watch also for moose, black bears,

An aerial view of the Nowitna shows oxbow lakes created when the meandering stream changes its course.   USFWS photo

brown (grizzly) bears, caribou, coyotes, red foxes, lynx, wolves, beavers, mink, muskrats, and river otters. Major populations of marten and wolverines are found in the refuge.

Recreation: Camping and campfires are permitted on public lands. Fishing, hunting, powerboats, snowmobiles, and fixed-wing aircraft landings are permitted. Expect large populations of mosquitoes and other biting insects during summer months.

83a *Nowitna National Wild River.* This river is best to float

between June and September. The river is rated WW1–FWC; a popular trip length is 310 miles (500 km). The Nowitna may be reached by air taxi to the vicinity of Clearwater Creek, elevation 700 feet (200 m). The confluence with the Yukon River is 270 miles (430 km) away. The town of Ruby, elevation 135 feet (41 m), is 41 miles (66 km) farther down the Yukon. An alternate river trip begins at the Sulatna River crossing, elevation 350 feet (110 m), 11 miles (18 km) south of Ruby on the Placerville Road. (This road is not connected to the state highway system.) Float the Sulatna to the Nowitna, WW1–FWC, and continue to the Yukon, ending at Ruby, a total distance of 230 miles (370 km).

Weather and conditions: In a subarctic continental climate, the area enjoys warm, dry summers and endures cold, dry, severe winters. (See the Galena weather table.) Winds are normally light.

Caution: Within the boundaries of this roadless, undeveloped refuge, respect private lands and ask permission before trespassing.

Directions/access: Ruby, Galena, and Tanana all have scheduled air service, general stores, and limited lodging; air taxis operate from Galena and Tanana.

84 Quartz Lake State Recreation Area

Location: North of Delta Junction
Size: 600 acres (240 hectares)
High point: 1269 feet (387 m)
Low point: 75 feet (23 m)
Best time of year: Foot, May–October; boat, June–September; ski, February–April
Daylight: June 21: 21 ½ hours

December 22: 4 ½ hours
Activities: Sport-fishing, boating, picnicking, swimming, hiking, ski touring
USGS map: Big Delta A-4
Established: 1975
Managed by: Alaska Division of Parks and Outdoor Recreation

Set among boreal-forested hills, Quartz Lake, Lost Lake, and their marshy and rolling lowlands are popular recreation spots for Fairbanks and Delta Junction residents. The 3-mile road to Quartz Lake from the Richardson Highway was once part of a dogsled trail used by locals traveling south to Healy and the Tanana River, when the area was used for mink farming and fur trapping.

Picnicking at Quartz Lake State Recreation Area   ASP photo by Neil Johannsen

Fauna: Watch for muskrats in the water and shorebirds. The boreal forest supports moose, black bears, red foxes, snowshoe hares, lynx, porcupines, grouse, flying squirrels, and red squirrels.

Recreation: Quartz Lake State Recreation Area is an excellent destination for families with children and those who want developed campground facilities. Facilities include picnic tables, a boat ramp, and toilets. Camping is permitted only in camp-grounds (21 units); campfires may be built only in the fire pits provided. Powerboats are permitted on the lake; snowmobiles, horses, off-road vehicles, and aircraft are allowed. Hunting is permitted but not within 0.5 mile of a developed facility, such as the campground.

233

Weather and conditions: Expect warm, dry summers with occasional thunder-showers and a few cool, overcast, drizzly days. In this subarctic continental climate, winters are cold, dry, and severe. (See the Fairbanks weather table.) Winds are light.

Caution: Swimmers may pick up "swimmer's itch" when lake waters are warm.

Directions/access: The recreation area is accessible by automobile or scheduled bus (Fairbanks–Delta Junction route) from Mile 277.9 Richardson Highway, 12 miles (19 km) northwest of Delta Junction. A 2.6-mile (4.2-km) side road leads north to Quartz Lake. Rental cars are available in Fairbanks; restaurants and lodging can be found along the road and in Delta Junction and Fairbanks.

85 Steese National Conservation Area

Location: Northeast of Fairbanks
Size: 1,220,000 (494,000 hectares)
High point: 5580 feet (1700 m)
Low point: 850 feet (260 m)
Best time of year: Foot, June–September; boat, May–September; ski, February–April
Daylight: June 20–22, the midnight sun is visible above 3600 feet (1100 m) at this latitude; at sea level, 21½ hours

December 22: 3 hours
Activities: River running, gold-panning, hiking
USGS maps: Charley River, Circle
Established: 1980
Managed by: Bureau of Land Management

Established to maintain the environmental quality of a portion of the rolling Tanana–Yukon uplands, yet allow multiple use and sustained yields, the conservation area permits mineral exploration and development. Several gold-mining operations currently are at work. Over the years, miners have unearthed fossil remains of mastodons and other pre-glacial mammals.

Prominent peaks are Mount Prindle, elevation 5286 feet (1611 m); Lime Peak, elevation 5062 feet (1543 m); Pinnell Mountain, elevation 4721 feet (1439 m).

Flora and fauna: In two units straddling the Steese Highway, the conservation area contains broad treeless summits, covered by dry alpine tundra above 3500 feet (1100 m), that beckon the hiker, dropping to spruce–birch–aspen-forested valleys with clear streams. In this area of discontinuous permafrost, look for ice lenses exposed in unstable soil areas along eroding stream banks.

Watch for wildlife of the uplands: moose, caribou, brown (grizzly) bears, black bears, wolves, coyotes, wolverines, red foxes, lynx, porcupines, and beavers. The area contains the highest population of forest grouse in Alaska, including ruffed, sharp-tailed, and spruce grouse and willow, rock, and white-tailed ptarmigan.

Recreation: Backcountry camping and campfires are permitted, but be particularly careful with fire during dry periods. The Pinnell Mountain National Recreation Trail, 27 miles (43 km) long, follows the south border of the northern unit across a series of alpine ridgetops. The trail is above timberline in its entirety and is well-marked with wooden mileposts and rock cairns; Birch Creek National Wild and Scenic River

Pinnell Mountain Trail offers sensational views of the countryside.   APLIC photo

meanders through the southern unit. The conservation area includes a wheelchair-accessible trail and viewing deck at the eastern end of the Pinnell Mountain National Recreation Trail, accessible from Mile 107 Steese Highway. Access to Twelvemile Summit begins at Mile 85.6. There are parking areas and trail registers at both trailheads. Two small emergency shelters also are available along the trail. The trail is closed to all motorized vehicles.

Fishing, hunting, firearms, horses, fixed-wing aircraft, powerboats, and snowmobiles are all permitted. The public may pan for gold in Birch Creek.

85a *Birch Creek National Wild and Scenic River.* This river
is rated WW 1–3. Managed by the Bureau of Land Management, Birch Creek was designated a Wild and Scenic River in 1980. The annual high-water month is July; the best time of year to visit is May through July.

With its headwaters near timberline in the rolling Yukon–Tanana uplands, Birch Creek winds through boreal-forested valleys eventually to emerge in the wetlands of the Yukon River valley in the Yukon Flats National Wildlife Refuge. Although it flows through uninhabited wilderness, the creek often is extremely muddy from placer gold mining in its headwaters and tributaries. Near and below the Steese Highway bridge at Mile 147, which marks the end of the Wild River designation, Birch Creek is a slow meandering stream, with occasional sloughs and old river channels obscuring the main channel. About 150 miles (240 km) below the bridge, the river divides into two channels that enter the Yukon River 20 miles (32 km) apart. The distance from the access at Mile

235

Climbing the outcrop known as the Granite Tors ASP photo

94 Steese Highway to the take-out at Mile 147 Steese Highway, at the bridge, is about 125 miles (200 km). (An earlier take-out is possible at Mile 140.) Continuing down Birch Creek and the Yukon River to the Dalton Highway bridge adds another 300 miles (480 km).

During periods of low water, the upper 8 miles (13 km) of the river may require lining and extensive dragging, particularly in late summer. The WW3 rapids about 6 miles (10 km) below Clums (Coulombes) Fork can be dangerous and should be lined or portaged. Numerous sweepers hang from the banks.

To reach the river, drive the Steese Highway north of Fairbanks to Mile 94, where a short side road leads to a parking area and access to the main fork of Birch Creek, elevation 2000 feet (600 m). Take out at Jumpoff Creek, Mile 140 Steese Highway, or at the Steese Highway bridge over Birch Creek at Mile 147, elevation 600 feet (200 m). Food and lodging are available at Central and Circle Hot Springs.

Weather and conditions: Summers are warm and dry; winters are cold, dry, and severe in this subarctic continental climate. (See the Fairbanks weather table.) Winds normally are light. Snow can fall on the summits in any month. Avoid these peaks and other open areas during summer lightning storms.

Caution: Expect large populations of mosquitoes and other biting insects from June through August. Numerous mining claims exist throughout; you are legally permitted to cross them so long as you do not interfere with mining operations. For your own safety, ask before crossing, if possible, and do not pick up anything from the ground.

Directions/access: Other than unimproved miners' roads, no public roads penetrate the conservation area, but access is easily available from the Pinnell Mountain trailhead, Mile 85.6 Steese Highway; on Twelvemile Summit, at Mile 94, an access road to Birch Creek; on Eagle Summit, at the Mile 107 Pinnell Mountain trailhead; and at the Mammoth Creek bridge, Mile 116. Scheduled air service, food, and lodging are available at Central, Circle, and Circle Hot Springs; air taxis operate from Fairbanks, Circle, and Circle Hot Springs.

---

86 Tetlin National Wildlife Refuge

Location: Southeast of Tok
Size: 700,053 acres (280,021 hectares)
High point: 8000 feet (2400 m)
Low point: 1650 feet (503 m)
Best time of year: Foot, May–October; boat, June–September; ski, February–April
Daylight: June 21: 20 hours

December 22: 5 hours
Activities: Fishing, boating, hunting, hiking, photography, birding
USGS maps: Nabesna, Tanacross
Established: 1980
Managed by: U.S. Fish and Wildlife Service

Tetlin is one of the coldest areas on the North American continent. Nearby Snag, Yukon Territory, has registered minus 81 degrees F (minus 63 degrees C). The undulating alluvial plain, with extensive marshes and numerous lakes, was once the bottom of an Ice Age lake. Today, bordered by the Alaska Highway on the north and Canada on the east, the refuge lowlands rise in the south to rolling uplands and the foothills of the Alaska Range.

Flora and fauna: The refuge is an excellent example of an interior Alaska boreal forest ecosystem. Some sections of its highly productive wetlands contain 600 nesting ducks per square mile. Seventeen species of ducks, including ring-necks, redheads, and blue-winged teal, nest here, as do large populations of sharp-tailed grouse, ptarmigan, and raptors. Up to 300,000 sandhill cranes visit the refuge during fall migration. Watch

Yarger Lake in Tetlin National Wildlife Refuge   USFWS photo

also for moose, black bears, brown (grizzly) bears, coyotes, red foxes, lynx, Dall sheep, wolves, wolverines, snowshoe hares, beavers, and other furbearers.

Recreation: The refuge is undeveloped. Camping and campfires are unrestricted, but be careful with fires, especially during dry periods. Fishing, hunting, horses, powerboats, snowmobiles, and fixed-wing aircraft are all permitted; all-terrain vehicles are restricted to designated trails. Expect large populations of mosquitoes and other biting insects from June through August. Avoid disturbing waterfowl during breeding and nesting season.

Water travel: Nabesna River, WW2–FWA, from Nabesna to Northway, 66 miles (106 km); Chisana-Nabesna Rivers, FWB, from Northway Road to about Mile 1280 Alaska Highway, near Bitter's Creek, 20 miles (32 km).

Weather and conditions: Summers in this subarctic continental climate are warm and dry; winters are cold, dry, and severe. (See the Northway weather table.) Winds generally are light.

Directions/access: The refuge is easily accessible from the Alaska Highway between Mile 1221.3 and Mile 1286.5. Scheduled buses travel the highway frequently, particularly in the summer, en route to Haines or Whitehorse from Tok, Fairbanks, and Anchorage. Rental automobiles are available in Fairbanks and Tok; air taxis are based in Northway, Tanacross, and Tok. Stores, restaurants, and lodging are found at roadside businesses and at Northway and Tok.

87 White Mountains National Recreation Area

Location: North of Fairbanks
Size: 1,000,000 acres (405,000 hectares)
High point: 5286 feet (1611 m)
Low point: 800 feet (200 m)
Best time of year: Foot, June–
September; boat, May–September;
ski, February–April
Daylight: June 20–22, the
midnight sun is visible above 3600
feet (1100 m) at this latitude;
at sea level, 22 hours
December 22: 3 hours
Activities: Camping, hiking, ski touring,
mountain biking, skijoring, dog
mushing, boating, gold panning
USGS maps: Circle, Livengood
Established: 1980
Managed by: Bureau of Land
Management

Spectacular white limestone pinnacles and rolling, gentle mountains characterize the White Mountains, a part of the Tanana–Yukon uplands. The summits above 3500 feet (1100 m) are inviting dry tundra, with easy walking. Beaver Creek National Wild and Scenic River is the principal drainage. Prominent peaks include Mount Prindle, elevation 5286 feet (1611 m); Lime Peak, elevation 5062 feet (1543 m); Cache Mountain, elevation 4772 feet (1455 m); Wickersham Dome, elevation 3207 feet (977 m). A panoramic view from the summit of Wickersham Dome is only 3 miles (5 km) from the highway.

Mushing the winter trails through the White Mountains   BLM photo

Flora and fauna: Forested valleys are punctuated by treeless subarctic bogs. In this area of discontinuous permafrost, erosion along stream banks occasionally exposes ice lenses, blocks of ice embedded in the frozen ground. Animals of the boreal forest include moose, black bears, brown (grizzly) bears, caribou, wolves, wolverines, red foxes, coyotes, lynx, porcupines, and beavers. Keep an eye out for grouse and ptarmigan, and watch for Dall sheep on the treeless summits above the river. In Beaver Creek, grayling inhabit the upper river; below Victoria Creek, you can fish for northern pike and whitefish.

Recreation: The recreation area includes three trailheads that lead to nine trails, comprising more than 200 miles of trails that are especially good for winter recreation. Nine public-use recreational cabins (reservations necessary, fee) and a trail shelter are accessible with snowmobiles or mountain bikes after parking at a trailhead. The cabins range from 7 miles to 44 miles from the road, spaced about 10 miles apart. Three campgrounds, one including wheelchair-accessible facilities, also have been developed. Backcountry camping, campfires, fishing, hunting, firearms, horses, fixed-wing aircraft, powerboats, and snowmobiles are all permitted throughout the recreation area. Expect large populations of mosquitoes and other biting insects in summer months. Commercial mining is permitted within the recreation area. Although you are legally permitted to cross the numerous mining claims, do not interfere with mining operations or pick up anything from the ground. If possible, ask before crossing.

87a *Beaver Creek National Wild and Scenic River.* This
River was designated in 1980 and is managed by the Bureau of Land Management. The river rating is WW1–FWB. A popular trip length is 130 miles (210 km), and the best time to visit is between May and September. The water typically is at its highest level in May.

A clear, gentle wilderness stream, the Beaver winds through rich boreal forests in

An aerial view of the White Mountains   BLM photo

the rounded White Mountains of the Interior. White limestone cliffs and pinnacles line portions of the river. At "Big Bend," warm springs keep the river open all winter, providing good late-season grayling fishing. From Nome Creek to the flats below Victoria Creek is about 130 miles (210 km). To continue on Beaver Creek and down the Yukon River, leaving the Yukon at the Dalton Highway bridge, is another 270 miles (430 km).

The Beaver has no large rapids or serious obstacles, although the upper river flows frequently over exposed bedrock. The current in the lower river below Victoria Creek is extremely slow as it meanders through the Yukon Flats National Wildlife Refuge. Often the water has a harmless brown tint leached from the bog vegetation.

To reach the river, drive to Mile 42 on the Steese Highway north of Fairbanks. A 15-mile (24-km) unimproved gravel miners' road near Belle Creek leads to the Nome Creek tributary, elevation 1700 feet (520 m). Upstream an alternate access is at the 2100-foot (640-m) level via a 7-mile (11-km) unimproved road along U.S. Creek from Mile 58 Steese Highway. Leave the river by air taxi, landing on the river or on gravel bars in the flats, elevation 700 feet (200 m), below Victoria Creek. Air taxis, rental cars, food, and lodging are available at Fairbanks.

Weather and conditions: The climate is a subarctic continental one; summers are usually warm and dry, although temperatures can drop and snow can fall on summits. Avoid peaks and other open areas during summer lightning storms. Winters are cold, dry, and severe. (See the Fairbanks weather table.) Winds normally are light.

Directions/access: Although no maintained roads enter the recreation area, it is accessible from both the Elliott and Steese Highways by trail or primitive road. Access to the Nome Creek tributary of Beaver Creek is via two unimproved gravel mining roads that leave the Steese Highway, one 15 miles (24 km) long, at Mile 42 near Belle Creek, and one 7 miles (11 km) long, at U.S. Creek, Mile 58. The 20-mile (32-km) Summit Trail to Beaver Creek is a summer trail that leaves the Elliott Highway at Mile 28. It is for nonmotorized vehicles only. Winter trails include the Colorado Creek Trail, which begins at Mile 57 Elliott Highway, and the McKay Creek Trail, at Mile 42.5 Steese Highway. Food is available at Fairbanks, Fox, and Livengood. Food, lodging, rental cars, and air taxis can be found in Fairbanks.

88 Yukon-Charley Rivers National Preserve

Location: East of Fairbanks
Size: 2,260,000 acres (915,000 hectares)
High point: 6435 feet (1961 m)
Low point: 600 feet (180 m)
Best time of year: Foot, June–September; boat (Yukon River, June–August; Charley River, June–September); ski, February–April

Daylight: June 21: 22 hours
   December 22: 3½ hours
Activities: Hiking, boating, photography, fishing, hunting, snowmobiling
USGS maps: Big Delta, Charley River, Circle, Eagle
Established: 1978; amended 1980
Managed by: National Park Service

A pleasant, undisturbed wilderness watershed of low mountains and clearwater rivers, the preserve straddles the placid Yukon River. The Yukon historically was, and still is, an important transportation route, summer and winter, in a region only occasionally penetrated by roads. The nearby small towns of Eagle and Circle, on the south bank, were prominent centers of activity during the heyday of the Klondike and Nome gold rushes. Decaying cabins from that era can still be found among the tall magenta fireweed lining the banks. Originally established as a national monument, the area was designated a Preserve with a Wild River in 1980.

Although the Yukon's banks abound with history and artifacts, the Charley River basin was not of particular interest to gold-seekers because it produced little "color."

Flora and fauna: The many branches of the Charley, flowing from open tundra upland through forested valleys, have seldom been visited. One of the clearest streams in Alaska, it has shallow, braided upper reaches and a middle section that skirts steep rock bluffs in a spruce–birch–aspen forest to tumble over boulders and through pools. The lower river meanders through muskeg and black spruce woods. Wildlife is typical of the boreal forest and includes moose, lynx, black bears, brown (grizzly) bears, wolves, wolverines, and beavers. The entire Charley River area is part of the range of the Fortymile caribou herd, which uses the headwaters as a calving area. The hillsides and bluffs along the Charley are Dall sheep range. Watch for nesting peregrine falcons on the bluffs above the Yukon, but don't disturb this endangered species.

Recreation: Camping and campfires are permitted throughout this undeveloped preserve, but be careful where you camp on the Charley; rainstorms in the headwaters can rapidly raise the water level downriver without warning. Prepare for large numbers of mosquitoes and other biting insects in summer months. Fishing, hunting, firearms, horses, fixed-wing aircraft, helicopters (by permit), powerboats, and snowmobiles are all permitted; off-road vehicles are not.

Fly-fishing on the Charley River   YCRNP photo

88a *Charley National Wild River.* This river is rated WW4–FWC.

The best time of year to float is June through September, and a popular trip length is 140 miles (230 km). The entire river and its tributaries are designated as Wild River. To float the Charley River, take an air taxi to the upper Charley airstrip, elevation 2400 feet (730 m), on the main river about 20 miles (32 km) above Crescent Creek. The WW3–4 rapids between the airstrip and Crescent Creek may have to be lined or portaged, especially at high water during spring runoff or at low water. An alternate access point is at the Crescent Creek confluence, elevation 1900 feet (580 m), via helicopter from Circle. From the airstrip to the Yukon River, elevation 700 feet (210 m), is about 88 miles (140 km); Circle, elevation 597 feet (182 m), is another 63 miles (100 km) down the Yukon.

An easier boat trip is a float down the Yukon from Eagle, elevation 865 feet (264 m), to Circle, a distance of about 150 miles (240 km). Take time to explore up side rivers and hike a bit. Be alert for williwaws—sudden violent winds spilling over mountains onto the river that can raise whitecaps and large waves capable of capsizing canoes.

Weather and conditions: Expect warm, dry summers interspersed with periods of rain and drizzle in this subarctic continental climate. Winters are cold, dry, and severe. (See the Eagle weather table.) Winds generally are light.

Caution: Private lands and cabins line the Yukon River. Do not disturb them, or fish nets, fish wheels, or other private equipment—local residents depend upon subsistence foods for survival.

Directions/access: Both Eagle, at Mile 161 Taylor Highway, and Circle, Mile 162 Steese Highway, are accessible by automobile from about March 15 to October 15. The Steese is maintained in winter; the Taylor is not. Both towns have scheduled air service, air taxis, charter flights, food, and lodging. Charter helicopters are available in Circle.

89 Yukon Flats National Wildlife Refuge

Location: Surrounding Fort Yukon
Size: 8,630,000 acres (3,452,000 hectares)
High point: 4177 feet (1273 m)
Low point: 300 feet (90 m)
Best time of year: Foot, late May–September; boat, late May–September; ski, February–April
Daylight: June 21: 24 hours December 22: 2 ½ hours

Activities: Boating, hiking, camping, photography, fishing, hunting, snowmobiling, river running
USGS maps: Beaver, Bettles (Evansville), Black River, Chandalar, Charley River, Christian, Circle, Fort Yukon, Livengood
Established: 1980
Managed by: U.S. Fish and Wildlife Service

Here on the Arctic Circle the early summer sun circles the horizon, giving the flats 24 hours of sunlight daily. In this "solar basin," summer temperatures often soar above

An aerial view of the Yukon Flats   USFWS photo by M. LeFever

90 degrees F (32 degrees C), but a record low of minus 75 degrees F (minus 59 degrees C) has occurred in January. More than 200 miles (320 km) of the Yukon River flows through the refuge at a gradient of 1 foot per mile (0.2 m/km). Fort Yukon, 1 mile (2 km) above the Arctic Circle, was established by the Hudson's Bay Company in 1847 to compete with the Russians for the lucrative fur trade; today the town is the largest settlement in northeastern Alaska.

Flora and fauna: The refuge takes in part of the vast floodplain of the Yukon River and its associated lowlands, with extensive wetlands, marshes, 40,000 lakes, and 25,000

miles (40,000 km) of rivers, and also includes the surrounding gentle, forested mountains. More than 100 bird species have been identified here. One of North America's
most productive wildlife habitats, the area has the greatest overall nesting density of
ducks in Alaska. Most abundant are pintails, scoters, widgeons, and scaup; 10 to 15
percent of the continent's canvasback ducks breed here. Watch for caribou in the
uplands, and, throughout, moose, black bears, brown (grizzly) bears, coyotes, wolves,
wolverines, red foxes, snowshoe hares, marten, mink, muskrats, beavers, and river
otters.

Recreation: The roadless refuge has no recreational development for visitors.
Camping is unrestricted on public lands, but since extensive private lands line the rivers,
especially near villages, try to ask before using an area. Campfires normally are permitted, although restrictions may be in effect during dry periods. Fishing, hunting,
powerboats, fixed-wing aircraft, and snowmobiles are permitted. Expect large populations of mosquitoes and other biting insects during summer months.

Water travel: Beaver Creek National Wild and Scenic River, WW1–FWB (see No.
87, White Mountains National Recreation Area); Birch Creek National Wild and Scenic
River, FWC within the refuge (see No. 85, Steese National Conservation Area, for upper
river description); Black River, WW1–FWA, from lakes near Grayling Fork to Fort
Yukon, 290 miles (470 km); Chandalar River, North Fork, WW3–FWA, from Chandalar
Lake to Venetie, 130 miles (210 km); Chandalar River, East Fork, WW2–FWA, from
Arctic Village to Venetie, 170 miles (270 km); Porcupine River, WW1–FWB, from upper
Porcupine River or Summit Lake on Bell River, Yukon Territory, to Fort Yukon, 300 miles
(480 km) (you must contact both U.S. and Canadian customs offices for clearance prior
to your trip—see Information Sources in the Appendix for addresses); Sheenjek River,
WW2–FWB (see No. 97, Arctic National Wildlife Refuge and Wilderness); Yukon River,
FWC, from Circle to the Dalton Highway bridge, 240 miles (390 km).

Weather and conditions: In this subarctic continental climate, expect warm,
dry summers, and cold, dry, severe winters. Fort Yukon holds the state's high temperature record of 100 degrees F (38 degrees C). (See the Fort Yukon weather table.) Winds
normally are light.

Directions/access: The southwestern section of the refuge is accessible from the
Dalton Highway near the Yukon River bridge; a public boat ramp is at Mile 56.6, at the
north end of the bridge. Boaters may also reach the refuge via the Yukon River from
Circle, at the north end of the Steese Highway. Scheduled air service stops at Beaver,
Chalkyitsik, Fort Yukon, and Stevens Village. Air taxis, boat charters, restaurants, and
lodging are available in Fairbanks, Circle, and Fort Yukon; most of the villages have
general stores.

WESTERN/BERING SEA COAST

The flat, treeless plain bordering the Bering Sea north of the Alaska Peninsula and continuing northward to Point Hope on the Chukchi Sea has a climate controlled by the nearness of open ocean. Maritime influences create cool summers, with considerable cloudiness, fog, and drizzle near the coast. At increasing distances from the coast, continental masses begin to dominate the weather. Winter temperatures vary between 0 degrees F (minus 18 degrees C) and freezing so long as open water remains offshore; lower temperatures occur once the ocean has frozen in January. Seas in the southern extent of the region normally are blocked by significant ice formation from December through April; in the north, ice halts shipping from October through June.

Despite extensive overcast, precipitation is light. Summer showers bring the largest amount; snow, sometimes wet and heavy, falls from late September to May. Winds blow moderately and steadily along the coast, frequently reaching gale force.

Much of the area is covered by moist tundra. Cottongrass tussocks predominate, with pockets of dwarf shrubs or alder–willow thickets. Where the land is flat with much underlying permafrost and standing water, many shallow lakes dot the wetlands, particularly in the Yukon–Kuskokwim delta. Here the vegetation is primarily a sedge–cottongrass mat, but with few tussocks.

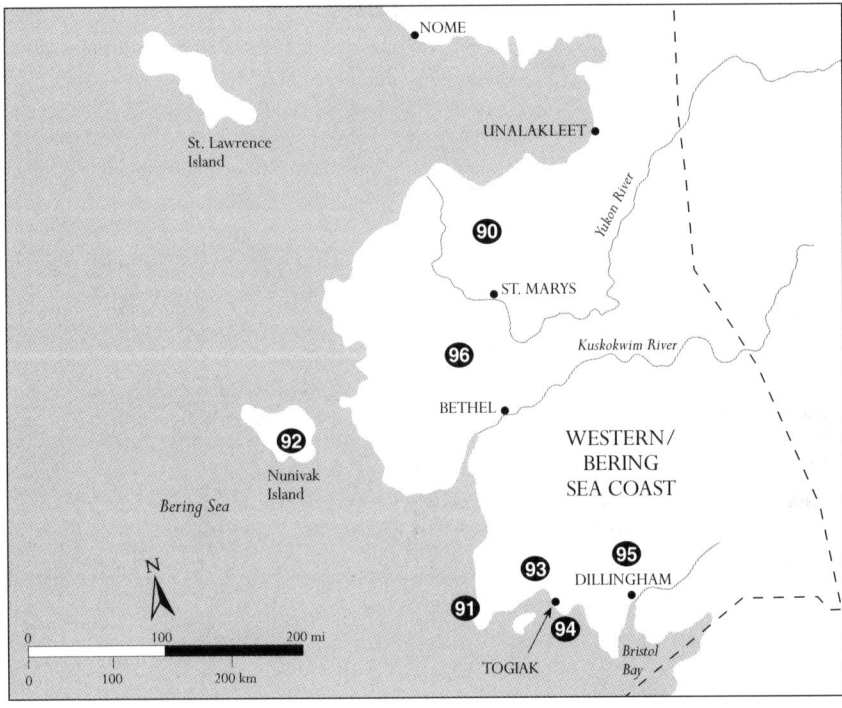

90 Andreafsky Wilderness, Yukon Delta National Wildlife Refuge

Location: Northwest of St. Marys

Size: 1,100,000 acres (445,000 hectares)

High point: 3408 feet (1039 m)

Low point: 25 feet (8 m)

Best time of year: Foot, late May–September; boat, late May–September; ski, February–April

Daylight: June 21: 20½ hours

December 22: 5 hours

Activities: Boating, fishing, hunting, ski touring, backpacking

USGS maps: Holy Cross, Kwiguk, St. Michael, Andreafsky, Unalakleet

Established: 1980

Managed by: U.S. Fish and Wildlife Service

A wilderness section of the Yukon Delta National Wildlife Refuge, Andreafsky contains two of the most important salmon-spawning streams in the entire Yukon drainage, the Andreafsky and its East Fork.

Flora and fauna: In parallel valleys, the clear waters of the Andreafsky River and its East Fork flow through tundra-covered uplands to meander through balsam poplar and white spruce forests lower down. Area Eskimos once commercially herded reindeer here, but the herds were later abandoned. The animals joined local migrating caribou to interbreed, producing strangely marked wild offspring. The wilderness supports abundant populations of large mammals, notably brown (grizzly) bears that fish the rivers for salmon in July and August. Watch also for black bears, moose, beavers, arctic foxes, red foxes, lynx, river otters, wolves, and wolverines.

Recreation: An area without recreational development, Andreafsky attracts river runners, fishermen, hunters, backpackers, and ski tourers. Fixed-wing aircraft may land within the wilderness; powerboats and snowmobiles are permitted. Camping is unrestricted, but avoid areas heavily used by bears. Campfires are permitted, but use a camping stove in tundra areas or build fires on river gravel.

River otters are among the wildlife that inhabit the Andreafsky Wilderness. ASP photo

90a Andreafsky National Wild River.

This river is rated WW2–FWB; the East Fork is WW1–2. A popular trip length is 100 miles (160 km). The Andreafsky is reached by air taxi to upriver lakes or, for the East Fork, an upriver location at the 500- to 1000-foot (150- to 300-m) elevation. The trip ends at St. Marys, at the confluence of the Andreafsky and Yukon Rivers, elevation 20 feet (6 m). All but the lower 20 to 30 miles (30 to 50 km) is designated Wild River.

Weather and conditions: Due to its proximity to salt water, the wilderness has a subarctic climate that is transitional between maritime and continental. Expect cool summers, with some fog and some warm days; winters are cold, dry, and severe. (See the Bethel weather table.) Winds are moderate to light.

Directions/access: St. Marys, a transportation center for the lower Yukon River area, provides modern visitor facilities, frequent scheduled flights from Anchorage, and air taxi service.

---

91 Cape Newenham State Game Refuge

Location: Southwest of Dillingham

Size: 15,360 acres (6144 hectares)

High point: 649 feet (195 m)

Low point: Sea level

Best time of year: Foot, June–September; boat, June–September; ski, January–April

Daylight: June 21: 18½ hours

December 22: 6 hours

Activities: Birding, photography, hunting, fishing

USGS maps: Hagemeister Island C-5, C-6, C-7, D-5, D-6

Established: 1960

Managed by: Alaska Department of Fish and Game

Located just north of Cape Newenham, on the shores of the Bering Sea, Chagvan Bay is a shallow estuary with large eelgrass beds. The refuge was established to protect the Chagvan Bay waterfowl habitat and is located within Togiak National Wildlife Refuge. In the local language of Yup'ik Eskimo, *chagvan* means "briskly flowing water," an apt name considering the tidal action here.

Flora and fauna: Eelgrass grows in abundance along the shores. The bay is an important stopover for hundreds of thousands of ducks, geese, and shorebirds headed to or from nesting areas. Among them are black brant, emperor geese, Taverner's Canada geese, and pintails. Other birds include greater white-fronted geese, northern shoveler, scaup, mallard, American green-winged teal, red-breasted merganser, black scoter and white-winged scoter, harlequin, oldsquaw, and all three species of eider. Offshore, watch for sea lions, harbor seals, and walrus. Gray and beluga whales are occasionally spotted as well. Brown (grizzly) bears may be seen along the beaches. Other furbearers include river otters, mink, red fox, and wolverine.

Recreation: The refuge is undeveloped for public recreation. Main uses include subsistence hunting and fishing by residents of Togiak, Goodnews, and Platinum. A commercial herring fishery has developed in the waters offshore.

Shallow Chagvan Bay is the primary feature of Cape Newenham, which attracts migrating ducks, geese, and shorebirds.   USFWS photo

Weather and conditions: Expect cool, foggy summers near the coast. Winters are cold, dry, and severe in this subarctic maritime continental climate. (See the King Salmon weather table.) Winds are moderate and continuous.

Directions/access: There is no developed access to the refuge. Residents of nearby Platinum and Goodnews travel here by beach and boat; from Togiak, villagers travel here by snowmobile. Scheduled air service, or air taxi service, is available to any of the three communities from Dillingham or Bethel. Lodging, restaurants, and grocery stores may be found in Togiak, Goodnews, Dillingham, and Bethel.

92 Nunivak Wilderness, Yukon Delta National Wildlife Refuge

Location: On Nunivak Island
Size: 600,000 acres (243,000 hectares)
High point: 1675 feet (511 m)
Low point: Sea level
Best time of year: Foot, June–August; boat, June–August; ski, February–April
Daylight: June 21: 19 hours

December 22: 6 hours
Activities: Hiking, fishing, hunting, photography
USGS maps: Cape Mendenhall, Nunivak Island
Established: 1929; amended 1980
Managed by: U.S. Fish and Wildlife Service

Once ranging freely across the North American tundra, the musk ox was an easy target for rifle-wielding explorers and Eskimos; the last survivors in Alaska, a herd of 13, were killed about 1865. In an attempt to reestablish the musk oxen, 34 animals were

Musk oxen are prized for their ultrasoft underwool, which is spun and woven into hats and scarves.   USFWS photo

brought from Greenland in 1935, studied at the University of Alaska at Fairbanks for 5 years, and then moved to predator-free Nunivak Island. By 1968, the free-roaming herd on this treeless, windswept island had increased to 750, and animals were transplanted to other areas of Alaska: Nelson Island, Barter Island, Kavik River, and Cape Thompson. In 1980, the State of Alaska transferred ownership of some of the herds to Oomingmak, an Eskimo cooperative formed to manufacture and distribute luxury, handcrafted garments made from qiviut, the extraordinarily soft underhair of the animal. Since the island can support a herd of only about 500 animals, musk ox hunting, with permits selected by lottery, has continued since 1975.

Caribou formerly lived on the island but, according to Eskimo legend, "walked away into the sky" about 1880. Reindeer were brought to the island in 1920 and today number about 4000. The herd is the property of the islanders, supplying meat, hides, and antlers for food, clothing, and crafts. The Eskimos of Mekoryuk, on the north side of the island, have a close tie with the wilderness, whose lands and waters they have hunted for thousands of years; the tradition continues today.

The entire island, except for privately held lands, is included in the Yukon Delta National Wildlife Refuge, with the southern half, 600,000 acres (243,000 hectares), designated as Wilderness. A tundra-topped volcanic island with rolling hills, Nunivak has volcanic cones, sand dunes, beaches, sea cliffs, salt-water lagoons, lakes, and streams.

Flora and fauna: The wilderness contains large eelgrass beds—a food source for migrating waterfowl—and extensive seabird rookeries, and is the wintering ground for the McKay's snow bunting. Mink, red foxes, and arctic foxes are found on the island. Sea lions, seals, walruses, and whales are offshore.

Recreation: There is no recreational development within the wilderness. Several private adventure guide services operate out of Mekoryuk. Camping is permitted throughout; firewood is scarce. Fishing, hunting, powerboats, snowmobiles, and fixed-wing aircraft are permitted.

Weather and conditions: Hypothermia is a constant danger on this wet, windswept island; prepare for long periods of rain and fog. In the subarctic maritime climate, summers are cooler than in Bethel, foggy, and overcast; winters are cold and dry. (See the Nunivak Island weather table.)

Caution: Winds are strongest from August through October. Frequent, violent, and long-lasting storms make boating hazardous in the Bering Sea.

Directions/access: Mekoryuk, the only community on the island, is connected to the mainland by scheduled air service; the nearest air taxi operation is in Bethel. Mekoryuk has a store but no commercial lodging, although arrangements can be made. Call the NIMA Corp., the village corporation, at (907) 827-8313.

93 Togiak National Wildlife Refuge and Wilderness

Location: West of Dillingham
Size: 4,097,431 acres (1,638,972 hectares)
High point: 5500 feet (1700 m)
Low point: Sea level
Best time of year: Foot, June–September; boat, June–September; ski, January–April
Daylight: June 21: 18½ hours

December 22: 6 hours
Activities: Camping, fishing, hunting, snowmobiling, river running
USGS maps: Bethel, Dillingham, Goodnews, Hagemeister Island, Nushagak Bay
Established: 1980
Managed by: U.S. Fish and Wildlife Service

Protecting major salmon-spawning streams and important seabird-nesting areas, the refuge stretches from restless ocean shores to the treeless tundra uplands of the Ahklun Mountains. The area, which has been occupied for 5000 years by Yup'ik Eskimos and Aleut Indians, has also seen Captain James Cook, Russian explorers, and numerous U.S. miners. Today, residents of the area continue to use the resources of the refuge for their subsistence needs.

The former Cape Newenham National Wildlife Refuge, established in 1969, is now included in Togiak National Wildlife Refuge. Cape Newenham State Game Refuge, established in 1960 to protect the Chagvan Bay waterfowl habitat and now located within Togiak National Wildlife Refuge, continues to be administered by the Alaska Department of Fish and Game. The northern half of Togiak NWR, 2,270,000 acres (919,000 hectares), has been designated as Wilderness.

Flora and fauna: The largest seabird colonies are found at Cape Newenham and Cape Pierce, where more than a million birds are found offshore in the summer. Waterfowl use the marshy lowlands, lagoons, and numerous lakes of the southern part of the refuge as well as the lowlands along the Togiak River. Common mammals of the

Horned puffins   ASP photo by Robert Angell

refuge uplands are brown (grizzly) bears, moose, wolves, wolverines, and, offshore, sea otters, seals, sea lions, walruses, and whales.

Recreation: Camping is unrestricted and campfires are permitted in this undeveloped roadless refuge; a camping stove is recommended. Avoid attracting or interfering with bears, which are most likely to be found along streams with spawning salmon. Expect large populations of mosquitoes and other biting insects in summer months. Carry extra food since fog, storms, or wind often delay planned air pickup. Fishing, hunting, horses, powerboats, snowmobiles, and fixed-wing aircraft landings are permitted. Numerous private landholdings exist within the refuge.

Water travel: Kanektok River, WW3–FWC, from Kagati Lake to Quinhagak, 80 miles (130 km); Togiak River, WW2–FWC, from Togiak Lake to Togiak, 60 miles (100 km), WW1–2, from Upper Togiak Lake to Togiak Lake, 10 miles (16 km); Goodnews River, WW3–FWC, from Goodnews Lake to Goodnews Bay, 60 miles (100 km).

Weather and conditions: Expect cool, foggy summers near the coast, warmer summers inland. Winters are cold, dry, and severe in this subarctic maritime continental climate. (See the King Salmon weather table.) Winds are moderate and continuous along the coast, lighter inland.

Directions/access: The refuge is reached by air, with scheduled service to Dillingham, Goodnews, Manokotak, Platinum, Quinhagak, Togiak, and Twin Hills. Air taxis are available at Dillingham. Manokotak, Quinhagak, Togiak, and Dillingham have stores; the latter two also have restaurants and lodging.

94 Walrus Islands State Game Sanctuary

Location: In Bristol Bay south of Togiak
Size: 162,200 acres (64,880 hectares)
High point: 1400 feet (430 m)
Low point: Sea level
Best time of year: June–August
Daylight: June 21: 18½ hours
    December 22: 6 hours

Activities: Wildlife-viewing, photography
USGS maps: Hagemeister Island C-1,
    C-2, D-I; Nushagak Bay
Established: 1960
Managed by: Alaska Department of Fish
    and Game

When the pack ice retreats north in the spring, Alaska's migratory wildlife returns home from wintering farther south. Seabirds, of course, return to the Walrus Islands' rocky cliffs, but the most spectacular sight is the 8000 to 12,000 Pacific walruses that haul out on Round Island. Meanwhile, sea lions sun on the southern tip of the island and red foxes den on the grassy slopes.

A seven-island sanctuary that includes Round, High, Crooked, and Summit Islands, the refuge was established to protect the last major walrus hauling grounds in the southern Bering Sea.

Flora and fauna: The treeless islands are steep, with many sea cliffs. Watch the waters of Bristol Bay for dolphins, porpoises, seals, and whales. Each summer, the islands

The remote Round Island walrus colony is visited by permit only.   ASP photo

support thousands of seabirds, including common murres, black-legged kittiwakes, pelagic cormorants, parakeet auklets, horned and tufted puffins, pigeon guillemots, and glaucous-winged gulls.

Recreation: Round Island, focal point for most visitors, has public viewing and public access facilities that are staffed for part of the year. Camping is restricted to specific areas, and fresh water is abundant. Fishing, hunting, and firearms are prohibited; use of fixed-wing aircraft and boats is restricted.

Weather and conditions: Violent storms with winds up to 75 mph (120 kph) hit the islands during the summer. Be sure your equipment and clothing are strong, warm, and waterproof. Many shredded tents have been hauled from the island. A good rain parka, pants, and waterproof boots are a necessity; bring clothes that are warm even when wet. Hypothermia is a serious danger here. Bring a minimum of 4 days' extra food; storms have delayed pickup for up to 2 weeks. Visitors must be strong, in good health, and prepared for a rugged wilderness experience.

In this subarctic maritime climate, summers normally are cool, foggy, and overcast; winters are cold, foggy, and overcast. (See the King Salmon weather table.)

Directions/access: The islands are extremely isolated and hard to reach. There are no good anchorages. Most visitors arrive by air taxi from Dillingham or by charter boat from Togiak. Both towns have scheduled air service and food. Dillingham, a transportation hub, has lodging and a larger selection of stores and services.

Permits are required to visit Round Island and adjacent waters between May 1 and September 1. There are set conditions by which visitors must abide to ensure that walrus will not abandon haul-out sites. Permits are obtainable from department offices in Dillingham, Anchorage, and King Salmon; specify dates desired. Up to 30 permits (15 overnight and 15 day visitors) at a time can be issued.

95 Wood-Tikchik State Park

Location: North of Dillingham
Size: 1,547,600 acres (619,040 hectares)
High point: 5026 feet (1532 m)
Low point: 40 feet (12 m)
Best time of year: Foot, mid-June–September; boat, mid-June–September; ski, February–April
Daylight: June 21: 19 hours December 22: 6 hours

Activities: Hiking, backpacking, kayaking, lake boating, ski touring, fishing, hunting, river running
USGS maps: Bethel, Dillingham, Goodnews, Taylor Mountains
Established: 1978; amended 1985
Managed by: Alaska Division of Parks and Outdoor Recreation

Spectacular glacier-carved lakes interconnect among tundra-covered craggy mountains. The park takes in six principal lakes, with Lake Nerka the largest, 29 miles (47 km) long, and Lake Nuyakuk the deepest, at 930 feet (280 m). Both lake systems are important salmon-spawning areas for the Bristol Bay salmon fishery. Although the Wood River and Tikchik Lakes area has long been used by local Eskimos for fishing, hunting,

Milk Creek and Chikuminuk Lake are part of the multiple lakes and connecting waterways in Wood–Tikchik State Park.   ASP photo

and trapping, its first contact with the outside world was in 1818, when Russian fur traders established a trading post near present-day Dillingham.

Flora and fauna: In addition to the five species of Pacific salmon, wildlife common to the area includes moose, black bears, brown (grizzly) bears (especially along the Tikchik River), caribou, beavers, muskrats, river otters, red foxes, wolverines, marmots, golden eagles, ptarmigan, and numerous migratory waterfowl species.

Recreation: An undeveloped wilderness park, Wood–Tikchik attracts hikers and backpackers, kayakers, lake boaters, river runners, ski tourers, fishermen, and hunters. Camping and the use of powerboats and snowmobiles are permitted; off-road vehicles are not. Fixed-wing aircraft may land only at designated locations. Expect large populations of mosquitoes and other biting insects in summer months.

Water travel: Nuyakuk River, WW2–FWB, from Tikchik Lake to Koliganek, 56 miles (90 km) (portage around the waterfall); Tikchik River, WW1–FWC, Nishlik Lake to Tikchik Lake, 60 miles (97 km); Wood River, WW2–FWB, Lake Kulik to Aleknagik, 86 miles (138 km).

Weather and conditions: Cool overcast summers and cold overcast winters are typical of this subarctic climate, transitional between the maritime and continental. (See the King Salmon weather table, although King Salmon's climate is somewhat more maritime.) Winds generally are moderate, occasionally strong. The terrain generally is brushy to about 1100 feet (330 m); trees seldom extend beyond 900 feet (300 m) elevation. Prominent peak: Mount Waskey, elevation 5026 feet (1532 m).

Caution: Boaters should be alert for sudden winds that can whip up large waves on the lakes. Private lands exist within the park and should be respected.

Directions/access: The park is most easily reached by air taxi from Dillingham or chartered boat from Aleknagik. Both towns have scheduled air service. They are also connected by road, but not to the contiguous state highway system. Meals, lodging, and a variety of stores are available in Dillingham. Wilderness fishing and hunting lodges in the area offer comfortable accommodations, but require reservations.

96 Yukon Delta National Wildlife Refuge

Location: Surrounding Bethel
Size: 19,131,646 acres (7,652,658 hectares)
High point: 4550 feet (1387 m)
Low point: Sea level
Best time of year: Foot, late May–September; boat, late May–September; ski, February–April
Daylight: June 21: 19½ hours December 22: 5½ hours
Activities: Boating, hiking, camping, birding, photography, wildlife-

viewing, fishing, hunting, snowmobiling, river running
USGS maps: Baird Inlet, Bethel, Black, Cape Mendenhall, Goodnews, Holy Cross, Hooper Bay, Kuskokwim Bay, Kwiguk, Marshall, Nunivak Island, Russian Mission, St. Michael, Unalakleet
Established: 1980
Managed by: U.S. Fish and Wildlife Service

Formed by the Yukon and Kuskokwim rivers as they empty into the Bering Sea, this delta, largest in the United States, is one of the most important waterfowl breeding areas in North America, used by millions of migratory birds.

The center of today's Yup'ik culture, the Yukon–Kuskokwim delta contains the largest concentration of Eskimos in Alaska. Living within the heart of the refuge, they continue to use the lands and rivers for subsistence fishing, hunting and trapping—a centuries-old tradition. Extensive private lands exist within the refuge boundaries, especially along rivers and near villages.

Three previously established national wildlife refuges are included in the Yukon Delta National Wildlife Refuge (NWR): Clarence Rhodes NWR, established in 1960, Hazen Bay NWR, established in 1937, and Nunivak NWR, established in 1929. The Nunivak NWR area was designated as Wilderness within the Yukon Delta NWR in 1980, as was a new area, Andreafsky Wilderness. These wildernesses are treated separately in this book (see descriptions No. 92 and 90, respectively).

Flora and fauna: Bird population in the wetlands have changed in the last few decades as waterfowl managers have sought to ensure healthy populations while allowing subsistence and sport hunting practices to continue. In the wetlands nest all of the world's cackling Canada geese, which number more than 200,000 and are on the rise after a sharp decline. (From the 1960s to the mid-1980s, that population fell from more than 400,000 to less than 30,000.) Also nesting in the Yukon–Kuskokwim Delta are 340,000 white-fronted geese, about 100,000 Pacific black brant, and more than 80,000 tundra swans. About 40,000 emperor geese nest here, but that number is unsatisfactory

An aerial view of theYukon Delta   USFWS photo by M. LeFever

to the waterfowl managers, as there were about 140,000 birds in the 1960s. The same concern extends to spectacled eiders. While there were 3000 to 4000 nesting pairs in the late 1990s, in the early 1970s, they numbered 50,000 pairs.

At least 170 species of birds and 43 species of mammals are found regularly in the refuge, of particular note the large populations of furbearers—beavers, red foxes, arctic foxes, marten, mink, muskrats, river otters, and weasels. Wolves, wolverines, and moose are found throughout the eastern portion of the refuge; musk oxen have been established on Nunivak and Nelson Islands. The waterways of the delta are spawning areas for a major salmon fishery.

Containing extensive wet-tundra flatlands, lakes, and ponds, the refuge rises to rolling uplands in the northern and southeastern portions. It is primarily treeless, though forested areas are found inland. Most of the refuge is underlain by continuous permafrost; the coastal areas flood annually.

Recreation: The refuge has no development for recreational visitors. Camping is unrestricted on public lands, but the traveler has the responsibility of identifying which lands are public. Assume that most land along navigable waterways and near villages is private. Ask where you may camp. Do not disturb cabins, fish camps, or equipment. Although the area is treeless, sufficient driftwood for campfires lines the shores of major rivers and the coast. Dry land for campsites and fire pits may be difficult to find in many areas. Fishing, hunting, powerboats, snowmobiles, and aircraft are permitted on public lands. Expect hungry mosquitoes and other biting insects during summer months.

Water travel: Andreafsky National Wild River, WW3–FWB (see description No. 98); Aniak River, WW2–FWB, from Aniak Lake to Aniak, 110 miles (180 km); Kisaralik

River, WW3–FWC, from Kisaralik Lake to Bethel, 160 miles (260 km); Yukon and Kuskokwim Rivers, FWR in the refuge, a gradient less than 0.35 feet per mile (0.062 m/km).

Weather and conditions: Near the coast, weather is typical of the subarctic maritime climate with cool, foggy, summers and cold, dry, severe winters. Further inland, continental forces take effect, with warmer, sunnier summers; winters are severely cold. (See the Bethel weather table.) Winds, constant and generally moderate near the coast, are lighter inland.

Directions/access: Access to the refuge is by air, with daily service to every village on the delta. Bethel is the gateway community, with smaller aircraft connections into villages such as Akiachak, Akiak, Alakanuk, Aniak, Atmautluak, Cape Romanzof, Chefornak, Chevak, Eek, Emmonak, Hooper Bay, Kalskag, Kasigluk, Kipnuk, Kongiganak, Kotlik, Kwethluk, Kwigillingok, Marshall, Mekoryuk, Mountain Village, Napakiak, Napaskiak, Newtok, Nightmute, Nunapitchuk, Russian Mission, St. Marys, Scammon Bay, Stebbins, Toksook Bay, Tuluksak, Tuntutuliak, and Tununak. Air taxis operate from Aniak, Bethel, Emmonak, Hooper Bay, and St. Marys. It's important to note that most villages do not have accommodations for visitors. Most have stores; the larger ones may have a cafe and lodging. (See Table 1, "Access and Services," Appendix.) Bethel and St. Marys are transportation hubs for the area, with modern visitor facilities.

ARCTIC

The North Slope and the north side of the Brooks Range normally are influenced by arctic air masses, resulting in a cold climate throughout the year. Although temperatures normally are comfortable from June through mid-August, freezing temperatures can occur even in summer. Winter lasts 9 months and temperatures are low. Coastal waters contain large masses of ice even in summer.

Precipitation is light throughout the year, appearing in the summer as drizzle and fog. Snow, generally powdery and wind-drifted, covers the ground from September through May. The greatest number of clear days occurs in February and March; cloudiness is most likely July through September. Winds frequently reach gale force and blow more or less continually. Summer days are 24 hours long; winter days consist of a few hours of twilight.

Except for a few isolated stands of trees on river gravel floodplains, the area is treeless. Willow bushes grow profusely in riverbeds. The flat northern coastal areas, underlain by continuous permafrost, are covered by wet tundra with many north–south-oriented shallow lakes. One frequently can observe "patterned ground"—irregular polygon-shaped patterns on the soil, varying from 3 to 90 feet (1 to 27 m) in diameter, formed by repeated freeze–thaw cycles.

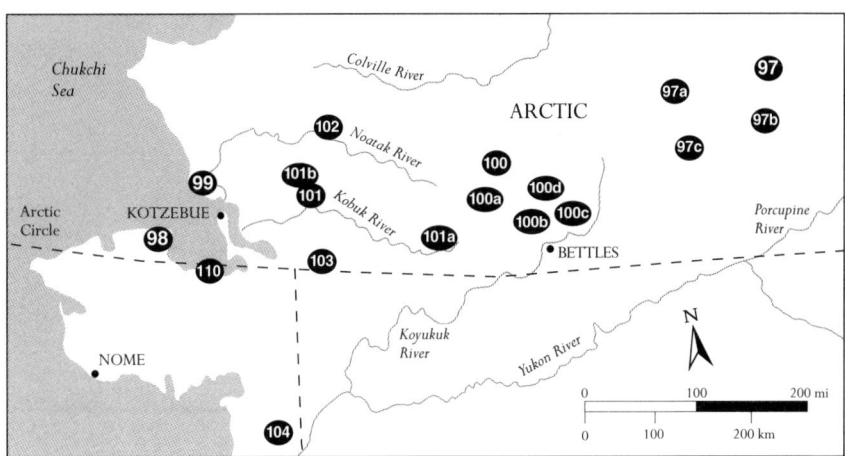

97 Arctic National Wildlife Refuge and Wilderness

Location: North of Fort Yukon
Size: 19,575,711 acres (7,830,284 hectares)
High point: 9050 feet (2758 m)
Low point: Sea level
Best time of year, North Slope: Foot, June–September; boat, late June–August on rivers, mid-July–August along the Arctic coast; ski, March–April
Best time of year, South Slope: Foot, June–September; boat, late May–September; ski, March–April
Daylight: June 21: 24 hours

December 22: 0 hours, with 5 hours of twilight
Activities: Hiking, camping, hunting, fishing, river running, boating
USGS maps: Arctic, Barter Island, Black River, Chandalar, Christian, Coleen, Demarcation Point, Flaxman Island, Mt. Michelson, Philip Smith Mountains, Sagavanirktok, Table Mountain
Established: 1960
Managed by: U.S. Fish and Wildlife Service

From the barrier islands and salt-water lagoons on the Arctic Ocean coast, to the rich boreal forests in valleys of the southern Brooks Range, the refuge and wilderness protect a unique cross-section of arctic and subarctic wildlife habitats. Containing the highest peaks of the Brooks Range, the refuge straddles a 220-mile- (350-km-) long section of the eastern range and includes large drainages on both sides, among them three national wild rivers: the Ivishak, Sheenjek, and Wind. Throughout, land surfaces

An unnamed lake east of the Sheenjek River in Arctic National Wildlife Refuge and Wilderness
USFWS photo by D. Cline

are molded by severe surface freeze–thaw cycles and deeply buried permafrost. Irregular polygon-shaped patterns are particularly conspicuous. Low mounds called *pingos*, "dripping" shapes produced by sliding surface soil, and leaning trees called "drunken forests" may also be seen.

With its name change in 1980, the former Arctic National Wildlife Range also was enlarged, with most of the original range becoming an 8,000,000-acre (3,000,000-hectare) Wilderness. Prominent mountain peaks include Mount Isto, elevation 9050 feet (2758 m); Mount Chamberlin, elevation 9020 feet (2749 m); and Mount Michelson, elevation 8855 feet (2699 m).

Flora and fauna: North of the Brooks Range lie the treeless tundra-covered foothills and flatlands of the Arctic coastal plain. To the south, treeless mountain ridges drop to rich conifer–hardwood forests in the river valleys. By arctic standards, wildlife is abundant. The 125,000-animal Porcupine (River) caribou herd winters on the south side of the Brooks Range in both Alaska and Yukon Territory; in spring, the herd moves north to the coastal plain where cows calve in early June. Except for pregnant females that den ashore in winter, polar bears remain on the offshore ice pack.

Moose, brown (grizzly) bears, wolves, wolverines, and red foxes are found throughout most of the area, while black bears, coyotes, lynx, porcupines, and beavers prefer forest habitats. Dall sheep and marmots like the high mountain country; musk oxen and arctic foxes roam the northern slope. Offshore in the Arctic Ocean swim ringed seals, bearded seals, bowhead and beluga whales, and occasionally spotted seals, walrus, and gray whales. This is fine country for raptors: watch for peregrine falcons, gyrfalcons, rough-legged hawks, golden eagles, and snowy owls as they hunt for lemmings, voles, snowshoe hares, and ground squirrels. The refuge's migratory birds travel to all parts of the world, including Antarctica.

Recreation: Long a mecca for backpackers, river runners, wildlife observers, and other wilderness travelers, the refuge offers excellent hiking terrain for the most part, in mountain valleys with many clear-running streams. Camping is unrestricted in this undeveloped area, and campfires are permitted, but since the existing forests grow so slowly and much of the refuge is treeless, visitors are asked to use camping stoves.

Fishing, hunting, powerboats, and fixed-wing aircraft are all permitted. Pack lots of mosquito repellent, and perhaps a head net, for summer trips.

Water travel: By late July, the sea ice has usually broken up enough to permit small-boat travel along the coast. Peters and Schrader Lakes usually are ice-free by July 20. Extensive overflow ice (*aufeis*) accumulates on many of the floodplains and remains much of the summer; float the channels through the ice cautiously.

97a *Ivishak National Wild River.* Rated WW1–FWC, the Ivishak was designated a Wild River in 1980 and, like the other Wild Rivers, is managed by the U.S. Fish and Wildlife Service. Annual high water is in June; best time of year to float it is in July.

A highly braided swift river on the treeless arctic tundra, the Ivishak flows north toward the Arctic Ocean. The upper half of the river flows through tundra-covered mountains with excellent hiking terrain. By continuing down the Sagavanirktok River, the boater traverses a cross-section of Alaska's North Slope, from the crest of the Brooks Range north to the Arctic Ocean. Wild River designation extends for the first 45 miles (72 km). From Porcupine Lake to the Sagavanirktok River is 95 miles (150 km); to Deadhorse another 55 miles (88 km). In the Inupiat Eskimo language, *Ivishak* means "red earth"; *Sagavanirktok* means "swift current."

To reach the river, take an air taxi to Porcupine Lake (elevation 3000 feet (910 m). Leave the river by air taxi from lakes or gravel bars on the lower Ivishak, elevation 600 feet (180 m), or by automobile from the Dalton Highway just north of Pump Station 2, at about Mile 370, where the Sagavanirktok River closely parallels the road. An alternative take-out point is 55 miles (89 km) downstream at Deadhorse, elevation 43 feet (13 m), the airport and commercial center for the Prudhoe Bay oil field development.

97b *Sheenjek National Wild River.* Rated WW2–FWB, the
Sheenjek was designated a Wild River in 1980. The best time to visit is July through mid-September. The most popular trip length is 270 miles (430 km). High water is mid-May through June.

A gentle clearwater river flowing through a broad valley, the Sheenjek skirts some of the highest peaks in the Brooks Range. Providing a long, relatively easy float through some of Alaska's finest wilderness, the river rises on the Arctic Divide and flows south from open tundra through subarctic boreal forest to the Yukon River wetlands.

Overflow ice accumulates in headwater areas, so scout ahead to be sure the channel is open all the way through. From Ambresvajun (Last) Lake to Fort Yukon is 220 miles (350 km), the first 80 miles (130 km) designated Wild River.

The most popular float trip begins at Ambresvajun (Last) Lake, elevation 2400 feet (730 m), Kuirzinjik (Lobo) Lake, elevation 2200 feet (670 m), or upper river bars, with access by air taxi. Leave the river by air taxi from the lower Sheenjek or the Porcupine River, elevation about 450 feet (140 m), or continue to Fort Yukon. Be sure to beach the boats at Suckel Creek, elevation 420 feet (130 m), a tributary of the Porcupine River just north of Fort Yukon, where a short road leads to the town. The actual confluence of the Porcupine with the Yukon River is 2 miles (3 km) downstream from Fort Yukon.

97c *Wind National Wild River.* Designated a Wild River in 1980, the
Wind is rated WW1–3 with annual high water in May. The best time to visit is July through mid-September.

A swift, challenging, scenic river with headwaters on the Continental Divide in the rugged heart of the Brooks Range, the Wind flows south through a U-shaped valley to meet the broad, forested floodplain of the Chandalar River. The entire length of the Wind is designated as Wild River. Check the water level of the Wind before waving goodbye to the air taxi—the river rating was determined at high water conditions.

Most paddlers continue down the East Fork of the Chandalar River to Venetie. Below the Wind, the East Fork is primarily WW1, with the possibility of some WW2 at low water levels, and may require lining around boulders. Private lands of the Venetie

The course of a meandering stream is visible even in winter.   USFWS photo by Jo Goldmann

Indian Reservation lie east of the East Fork, with the river as the boundary. From Center Mountain Lake to Big Rock Mountain Lake is 80 miles (130 km), and on to Venetie another 100 miles (160 km).

To reach the river, take a floatplane to the lake, elevation 2800 feet (850 m), near Center Mountain. The trip can end with an air taxi pickup on the lake, elevation 1600 feet (490 m), northeast of Big Rock Mountain on the East Fork, or it can continue to Venetie, elevation 300 feet (90 m), which has scheduled air service. Air taxis are based at Fort Yukon, which also has scheduled air service, food, and lodging.

Weather and conditions: The weather north of the Arctic Divide is typical of an arctic maritime climate—cool, dry, and often foggy summers; cold, dry, severe winters. Winds are constant and moderate to strong. South of the Arctic Divide, a subarctic continental climate prevails, with warm, dry summers (somewhat cooler in the mountains, with snow possible at any time) and cold, dry, severe winters. Winds, except in exposed mountain areas, generally are light. (See the Wiseman and Galbraith weather tables.)

Directions/access: This remote, roadless area normally is accessed by air. Air taxis operate from Barter Island (Kaktovik) and Fort Yukon. Scheduled airlines serve Arctic Village, Barter Island, Deadhorse (Prudhoe Bay), Fort Yukon, and Venetie, communities that also have small general stores. Familiarize yourself with village regulations regarding alcohol consumption and transport before you travel. The Dalton Highway skirts the refuge. (See the Dalton Highway description, No. 71.) Mile 211 is about 40 miles (60 km) south of the nearest refuge boundary and 155 miles (249 km) north of the Yukon River. Arctic Village, Deadhorse, and Fort Yukon have lodging.

98 Bering Land Bridge National Preserve

Location: Southwest of Kotzebue
Size: 2,767,520 acres (1,120,000 hectares)
High point: 3380 feet (1030 m)
Low point: Sea level
Best time of year: Foot, June–October; boat, June–September; ski, March–April
Daylight: June 21: 23 hours

December 22: 1 hour
Activities: Camping, hunting, fishing, snowmobiling, wildlife-viewing, photography
USGS maps: Bendeleben, Kotzebue, Shishmaref, Teller
Established: 1980
Managed by: National Park Service

More than 10,000 years ago, humans and many plants and animals are thought to have migrated to North America from Asia across a neck of land now inundated by the Bering Sea. A drop in sea level of only 100 feet (30 m) would re-create a similar "bridge" today connecting Alaska and Russia.

Only 60 miles (100 km) from the Siberian mainland, the preserve contains sea cliffs, lagoons, clear lakes and streams, granite tors, hot springs, lava beds, and significant archaeological sites. Inland, the vast coastal wet-tundra flatlands rise to the rolling treeless uplands of the Bendeleben Mountains. Today, local Eskimos use the area extensively for subsistence hunting and fishing—a primary reason for establishing this preserve.

Many thousands of years ago, the Bering Land Bridge once connected Asia with North America.   APLIC photo

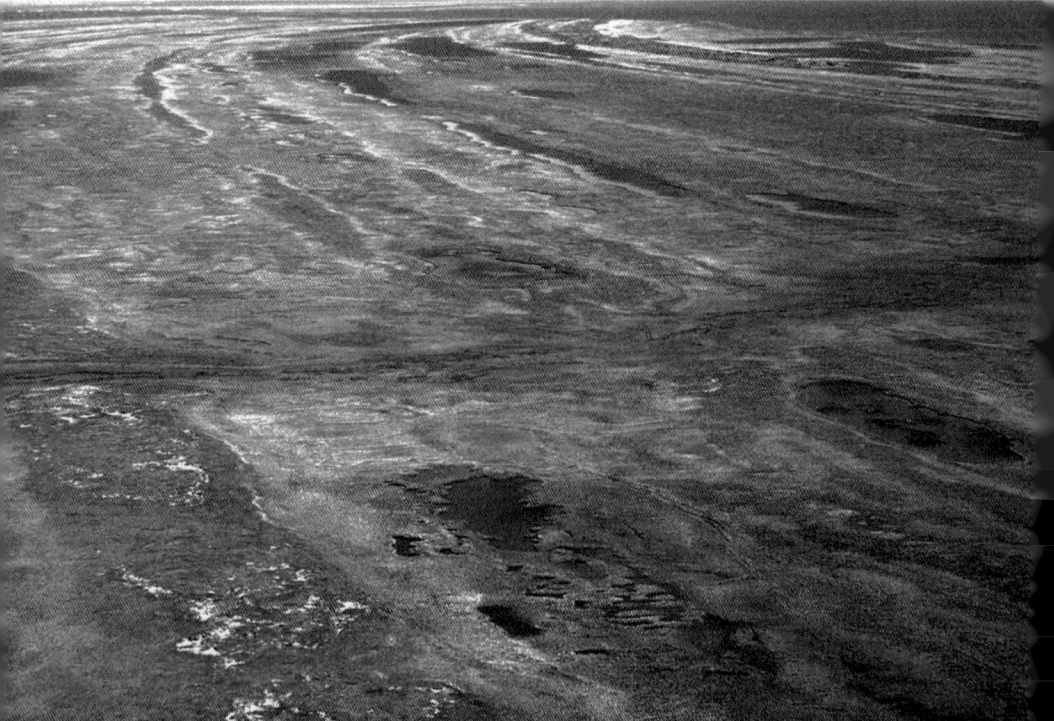

Flora and fauna: Musk oxen have been reestablished in the area surrounding Ikpek Lagoon. The ecological niche normally occupied by caribou has been filled by Eskimo-owned reindeer, a close relative of the gentle tundra traveler. Watch also for moose, brown (grizzly) bears, wolves, wolverines, arctic foxes, red foxes, and, on offshore ice floes, polar bears. Seals, walrus, and whales swim the coastal waters. The shoreline is a major migration route for seabirds and migratory waterfowl, many of which nest on the coastal flatlands.

Recreation: The preserve contains no roads or recreational development. Camping is unrestricted on public lands. Respect the extensive private landholdings, most of which are along the coast and may not be marked. Do not enter cabins or other private structures. Campfires technically are permitted, but wood is scarce, especially inland. Expect mosquitoes in July and August. Prepare for periods of rain and strong winds; hypothermia is a constant danger. Fog or winds can delay your air pickup, so carry extra food. Hunting, fishing, firearms, fixed-wing aircraft, powerboats, and snowmobiles are all permitted.

Weather and conditions: In this arctic maritime climate, summers can be cool, foggy, and overcast, with warmer temperatures and more sun inland. Winters are cold, dry, and severe. (See the Kotzebue weather table.) Winds are constant and moderate, frequently strong.

Directions/access: Access to the preserve is by air taxi from Kotzebue or Nome or by charter boat from Shishmaref or Deering. Scheduled air service lands at Kotzebue, Nome, Shishmaref, Deering, and Wales. The villages have small general stores but limited supplies. Restaurants and lodging are available in Kotzebue and Nome.

99 Cape Krusenstern National Monument

Location: Northwest of Kotzebue
Size: 540,000 acres (219,000 hectares)
High point: 2285 feet (696 m)
Low point: Sea level
Best time of year: Foot, June–September; boat, June–August; ski, March–April
Daylight: June 21: 24 hours

December 22: 0 hours, with 6 hours of twilight
Activities: Backcountry hiking, camping, photography
USGS maps: Kotzebue, Noatak
Established: 1978
Managed by: National Park Service

Curving in graceful arcs parallel to the Chukchi Sea shore, 114 beach-sand ridges, deposited over time by the ocean, hide an unusual archaeological site in the far Arctic. The ridges contain artifacts from every known Eskimo occupation of North America in chronological order, dating from 6000 B.C. Some of the artifacts relate to cultures never before described. (Collecting artifacts or bones is prohibited.) Beach ridges continue to form today, mainly at Sheshalik Spit, where local Eskimos fish and hunt marine mammals much as their ancestors did.

Flora and fauna: Five large lagoons and many small lakes dot the wide coastal

An aerial view of Cape Krusenstern APLIC photo

plain of wet tundra. Farther inland, rolling hills topped by dry tundra are connected by large areas of tussock grass, discouraging all but the hardiest foot traveler. Permafrost underlies the area, and only the top 20 inches (50 cm) of soil thaws each year. (During the Pleistocene epoch, when the cape was part of the Bering Land Bridge, the seas and land are thought to have been ice-free.)

Musk oxen, earlier exterminated, have been reestablished in the Mulgrave Hills, joining other mammals of the tundra: caribou, moose, brown (grizzly) bears, red foxes, arctic foxes, wolverines, and wolves. Watch for Dall sheep in the Igichuk Hills and, offshore, polar bears, seals, walrus, and whales.

Recreation: The area is without recreational development. Camping is unrestricted on public lands except in archaeological zones. Respect private lands (extensive along the coast, particularly on the spit) and any structures or possessions that might be on them. Ask locally before selecting a campsite. Drinking water is hard to find near the ocean since the lagoons are brackish and may contain rotting fish. A few small lakes are fresh enough to drink from. Plan to use a camping stove; strong winds and the scarcity of firewood can make campfires impractical. If you build a fire, do so on beach sand, not on tundra or other areas underlain with peat. Fishing, firearms, fixed-wing aircraft, powerboats, and snowmobiles are permitted within the monument; sport hunting is not, although the area is used by the local people for subsistence food gathering.

Weather and conditions: Summers are cool, cloudy, and often foggy, with more sun and warmer temperatures inland. Winters are cold, dry, and severe. (See the Kotzebue weather table.) Winds are constant and moderately strong most of the time, very strong during storms.

Caution: Hypothermia is a constant danger—prepare for long periods of rain and strong winds. Since fog or winds can delay a planned air or water pickup, carry extra food. Those inexperienced in the Arctic should not plan winter visits.

Directions/access: Access to the monument is by light plane or boat, both of which can be chartered in Kotzebue. If you cross from Kotzebue in your own hand-powered boat, be extremely cautious on this frigid, hazardous water. Scheduled air service is available to Kotzebue, Kivalina, and Noatak, all of which have food supplies. Lodging is available at Kotzebue.

100 Gates of the Arctic National Park and Preserve

Come on edge June, 2012

Location: In the Brooks Range

Size: 8,090,000 acres (3,274,000 hectares)

High point: 8510 feet (2594 m)

Low point: 300 feet (90 m)

Best time of year: Foot, mid-June–September; boat, July–August; ski, March–April

Daylight: June 21: 24 hours
December 22: 0 hours, with 5 hours of twilight

Activities: Hiking, river running, mountaineering

USGS maps: Ambler River, Chandalar, Chandler Lake, Hughes, Killik River, Philip Smith Mountains, Survey Pass, Wiseman

Established: 1980

Managed by: National Park Service

A scenic, remote, undeveloped parkland astride the Arctic Divide in the Brooks Range, Gates of the Arctic is one of the finest large wilderness areas in the world. The rugged but not intimidating mountains hold a few glaciers (small by Alaska standards), clearwater rivers, alpine lakes, and mile after mile of inviting tundra-covered slopes. North of the divide, the area is treeless; the lower valleys on the south side are forested. Access to the Arrigetch Peaks area is from the Alatna River. Of the parkland's total size, 7,052,000 acres (2,854,000 hectares) are designated as Wilderness.

Robert Marshall first explored the central Brooks Range in 1929 and eloquently described it in his book *Alaska Wilderness.* He romantically designated as the "Gates of the Arctic" the two peaks, Boreal Mountain and Frigid Crags, that stand as sentinels on the North Fork of the Koyukuk River 100 miles (160 km) north of the Arctic Circle. Other prominent peaks are Mount Igikpak, elevation 8510 feet (2594 m); Mount Doonerak, elevation 7457 feet (2273 m); Cockedhat Mountain, elevation 7610 feet (2320 m); Boreal Mountain, elevation 6666 feet (2032 m); Frigid Crags, elevation 5550 feet (1692 m); and Arrigetch Peaks, elevation 7500 feet (2300 m).

Flora and fauna: Wildlife typical of this arctic/subarctic zone includes Dall sheep, caribou, moose, brown (grizzly) bears, black bears, wolves, wolverines, red foxes, coyotes, lynx, beavers, snowshoe hares, hoary marmots, marten, mink, muskrats, river otters, porcupines, arctic ground squirrels, red squirrels, and northern flying squirrels. Hawks, owls, and ptarmigan are frequently seen. Since vegetation grows so slowly here, the land supports a lower density of animals than is found farther south.

Hiking in Gates of the Arctic National Park and Preserve   APLIC photo

Recreation: A popular area for hiking, river running, and mountaineering, the parkland is getting increasing use in the winter by ski touring parties and dog mushers. Camping is unrestricted, but every effort should be made to avoid destroying the fragile vegetation or leaving any sign of use. Camping stoves are preferred since northern wood grows so slowly. Fishing, firearms, horses, and fixed-wing aircraft are permitted throughout; hunting is permitted in the preserve only, not in the park. Expect hungry mosquitoes until mid-August.

Water travel: Six national wild rivers lie wholly or partially within the park: Alatna, John, Kobuk (see description No. 101), North Fork of the Koyukuk, Tinayguk, and Noatak (see description No. 102). All six were named Wild Rivers in 1980 and all are managed by the National Park Service.

100a *Alatna National Wild River.* The Alatna is rated WW3–FWB; popular trip lengths are 74 miles (120 km) to 260 miles (420 km). Annual high-water months are July through August; the best time to float is July through September. A clearwater river winding through the heart of the Brooks Range, the Alatna drains south from the treeless Arctic Divide to the Koyukuk River lowlands. Flowing through rugged alpine mountains in its upper reaches, then past quiet lakes, it finally meanders in long swings across the broad, forested valley floor. The Arrigetch Peaks area is reached from the Alatna River near Circle Lake or from Takahula Lake.

One of the popular float trips begins near the headwaters at a series of unnamed alpine lakes and ends at the village of Allakaket, about 260 miles (about 420 km)

downstream. Shorter sections can also be run, but check with your air taxi pilot for access. Wild River designation extends from the headwater lakes to the Gates of the Arctic National Park boundary, a distance of about 90 miles (140 km). The river presents no serious obstacles to boaters, although the section from the headwater lakes to Unakserak River may require considerable lining.

There are no visitor facilities or marked trails. Sport-fishing is permitted in the Alatna River valley; sport hunting is not.

To reach the river, take a scheduled air carrier from Fairbanks to Bettles (Evansville), then charter an air taxi to the river. Popular river access points are unnamed lakes at elevation 2800 feet (850 m), at the headwaters of the Alatna River, and Circle Lake, elevation about 900 feet (about 300 m), near Arrigetch Creek. Floatplanes also land on Takahula Lake, elevation 810 feet (250 m); a short portage trail leads to the river. Leave the river by air taxi from Malamute Fork, elevation 700 feet (200 m), or by scheduled air carrier from Allakaket, elevation 400 feet (100 m). Bettles (Evansville) and Allakaket have stores; Bettles (Evansville) has a lodge with food service and showers.

100b *John National Wild River.* The best time of year to float the John

is July through September; high water is July and August. It is rated WW1–3 from Anaktuvuk Pass; WW1–2 from Hunt Fork. A scenic clearwater river winding from a remote rugged mountain wilderness, the John drops gently from treeless alpine headwaters to richly forested lowlands. The valley is narrow enough to bring the mountains close to the river. Hiking is excellent in the upper river area. From Hunt Fork to Bettles (Evansville) is about 100 miles (160 km). Since the John enters the Koyukuk about 5 miles (8 km) downstream from Bettles (Evansville), allow a day to line upriver.

Above Hunt Fork, water levels normally are too low to float, although some boaters have portaged and lined from Anaktuvuk Pass. Expect some WW3 rapids, for experienced boaters only. A strenuous but rewarding alternative is to hike the 40 miles (64 km) from Anaktuvuk Pass, arriving in time to meet the boats when they are flown into Hunt Fork Lake. Expect some difficult stream crossings.

The name "Anaktuvuk" is said to come from the Eskimo word *anaqtoq* ("dung"), referring to the presence of caribou. Not surprisingly, the John River valley is a major migration route between their summer and winter ranges.

To reach the river, take an air taxi from Bettles (Evansville) to Hunt Fork Lake, elevation 1149 feet (350 m). Leave the river by air taxi from Old Bettles (Evansville), elevation 600 feet (200 m), at the mouth of the John, or line upstream to Bettles (Evansville).

100c *North Fork, Koyukuk National Wild River.* Rated

WW1–2, the North Fork of the Koyukuk is best visited between July and September; high-water months are July and August. A popular trip length is 100 miles (160 km). A clearwater river surrounded by rugged mountain scenery, the North Fork of the Koyukuk drains south-facing slopes of the central Brooks Range. In its upper reaches, it flows past Doonerak Mountain and through the Gates of the Arctic, which are Boreal

Mountain and Frigid Crags. Take a few days to explore the upper river before beginning the float downstream.

From the Redstar Creek lakes to Bettles (Evansville) is about 100 miles (160 km). Boaters have flown into Summit Lake at the headwaters of the North Fork, but if you do so, expect a difficult portage and considerable lining well past Doonerak Mountain. The distance from the lake to Redstar Creek is about 60 miles (100 km). After Squaw Rapids, WW2, at the confluence of the Glacier River, the river enters a broad valley with wetlands and low rolling hills. Except at the extreme headwaters, the river valley is forested.

To reach the river, take an air taxi from Bettles (Evansville) to Summit Lake, elevation 3500 feet (1100 m), or Redstar Creek lakes, elevation 1500 feet (460 m). Park Service personnel suggest hiking from Summit Lake through the Gates of the Arctic, and arranging to pick up boats or rafts where the river is deep enough to float. End the float trip at Bettles (Evansville), elevation 600 feet (180 m), which has scheduled air service, food, lodging, and a general store.

100d *Tinayguk National Wild River.* The Tinayguk is rated WW2; a popular trip length is 120 miles (190 km). The best time to float it is July through September; annual high-water months are July and August. A small, clear river flowing through a glacier-carved alpine valley in the Brooks Range, the Tinayguk has extensive rocky rapids, especially at low water. Heading in the rugged Endicott Mountains and flowing southward from the Arctic Divide, the river drains into the North Fork of the Koyukuk National Wild River. Only a few scattered stands of spruce in the valley bottom dot the sweep of the tundra. The Tinayguk is a remote valley not often visited, and its entire river length is designated as Wild River. From the Savioyok Creek confluence to Bettles (Evansville) is about 120 miles (190 km). About 35 miles (56 km) of this distance is on the Tinayguk.

The river is reached by taking a light plane from Bettles (Evansville) to gravel bars in the vicinity of Savioyok Creek, elevation 2000 feet (600 m), or by hiking over Inukpasugruk Creek from Anaktuvuk Pass community, a distance of 16 miles (26 km). End a float trip at Bettles (Evansville).

Other rivers: Ambler River, WW2–3, from the upper river to Ambler, 80 miles (130 km); Anaktuvuk River, WW3–FWA, from Cache Lake to the Colville River, 120 miles (190 km); Etivluk River, WW2–FWB, Nigtun Lake to Umiat, 160 miles (260 km); Killik River, WW1–3, from the lake at headwaters of Easter Creek to Umiat, 120 miles (190 km); Nigu River, WW3–FWB, from the lake in the pass drained by Nigu and Alatna Rivers to Umiat, 220 miles (350 km).

Weather and conditions: Weather in the parkland varies significantly with location. South of the Arctic Divide and below 2500 feet (760 m), a subarctic continental climate prevails: summers are warm and dry in the lowlands, cooler with more precipitation in the mountains. Winters are cold, dry, and severe, and warmer in the mountains than in the lowlands. (See the Wiseman weather table.) Winds generally are light. Drainages north of the Arctic Divide, below 2500 feet (760 m), have an arctic climate, with cool, dry summers and cold, dry, severe winters. (See the Galbraith weather table.) Winds are light to moderate and frequent. In the higher mountains, above 2500 feet (760 m), summers normally are cool, with frequent overcast skies. Winters are cold and dry, and while temperatures are not so severe as in the southern lowlands, winds can be moderate to strong.

Caution: Numerous private landholdings and mining claims exist within the parkland boundaries; respect private property and do not enter cabins. This is a remote area, not suitable for casual visits; plan your trip carefully.

Directions/access: The parkland is commonly reached by air taxi from Bettles (Evansville), although the village of Anaktuvuk Pass, lying within the park, is served by scheduled airline. Motorists on the rigorous Dalton Highway can reach the park from Wiseman and points north along the Dietrich River. (See the Dalton Highway description, No. 71.) Wiseman, Ambler, and Kobuk have scheduled air service; Ambler also has an air taxi. Bettles (Evansville) has lodging and a dining room; all of the villages have general stores.

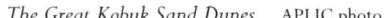

101 Kobuk Valley National Park

Location: Northwestern Alaska, east of Kotzebue
Size: 1,702,000 acres (688,800 hectares)
High point: 4760 feet (1450 m)
Low point: 50 feet (15 m)
Best time of year: Foot, June–September; boat, June–September; ski, March–April

Daylight: June 21: 24 hours
December 22: 1 hour
Activities: Hiking, river running, birding
USGS maps: Ambler River, Baird Mountains, Selawik, Shungnak
Established: 1978
Managed by: National Park Service

Nestled at the southern base of the gentle western Brooks Range, the Kobuk River meanders quietly through a broad forested valley that harbors an amazing treasure: sand dunes. The largest group of barchans—shifting, crescent-shaped dunes—covers 25

The Great Kobuk Sand Dunes   APLIC photo

square miles (65 square km). In this little Sahara in the Arctic, summer air temperatures can soar close to 100 degrees F (38 degrees C). Today's dunes are an exposed portion of a much larger dune field formed by glaciers to the north during the last Ice Age and now stabilized by subarctic vegetation.

The Kobuk Valley region remained ice-free during the glaciation and supported an arctic steppe environment, with grasslands that attracted the large mammals of the Pleistocene. While the animals have vanished, several plants of that epoch have survived on the dunes.

The Kobuk Valley has been used by people for subsistence needs and as a transportation corridor since the Pleistocene. Onion Portage, a shortcut across a sweeping loop in the Kobuk River channel, is one of North America's most important archaeological sites, containing more than 30 layers of artifacts dating as far back as 12,000 years and correlating closely with the beach-ridge artifacts found at Cape Krusenstern National Monument.

Flora and fauna: The park sits astride the transition between boreal forest and the treeless arctic tundra that extends westward to the Chukchi Sea. The Salmon National Wild River drains southward from the Baird Mountains into the Kobuk River.

Used by the western Arctic caribou herd both summer and winter, the valley also is a major junction of the Asiatic and North American migratory bird flyways. Other animals of the park include moose, brown (grizzly) bears, black bears, Dall sheep, wolves, wolverines, and lynx.

Recreation: In this undeveloped park, camping is not restricted except in sensitive archaeological areas and on Native lands; campfires are permitted. Numerous private lands exist within the boundaries, especially along the river; please respect them. Expect large numbers of mosquitoes and other biting insects in summer months. Fishing, firearms, fixed-wing aircraft, powerboats, and snowmobiles are all permitted; sport hunting is not. Good hiking terrain is found in the sand dunes and in the Baird and Waring Mountains.

101a *Kobuk National Wild River.*

This river is rated WW1–FWB with some portaging. A popular trip length is 140 miles (225 km); annual high-water months are July and August. The best time to float the Kobuk is July through September. A gentle woodland river that drains mountain-rimmed Walker Lake, the Kobuk flows through two scenic canyons in the southern Brooks Range foothills to meander across a broad wetland valley near Kobuk village. The upper reaches offer excellent walking and good mountain vistas, but extensive low-elevation hiking is difficult because of forest underbrush and tussock grass. From Walker Lake to Kobuk village is 140 miles (225 km).

Just downstream from Walker Lake, a short stretch of WW3–4 white water can be lined or portaged on the east bank. The Lower Kobuk Canyon, with 1 mile (2 km) of WW2–3 rapids, can be lined along the west bank. Below Pah River, local villagers use the river, winter and summer, for travel between villages and for access to fishing and hunting grounds. Numerous private lands, which may not be posted, line the Kobuk; travel quietly and courteously and respect private property.

To reach the river, take an air taxi from Bettles (Evansville) or Ambler to Walker

Lake, elevation 637 feet (194 m). Float to Kobuk village, elevation 175 feet (53 m), or villages downstream. Scheduled air service serves Bettles (Evansville), Kobuk, Shungnak, Ambler, and most villages beyond, all of which have general stores. Bettles (Evansville) has lodging as well.

101b *Salmon National Wild River.* Designated a Wild River in

1980, the Salmon is managed by the National Park Service. It is rated WW1–FWA, and a popular trip length is 140 miles (230 km). The best time to float it is July through September; annual high-water months are July and August. Rising in the rolling tundra-covered Baird Mountains of the western Brooks Range, the Salmon descends through a poplar–spruce forest to meander finally into the Kobuk River. In its upper navigable reaches, below Anaktok and Sheep Creeks, this clear small river alternates short, shallow pools and riffles. Downriver, the pools lengthen and the river deepens. Plan to spend some time hiking the tundra country above the confluence. From Anaktok and Sheep Creeks to the village of Kiana is about 90 miles (140 km). The entire length is designated as Wild River. There are large amounts of private land along the lower river.

To get to the river, take an air taxi to gravel bars near the confluence of Anaktok and Sheep Creeks, elevation 1700 feet (520 m) or higher. Leave the river at the village of Kiana, elevation 10 feet (3 m). Air taxis, scheduled air service, food, and lodging are available at both Kotzebue and Kiana.

Weather and conditions: A subarctic continental climate brings summers that are often warm and dry, winters that are cold, dry, and severe. (See the Kotzebue weather table.) Strong winds can make float travel difficult.

Directions/access: A roadless area, the park can be reached by air taxi or boat. Ambler, Kiana, and Kotzebue all have air taxis, charter boats, lodging, scheduled air service, and food. Private tour operators in Kiana provide guided river trips.

---

102 Noatak National Preserve

Location: Northeast of Kotzebue
Size: 6,550,000 acres (2,650,000 hectares)
High point: 4915 feet (1498 m)
Low point: 100 feet (30 m)
Best time of year: Foot, mid-June–September; boat, mid-June–August; ski, March–April
Daylight: June 21: 24 hours

December 22: 0 hours, with 5 hours of twilight
Activities: River running, hiking, birding, fishing, hunting
USGS maps: Ambler River, Baird Mountains, Delong Mountains, Howard Pass, Killik River, Misheguk Mountain, Noatak
Established: 1978
Managed by: National Park Service

Far above the Arctic Circle, the treeless sweep of gentle mountains emphasizes the moods of the arctic sky. The endless summer days create a tranquil pace of life. The preserve, along with the western part of Gates of the Arctic National Park, protects

The Noatak River   APLIC photo

almost the entire watershed of the Noatak River, one of the finest large wilderness areas in North America. Except for about 700,000 acres (about 280,000 hectares) near the village of Noatak, the entire preserve is designated as Wilderness. Originally established as a national monument, the area became a national preserve in 1980. Although remote, the preserve attracts many boaters and hikers; it is a gentle wilderness in danger of being trampled by those who come to embrace it.

Wildlife, although abundant by Arctic standards, is limited by the slow-growing northern vegetation. Watch for the western Arctic caribou herd en route between its wintering grounds along the Kobuk River and its summer calving areas north of the Brooks Range. Dall sheep graze mountain slopes throughout the preserve. Look also for moose, brown (grizzly) bears, black bears, wolves, wolverines, and red foxes. The vast treeless tundra makes bird-watching especially rewarding.

Weather and conditions: Summers are often warm and frequently hot in this subarctic solar basin, but prepare also for cold, rainy weather with the possibility of light snow. Near the coast, expect a maritime influence with more overcast skies and fog. Winters are cold, dry, and severe. (See the Kotzebue weather table.) Winds generally are light, but can be strong, making float travel difficult when winds come from the west.

Recreation: Camping is permitted throughout the preserve and is best on river bars and dry tundra knobs. Since northern wood grows so slowly, use a camping stove in this treeless country. If you do build a campfire, build it on river gravel only; tundra wildfires are a serious problem during long, hot summer days. Fishing, hunting, firearms, fixed-wing aircraft, powerboats, and snowmobiles are all permitted.

102a Noatak National Wild River.

This river is rated WW 1–2. A popular trip length is 350 miles (560 km), and mid-June through August is the best time of year. The river, which is managed by the National Park Service, drains westward through a broad, gently sloping valley in the Brooks Range to empty into the Chukchi Sea near Kotzebue. Numerous tributary valleys, especially along the upper half of the river, beckon the hiker. From its headwaters on glacier-pocked Mount Igikpak in Gates of the Arctic National Park, the river flows through narrow canyons, beside steep-walled peaks, across broad lake-dotted basins, and down two canyons to open as a wide braided river on a forested floodplain. The Wild River designation ends at the Kelly River, 33 miles (53 km) above Noatak village. Below Noatak, the river flows through the Igichuk Hills to spread in a wide wetland delta. If you choose to paddle to Kotzebue, be cautious on the delta mudflats and on the frigid, hazardous waters of Hotham Inlet. From Lake Matcharak in Gates of the Arctic National Park to Noatak village is about 350 miles (560 km).

Caution: Travel with care in this extremely remote area. Take extra food, since fog in Kotzebue or clouds over the mountains toward Bettles (Evansville) can delay air pickup. Large numbers of hungry mosquitoes hatch in summer, so carry head nets and a good supply of repellent. Numerous private lands line the lower Noatak within the preserve; try not to camp on private property.

Directions/access: Access to this vast, roadless area is normally by air taxi from Bettles (Evansville) or Kotzebue, both of which have scheduled air service, food, and lodging. Access to float the Noatak River is by air taxi from Bettles (Evansville) or Kotzebue to Lake Matcharak, elevation 1600 feet (488 m), to lakes farther upstream, or to river bars. Pickup can be made from Kotzebue by light aircraft on lakes near the lower river, on the river itself, or on gravel bars—or continue to Noatak village, elevation 50 feet (15 m), which has scheduled air service.

103 Selawik National Wildlife Refuge and Wilderness

Location: East of Kotzebue
Size: 2,150,002 acres (860,001 hectares)
High point: 2021 feet (616 m)
Low point: Sea level
Best time of year: Foot, mid-June–September; boat, July–September; ski, March–April
Daylight: June 21: 24 hours

December 22: 2½ hours
Activities: River running, hiking, birding, fishing, hunting
USGS maps: Selawik, Shungnak
Established: 1980
Managed by: U.S. Fish and Wildlife Service

An extensive system of estuaries, brackish lakes, and wetlands along the lower Kobuk and Selawik Rivers and the uplands of the Selawik River valley, the delta provides prime feeding and nesting habitat for migratory birds from six continents.

Male and female caribou alike grow and shed their antlers annually. USFWS photo by Jo Goldmann

Flora and fauna: Snow geese and sandhill cranes stop en route from northern Siberia to winter in California and Mexico; wheatears fly to Africa; other birds travel to China, India, and Australia. The refuge lands are the only recorded North American nesting area for the Asiatic whooper swan. The Eskimo curlew, now thought to be extinct, was once found in the Kobuk–Selawik area; perhaps it still survives somewhere in this remote region. Birds most commonly found in the refuge are pintails, scaup, cackling Canada geese, lesser Canada geese, white-fronted geese, whistling swans, and all four species of North American loons.

In the uplands, extensive areas of boreal forest with lichen ground cover attract wintering caribou of the western Arctic herd. Where once the woolly mammoth and the saber-toothed tiger roamed, today's refuge inhabitants include moose, black bears, brown (grizzly) bears, arctic foxes, red foxes, lynx, wolves, wolverines, beavers, marten, mink, muskrats, and river otters.

Recreation: In this undeveloped refuge, camping is unrestricted, although campsites are not plentiful in the wetlands. Campfires are permitted, but wood is scarce. Expect large populations of mosquitoes and other biting insects throughout the summer months. Numerous private lands exist within the refuge boundaries. Fishing, hunting, powerboats, snowmobiles, and fixed-wing aircraft are all permitted.

103a *Selawik National Wild River.* This river, a key habitat for the Alaskan sheefish, rises amid spruce forests in the eastern extension of the refuge in the Purcell Mountains. Then, meandering slowly through treeless pingo-dotted wetlands, it enters Selawik Lake, an expansive body of water only 5 to 15 feet (2 to 5 m) deep. The

river is rated WW1; a popular trip length is 230 miles (370 km). The best months for a float are July through September. Designated a Wild River in 1980, the Selawik is managed by the U.S. Fish and Wildlife Service.

Weather and conditions: Summers in the refuge are cool and foggy near the coast, but warmer inland, in this subarctic climate that is transitional between maritime and continental. Winters are cold, dry, and severe. (See the Kotzebue weather table.) Winds normally are moderate, but can be strong near the coast.

Directions/access: Access to the refuge is by air or boat. Air taxis operate from Kiana and Kotzebue; informal boat charters are available at most villages. Kotzebue, Kiana, Noorvik, and Selawik have scheduled air service and general stores. Kotzebue, a transportation and distribution center for northwestern Alaska, provides modern lodgings.

104 Unalakleet National Wild and Scenic River

Location: Western Alaska, east of Unalakleet
River rating: WW2–FWB
Popular trip length: 70 miles (110 km)
Best time of year: June–September
Annual high water: Late May
Daylight: June 21: 21½ hours

December 22: 4 hours
USGS maps: Norton Bay A-2; Unalakleet D-2, D-3, D-4
Designated as Wild River: 1980
Managed by: Bureau of Land Management

A clearwater river, the Unalakleet flows through a broad valley in the rolling tundra-covered Nulato Hills and Kaltag Mountains to empty into the Bering Sea.

The river and its surrounding lands are used extensively by local Eskimos for subsistence fishing and hunting. The old Kaltag Trail, a gold rush sled trail now part of the present Iditarod National Historic Trail, parallels the river from headwaters to Unalakleet. From the Tenmile Creek confluence to the village of Unalakleet is about 70 river miles (110 km).

Flora and fauna: Scattered stands of spruce, birch, and poplar dot the valley. Numerous brown (grizzly) bears fish the river for salmon from mid-June to mid-July. Other wildlife of the valley includes moose, caribou, black bears, wolves, wolverines, red foxes, arctic foxes, lynx, and many species of migratory birds.

Recreation: Camping is unrestricted; campfires, hunting, firearms, snowmobiles, fixed-wing aircraft, and powerboats are permitted. Fishing is excellent for salmon, grayling, and char. Expect large populations of mosquitoes and other biting insects in summer months. Most lands below the Chiroskey River confluence are private.

Weather and conditions: Summers are cool, foggy, and overcast near the coast, warmer and drier inland in this subarctic maritime climate. (See the Nome weather table.) Winds generally are moderate.

Directions/access: Begin your trip by taking a charter boat from Unalakleet to the upper limit of navigation, which is usually at about Tenmile Creek, elevation 300 feet (90 m). Float back down to Unalakleet, at sea level, which has scheduled air service, food, and lodging.

This remote BLM cabin is available by reservation for visitors to the Unalakleet River.   BLM photo

ALASKA MARITIME NATIONAL WILDLIFE REFUGE

A mind-boggling assortment of more than 2500 islands, rocks, spires, reefs, and headlands make up the 3,435,640-acre Alaska Maritime National Wildlife Refuge, established to protect seabirds and marine mammals and their habitats, from farthest north Alaska to the southern tip of the Panhandle.

More than 20 million seabirds, about two-thirds of Alaska's total, use the refuge— more than the sum of all other seabird populations in the Northern Hemisphere. Some of the marine birds are unique to North America, including eight species that breed only in Alaska. Most abundant are murres, auklets, storm petrels, puffins, kittiwakes, fulmars, gulls, cormorants, murrelets, and guillemots. Also protected by the refuge are most of Alaska's sea otters (about 150,000 animals), 70,000 sea lions, and substantial numbers of walrus, seals, and whales.

Ten former refuges, established prior to 1980, are incorporated into the Alaska Maritime National Wildlife Refuge. To indicate the diversity of the refuge lands, these ten, plus one more area added in 1980, are treated separately in this book.

In general, visitors are not encouraged. Human activity is disruptive to bird nesting, breeding, and rearing of young. In some areas, visitor restrictions may be in effect. Camping is permitted in most areas, although it is practical only on larger islands and mainland areas. Campfires may be built, but most areas are treeless, wet, and windswept.

The Alaska Maritime National Wildlife Refuge is mostly undeveloped. Since some parts of the refuge are closed to hunting, powerboats, snowmobiles, and fixed-wing

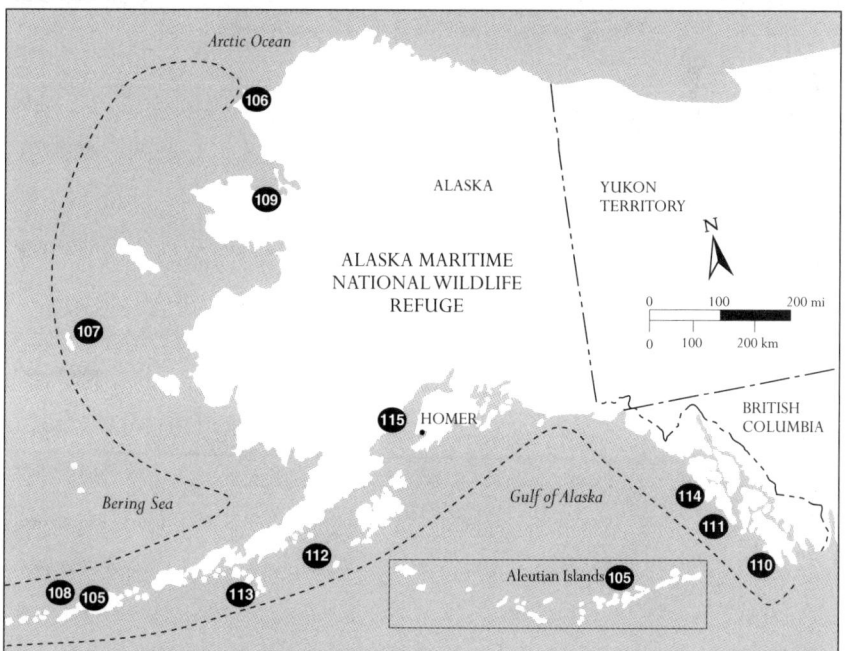

The refuge headquarters and visitors' center is based in Homer.   USFWS photo

aircraft, check with the refuge manager before visiting. A visitors' center and small bookstore in Homer operate daily during the summer months; limited hours in the winter. Programs include displays, naturalists on board some state ferries, videos, slide shows, guided birding tours, and beach walks.

Most of the refuge lands and waters are extremely remote and hard to reach. Frequent violent and long-lasting storms make boating and air travel hazardous; there are few anchorages, protected waters, or airfields. Refer to individual subunit descriptions that follow or contact the refuge manager in Homer for further access information.

For birders interested in specific population figures, counting methods, and field notes, all of which are in the Beringia Seabird computer database, contact the USFWS in Anchorage at (907) 786-3691.

105 Aleutian Islands Subunit

Location: In the Aleutian Islands
Size: 2,720,400 acres (1,100,900 hectares)
High point: 9372 feet (2857 m), Shishaldin Volcano on Unimak Island
Low point: Sea level
Best time of year: Foot, May– September; boat, June–August; ski (marginal), January–March
Daylight: June 21: 17 hours December 22: 7½ hours

Activities: Hiking, camping, wildlife-viewing, photography, fishing, boating, limited hunting
USGS maps: (West to east) Attu, Kiska, Rat Islands, Gareloi Island, Adak, Atka, Seguam, Amukta, Samalga Island, Umnak, Unalaska, Unimak, False Pass, Cold Bay
Established: 1913; amended 1980
Managed by: U.S. Fish and Wildlife Service

The Aleutian Islands, a long chain of ocean-bound volcanoes stretching 1100 miles (1800 km) across the North Pacific Ocean toward Russia, contain great numbers of sea otters, seals, and sea lions, and some of the world's largest seabird rookeries. Kiska is home to the world's largest known colony of crested and least auklets. At least a half-million northern fulmars nest on Chagulak Island. The tiny island of Kaligagan supports more than 100,000 breeding tufted puffins. The largest tufted puffin colony in the state is just to the west on Egg Island, where 163,000 of the birds nest.

Biologically, the Aleutians are stepping-stones between the Asian and North American continents; the western islands have Asian vegetation features, while the eastern islands have plant life typical of the North American mainland. Of the 227 species of birds recorded on the islands, 79 are of Asian origin.

Large concentrations of waterfowl use the islands, both during migrations and as nesting and wintering grounds. One-half of the world's emperor geese winter here. The Aleutian Canada goose, one of the world's rarest birds, has been exterminated by foxes on all but tiny, remote Buldir and Chagulak Islands.

When visited by the first Europeans—Vitus Bering and his crew, in 1741—the islands already were home for the gentle Aleuts. Two years later, Russian fur traders swarmed in, plundering from the Aleuts and enslaving them to harvest sea otters. Partly due to newly introduced diseases, the Aleut population dropped from about 20,000 to fewer than 2500 by 1850. The sea otter population was nearly exterminated by 1911 through the efforts of both Russian and U.S. traders. Today, the Aleut population is healthy, and the sea otters are increasing in numbers.

Many of the islands contain abandoned military installations and other remnants of World War II battles against Japanese invaders. At press time, the installation at Adak was in the process of transforming from a naval base to a private community. The facility at Shemya is closed.

Originally known as the Aleutian Islands National Wildlife Refuge, in 1980 the area was redesignated as part of the newly formed Alaska Maritime National Wildlife Refuge. It includes 2,210,000 acres (894,000 hectares) of Wilderness.

Flora and fauna: The islands, many with active volcanoes, rise directly from the ocean, skirted with treeless grasslands and tundra-covered slopes; the highest are Shishaldin Volcano, elevation 9372 feet (2857 m), on Unimak Island and Makushin Volcano, elevation 6680 feet (2036 m), on Unalaska Island. Almost all land mammals on the islands have been introduced by man. Commercial fur farming from 1915 into the 1940s brought the arctic fox; now wild, the foxes prey upon the native fauna. Caribou have been introduced on Adak; reindeer have been introduced on Atka and Unimak Islands. Only Unimak, a short 0.5 mile (0.8 km) from the mainland, supports naturally occurring caribou, as well as brown (grizzly) bears, wolves, wolverines, red foxes, arctic foxes, and river otters.

Recreation: Commercial lodging is available at Dutch Harbor. Camping and campfires are permitted throughout the refuge; plenty of driftwood, often wet, can be found along the coast, but plan to use a camping stove inland. Portions of several islands are Native-owned; be certain of land status before you set up camp—better yet, check in with the refuge office at (907) 235-6546 before embarking on your trip. Fishing, hunting, and fixed-wing aircraft are permitted generally; some areas are closed to powerboats and snowmobiles.

Weather and conditions: The North Pacific Ocean and the Bering Sea produce a maritime climate at its foggiest; the Aleutians create a barrier between the frigid Bering

Backpacking on Adak USFWS photo

Sea and the warm Japanese and California currents arriving from the south. Summers are cool and wet; winters are mild and wet. (See the Atka and Cold Bay weather tables.) Winds are constant and moderate to strong; frequently storm follows storm, accompanied by violent wind squalls.

Caution: Due to the frequent storms, fog, and lack of protected waters, boating is hazardous. Hypothermia is an ever-present danger.

Directions/access: Access to the refuge is normally by air; allow extra time and food for delays caused by weather. Atka, Akutan, Cold Bay, Dutch Harbor/Unalaska, False Pass, and Nikolski have scheduled air service; air taxis are available at Cold Bay and Dutch Harbor. The southwestern Alaska state ferry visits Cold Bay bimonthly. Stores and/or restaurants can be found at Akutan, Nikolski, Cold Bay, and Dutch Harbor.

Because of the distances involved, a visit to the refuge can be expensive and requires careful preparation. Persevere: Many travelers feel the Aleutians are the most fascinating part of Alaska.

106 Ann Stevens-Cape Lisburne Subunit

Location: Northwest of Kotzebue
Size: 20,000 acres (8100 hectares)
High point: 2034 feet (620 m)
Low point: Sea level
Best time of year: June–September
Daylight: June 21: 24 hours
    December 22: 0 hours, with 5 hours
    of twilight
Activities: Birding, camping, fishing, hunting, snowmobiling
USGS map: Point Hope
Established: 1980
Managed by: U.S. Fish and Wildlife Service

The headlands of Cape Lisburne project from the far northwest corner of Alaska into the frigid Chukchi Sea. Precipitous rock cliffs provide no harbors or anchorages in this area of drifting ice and strong ocean currents. A U.S. Air Force early-warning site perches on the cape. The refuge was named in memory of Ann Stevens, wife of one of Alaska's U.S. senators.

At nearby Cape Thompson, early sailors listened for the commotion of cliff-nesting seabirds to help them avoid the headlands in the thick fogs characteristic of the region. In the early 1960s, scientists for the Atomic Energy Commission's Project Chariot extensively studied the flora, fauna, climate, and geology of the area to determine the feasibility of excavating a deep-water seaport with nuclear explosions; the harbor was not built.

Flora and fauna: More than 210,000 seabirds nest on the cliffs, primarily thick-billed murres, common murres, and black-legged kittiwakes. On the headlands, covered by tundra and dotted with small streams and ponds, the wildlife is typical of the far Arctic—caribou, moose, brown (grizzly) bears, wolves, wolverines, arctic foxes, red foxes, and musk oxen. Common sea mammals are seals, walruses, and whales.

Recreation: Cape Lisburne has one airstrip. No recreational facilities have been built, but camping is unrestricted. Campfires are not practical; use a camping stove. Fishing, hunting, and snowmobiles are permitted; aircraft may land in the area, but are prohibited near the seabird cliffs during nesting. Take warm, windproof clothes and adequate rain gear. Since fog, storms, or winds often delay pickup by air, pack extra supplies.

Weather and conditions: In this arctic maritime climate, cool, cloudy, foggy summers and cold, dry, severe winters are the rule. (See the Kotzebue weather table.) Winds usually are constant and strong, especially over the cliffs.

Boaters in the waters off Kotzebue   Tricia Brown photo

Directions/access: Access to the area is by air. Cape Lisburne, Kotzebue, and Point Hope have scheduled air service; air taxis operate from Kotzebue. Stores, restaurants, and lodging are available in Kotzebue and Point Hope.

107 Bering Sea Subunit

Location: In the Bering Sea
Size: 86,000 acres (34,400 hectares)
High point: 1505 feet (459 m) on
St. Matthew Island
Low point: Sea level
Best time of year: June–September
Daylight: June 21: 19 hours

December 22: 6 hours
Activities: Visitation is discouraged
USGS map: St. Matthew
Established: 1909; amended 1980
Managed by: U.S. Fish and Wildlife
Service

These three extremely remote islands in the Bering Sea—St. Matthew, Hall, and Pinnacle—are used by marine mammals and large numbers of seabirds, primarily cormorants, murres, puffins, auklets, gulls, common eiders, and oldsquaw ducks. The islands are also the major U.S. nesting grounds for the McKay's bunting.

The islands originally supported a dense polar bear population, but by 1899 hunters had eradicated the animals. Bering Sea National Wildlife Refuge was established to preserve the remaining wildlife. In 1980, the refuge was designated a part of the Alaska Maritime National Wildlife Refuge.

A sea lion colony　　APLIC photo

During World War II, reindeer were introduced onto St. Matthew Island as an emergency food supply for resident military personnel who manned weather stations and navigational equipment. Left alone after the war, the reindeer overpopulated the island, stripping the vegetation, until a sudden die-off occurred in 1964, reducing the population to less than 100. Eventually the herd died off completely.

Recreation: Restrictions may be in effect; contact the refuge manager before going to the islands. Hunting is not permitted. No development exists other than an abandoned military airstrip.

Weather and conditions: The subarctic maritime climate brings cool, foggy summers and cold, dry winters. (See the Nunivak Island weather table.) Winds are strong. The Bering Sea is ice-free by June.

Directions/access: The islands have no good anchorages. Frequent and long-lasting storms and fog make flying and boating hazardous.

108 Bogoslof Subunit

Location: Southwestern Alaska, in the Aleutian Islands north of Umnak Island

Size: 180 acres (72 hectares)

High point: 360 feet (110 m), on Bogoslof Island

Low point: Sea level

Best time of year: May–September

Daylight: June 21: 18 hours
December 22: 7 hours

Activities: Visitation is discouraged

USGS map: Umnak

Established: 1909; amended 1980

Managed by: U.S. Fish and Wildlife Service

"Bogoslof! Bogoslof!" ("God's voice!") shouted the Aleuts as the island rose from the sea during a fiery eruption. Bogoslof Island, formed in 1706, and Fire Island, formed in 1883, are of particular interest to biologists because they came into existence within recent historic time. During World War II, a military outpost was established on Bogoslof. Designated a National Wildlife Refuge early in the century, Bogoslof became a part of the Alaska Maritime National Wildlife Refuge in 1980.

Flora and fauna: Treeless Bogoslof consists of a vegetated lava dome with the one rugged spire of Castle Rock, black lava cliffs, and sandy bouldered beaches. Fire Island is a single, barren pinnacle that rises 40 feet (12 m) above the sea. These two remote, rocky islands are habitat for more than 90,000 seabirds—primarily murres, puffins, kittiwakes, and gulls—and about 500 Steller's sea lions.

Recreation: Visits to this undisturbed sanctuary are limited to those with scientific or educational purposes. Hunting, firearms, and aircraft are not permitted. Contact the refuge manager before planning a trip.

Weather and conditions: The weather is typical of a maritime climate: cool, wet, foggy summers and mild, wet, foggy winters. (See the Cold Bay weather table.) Here the Bering Sea is ice-free the entire year. Winds usually are constant and strong, and severe storms are frequent.

Bogoslof Island   USFWS photo by Mary Clemens

Caution: Frequent, violent, and long-lasting storms make boating and flying dangerous.

Directions/access: The islands are isolated and hard to reach. They are undeveloped, and there are no anchorages or airstrips. Dutch Harbor/Unalaska is the nearest community that has scheduled air service, air taxis, stores, restaurants, and lodging.

109 Chamisso Subunit

Location: Northwestern Alaska, southeast of Kotzebue
Size: 3000 acres (1200 hectares)
High point: 246 feet (75 m), on Chamisso Island
Low point: Sea level
Best time of year: June–September

Daylight: June 21: 24 hours
December 22: 3 hours
Activities: Visitation is discouraged
USGS maps: Selawik A-6, B-6
Established: 1912; amended 1980
Managed by: U.S. Fish and Wildlife Service

Established as a refuge to protect seabird nesting sites, Chamisso and Puffin Islands and nearby islets are used by large populations of horned puffins, thick-billed murres, and black-legged kittiwakes. Most of the nesting sites are on Puffin Island, which drops steeply to tidewater; the cliffs have long been a source of murre and kittiwake eggs for local Eskimos, who are permitted to continue gathering them for subsistence. Horned puffins usually nest in rock crevices and boulder piles, but on Puffin Island they have dug underground burrows similar to those of tufted puffins.

Chamisso, the larger island, was named for Adelbert von Chamisso, botanist on the Russian ship *Rurik,* which first visited the islands in 1815 under the command of Otto von Kotzebue. Originally designated a National Wildlife Refuge, Chamisso became a part of the Alaska Maritime National Wildlife Refuge in 1980.

Flora and fauna: With a large sandspit and a low shoreline, tundra-covered Chamisso Island has fewer nesting seabirds. The waters of Spafarief Bay contain walrus, seals, porpoises, and whales; in winter an occasional arctic fox may trot across the frozen bay from the mainland.

Recreation: Human visitors are not encouraged on the refuge during nesting season. Contact the refuge manager before planning a trip, since visitor restrictions may be in effect. The refuge is undeveloped.

Weather and conditions: In this Arctic maritime climate, cool, cloudy, foggy summers and dry, cold, severe winters are the norm. (See the Kotzebue weather table.)

Caution: With frequent fog and strong winds, hypothermia is a danger. Long-lasting storms make boating hazardous, and there are no good anchorages.

Directions/access: Kotzebue is the closest major settlement, with stores, restaurants, lodging, scheduled air service, and air taxis. Deering, a small village southwest of the refuge, has a store and scheduled air service.

The sand spit at Chamisso Island　USFWS photo

The upland muskeg on Forrester Island USFWS photo by D. L. Spencer

110 Forrester Island Subunit

Location: Southeast Alaska, southwest of Craig

Size: 20,600 acres (8240 hectares)

High point: 1340 feet (408 m), on Forrester Island

Low point: Sea level

Best time of year: May–September

Daylight: June 21: 17½ hours December 22: 7 hours

Activities: Visitation is discouraged

USGS map: Dixon Entrance D-5

Established: 1912; amended 1980

Managed by: U.S. Fish and Wildlife Service

Three islands, Forrester, Lowrie, and Petrel, and numerous offshore rocks make up this remote seabird refuge in the Gulf of Alaska near Dixon Entrance, a critical habitat for more than a million birds. The refuge became part of the Alaska Maritime National Wildlife Refuge in 1980.

Flora and fauna: On islands seemingly deserted by day, huge populations of Leach's storm petrels, fork-tailed storm petrels, Cassin's auklets, and rhinoceros auklets nest in underground burrows, emerging only after dark to feed in the open ocean.

Forrester Island, whose mountainous steep slopes are heavily forested, has dense underbrush, many cliffs, and few beaches. Petrel Island, 300 feet (100 m) high, is also densely forested atop precipitous sea cliffs. Lowrie Island is 250 feet (75 m) high and essentially flat.

Recreation: Since nearly all available soil is honeycombed with the burrows, which are up to 15 feet (5 m) long, a single person walking on an island collapses many tunnels. Visitor restrictions may be in effect, so contact the refuge manager before planning a trip.

Weather and conditions: The islands have a maritime climate, with cool, wet summers and mild, wet winters. (See the Annette Island weather table.) Winds are variable.

Directions/access: Undeveloped, the islands have no anchorages or airstrips.

111 Hazy Islands Subunit

Location: Southeast Alaska, south of Sitka
Size: 1900 acres (760 hectares)
High point: Estimated 500 feet (150 m)
Low point: Sea level
Best time of year: May–September
Daylight: June 21: 17½ hours

December 22: 7 hours
Activities: Visitation is discouraged
USGS map: Craig
Established: 1912
Managed by: U.S. Fish and Wildlife
Service

Far offshore in the Gulf of Alaska, this refuge consists only of four or five exposed rocks with little vegetation, but it provides a predator-free nesting area for large numbers of common murres, glaucous-winged gulls, pigeon guillemots, tufted puffins, and horned puffins. Brandt's cormorants, which nest on only one other island in Alaska, are also found here.

Recreation: The rocks, 10 miles (16 km) west of Coronation Island Wilderness, are isolated, without landing or camping sites, shelter, or water. Frequent storms and violent wind squalls make boating hazardous. Visitors are not encouraged; restrictions

Big Hazy Islet is one of several small islands that make up the unit.   USFWS photo

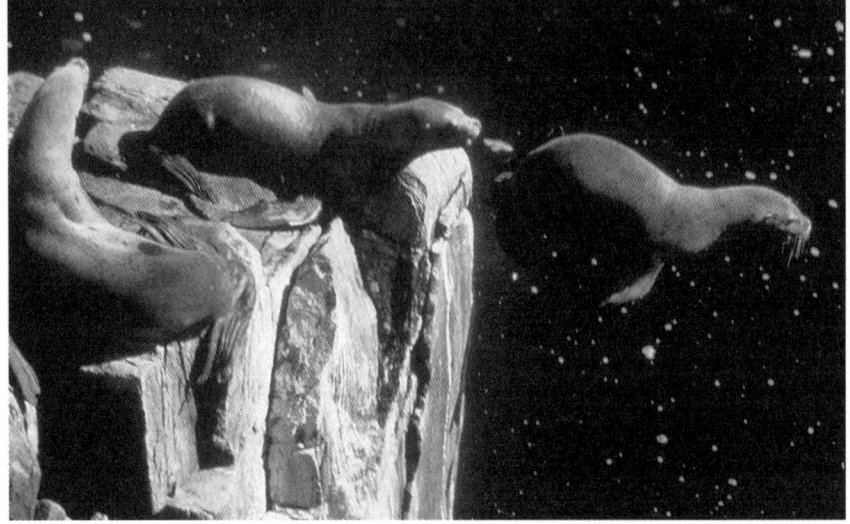

Sea lions launch off a low cliff.   ASP photo

may be in effect, so contact the refuge manager in Homer before planning a trip. Originally a separate refuge, the islands became a part of the Alaska Maritime National Wildlife Refuge in 1980.

Weather and conditions: The maritime climate brings cool, wet summers and mild, wet winters. (See Sitka weather table.) Winds are moderate to strong.

Directions/access: The Hazy Islands are extremely remote and hard to reach. Air taxis operate from Ketchikan, Petersburg, Sitka, and Wrangell; boat charters are available at most coastal communities. Food and lodging are found at Craig, Ketchikan, Klawock, Petersburg, Sitka, and Wrangell.

112 Semidi Subunit

Location: Southwest Alaska, southwest of Kodiak Island

Size: 257,000 acres (102,800 hectares)

High point: 1024 feet (312 m), on Aghiyuk Island

Low point: Sea level

Best time of year: May–August

Daylight: June 21: 18 hours

December 22: 7 hours

Activities: Birding, wildlife-viewing, photography

USGS map: Sutwik A-3

Established: 1932

Managed by: U.S. Fish and Wildlife Service

A group of islands in the stormy Gulf of Alaska, the wilderness refuge is home for millions of pelagic seabirds, some of the largest seabird colonies in North America.

Flora and fauna: Precipitous cliffs up to 200 feet (60 m) high attract murres, kittiwakes, puffins, fulmars, and parakeet auklets. The area also is used by sea otters, sea lions, seals, dolphins, porpoises, and whales. Consisting of nine major treeless islands, numerous small islets, rocks, and submerged lands, the Semidi group was redesignated as part of the Alaska Maritime National Wildlife Refuge in 1980.

Recreation: Devoid of development, the islands are remote and hard to reach. There are no anchorages or airstrips, and the waters are not well charted. Violent storms make boating hazardous. Recreational use of the refuge is discouraged during nesting periods, since the birds are highly sensitive to disturbance. Visitor restrictions may be in effect, so contact the refuge manager in Homer before traveling to the islands.

Weather and conditions: In this maritime climate, the ocean waters are ice-free the entire year, with cool, wet summers and mild, wet winters. (See the Cold Bay weather table.) The area receives three times the precipitation of Cold Bay. Winds generally are strong; frequent severe storms are accompanied by gale-force winds.

Directions/access: Kodiak and Sand Point have stores, restaurants, lodging, scheduled air service, and air taxis, and are ports of call for the southwestern Alaska state ferry.

113 Simeonof Subunit

Location: Southwest Alaska, in the Shumagin Islands
Size: 26,046 acres (10,540 hectares)
High point: 1436 feet (438 m)
Low point: Sea level
Best time of year: May–September
Daylight: June 21: 18 hours
December 22: 7 hours
Activities: Birding, wildlife-viewing, photography
USGS map: Simeonof Island
Established: 1958
Managed by: U.S. Fish and Wildlife Service

In the Gulf of Alaska, 58 miles (93 km) south of the Alaska Peninsula, Simeonof originally was established as a wildlife refuge to protect sea otters and the extensive kelp beds that are their habitat. The Shumagin Islands contain the greatest diversity of seabirds in the entire Alaska Maritime National Wildlife Refuge system—of the 35 species of seabirds that breed in Alaska, 21 breed in the Shumagins. There are almost a million

Red foxes are among the small furbearers that live on Simeonof.   ASP photo

breeding birds, especially murres, puffins, auklets, murrelets, kittiwakes, gulls, cormorants, and storm petrels.

One of about 30 named islands in the Shumagin Island group, Simeonof was used for cattle and fox ranching from 1896 to 1930, then abandoned. Cattle were reintroduced in 1962 but they all have been removed.

Flora and fauna: With its gently sloping shores and white sand beaches, Simeonof Island attracts relatively few seabirds. Nearby Murie Inlet, with nesting gulls and arctic terns, is also included in the refuge; the two islands and nearby tidal waters, along with the rest of the Shumagins, became part of the Alaska Maritime National Wildlife Refuge in 1980. Many of the islands have rocky, precipitous sea cliffs. They are treeless, except where Sitka spruce have been introduced; extensive brush grows below 1000 feet (300 m). Arctic and red foxes and river otters, all predatory on seabirds, are found on the islands. So are ground squirrels, ptarmigan, and migratory waterfowl, and black brant and emperor geese winter over here. Sea otters, seals, sea lions, and whales use the Gulf waters. Although the islands were the site of the first contact between Alaska Natives and the outside world in 1741, their plant and animal life has only recently been studied.

Recreation: Simeonof Island has no recreational development. Although it has an excellent harbor with good anchorage, the island is isolated and hard to reach; fog and frequent, long-lasting storms make boating hazardous. Human visitors are requested not to disturb nesting birds.

Weather and conditions: Although the weather in the Shumagin Islands is somewhat better than in the Aleutians, the maritime climate brings nearly constant overcast, cool, wet summers and mild, wet winters. (See the Cold Bay weather table.) Ocean waters are ice-free the entire year. Winds generally are strong, with gale-force winds accompanying storms.

Directions/access: Contact the refuge manager in Homer before traveling to the islands. Scheduled air service lands at Sand Point, which has air taxis, boat charters, a store, a restaurant, and lodging. The southwestern Alaska state ferry occasionally docks at Sand Point.

114 St. Lazaria Subunit

Location: Southeast Alaska, southwest of Sitka

Size: 620 acres (248 hectares)

High point: 281 feet (86 m)

Low point: Sea level

Best time of year: May–September

Daylight: June 21: 18 hours

December 22: 6½ hours

Activities: Birding, photography

USGS map: Port Alexander

Established: 1909; amended 1980

Managed by: U.S. Fish and Wildlife Service

Originally named Robin Islands by the first explorers in 1780, the two volcanic outcroppings are connected by a low, tide-washed saddle; steep cliffs that ring the knobs

An aerial view of St. Lazaria Island   USFWS photo

make landing and access difficult. In 1809, the Russians renamed the island St. Lazaria. Designated a Wilderness Area in 1970, the refuge was added to the Alaska Maritime National Wildlife Refuge system in 1980.

Flora and fauna: A prime breeding habitat for more than a million seabirds, the refuge originally was established by President Teddy Roosevelt to protect an extremely fragile nesting area. One of the state's largest populations of Leach's storm petrels and fork-tailed storm petrels nest in burrows amid the spruce and hemlock roots, emerging only at night to feed in the open ocean.

Also found in this wilderness refuge are burrowing tufted puffins, rhinoceros auklets, and crevice-nesting pigeon guillemots, common murres, glaucous-winged gulls, and pelagic cormorants, as well as many other sea and land birds. Both burrowing and cliff-nesting birds leave their nests when disturbed, giving local gulls a chance to feed on the untended eggs and chicks.

Recreation: Visitors are requested not to walk on the island, since tunnels of burrowing birds collapse easily underfoot; special permits are required to land. Visitors are asked to view birds from boats without disturbing them.

Weather and conditions: As is typical of a maritime climate, the area experiences frequent overcast skies, with cool, wet summers and mild, wet winters. (See the Sitka weather table.) Winds normally are moderate to strong.

Directions/access: Sitka, 15 miles (24 km) away, provides stores, restaurants, lodging, air taxis, and charter boats. A port of call for the southeastern Alaska state ferry and most cruise ships, the city also is served by frequent scheduled air service.

115 Tuxedni Subunit

Location: Southcentral Alaska, northwest of Homer
Size: 15,400 acres (6160 hectares)
High point: 2674 feet (815 m), on Chisik Island
Low point: Sea level
Best time of year: May–September
Daylight: June 21: 19 hours

December 22: 6 hours
Activities: Birding, camping, photography
USGS maps: Kenai A-7, A-8
Established: 1909; amended 1980
Managed by: U.S. Fish and Wildlife Service

Two islands, Chisik and Duck, at the mouth of Tuxedni Bay, protect major seabird colonies, bald eagles, and peregrine falcons. Chisik Island rises ramp-like from Cook Inlet, with a cannery and sandy beaches on the south end and 400-foot (100-m) sea cliffs on the north. The view of the nearby volcanoes Iliamna and Redoubt from the refuge is outstanding.

Flora: A nearly impenetrable jungle of alder, salmonberry, and other brush cloaks the lower slopes and fills spruce-forest clearings; summit areas are alpine tundra. Duck Island is a 6-acre (2-hectare) rocky islet with little vegetation.

Recreation: Camping, campfires, and fishing are permitted; hunting is not.

Weather and conditions: The refuge enjoys a maritime climate, with cool, overcast summers and mild, overcast winters. (See the Homer weather table.) Winds generally are light.

Directions/access: Access to the refuge is by air or water, although the use of small boats on the treacherous waters of Cook Inlet is not recommended because of sudden winds, large waves, and strong tides. Air taxis, stores, restaurants, and lodging are available in Homer, Kenai, and Soldotna.

Sea otters are among the marine mammals in the waters around Tuxedni.   ASP photo

$\mathcal{A}$DDITIONAL AREAS OF INTEREST

For more information on these areas of interest, see Table 2.

Key to Abbreviations

Cmpgnd.	Campground	SGS	State Game Sanctuary	SRA	State Recreation Area
NHS	National Historic Site	SHP	State Historical Park	SRS	State Recreation Site
PUF	Public Use Facility	SHS	State Historic Site	SWR	State Wildlife Refuge
SCHA	State Critical Habitat Area	SMP	State Marine Park	SWS	State Wildlife Sanctuary
SGR	State Game Refuge	SP	State Park	ST	State Trail

$\mathcal{A}$laska $\mathcal{D}$epartment of $\mathcal{F}$ish and $\mathcal{G}$ame

Name	Location / Office	Size / Date Formed	To Protect
Southeast Alaska			
Chilkat River SCHA	North of Haines Haines	4730 acres 1972	Uplands; eagle nesting and feeding
Dude Creek SCHA	West of Gustavus Douglas	4080 acres 1988	Lands and waters; lesser sandhill cranes
Southcentral Alaska			
Anchor River/Fritz Creek SCHA	North of Homer Homer	18,600 acres 1985/1990	Lands and waters; moose
Clam Gulch SCHA	West of Clam Gulch Soldotna	2820 acres 1976	Tidelands and submerged lands; razor clams
Copper River Delta SCHA	Southeast of Cordova Cordova	615,900 acres 1978	Lands, tidelands, submerged lands, waters; waterfowl, shorebirds, fish
Fox River Flats SCHA	Northeast of Homer Homer	6780 acres 1972	Uplands; waterfowl
Kachemak Bay SCHA	Kachemak Bay Homer	228,800 acres 1972/1993	Tidelands and submerged lands; shellfish, crab, and fish
Kalgin Island SCHA	West of Kenai Soldotna	3520 acres 1972	Uplands, tidelands, and submerged lands; waterfowl
Little Susitna River PUF (See description of Susitna Flats SGR, No. 55.)	Mile 18, Knik–Goose Bay Rd.	245 vehicle spaces 1989	Campground, water, handicap toilets, boat launch, fishing, sanitary dump station
Homer Airport SCHA	Homer	294 acres 1996	Moose enhancement; recreation
Redoubt Bay SCHA	West of Kenai Soldotna	164,400 acres 1989	Uplands, tidelands, and submerged lands; tule geese
Willow Mountain SCHA	North of Wasilla Palmer	22,500 acres 1989	Uplands; moose winter habitat
Interior Alaska			
Delta Junction Bison Range Area	SE of Delta Jct. Delta	89,700 acres 1979	Protection and feeding; bison
Southwest Alaska			
Cinder River SCHA	Northeast of Cold Bay King Salmon	25,800 acres 1972	Uplands, tidelands, and submerged lands; waterfowl

Name	Location/Office	Size/ Date Formed	To Protect
Egegik SCHA	Northeast of Cold Bay King Salmon	8250 acres 1972	Uplands, tidelands, and submerged lands; waterfowl
Pilot Point SCHA	Northeast of Cold Bay King Salmon	46,600 acres 1972	Uplands, tidelands, and submerged lands; waterfowl
Port Heiden SCHA	Northeast of Cold Bay King Salmon	72,120 acres 1972	Uplands, tidelands, and submerged lands; waterfowl
Port Moller SCHA	Northeast of Cold Bay King Salmon	131,300 acres 1972	Uplands, tidelands, and submerged lands; waterfowl
Tugidak Island SCHA	Southwest of Kodiak Kodiak	53,600 acres 1988	Uplands, tidelands, and waters; marine mammals, shellfish, fish, birds

Alaska Department of Natural Resources

Name	Location/Office	Size/ Date Formed	Purpose
Caribou Creek Rec. Mining Area	Northeast of Palmer Anchorage	800 acres 1990	Recreational mining and gold panning
Ernie Haugen Public Use Area	Near Ketchikan Juneau (DL)	420 acres 1989	Recreation
Goldstream Public Use Area	Northeast of Fairbanks Fairbanks (DL)	3000 acres 1990	Recreation
Haines State Forest	Surrounding Haines Juneau (DF)	247,000 acres 1982	Forest management/recreation
Hatcher Pass Public Use Area	North of Palmer Anchorage	5100 acres 1986	Recreation
Matanuska Valley Moose Range	Northeast of Palmer Anchorage	132,500 acres 1984	Recreation; maintain, improve, enhance moose and other wildlife habitat
Nelchina Public Use Area	West of Glennallen Anchorage	2,350,000 acres 1988	Recreation
Susitna Valley Recreational Rivers: Alexander Creek, Kroto Creek/Moose Creek, Lake Creek, Little Susitna River, Talachulitna River, and Talkeetna River	Northwest of Wasilla Anchorage	259,000 acres 1988	Recreation
Tanana Valley State Forest	Southeast of Fairbanks Fairbanks (DF)	2,033,000 acres 1983	Forest management/recreation

Alaska Division of Parks and Outdoor Recreation

Name	Location/Office	Size	Facilities/Purpose

Southeast Alaska (Managed by Southeast Region Office, Juneau)

Ketchikan area

Name	Location/Office	Size	Facilities/Purpose
Refuge Cove SRS	Mile 8.7 N. Tongass Hwy.	13 acres	Picnicking, toilets, fishing
Settlers Cove SRS	Mile 18 N. Tongass Hwy.	38 acres	Campground, water, handicap toilets, trails, fishing
Dall Bay SMP	Gravina Island	585 acres	Undeveloped, fishing
Grindall Island SMP	Kasaan Peninsula	240 acres	Toilets, fishing
Black Sands Beach SMP	Gravina Island	640 acres	Undeveloped, fishing

Name	Location	Size	Facilities/Purpose
Wrangell/Petersburg area			
Thom's Place SMP	Wrangell Island	1198 acres	Undeveloped, fishing
Joe Mace Island SMP	Sumner Strait	62 acres	Undeveloped, fishing
Beecher Pass SMP	Mitkof Island	660 acres	Undeveloped, fishing
Security Bay SMP	Chatham Strait	500 acres	Undeveloped, fishing
Sitka area			
Pioneer Park SRS	Mile 2 Halibut Point Rd.	3 acres	Picnic shelters, water, toilets, trail
Halibut Point SRS	Mile 4.4 Halibut Point Rd.	22 acres	Picnic shelters, water, toilets, trail, fishing, historical features
Magoun Island SMP	Krestof Sound	1135 acres	Undeveloped, fishing
Big Bear/Baby Bear SMP	Peril Strait	1023 acres	Undeveloped, fishing
Juneau area			
Wickersham SHS	213 Seventh Ave.	0.5 acres	Tours, handicap toilets
Gruening SHS	Mile 24.8 Glacier Hwy.	12 acres	Fishing
Juneau Trail System ST	Juneau Area	15 acres	Trails, fishing, historical features
Johnson Creek SRS	Mile 15.5 N. Douglas Hwy.	65 acres	Undeveloped
Taku Harbor SMP	Stephens Passage	700 acres	Undeveloped, fishing
Oliver Inlet SMP	Admiralty Island	560 acres	Toilets, trail, boat launch, cabin
Funter Bay SMP	Admiralty Island	162 acres	Undeveloped, fishing
St. James Bay SMP	Lynn Canal	1022 acres	Undeveloped, fishing
Shelter Island SMP	Lynn Canal	3560 acres	Picnic sites, toilets, trails, fishing
Sullivan Island SMP	Lynn Canal	2163 acres	Undeveloped, fishing
Haines area			
Portage Cove SRS	Mile 1 Beach Rd.	7 acres	Campground, water, toilets, fishing
Chilkoot Lake SRS	Mile 10 Lutak Rd.	80 acres	Campground, picnic shelters, water, handicap toilets, boat launch, fishing, historical features
Mosquito Lake SRS	Mile 27 Haines Hwy.	5 acres	Campground, water, toilets, boat launch, fishing
Chilkat Islands SMP	Lynn Canal	6560 acres	Undeveloped, fishing

Southcentral Alaska (Managed by Chugach/Southwest Area Office, Anchorage)

Name	Location	Size	Facilities/Purpose
Anchorage area			
Potter Section House SHS	Mile 115 Seward Hwy.	0.5 acres	Water, handicap toilets, railroad museum, gift shop

Kenai Peninsula (Managed by Kenai Peninsula Area Office, Soldotna)

Name	Location	Size	Facilities/Purpose
Sterling/Soldotna/Kenai area—Kenai River Special Management Area			
Kenai Keys SRA	Mile 78 Sterling Hwy.	193 acres	Undeveloped, fishing
Bing's Landing SRS	Mile 80 Sterling Hwy.	126 acres	Campground, water, handicap toilets, boat launch, fishing, trails
Izaak Walton SRS	Mile 81 Sterling Hwy.	8 acres	Campground, water, handicap toilets, boat launch, fishing

Name	Location	Size	Facilities/Purpose
Morgan's Landing SRA	Mile 85 Sterling Hwy.	279 acres	Campground, water, handicap toilets, fishing, information, trails
Kenai River Islands SRS	River Miles 11–41	69 acres	Undeveloped, fishing
Big Eddy SRS	Mile 1.8 Kenai Spur Rd.	16 acres	Handicap toilets, fishing
Funny River SRS	Mile 10 Funny River Rd.	336 acres	Campground, water, handicap toilets, fishing
Nilnunqua SHS	Funny River Rd.	42 acres	Undeveloped
Slikok Creek SRS	Mile 20 Kalifonsky Beach Rd.	40 acres	Picnicking, handicap toilets, fishing
Ciechanski SRS	Ciechanski Rd.	34 acres	Handicap toilets, fishing
Kenai River Flats SRS	Mile 16 Kalifonsky Beach Rd.	832 acres	Toilets, fishing
Scout Lake SRS	Mile 85 Sterling Hwy.	195 acres	Campground, picnic shelter, water, handicap toilets, trails, fishing
Crooked Creek SRS	Cohoe Loop Rd., 2 miles from north jct. with Sterling Hwy.	49 acres	Campground, water, toilets, trails, fishing
Kasilof River SRS	Mile 109 Sterling Hwy.	50 acres	Campground, water, handicap toilets, trails, fishing, boat launch

Homer area

Stariski SRS	Mile 151 Sterling Hwy.	30 acres	Campground, picnic shelter, water, handicap toilets

Seward area

Thumb Cove SMP	Resurrection Bay	720 acres	Undeveloped, fishing
Sunny Cove SMP	Resurrection Bay	960 acres	Undeveloped, fishing
Sandspit Point SMP	Eldorado Narrows	560 acres	Undeveloped, fishing
Driftwood Bay SMP	Day Harbor	1480 acres	Undeveloped, fishing
Safety Cove SMP	Day Harbor	960 acres	Undeveloped, fishing

Prince William Sound (Managed by Kenai Peninsula Area Office, Soldotna)

Whittier Area

Decision Point SMP	Passage Canal	460 acres	Undeveloped, fishing
Entry Cove SMP	Point Pigot	370 acres	Undeveloped, fishing
Surprise Cove SMP	Cochrane Bay	2280 acres	Undeveloped, fishing
Zeigler Cove SMP	Port Wells	720 acres	Undeveloped, fishing
Bettles Bay SMP	Port Wells	680 acres	Undeveloped, fishing
Granite Bay SMP	Esther Island	2105 acres	Undeveloped, fishing
South Esther Island SMP	Esther Island	3360 acres	Undeveloped, fishing
Horseshoe Bay SMP	Latouche Island	970 acres	Undeveloped, fishing

Valdez/Cordova area

Shoup Bay SMP	Valdez Arm	4560 acres	Undeveloped, fishing
Sawmill Bay SMP	Valdez Arm	2320 acres	Undeveloped, fishing
Jack Bay SMP	Valdez Arm	811 acres	Undeveloped, fishing
Canoe Passage SMP	Hawkins Island	2735 acres	Undeveloped, fishing
Boswell Bay SMP	Hinchinbrook Island	799 acres	Undeveloped, fishing

Name	Location	Size	Facilities/Purpose
Kayak Island SMP	Gulf of Alaska	1437 acres	Undeveloped, fishing

Kodiak area (Managed by Kodiak Area Office, Kodiak)

Name	Location	Size	Facilities/Purpose
Buskin River SRS	Mile 4.5 W. Rezanof Dr.	196 acres	Campground, picnic shelter, water, handicap toilets, trails, fishing, sanitary dump station
Pasagshak SRS	Mile 40 Pasagshak River Rd.	20 acres	Campground, water, handicap toilets, fishing
Woody Island SRS	Woody Island	113 acres	Undeveloped, fishing

Matanuska-Susitna Valleys area (Managed by Mat-Su/Copper Basin Area Office, Wasilla)

Palmer/Wasilla area

Name	Location	Size	Facilities/Purpose
Finger Lake SRS	Bogard Road	47 acres	Campground, water, toilets, trails, boat launch, fishing
Wolf Lake SRS	Mile 2.5 Engstrom Rd.	23 acres	Campground, handicap toilets, handicap trail, fishing
Summit Lake SRS	Mile 19 Hatcher Pass Rd.	360 acres	Trail, handicap toilets
Big Lake South SRS	Mile 5.2 S. Big Lake Rd.	16 acres	Campground, water, handicap toilets, boat launch, fishing
Big Lake North SRS	Mile 5 N. Big Lake Rd.	19 acres	Campground, picnic shelter, water, handicap toilets, boat launch, fishing
Rocky Lake SRS	Mile 3.5 Big Lake Rd.	48 acres	Campground, water, toilets, boat launch, fishing

Willow/Talkeetna area

Name	Location	Size	Facilities/Purpose
Nancy Lake SRS	Mile 66.5 Parks Hwy.	36 acres	Campground, picnic shelter, water, handicap toilets, boat launch, fishing
Montana Creek SRS	Mile 97 Parks Hwy.	82 acres	Campground, water, handicap toilets, handicap trail, fishing

Palmer to Glennallen

Name	Location	Size	Facilities/Purpose
King Mountain SRS	Mile 76 Glenn Hwy.	20 acres	Campground, picnic shelter, water, toilets
Bonnie Lake SRS	Mile 83 Glenn Hwy.	129 acres	Campground, toilets, boat launch, fishing, not recommended for motorhomes
Long Lake SRS	Mile 85 Glenn Hwy.	480 acres	Campground, water, toilets, boat launch, fishing
Matanuska Glacier SRS	Mile 101 Glenn Hwy.	229 acres	Campground, water, handicap toilets, trail

Copper River Basin/Valdez (Managed by Mat-Su/Copper Basin Glennallen Office, Wasilla)

Name	Location	Size	Facilities/Purpose
Little Nelchina SRS	Mile 137.4 Glenn Hwy.	22 acres	Campground, toilets, trail, boat launch, fishing
Dry Creek SRS	Mile 118 Richardson Hwy.	372 acres	Campground, picnic shelter, toilets, trail, fishing
Porcupine Creek SRS	Mile 64 Tok Cut-Off	240 acres	Campground, water, handicap toilets, trail, fishing
Liberty Falls SRS	Mile 24 Edgerton Hwy.	10 acres	Campground, toilets, trail
Squirrel Creek SRS	Mile 80 Richardson Hwy.	350 acres	Campground, water, toilets, fishing

Name	Location	Size	Facilities/Purpose
Little Tonsina SRS	Mile 65 Richardson Hwy.	103 acres	Campground, water, toilets, fishing
Worthington Glacier SRS	Mile 29 Richardson Hwy.	113 acres	Picnic shelter, toilets, trails
Blueberry Lake SRS	Mile 23 Richardson Hwy.	192 acres	Campground, handicap toilets, trails, fishing

Fairbanks/Delta Junction/Tok area (Managed by Northern Region Office, Fairbanks)

Name	Location	Size	Facilities/Purpose
Chena River SRS	University Ave., Fairbanks	27 acres	Campground, picnic shelter, water, handicap toilets, sanitary dump station, boat launch, fishing, trails
Upper Chatanika River SRS	Mile 39 Steese Hwy.	73 acres	Campground, water, toilets, fishing
Salcha River SRS	Mile 323 Richardson Hwy.	61 acres	Campground, water, handicap toilets, boat launch, fishing
Birch Lake SRS	Mile 306 Richardson Hwy.	191 acres	Campground, toilets, boat launch, fishing
Delta SRS	Mile 267 Richardson Hwy.	7 acres	Campground, water, handicap toilets, picnic shelters
Clearwater SRS	Mile 1415 Alaska Hwy. or Mile 268 Richardson Hwy.	27 acres	Campground, water, toilets, boat launch, fishing
Donnelly Creek SRS	Mile 238 Richardson Hwy.	42 acres	Campground, water, trail
Fielding Lake SRS	Mile 200 Richardson Hwy.	600 acres	Campground, handicap toilets, boat launch, fishing
Moon Lake SRS	Mile 1332 Alaska Hwy.	22 acres	Campground, water, handicap toilets, boat launch
Eagle Trail SRS	Mile 109 Tok Cut-Off	320 acres	Campground, picnic shelter, water, toilets, trail
Tok River SRS	Mile 1309 Alaska Hwy.	38 acres	Campground, picnic shelter, water, handicap toilets, trail

Bureau of Land Management

Glennallen District Office

Name	Location	Size	Facilities/Purpose
Tangle Lakes Cmpgnd.	Mile 21.5 Denali Hwy.	60 acres	Campground, water, handicap toilets, boat launch, fishing
Tangle River Cmpgnd.	Mile 21.5 Denali Hwy.	3 acres	Campground, water, toilets, boat launch, fishing
Brushkana Cmpgnd.	Mile 104.5 Denali Hwy.	20 acres	Campground, picnic shelter, toilets, water
Sourdough Cmpgnd.	Mile 147 Richardson Hwy.	150 acres	Campground, handicap toilets, sanitary dump station, boat launch, fishing
Paxson Lake Cmpgnd.	Mile 175 Richardson Hwy.	90 acres	Campground, water, handicap toilets, sanitary dump station, boat launch, fishing

Fairbanks, Northern Field Office

Name	Location	Size	Facilities/Purpose
Arctic Circle Site	Mile 115 Dalton Hwy.	5 acres	Undeveloped campground above wayside, outhouse
Cripple Creek Cmpgnd.	Mile 60 Steese Hwy.	15 acres	Campground, water, toilets, cabin, fishing, handicap trail

Name	Location	Size	Facilities/Purpose
Eagle Cmpgnd.	Mile 160 Taylor Hwy.	80 acres	Campground, toilets
Galbraith Lake Site	Mile 275 Dalton Hwy.	5 acres	Undeveloped campground, outhouse
Marion Creek Cmpgnd.	Mile 180 Dalton Hwy.	1.5 acres	Campground, toilets, water
Pinnell Mountain Nat'l Recreation Trail	Mile 86/Mile 107 Steese Hwy.	27 miles	Trail, 27 miles long, wheelchair access and viewing deck
Salmon Lake Cmpgnd.	Mile 40 Nome–Taylor Rd.	5 acres	Campground, toilets, boat launch, fishing
Sixty-Mile Site	Mile 60 Dalton Hwy.	5 acres	Undeveloped campground, outhouse, water
Walker Fork Cmpgnd.	Mile 82 Taylor Hwy.	60 acres	Campground, water, toilets, trail, fishing, gold panning
West Fork Cmpgnd.	Mile 48.5 Taylor Hwy.	20 acres	Campground, handicap toilets, fishing

U.S. Forest Service

Wilderness areas within the Tongass National Forest. (See description of Tongass National Forest, No. 24.)

Name	Location/ Office	Size/ Date Formed	Primary Use
Chuck River Wilderness	Endicott Arm Juneau District	72,503 acres 1990	General recreation
Karta Wilderness	Prince of Wales Island Thorne Bay	38,046 acres 1990	General recreation
Kootznoowoo Wilderness	Admiralty Island Juneau District	955,632 acres 1990	(See description of Admiralty Island National Monument, No. 1.)
Kuiu Wilderness	Southeast of Sitka Petersburg	60,576 acres 1990	Boating
South Etolin Island Wilderness	South of Wrangell Ketchikan	83,642 acres 1990	Beach-combing, boating, hunting

Appendix

Land Managers

To make sense of the overwhelming diversity of rules and regulations, let's look briefly at each of the land managing agencies and the philosophies behind their decisions. See Table 2 in the Appendix for information about specific land units.

The Alaska Department of Fish and Game oversees the state's wildlife resources, from research to the establishment of harvest levels to the enforcement of fishing, hunting, and trapping regulations. Land units managed by other governmental agencies may have more restrictive hunting, fishing, and trapping laws, but in the absence of such restrictions, Alaska Department of Fish and Game regulations apply. A number of land areas are under more restrictive regulations by the Alaska Department of Fish and Game to protect wildlife and wildlife habitat. *Refuges* and *critical habitat areas* permit most recreational activities when wildlife and habitat are not adversely affected. *Sanctuaries* protect extremely critical wildlife populations or habitats, prohibit hunting, and severely restrict human activities.

The Alaska Department of Natural Resources manages state land conservation units not assigned to another state land manager. Protection of recreational values is a major priority.

The Alaska Division of Parks manages its land units to provide for public recreational opportunities. *State parks* are relatively large areas managed to protect the resources of the land while providing for a wide range of recreational opportunities. For public safety or because of the impact on specific lands, wildlife, or recreational values, some activities may be restricted or limited to specific areas. *State marine parks* are mostly undeveloped and accessible only by water. *State historical parks* and *state historic sites* preserve, interpret, or commemorate a part of Alaska's history or prehistory. *State recreation areas* and *state recreation sites* have developed facilities to encourage public use, providing picnic areas, campgrounds, trails, boat ramps, and interpretive activities and displays.

The Bureau of Land Management's objective is to provide maximum public benefits from the land through multiple use by many interest groups. Wildlife resources are managed by the Alaska Department of Fish and Game, while BLM oversees the land, maintaining federal land records and fighting forest and tundra fires statewide. Federal public lands not contained within another specific management unit are under the care of BLM. Two land classifications have been created to protect land and recreational values beyond the usual BLM guidelines: *national recreation areas* and *national conservation areas*. Most recreational activities are permitted within the units. The difference between the two classifications lies with mining. In both, valid mining claims in existence when a unit was established are honored. Lands are withdrawn from further mineral entry in national recreation areas, whereas within a conservation area, additional mineral entry can occur at some future time.

The National Park Service is charged with the protection and preservation of the land, its resources, and its cultural values so that they may be passed on undisturbed to future generations. At the same time, the lands are to be used by people for recreation and enjoyment. In a departure from earlier National Park Service policy, most of their parklands created in 1980 provided for subsistence use by rural Alaskans for hunting, the gathering of food and firewood, and the use of rural transportation forms—powerboats, airplanes, and snowmobiles. In general, these *national parks, national wildernesses,* and *national monuments* permit the recreational visitor to fish, carry firearms, and use horses, powerboats, fixed-wing aircraft, and snowmobiles; recreational hunting, trapping, and off-road vehicles are not permitted. National Park Service units established prior to 1980 retain their original regulations. *National preserves* permit recreational hunting and trapping in addition to the uses listed above.

The U.S. Fish and Wildlife Service protects wildlife and its habitat on its land units. Other activities may be permitted if they are compatible with wildlife management. *National wildlife refuge* regulations permit most recreational uses. Regulations in *refuge wilderness* areas are similar, but occasionally more restrictive.

The U.S. Forest Service manages the *national forests* for multiple use. Most recreational activities are permitted, but where user values conflict, lands are zoned for or against a specific use. To protect outstanding scenic lands and wildlife habitats, a number of *wildernesses, monuments,* and *monument wildernesses* have been established. The recreational visitor will find essentially no additional use restrictions on these lands. The designations, instead, limit development of recreational facilities and commercial use of the land's resources.

Addresses

You are encouraged first to contact one of the Public Land Information Centers (addresses under Information Sources) for brochures and campground and other information. They can refer you to the proper contact for additional information.

Note: Unless otherwise noted, all addresses listed below are in Alaska, postal abbreviation AK; numbers in parenthesis following a street or mailing address are zip codes.

For addresses of specific parklands described in this book, use the Key to Addresses of Described Parklands to find the agency and office location listed below.

Alaska Department of Fish and Game (ADF&G)

Home page: www.state.ak.us/local/akpages/FISH.GAME/adfghome.htm

Anchorage Regional Office: 333 Raspberry Rd. (99518-1599). Phone: (907) 344-0541; hunting/ fishing recording: (907) 349-4687; wildlife conservation: (907) 267-2182

Angoon: 700 Aan Deinaa Aat, P.O. Box 211 (99820-0211). Phone: (907) 839-2243

Barrow: 1265 Agvik St., P.O. Box 1284 (99723-1284). Phone: (907) 852-3464

Bethel: 460 Ridgecrest Dr., Room 215, P.O. Box 146 (99559). Phone: (907) 543-2979

Cold Bay: 1 Russell Creek Rd., P.O. Box 50 (99571-0050). Phone: (907) 532-2419

Cordova: 401 Railroad Ave., P.O. Box 669 (99574-0669). Phone: (907) 424-3212

Delta Junction: Mile 266.5 Richardson Hwy., P.O. Box 605 (99737-0605). Phone: (907) 895-4484

Dillingham: 546 Kenny Wren Rd., P.O. Box 230 (99576-0230). Phone: (907) 842-5227

Douglas: Southeast Regional Office: 802 3rd St., P.O. Box 240020 (99824-0020). Phone: (907) 465-4293; sport-fishing information: (907) 465-4270; wildlife conservation: (907) 465-4265

Dutch Harbor: P.O. Box 920587 (99692-0587). Phone: (907) 581-1219

Fairbanks Regional Office: 1300 College Rd. (99701-1599). Phone: (907) 459-7200; sport-fishing information: (907) 459-7385; hunting information: (907) 459-7306; wildlife conservation: (907) 459-7213

Fort Yukon: c/o 1300 College Rd., Fairbanks (99701). Phone: (907) 662-2614 or 459-7213

Galena: P.O. Box 209 (99741-0209). Phone: (907) 656-1663

Glennallen: Mile 186.3 Glenn Hwy., P.O. Box 47 (99588-0047). Phone (907) 822-3309

Haines: Mile 1 Haines Hwy., P.O. Box 330 (99827-0330). Phone: (907) 766-2625

Homer: 3298 Douglas St. (99603-8027). Phone: (907) 235-8191

Juneau Headquarters: 1255 W. 8th St., P.O. Box 25526 (99802-5526). Phone: (907) 465-4112; sport-fishing information: (907) 465-4116; wildlife conservation: (907) 465-4190

Ketchikan: 2030 Sea Level Dr., Suite 205 (99901). Phone: sport-fishing information: (907) 225-2859; wildlife conservation: (907) 225-2475

King Salmon: Main Street, P.O. Box 37 (99613-0037). Phone: (907) 246-3340

Klawock: P.O. Box 271 (99925-0271). Phone: (907) 755-2485

Kodiak: 211 Mission Rd. (99615-6399). Phone: (907) 486-1825; fishing/hunting recording: (907) 486-5176; wildlife conservation: (907) 486-1880

Kotzebue: 240 5th Ave., P.O. Box 689 (99752-0689). Phone: (907) 442-3420

McGrath: P.O. Box 230 (99627-0230). Phone: (907) 524-3323

Nome: 320 E. Front St., Pouch 1148 (99762). Phone: sport-fishing information: (907) 443-5796; wildlife conservation: (907) 443-2271

Palmer: 1800 Glenn Hwy., Suite 4 (99645-6736). Phone: (907) 746-6300

Sand Point: P.O. Box 129 (99661-0129). Phone: (907) 383-2066

Sitka: 304 Lake St., Room 103 (99835-7563). Phone: sport-fishing information: (907) 747-5355; wildlife conservation: (907) 474-5449

Soldotna: 34828 Kalifornsky Beach Rd., Suite B (99669-8367). Phone: (907) 262-9368; sport-fishing recording: (907) 262-2737; escapement numbers recording: (907) 262-9097

Tok: P.O. Box 355 (99780-0355). Phone: (907) 883-2971

Wrangell: 215 Front St., P.O. Box 200 (99929-0200). Phone: (907) 874-3822

Yakutat: 1 Fish and Game Plaza, P.O. Box 49 (99689-0049). Phone: sport-fishing information: (907) 784-3222

Alaska Department of Natural Resources (ADNR)

Home page: www.dnr.state.ak.us

Anchorage: Public Information Center, 3601 C St., Suite 200, P.O. Box 107005 (99510-7005). Phone: (907) 269-8400

Fairbanks: (DF) Division of Forestry, 3700 Airport Way (99709). Phone: (907) 451-2700 (DL) Division of Land, 3700 Airport Way (99709). Phone: (907) 451-2700

Juneau: (DF) Division of Forestry, 400 Willoughby Ave. (99801). Phone: (907) 465-3379 (DL) Division of Land, 400 Willoughby Ave. (99801). Phone: (907) 465-3400

Alaska Division of Parks and Outdoor Recreation, Department of Natural Resources (ADP)

Home page: www.dnr.state.ak.us/parks/index.htm

Anchorage: Chugach State Park Office, Potter Section House, Mile 115 Seward Highway, HC 52, Box 8999, Indian (99540). Phone: (907) 345-5014

Eagle River Nature Center. Phone: (907) 694-2108

Wood–Tikchik Park, 3601 C St., Suite 1200 (99503). Phone: (907) 269-8698

Dillingham: (Summer only) Phone: (907) 842-2375

Fairbanks: Northern Area Office, 3700 Airport Way (99709-4613). Phone: (907) 451-2695

Juneau: Southeast Area Office, 400 Willoughby Ave., Fourth Floor (99801). Phone: (907) 465-4563

Kodiak: Kodiak District Office, 1400 Abercrombie Dr., Kodiak (99615). Phone: (907) 486-6339 or (907) 486-6550

Soldotna: Kenai/Prince William Sound Area Office, Mile 85 Sterling Hwy., P.O. Box 1247 (99669). Phone: (907) 262-5581

Wasilla: Mat-Su/Valdez–Copper River Area Office, Mile 0.7 Bogard Rd., HC 32 Box 6706 (99687-9719). Phone: (907) 745-3975

Bureau of Land Management, U.S. Department of the Interior (BLM)

Home page: www.ak.blm.gov/

Alaska State Office: 222 W. 7th Ave., P.O. Box 13, Anchorage (99513). Phone: (907) 271-5960 Joint Pipeline Office (JPD). Phone: (907) 271-4336

Anchorage: Anchorage Field Office, 6881 Abbott Loop Rd. (99507). Phone: (907) 267-1246; fax: (907) 267-1267; home page: www.ak.blm.gov/ado/

Fairbanks: Northern Field Office,1150 University Ave. (99709-3844). Phone: (907) 474-2302; home page: www.ak.blm.gov/ndo/

Glennallen: Glennallen Field Office, P.O. Box 147 (99588). Phone: (907) 822-3217; home page: www.ak.blm.gov/gdo/

Juneau: Juneau Mineral Information Center, 100 Savikko Rd., Douglas (99824). Phone: (907) 364-1553; fax: (907) 364-1574

Kotzebue: Kotzebue Field Station, P.O. Box 1049 (99752). Phone: (907) 442-3430

Nome: Nome Field Station, P.O. Box 925 (99762). Phone: (907) 443-2177

Tok: Tok Field Station, P.O. Box 309 (99780). Phone: (907) 883-5121

Forest Service, U.S. Department of Agriculture (USFS)

Home page: www.fs.fed.us/r10

Forest Service Information Center: 101 Egan Dr., Juneau (99801). Phone: (907) 586-8751; fax: (907) 586-7928; TTY: (907) 586-7894

Southeast Alaska Visitor Center: Tongass National Forest, 50 Main St., Ketchikan (99901). Phone: (907) 228-6214; fax: (907) 228-6234; TTY: (907) 228-6237

Anchorage: Chugach National Forest, 3301 C St., Suite 300 (99503). Phone: (907) 271-2500. Cabin reservations: (800) 280-2267

Craig: Craig Ranger District, P.O. Box 500 (99921). Phone: (907) 826-3271

Cordova: Cordova Ranger Station, 612 Second St. (99574). Phone: (907) 424-7661

Girdwood: Girdwood Ranger Station, Alyeska Highway and Monarch Mine Road (99587). Phone: (907) 783-3242

Hoonah: Hoonah Ranger District, P.O. Box 135 (99829). Phone: (907) 945-3631

Juneau: Juneau Ranger District, 8465 Old Dairy Rd. (99801). Phone: (907) 586-8800 Admiralty Island National Monument, 8461 Old Dairy Rd. (99801). Phone: (907) 586-8790

Ketchikan: Ketchikan Ranger District and Misty Fiords National Monument, 3031 Tongass Ave. (99901). Phone: (907) 225-2148

Ketchikan Area Supervisor's Office, Federal Building, 648 Mission St. (99901). Phone (907) 228-6202

Petersburg: Petersburg Ranger District, P.O. Box 1328 (99833). Phone: (907) 772-3871
Stikine Area Supervisor's Office, P.O. Box 309, 201 12th St. (99833). Phone: (907) 772-3841

Seward: Seward Ranger District, 334 Fourth Ave. (99664). Phone: (907) 224-3374

Sitka: Sitka Ranger District, 201 Katlian St., Suite 109 (99835). Phone: (907) 474-4220.
Chatham Area Supervisor's Office, 204 Siginaka Way (99835). Phone: (907) 747-6671

Thorne Bay: Thorne Bay Ranger District, P.O. Box I (99919). Phone: (907) 828-3304

Wrangell: Wrangell Ranger District, P.O. Box 51 (99929). Phone: (907) 874-2323

Yakutat: Yakutat Ranger District, P.O. Box 327 (99826). Phone: (907) 784-3359

National Park Service, U.S. Department of the Interior (NPS)

Home page: www/nps.gov/

Alaska Regional Office: 2525 Gambell St., Anchorage (99503). Phone: (907) 257-2696

Anchorage: Lake Clark National Park, Alaska Pacific University, Grace Hall, Suite 311, 4230 University Dr. (99508). Phone: (907) 271-3751

Copper Center: P.O. Box 439 (99573). Phone: (907) 822-5234

Denali National Park: P.O. Box 9 (99755). Phone: (907) 683-2294

Eagle: P.O. Box 167 (99738). Phone: (907) 547-2234

Fairbanks: Gates of the Arctic, P.O. Box 74680 (99707). Phone: (907) 456-0281.

Yukon–Charley Rivers: P.O. Box 74680 (99707). Phone: (907) 456-0281

Gustavus: P.O. Box 140 (99826). Phone: (907) 697-2232

King Salmon: P.O. Box 7 (99613). Phone: (907) 246-3305

Kotzebue: P.O. Box 1029 (99752). Phone: (907) 442-3890

Nome: P.O. Box 220 (99762). Phone: (907) 443-2522

Seward: P.O. Box 1727 (99664). Phone: (907) 224-3175

Sitka: P.O. Box 738 (99835). Phone: (907) 747-6281

Skagway: P.O. Box 517 (99840). Phone: (907) 983-2921

U.S. Fish and Wildlife Service, U.S. Department of the Interior (USFW)

Home page: www.r7.fws.gov/

Alaska Regional Office: 1011 E. Tudor Rd., Anchorage (99503). Phone: (907) 786-3353

Adak: Aleutian Islands Unit/Alaska Maritime National Wildlife Refuge, P.O. Box 5251 (99546-5251). Phone: (907) 592-2406; fax: (907) 592-3472

Bethel: Yukon Delta National Wildlife Refuge/Nunivak National Wildlife Refuge and Wilderness/Andreafsky National Wilderness and Wild River, P.O. Box 346 (99559). Phone: (907) 543-3151; fax: (907) 543-4413

Cold Bay: Izembek National Wildlife Refuge, P.O. Box 127 (99571-0127). Phone: (907) 532-2445; fax: (907) 532-2549

Dillingham: Togiak National Wildlife Refuge, P.O. Box 270 (99576). Phone: (907) 842-1063; fax: (907) 842-5402

Fairbanks: Federal Bldg., 101 12th Ave. (99701). Phone: (907) 456-0219
Arctic National Wildlife Refuge (ANWR), P.O. Box 20 (99701). Phone: (907) 456-0253; fax: (907) 456-0428

Kanuti National Wildlife Refuge, 101 12th Ave., Room 112 (99701). Phone: (907) 456-0329; fax: (907) 456-0506

Yukon Flats National Wildlife Refuge, 101 12th Ave., Room 264 (99701). Phone: (907) 456-0440; fax: (907) 456-0447

Galena: Koyukuk National Wildlife Refuge/Nowitna National Wildlife Refuge, P.O. Box 287 (99741). Phone: (907) 656-1231; fax: (907) 656-1708

Homer: Alaska Maritime National Wildlife Refuge, 2355 Kachemak Drive, Suite 101 (99603-8021). Phone: (907) 235-6546; fax: (907) 235-7783

AMNWR Visitor Center, 451 Sterling Highway (99603). Phone: (907) 235-6961; bird hotline: (907) 235-PEEP

King Salmon: Alaska Peninsula National Wildlife Refuge/Becharof National Wildlife Refuge, P.O. Box 277 (99613). Phone: (907) 246-3339; fax: (907) 246-6696

Kodiak: Kodiak National Wildlife Refuge, 1390 Buskin River Rd. (99615). Phone: (907) 487-2600; fax: (907) 487-2144

Kotzebue: Selawik National Wildlife Refuge, P.O. Box 270 (99752). Phone: (907) 442-3799; fax: (907) 442-3124

McGrath: Innoko National Wildlife Refuge, P.O. Box 69 (99627). Phone: (907) 524-3251; fax: (907) 524-3141

Soldotna: Kenai National Wildlife Refuge, P.O. Box 2139 (99669-2139). Phone: (907) 262-7021; fax: (907) 262-3599

Tok: Tetlin National Wildlife Refuge, P.O. Box 779 (99780). Phone: (907) 883-5312; fax: (907) 883-5747

Other

Pribilof Islands, Tanadgusix Corp (TDX) of St. Paul Island: 1500 W. 33rd Ave., Suite 220, Anchorage (99503). Phone: (907) 278-2312

For a package tour to St. Paul Island, contact Reeve Aleutian Airways, Inc., 4700 W. International Airport Rd., Anchorage (99502). Phone: (907) 243-4700, (800) 544-2248 (outside Alaska). Home page: www.alaskabirding.com

Tours to St. George may be arranged through PenAir in Anchorage. Phone: (907) 243-2323, (800) 448-4226 (outside Alaska).

Key to Addresses of Described Parklands

Parkland Region/Name	Manager	Office Location	Parkland Region/Name	Manager	Office Location
Southeast			Klondike Gold Rush National Historical Park	NPS	Skagway
Admiralty Island Monument	USFS	Juneau District	Kootznoowoo Wilderness	USFS	Juneau District
Alaska Chilkat Bald Eagle Preserve	ADP	Juneau	Kuiu Wilderness	USFS	Juneau District
Baranof Castle Hill State Historic Site	ADP	Juneau	Maurelle Islands Wilderness	USFS	Thorne Bay
Chilkat State Park	ADP	Juneau	Mendenhall Wetlands State Game Refuge	ADFG	Douglas
Chuck River Wilderness	USFS	Juneau District	Misty Fiords National Monument	USFS	Ketchikan
Coronation Island Wilderness	USFS	Thorne Bay	Old Sitka State Historic Site	ADP	Juneau
Eagle Beach State Recreation Area	ADP	Juneau	Petersburg Creek–Duncan Salt Chuck Wilderness	USFS	Juneau District
Endicott River Wilderness	USFS	Juneau District	Pleasant–Lemesurier–Inian Islands Wilderness	USFS	Juneau District
Glacier Bay National Park	NPS	Gustavus	Point Bridget State Park	ADP	Juneau
Gruening State Historical Park	NPS	Juneau	Russell Fiord Wilderness	USFS	Yakutat
Karta River Wilderness	USFS	Thorne Bay	Sitka National Historical Park	NPS	Sitka

Parkland Region/Name	Manager	Office Location
South Baranof Wilderness	USFS	Sitka
South Etolin Island Wilderness	USFS	Ketchikan
South Prince of Wales Wilderness	USFS	Craig
Stan Price State Wildlife Sanctuary	ADFG	Douglas
Stikine–LeConte Wilderness	USFS	Wrangell
Tebenkof Bay Wilderness	USFS	Petersburg
Tongass National Forest	USFS	Juneau
Totem Bight State Historical Park	ADP	Juneau
Tracy Arm–Fords Terror Wilderness	USFS	Juneau District
Warren Island Wilderness	USFS	Thorne Bay
Wickersham State Historical Site	ADP	Juneau
West Chichagof–Yakobi Wilderness	USFS	Sitka

Southcentral / Gulf Coast

Parkland Region/Name	Manager	Office Location
Afognak Island State Park	ADP	Kodiak
Anchorage Coastal Wildlife Refuge	ADFG	Anchorage
Anchor River State Recreation Area	ADP	Soldotna
Caines Head State Recreation Area	ADP	Soldotna
Captain Cook State Recreation Area	ADP	Soldotna
Chilikadrotna National Wild River	NPS	Anchorage
Chugach National Forest	USFS	Anchorage
Chugach State Park	ADP	Anchorage
Clam Gulch State Recreation Area	ADP	Soldotna
Deep Creek State Recreation Area	ADP	Soldotna
Fort Abercrombie State Historical Park	ADP	Kodiak
Goose Bay State Game Refuge	ADFG	Anchorage
Gulkana National Wild and Scenic River	BLM	Glennallen
Iditarod National Historic Trail	BLM	Anchorage District
Independence Mine State Historical Park	ADP	Wasilla
Johnson Lake State Recreation Area	ADP	Soldotna
Kachemak Bay State Park and Wilderness Park	ADP	Homer
Kenai Fjords National Park	NPS	Seward
Kenai National Wildlife Refuge and Wilderness	USFW	Soldotna
Kepler–Bradley Lakes State Recreation Area	ADP	Wasilla
Kodiak National Wildlife Refuge	USFW	Kodiak
Lake Clark National Park and Preserve (LCNP)	NPS	Anchorage
Lake Louise State Recreation Area	ADP	Wasilla

Parkland Region/Name	Manager	Office Location
Mulchatna National Wild River	NPS	Anchorage
Nancy Lake State Recreation Area	ADP	Wasilla
Ninilchik State Recreation Area	ADP	Soldotna
Palmer Hay Flats State Game Refuge	ADFG	Palmer
Potter Section House Historic Site	ADP	Anchorage
Shuyak Island State Park	ADP	Kodiak
Susitna Flats State Game Refuge	ADFG	Anchorage
Tlikakila National Wild River	NPS	Anchorage
Trading Bay State Game Refuge	ADFG	Anchorage
Willow Creek State Recreation Area	ADP	Wasilla
Wrangell–St. Elias National Park and Preserve	NPS	Glennallen
Yakataga State Game Refuge	ADFG	Cordova

Aleutian Islands and Alaska Peninsula

Parkland Region/Name	Manager	Office Location
Alagnak National Wild River	NPS	King Salmon
Alaska Peninsula National Wildlife Refuge	USFW	King Salmon
Aniakchak National Monument and Preserve	NPS	King Salmon
Becharof National Wildlife Refuge and Wilderness	USFW	King Salmon
Izembek National Wildlife Refuge and Wilderness	USFW	Cold Bay
Izembek State Game Refuge	ADFG	Cold Bay
Katmai National Park and Preserve	NPS	King Salmon
McNeil River State Game Refuge and Sanctuary	ADFG	Anchorage
Pribilof Islands	*	St. Paul

* Municipalities of St. George and St. Paul, Tanadgusix and Tanaq corporations, and U.S. Fish and Wildlife Service, National Marine Fisheries Service

Interior

Parkland Region/Name	Manager	Office Location
Beaver Creek National Wild and Scenic River	BLM	Fairbanks
Big Delta State Historical Park	ADP	Fairbanks
Birch Creek National Wild and Scenic River	BLM	Fairbanks
Charley National Wild River	NPS	Fairbanks
Chena River State Recreation Area	ADP	Fairbanks
Creamer's Field Migratory Waterfowl Refuge	ADFG	Fairbanks
Dalton Highway	BLM	Fairbanks
Delta National Wild, Scenic, and Recreational River	BLM	Glennallen
Denali National Park and Preserve	NPS	Denali and
Denali State Park	ADP	Anchorage
Fort Egbert National Historic Site	BLM	Fairbanks

Parkland Region/Name	Manager	Office Location
Fortymile National Wild, Scenic, and Recreational River	BLM	Tok
Harding Lake State Recreation Area	ADP	Fairbanks
Innoko National Wildlife Refuge and Wilderness	USFW	McGrath
Kanuti National Wildlife Refuge	USFW	Fairbanks
Koyukuk National Wildlife Refuge and Wilderness	USFW	Galena
Lower Chatanika River State Recreation Area	ADP	Fairbanks
Minto Flats State Game Refuge	ADFG	Fairbanks
Nowitna National Wildlife Refuge	USFW	Galena
Quartz Lake State Recreation Area	ADP	Fairbanks
Steese National Conservation Area	BLM	Fairbanks
Tetlin National Wildlife Refuge	USFW	Tok
White Mountains National Recreation Area	BLM	Fairbanks
Yukon–Charley Rivers National Preserve	NPS	Fairbanks
Yukon Flats National Wildlife Refuge	USFW	Fairbanks

Western / Bering Sea Coast

Parkland Region/Name	Manager	Office Location
Andreafsky Wilderness, Yukon Delta National Wildlife Refuge	USFW	Bethel
Cape Newenham State Game Refuge	ADFG	Dillingham
Nunivak Wilderness, Yukon Delta National Wildlife Refuge	USFW	Bethel
Togiak National Wildlife Refuge and Wilderness	USFW	Dillingham
Walrus Islands State Game Sanctuary	ADFG	Dillingham
Wood-Tikchik State Park	ADP	Anchorage; Dillingham
Yukon Delta National Wildlife Refuge	USFW	Bethel

Arctic

Parkland Region/Name	Manager	Office Location
Alatna National Wild River	NPS	Fairbanks
Arctic National Wildlife Refuge and Wilderness (ANWR)	USFW	Fairbanks
Bering Land Bridge National Preserve	NPS	Nome
Cape Krusenstern National Monument	NPS	Kotzebue
Gates of the Arctic National Park and Preserve	NPS	Fairbanks
Ivishak National Wild River (ANWR)	USFW	Fairbanks
John National Wild River	NPS	Fairbanks
Kobuk Valley National Park	NPS	Kotzebue
Kobuk National Wild River	NPS	Fairbanks
North Fork, Koyukuk National Wild River	NPS	Fairbanks
Noatak National Preserve	NPS	Kotzebue
Salmon National Wild River	NPS	Kotzebue
Selawik National Wildlife Refuge and Wilderness and River	USFW	Kotzebue
Sheenjek National Wild River (ANWR)	USFW	Fairbanks
Tinayguk National Wild River	NPS	Fairbanks
Unalakleet National Wild and Scenic River	BLM	Anchorage
Wind National Wild River (ANWR)	USFW	Fairbanks

National Maritime Lands

Parkland Region/Name	Manager	Office Location
Alaska Maritime National Wildlife Refuge	USFW	Homer
Aleutian Islands Subunit	USFW	Homer
Ann Stevens–Cape Lisburne Subunit	USFW	Homer
Bering Sea Subunit	USFW	Homer
Bogoslof Subunit	USFW	Homer
Chamisso Subunit	USFW	Homer
Forrester Island Subunit	USFW	Homer
Hazy Islands Subunit	USFW	Homer
Semidi Subunit	USFW	Homer
Simeonof Subunit	USFW	Homer
St. Lazaria Subunit	USFW	Homer
Tuxedni Subunit	USFW	Homer

Information Sources

Public Lands Information Centers

Anchorage: 605 W. 4th Ave., Suite 105 (99501). Phone: (907) 271-2737
Fairbanks: 250 Cushman St., Suite 1A (99701). Phone: (907) 456-0527
Ketchikan: 3031 Tongass Ave. (99901). Phone: (907) 228-6220
Tok: Mile 1314 Alaska Hwy., P.O. Box 359 (99780). Phone: (907) 883-5667

General Information for Travelers

Books

Alaska Division of Tourism, P.O. Box 11081, Juneau (99811-0801). Phone: (907) 465-2010. Ask for the "Alaska Vacation Planner."

Alaska Northwest Books, P.O. Box 10306, Portland, OR 97210. Phones: (800) 452-3032, (503) 226-2402; fax: (503) 223-1410. Specializes in books about Alaska, including an annually updated edition of *The Alaska Almanac: Facts About Alaska.*

Epicenter Press, P.O. Box 82368, Seattle, WA 98028. Phone: (425) 485-6822; fax: (425) 481-8253. Umbrella Books travel series includes many Alaska titles.

The Milepost, updated annually. A guidebook essential and informative for travelers on the roads and ferries in Alaska and for getting to Alaska. Also *The Alaska Wilderness Guide,* covering off-road Alaska. Both from Alaskan Publications, 619 E. Ship Creek Ave., Suite 329, Anchorage (99501). Phone: (907) 272-6070; fax: (907) 258-5360.

Visitors Bureaus and Information Centers

Alaska Division of Tourism home page: www.commerce.state.ak.us/tourism/

Anchorage Convention and Visitors Bureau, 524 Fourth Ave., Anchorage (99501). Phone: (907) 276-4118; home page: www.anchorage.net

Bethel Visitor Center, P.O. Box 388, Bethel (99559). Phone: (907) 543-2798

Greater Copper Valley Visitor Information Center, P.O. Box 469, Glennallen (99588). Phone: (907) 822-5555

Cordova Visitors Center, P.O. Box 391, Cordova (99587). Phone: (907) 424-7443

Fairbanks Convention and Visitors Bureau, 550 First Ave., Fairbanks (99701). Phones: (907) 451-1724 or (800) 327-5774

Haines Visitor Information Center, City of Haines, P.O. Box 518, Haines (99827). Phone: (907) 766-2234

Juneau Convention and Visitors Bureau, 76 Egan Dr., Suite 300, Juneau (99801-1753). Phone: (907) 586-1737

Kachemak Bay Convention and Visitors Association, Box 1001, Homer (99603-1001). Phone: (907) 235-8897

Kenai Visitor Information Center, P.O. Box 1991, Kenai (99611-6935). Phones: (907) 283-1991 or (800) 535-3624; email: kptmc@alaska.net

Ketchikan Convention and Visitors Bureau, 131 Front St., Ketchikan (99901). Phone: (907) 225-6166

Kodiak Island Convention and Visitors Bureau, 100 Marine Way, Kodiak (99615). Phone: (907) 486-6545

Nome Convention and Visitors Bureau, P.O. Box 240, Nome (99762). Phone: (907) 443-5535

Petersburg Visitor Information, P.O. Box 649, Petersburg (99833). Phone: (907) 772-4636

Seward Visitor Information Cache, P.O. Box 749, Seward (99664). Phone: (907) 224-8051

Sitka Convention and Visitors Bureau, P.O. Box 1226, Sitka (99835). Phone: (907) 747-5940

Skagway Convention and Visitors Bureau, P.O. Box 415, Skagway (99840). Phone: (907) 983-2854; home page: www.skagway.org

Tok Visitor Center, P.O. Box 389, Tok (99780). Phone: (907) 883-5775

Unalaska/Port of Dutch Harbor Convention and Visitors Bureau, P.O. Box 545, Unalaska (99685). Phone: (907) 581-2612

Valdez Convention and Visitors Bureau, P.O. Box 1603, Valdez (99686). Phones: (907) 835-4636 or (800) 770-5954

Wrangell Convention and Visitors Bureau, P.O. Box 1078, Wrangell (99929). Phone: (907) 874-3800

Alaska Marine Highway System (Alaska State Ferry)

Home page: www.dot.state.ak.us/external/amhs/home.html

Department of Transportation

Main Office (for all reservations): P.O. Box 25535, Juneau (99802-5535). Phone: (800) 642-0066; fax: (907) 277-4829. From outside of Alaska: (800) 642-0066

Local Office Telephone Numbers

Anchorage: (907) 272-4482 or (907) 272-7116; fax: (907) 277-4829

Bellingham, WA: (360) 676-8445; recording: (360) 676-0212

Cordova: (907) 424-7333

Haines: Recording: (907) 766-2113; (907) 766-2111; (907) 766-2112

Homer: (907) 235-8449

Juneau: Recording: (907) 465-3940; (907) 465-3941

Ketchikan: (907) 225-6181

Kodiak: (907) 486-3800

Petersburg: (907) 772-3855

Prince Rupert, B.C., Canada: (604) 627-1744

Seldovia: (907) 234-7868

Seward: (907) 224-5485

Sitka: Recording: (907) 747-3300

Skagway: (907) 983-2229

Valdez: (907) 835-4436

Wrangell: (907) 874-3711

British Columbia Ferries

Service between Port Hardy and Prince Rupert.

British Columbia Ferry Corporation, 1112 Fort St., Victoria, BC V8V 4V2. Phone: (604) 386-3431 (Victoria); (604) 669-1211 (Vancouver); home page: www.bcferries.bc.ca/ferries

Inter-City Bus Lines

Alaska Direct Bus Lines, P.O. Box 501, Anchorage 99510. Phone: (800) 770-6652; (907) 277-6652 (Anchorage). Serves Anchorage, Beaver Creek, Y.T., Delta, Denali National Park, Dawson City, Y.T., Fairbanks, Glennallen, Haines Junction, Y.T., Skagway, Tok, Whitehorse, Y.T.

Alaskan Express (Gray Line of Alaska), 745 West 4th Ave., Anchorage (99501). Phone: (907) 277-5581; (800) 478-6388 (Alaska); (800) 544-2206 (outside Alaska). (Summer only. Serves Alyeska Prince Hotel, Anchorage, Delta Junction, Glennallen, Haines, Portage, Whittier, Seward, Skagway, Tok, and Valdez in Alaska; Beaver Creek, Haines Junction, Fraser/Log Cabin [Chilkoot Trail access], and Whitehorse in Canada.)

Parks Highway Express, P.O. Box 82884, Fairbanks (99708). Phone: (907) 479-3065 or (888) 600-6001. (Serves travelers between Fairbanks and Anchorage, including Denali National Park.)

Seward Bus Line, 3339A Fairbanks St., Anchorage (99503). Phone: (907) 278-0800 (Anchorage) or (907) 224-3608 (Seward). (Serves Anchorage, Bird Creek, Girdwood, Indian, Moose Pass, Portage, and Seward.)

Anchorage City Bus System

"The People Mover," Municipality of Anchorage, Transit Department, Customer Service, P.O. Box 196650 (99519-6650). Phone: (907) 343-6543

Fairbanks City Bus System

Metropolitan Area Commuter System (MACS), Fairbanks North Star Borough Transportation Department, 809 Pioneer Road, P.O. Box 71267, Fairbanks (99707-1267). Phone: (907) 459-1011

Railroads
Alaska Railroad

Home page: www.akrr.com

Anchorage: (main office) 411 W. 1st Ave., P.O. Box 107500 (99510).

Information/reservations: Passenger Services Dept. phone: (800) 544-0552; (907) 265-2494

Whittier shuttle: (907) 265-2607

Fairbanks: 280 N. Cushman St. (99701). Phone: (907) 458-6025

(Serves Anchorage, Denali National Park, Fairbanks, Portage, Seward, and Whittier. Vehicles are carried between Portage and Whittier. Local rural service available summers between Talkeetna and Hurricane Gulch.)

White Pass & Yukon Route

Home page: www.whitepassrailroad.com

Skagway: (main office) P.O. Box 435 (99840). Phone: (800) 343-7373 (USA); (800) 478-7373 (NW Canada); (907) 983-2217 (Skagway); (403) 668-RAIL (Whitehorse). (Operates between Skagway, Alaska, and Lake Bennett, B.C., Fraser, B.C., or Carcross, Y.T. Summers only. Chilkoot Trail hikers may book their return passage from Lake Bennett to Fraser or Skagway.)

Airlines. Consult local listings or see your travel agent.

Travelers' Current Road and Weather Information

Highway conditions and avalanche advisory, statewide information, touch-tone–selected recordings. Phone: (907) 273-6037 (Anchorage); (800) 478-7675

U.S. and Canada Customs Stations, Hours of Operation

U.S. Customs, Treasury Department, Skagway: (907) 983-2325

Canada Customs, Fraser, B.C.: (403) 821-4111

Alaska Time + 1 hour = Pacific (Canada) Time

	United States Customs		Canada Customs	
Highway	Location	Hours	Location	Hours
Alaska Hwy.	Mile 1222	24 hours, year-round	Mile 1170	24 hours, year-round
Haines Hwy.	Mile 40	7:00 A.M.–11:00 P.M., year-round	Mile 41	8:00 A.M.–midnight, year-round
Klondike Hwy.	Mile 6	8:00 A.M.–11:00 P.M., year-round	Mile 22	24 hours, year-round
Yukon Hwy. 9	Mile 66	8:00 A.M.–8:00 P.M., summers	Mile 66	9:00 A.M.–9:00 P.M., summers

United States Customs Service, Offices

Main Office: 605 W. 4th Ave., Room 205, Anchorage (99501). Phone: (907) 271-2675

Customs Stations

Alcan: HC 63, Box 1221, Tok (99780). Phone: (907) 774-2252

Dalton Cache: HC 60, Box 4000, Haines (99827). Phone: (907) 767-5511

Eagle: Yukon River entry point. Contact the Alcan office.

Fairbanks: Fairbanks International Airport, 6450 Airport Way, Suite 13 (99709). Phone: (907) 474-0307

Juneau: 1910 Alex Holden Way (99801). Phone: (907) 586-7211

Ketchikan: 105 Main St. (99901). Inside Passage entry point. Phone: (907) 225-2254

Poker Creek: Mile 66, Yukon Hwy. 9. Contact the Alcan office.

Sitka: 329 Harbor Dr., #206 (99835). Phone: (907) 747-3374

Skagway: P.O. 437 (99840). Phone: (907) 983-2325

Valdez: P.O. Box 217 (99686). Phone: (907) 835-3597

Wrangell: P.O. Box 561 (99929). Phone: (907) 874-3415

Alaska State Troopers, Department of Public Safety

Emergency: 911 (Not operational in some communities. Call Directory Assistance or check local phone directory.)

Anchorage Office: 5700 E. Tudor Rd. (99507). Phone: (907) 269-5511

Fairbanks Office: 1979 Peger Rd. (99709). Phone: (907) 451-5100

Juneau Office: 2760 Sherwood Lane (99801). Phone: (907) 465-4000

Ketchikan Office: P.O. Box 8700 (99901). Phone: (907) 225-5118

Tok: P.O. Box 335 (99780). Phone: (907) 883-5111

Royal Canadian Mounted Police Emergency Contacts

Alcan Office: Beaver Creek, Yukon Territory. Phone: (867) 862-5555

Dawson City: Yukon Territory. Phone: (867) 993-5555

Prince Rupert: British Columbia. Phone: 911, or for non-emergencies, (250) 627-0700

Whitehorse: Yukon Territory. Phone: 911

Specialized Information

Alaska Natives

Alaska Federation of Natives, Inc., 1577 C St., Suite 100, Anchorage (99501). Phone: (907) 274-3611

Alaska Native Heritage Center, corner of Muldoon Road and Glenn Highway; P.O. Box 213849, Anchorage (99521). Phone: (907) 263-5170; fax (907) 263-5575

Regional Native Corporations

Ahtna, Inc., P.O. Box 649, Glennallen (99588). Phone: (907) 822-3476

Aleut Corp., 400 Old Seward Hwy., #300, Anchorage (99503). Phone: (907) 576-4300

Arctic Slope Regional Corp., P.O. Box 129, Barrow (99723). Phone: (907) 852-8633

Bering Straits Native Corp., P.O. Box 1008, Nome (99762). Phone: (907) 443-5252

Bristol Bay Native Corp., P.O. Box 100220, Anchorage (99510). Phone: (907) 278-3602

Calista Corp., 301 Calista Ct., Suite A, Anchorage (99518). Phone: (907) 279-5516

Chugach Natives Inc., 560 E. 34th Ave., #200, Anchorage (99503). Phone: (907) 563-8866

Cook Inlet Region, Inc., P.O. Box 93330, Anchorage (99509). Phone: (907) 274-8638

Doyon, Ltd., 201 First Ave., Fairbanks (99701). Phone: (907) 452-4755

Koniag, Inc., 4300 B St., #407, Anchorage (99503). Phone: (907) 561-2668

NANA Regional Corp., 1001 E. Benson Blvd., Anchorage (99508). Phone: (907) 265-4100

Sealaska Corp., One Sealaska Plaza, #400, Juneau (99801). Phone: (907) 586-1512

The Thirteenth Corp., 4370 NE Halsey St., #130, Portland, OR 97213. Phone: (503) 287-5822

Boating

U.S. Coast Guard, Boating Safety Division, Cmdr. (B), 17th Coast Guard District, P.O. Box 25517, Juneau (99802-5517). Phone: (907) 463-2198

Rescue Coordination Center, phone: (800) 478-5555 or (907) 463-2000 (Juneau); (907) 271-6700 (24 hours, Marine Safety, Anchorage). Report accidents and casualties, water pollution, missing or inoperative marine navigational aids, or suspected violations of U.S. fisheries laws and gear conflicts.

Cooperative Extension Service

Anchorage: 2221 E. Northern Lights Blvd., Suite 118 (99508). Phone: (907) 279-5582

Fairbanks—Tanana District: 1255 Airport Way, Suite 203 (99701). Phone: (907) 452-1530; fax: (907) 456-6885

Juneau: 1108 F Street., Suite 130 (99801). Phone: (907) 586-8756; fax: (907) 465-8742

Federal Aviation Administration

Public Affairs Office, 222 W. 7th Ave., P.O. Box 14, Anchorage (99513-7587). Phone: (907) 271-5293

Flight Standards Division. Phone: (907) 271-5514

Guide Services, Licensing and Investigations

Alaska Department of Commerce & Economic Development, Division of Occupational Licensing, 3601 C St., Anchorage (99503). Phone: (907) 269-8160

Guide Services, Mountaineering and Wilderness

Alaska Wilderness Recreation and Tourism Assoc., P.O. Box 22827, Juneau (99802). Phone: (907) 463-3038; home page: www.alaska.net/~awrta/

Maps and Charts

Alaska Marine and Aeronautical Charts, Tide Tables, Tidal Current Tables, and Other Publications

Anchorage: Chart Sales Office, National Ocean Service, Federal Building, 222 W. 7th Ave., Room 109 (99513). Phone: (907) 271-5040. These publications are also available from chart agents and stores in many Alaskan communities.

Alaska Topographic Maps

Anchorage: Earth Science Information Center, U.S. Geological Survey, Alaska Pacific University Campus, 4230 University Dr., Room 101 (99508). Phone: (907) 786-7011. Also has reference library.

Denver: U.S. Geological Survey Information Services, Box 25286, Denver Federal Center, Denver, CO 80225. Phone: (800) 435-7627

Fairbanks: University of Alaska Fairbanks, Map Office, Geophysical Institute, 930 Koyukuk Drive (99775). Phone: (907) 474-6960

DeLorme Mapping. *Alaska Atlas & Gazetteer.* Yarmouth, Maine, 1992. A handy book of topographic maps of the entire state; available through local bookstores. DeLorme Mapping, 2 DeLorme Drive, Yarmouth ME (04096). Phone: (207) 846-7000.

Canadian Topographic Maps

Fairbanks: McCauley's Reprographics, Inc., 3419 Airport Way, Suite D (99703). Phone: (907) 452-8141

Ottawa: Canada Map Office, Natural Resources Canada, 615 Booth St., Ottawa, Ontario, Canada K1A 0E9. Phone: (613) 952-7000

Whitehorse: Mac's Fireweed Books, 203 Main St., Whitehorse, Yukon Territory, Canada Y1A 2B2. Phone: (800) 661-0508

Aerial Photographs

Anchorage: Aeromap U.S., 2014 Merrill Field Dr. (99501). Phone: (907) 272-4495

Earth Science Information Center, U.S. Geological Survey, Alaska Pacific University Campus, 4230 University Dr., Room 101 (99508). Phone: (907) 786-7011

Fairbanks: University of Alaska Fairbanks, Geo Data Center, Geophysical Institute, 930 Koyukuk Drive (99775). Phone: (907) 474-6960

Search and Rescue

Alaska Mountain Rescue Group, Fast Action Response Team. Recorded messages: (907) 566-2674
   In emergencies, contact Alaska State Troopers, phone 911 and ask for AMRG assistance.
Alaska Mountain Safety Center, 9140 Brewsters Dr., Anchorage (99516). Phone: (907) 345-3566
Civil Air Patrol, Wing Headquarters, P.O. Box 14, Elmendorf Air Force Base (99506). Phone:
   (907) 753-0518
U.S. Coast Guard emergency phone: (800) 478-5555

Weather Records

Home page: www.uaa.alaska.edu/enri/ascc_web/_home.html
Alaska State Climate Center, Environment and Natural Resources Institute, University of Alaska,
   707 A St., Anchorage (99501). Phone: (907) 257-2737; e-mail: auclima@uaa.alaska.edu

Youth Hostels

Hostelling International—Anchorage: 700 H St., Anchorage (99501). Phone: (907) 276-3635

Table 1: Access and Services, Selected Villages and Cities

Population of Alaska: 621,400 (July 1998) Source: AK Dept. of Labor

Key

- = Reported available
1 Certified December 1997, Alaska Department of Community and Regional Affairs. DCRA home page: www.ComRegAf.state.ak.us/ CF_ComDB.htm
2 See Figure 1, page 18.
3 See Figure 2, page 20. Most communities, including villages in the Bush, have taxicabs.
4 See Air Taxis in Getting Around, Part 1, of this book.
5 Merchandise selection in small communities is often extremely limited and dependent upon freight arrival schedules.
6 Both intra-city and inter-city service.
7 Intra-city service only.
8 Service to Glacier Bay National Park.
9 Via the Alaska State ferry system.
10 Accessible from an Alaska State ferry port.
11 On local road network; not connected to main highway system.
12 Winter road connects to Dalton Highway.
B = Bicycle rental.
H = Hostel.
L = Limited accommodations at school, city offices, or private homes.
V = Off-road vehicle rental.
•• = Base changing from Naval Air Station to a private community in 1999. Check DCRA homepage for updates.

Community	Zip	Population[1]	On road system[2]	Car rental	Boat rental	Scheduled bus service[3]	Railroad access[3]	Scheduled air service[3]	Air taxi base[3,4]	Ferry port[3]	Boat charter service	Store[5]	Meals	Lodging	Campground	Hospital or clinic	Other
Adak	98791	••															
Akhiok	99615	109						•						L			
Akiachak	99551	569						•				•		L		•	
Akiak	99552	316						•				•		L		•	
Akutan	99553	408			•			•		•	•	•		•	•	•	
Alakanuk	99554	671	•					•				•		L		•	
Aleknagik	99555	210	11					•			•	•	•	•		•	
Allakaket	99720	176						•				•		L		•	
Ambler	99786	315	•	•				•	•		•	•	•	•		•	V
Anaktuvuk Pass	99721	308						•				•			•	•	
Anchorage area	99502	258,782	•	•	•	6	•	•	•		•	•	•	•	•	•	B,H
Anchor Point	99556	1188	•					•			•	•	•	•	•	•	
Angoon	99820	587	9		•			•		•	•	•	•	•		•	
Aniak	99557	576		•				•	•		•	•	•	•		•	
Atqasuk	99791	259						•				•				•	
Anvik	99558	100			•			•			•	•	•	•		•	
Arctic Village	99722	117						•			•	•		L		•	
Atka	99502	115						•			•	•		L		•	
Atmautluak	99559	286			•			•		•	•	•		L			
Attu	99695	29													•		
Auke Bay	99821	(See Juneau)			•		•	•	•	•	•	•	•	•	•		
Barrow	99723	4397	11			7		•	•		•	•	•	•		•	
Beaver	99724	125						•				•				•	
Bethel	99559	5463		•	•	7		•	•		•	•	•	•	•	•	
Bettles (Evansville)	99726	48	12	•	•			•	•		•	•	•	•	•	•	
Big Lake	99652	2228	•		•		•				•	•	•	•	•		
Birch Creek	99790	35						•						L			

318

Community	Zip	Population[1]	Transportation									Services[5]					
			On road system[2]	Car rental	Boat rental	Scheduled bus service[3]	Railroad access[3]	Scheduled air service[3]	Air taxi base[3,4]	Ferry port[3]	Boat charter service	Store[5]	Meals	Lodging	Campground	Hospital or clinic	Other
Boundary	99780	9	•									•	•	•			
Brevig Mission	99785	274			•			•				•		L		•	
Buckland	99727	408						•				•				•	
Cantwell	99729	166	•			•	•					•	•	•	•		
Cape Lisburne	99790	36						•				(Military site)					
Central	99730	61	•					•				•	•	•	•		
Chalkyitsik	99788	100						•				•		L		•	
Chefornak	99561	423			•			•				•		L		•	V
Chevak	99563	741						•			•	•	•				
Chicken	99732	37	•									•	•	•			
Chignik	99564	121						•	•	•	•	•	•			•	
Chitina	99566	91	•						•		•	•	•	•	•		
Chuathbaluk	99557	112						•				•		L			
Circle	99733	86	•									•	•	•	•		
Circle Hot Springs	99730	33	•					•				•	•	•			
Clam Gulch	99568	108	•			•						•		•		•	
Cold Bay	99571	81		•				•	•	•	•	•	•	•		•	
Cooper Landing	99572	283	•			•			•		•	•	•	•	•		
Copper Center	99573	525	•			•					•	•	•	•	•		
Cordova	99574	2571	9	•	•			•	•	•	•	•	•	•		•	
Craig	99921	2145	10			•			•	•	10	•	•	•		•	
Crooked Creek	99575	144						•				•		•			
Deadhorse (See Prudhoe Bay)	99734	25	•					•	•			•	•	•			
Deering	99736	156						•				•					
Delta Junction	99737	884	•					•				•	•	•	•	•	H
Denali National Park	99755	184	•	•		•	•	•				•	•	•	•	•	
Dillingham	99576	2332			•	•		•	•		•	•	•	•	•		
Douglas	99824	(See Juneau)				7				10		•	•	•			
Dutch Harbor	99692	(See Unalaska)															
Eagle	99738	168	•		•			•	•		•	•	•	•	•	•	•
Eagle River	99577	9000	•			•			•			•	•	•	•	•	
Eek	99578	309						•			•	•		L		•	
Egegik	99579	132						•			•	•	•	L			
Ekwok	99580	120			•			•	•		•	•		L		•	V
Elfin Cove	99825	50			•			•			•	•	•	•			V
Elim	99739	306		•	•			•						L		•	V
Emmonak	99581	838						•	•			•	•	•		•	
Ester	99725	236	•			•						•	•	•	•		
Fairbanks/College area	99701	82,309	•	•	•	6	•	•	•		•	•	•	•	•	•	H
False Pass	99583	58			•			•	•		•	•		L		•	
Fort Yukon	99740	553			•			•	•	•		•	•	•		•	
Funter Bay	99850	15								•			•	•			
Gakona	99586	24	•			•						•	•		•		
Galena	99741	544		•	•			•	•		•	•	•	•		•	
Gambell	99742	670			•			•			•	•	•	•			V

			Transportation									Services[5]					
Community	Zip	Population[1]	On road system[2]	Car rental	Boat rental	Scheduled bus service[3]	Railroad access[3]	Scheduled air service[3]	Air taxi base[3,4]	Ferry port[3]	Boat charter service	Store[5]	Meals	Lodging	Campground	Hospital or clinic	Other
Girdwood	99587	1000	•			•						•	•	•			H
Glennallen	99588	488	•			•		•	•			•	•	•	•	•	
Golovin	99762	142						•	•			•				•	
Goodnews Bay	99589	256						•			•	•		L	•		
Grayling	99590	195						•	•			•		L		•	
Gulkana	99695	96	•					•	•			•				•	
Gustavus	99826	368			•	8		•	•		•	•	•	•	•	•	B
Haines	99827	1463	•	•		•		•	•	•	•	•	•	•	•	•	B,H
Healy	99743	641	•			•	•					•	•	•	•		
Hollis	99950	196	9			•				•							
Holy Cross	99602	277						•				•	•	•		•	
Homer	99603	4155	•	•	•	•		•	•	•	•	•	•	•	•	•	
Hoonah	99829	896	9					•	•	•	•	•	•	•	•	•	
Hooper Bay	99604	1039						•	•			•		•	•	•	
Hope	99605	135	•									•	•	•	•		
Hughes	99745	52			•	•		•				•		L		•	V
Huslia	99746	248						•				•		L		•	
Hydaburg	99922	405	10					•		10	•	•	•	•		•	
Hyder	99923	133	•		•	•		•	•	•	•	•	•	•	•	•	
Igiugig	99613	51						•	•			•	•	•			
Iliamna	99606	102		•	•			•	•			•	•			•	
Juneau area	99801	30,236	9	•	•	7		•	•	•	•	•	•	•	•	•	H
Kake	99830	783	9					•		•	•	•	•	•		•	
Kaktovik	99747	255						•	•		•	•	•	•		•	
Kalskag, Upper & Lower	99607	554						•				•	•	L		•	
Kaltag	99748	250						•				•	•			•	
Karluk	99608	48						•									
Kasigluk	99609	524						•			•	•		L	•	•	
Kasilof	99610	558	•			•						•	•	•			
Kenai	99611	7058	•	•	•	•		•	•			•	•	•	•	•	
Ketchikan	99901	8460	9	•	•			•	•	•	•	•	•	•	•	•	H
Kiana	99749	402				•		•	•		•	•	•			•	
King Cove	99612	703		•				•	•	•		•	•			•	
King Salmon	99613	480		•	•			•	•		•	•	•	•		•	
Kipnuk	99614	556						•				•		L		•	
Kivalina	99750	349			•			•				•		L		•	
Klawock	99925	659	10	•	•	•		•		10	•	•	•	•	•	•	
Kobuk	99751	102			•			•	•		•	•		•		•	
Kodiak City	99615	6859	9	•	•			•	•	•	•	•	•	•	•	•	
Kokhanok	99606	175						•				•		L		•	
Koliganek	99576	202						•				•					
Kongiganak	99559	348						•				•		L			
Kotlik	99620	552						•				•	•	L			
Kotzebue	99752	2964						•	•		•	•	•	•	•	•	
Koyuk	99753	296						•			•	•				•	
Koyukuk	99754	130						•				•		L		•	
Kwethluk	99621	667						•				•		L		•	

Community	Zip	Population[1]	On road system[2]	Car rental	Boat rental	Scheduled bus service[3]	Railroad access[3]	Scheduled air service[3]	Air taxi base[3,4]	Ferry port[3]	Boat charter service	Store[5]	Meals	Lodging	Campground	Hospital or clinic	Other
Kwigillingok	99622	324						•				•		L		•	
Lake Minchumina	99757	46						•				•		•			
Larsen Bay	99624	127						•	•					L			
Levelok	99625	128		•	•			•			•	•	•	L		•	V
Little Diomede	99762	176			•			•				•		L			V
Livengood	99790	100	•									•	•				
Manley Hot Springs	99756	94	•		•			•	•		•	•	•	•	•		
Manokotak	99628	396						•				•				•	
Marshall	99585	300			•			•				•					V
McCarthy	99588	33	•					•	•		•		•	•	•		
McGrath	99627	441			•			•	•		•	•	•	•		•	V
Mekoryuk	99630	192						•			•	•		L		•	
Metlakatla	99926	1502	9	•				•	•	•		•	•	•		•	
Minto	99758	251	•					•				•	•	•			
Moose Pass	99631	134	•			•		•				•	•	•	•		
Mountain Village	99632	793		•				•	•			•	•	L		•	
Naknek	99633	666		•	•			•	•		•	•	•	•		•	
Nanwalek	99697	180						•				•		L			
Napakiak	99634	373			•			•			•	•		L		•	
Napaskiak	99559	391						•				•		L			
Nenana	99760	372	•			•	•					•	•	•	•		
Newhalen	99606	191	11					•			•	•	•	•		•	
New Stuyahok	99636	454						•				•		•		•	
Newtok	99559	267						•				•				•	
Nightmute	99690	222						•				•		L			
Nikolai	99691	103						•			•	•		L		•	
Nikolski	99638	35						•				•	•			•	
Ninilchik	99639	675	•			•					•	•	•	•	•	•	
Noatak	99761	410						•				•		L		•	
Nome	99762	3706		•	•			•	•		•	•	•	•		•	
Nondalton	99640	227	11	•	•			•	•		•	•	•	•		•	V
Noorvik	99763	598		•	•			•			•	•	•	L		•	V
North Pole	99705	1619	•			•						•	•	•	•		
Northway	99764	237	•			•			•			•	•	•	•	•	
Nuiqsut	99789	459						•				•				•	
Nulato	99765	353		•	•			•	•		•	•		L	•	•	
Nunapitchuk	99641	479			•			•				•		L		•	V
Old Harbor	99643	292						•				•		L			
Ouzinkie	99644	252						•				•		L			
Palmer	99645	4161	•		•	•			•			•	•	•	•	•	
Paxson	99737	32	•			•							•	•	•		
Pelican	99832	149	9					•		•	•	•	•	•		•	
Petersburg	99833	3398	9	•	•			•	•	•	•	•	•	•		•	
Pilot Point	99649	87						•	•			•	•	L		•	
Pilot Station	99650	558			•			•	•			•		•		•	V
Platinum	99651	41						•				•		L			
Point Hope	99766	787		•	•			•			•	•	•	•		•	V

Community	Zip	Population[1]	Transportation									Services[5]					
			On road system[2]	Car rental	Boat rental	Scheduled bus service[3]	Railroad access[3]	Scheduled air service[3]	Air taxi base[3,4]	Ferry port[3]	Boat charter service	Store[5]	Meals	Lodging	Campground	Hospital or clinic	Other
Port Alsworth	99653	63			•			•	•		•	•	•				
Port Graham	99603	190										•		L			
Port Heiden	99549	126		•	•			•	•			•	•	L		•	
Port Lions	99550	242						•		•		•	•	•			V
Prudhoe Bay (transient work force)	99734	5000+	•					•	•			(See Deadhorse)					
Quinhagak	99655	612						•	•		•	•	•				
Rampart	99767	64						•				•					
Red Devil	99656	39				•		•	•			•	•	•			
Ruby	99768	204		•				•	•			•	•	•		•	
Russian Mission	99657	295						•				•		L			
St. George	99660	146		•				•				•	•	•		•	
St. Marys	99658	494						•				•	•	•		•	
St. Michael	99659	362						•				•		L		•	
St. Paul	99660	761						•				•	•	•		•	V
Sand Point	99661	830						•	•	•		•	•	•			
Savoonga	99769	632						•				•		•		•	V
Scammon Bay	99662	450		•				•				•		L		•	
Selawik	99770	746						•				•		L		•	
Seldovia	99663	281	9		•			•		•	•	•	•	•	•	•	
Seward	99664	3040	•	•	•	•	•	•	•	•	•	•	•	•	•	•	H
Shageluk	99665	152						•	•		•	•		L		•	
Shaktoolik	99771	226			•			•			•	•		•		•	V
Sheldon Point	99666	161			•			•			•	•		L		•	V
Shishmaref	99772	538						•			•	•		L		•	
Shungnak	99773	257						•			•	•	•	•			
Sitka	99835	8779	9	•	•	7		•	•	•	•	•	•	•	•	•	H
Skagway	99840	814	•	•			•	•	•	•	•	•	•	•	•	•	H
Skwentna	99667	80			•			•	•		•	•	•	•			V
Slana	99586	59	•			•						•	•				H
Sleetmute	99665	105						•	•		•	•		L		•	
Soldotna	99669	4134	•	•	•	•		•	•		•	•	•	•	•	•	
Stebbins	99671	548			•			•			•	•		•		•	V
Sterling	99672	5888	•		•	•					•	•	•	•	•		
Stevens Village	99774	100			•			•			•	•		L		•	
Stony River	99557	36						•			•	•		L		•	
Sutton	99674	473	•			•						•	•				
Takotna	99675	58						•	•		•	•		L		•	
Talkeetna	99676	366	•				•	•	•		•	•	•	•	•		
Tanacross	99776	88	•			•						•					
Tanana	99777	317		•				•	•			•	•	•		•	
Tatitlek	99677	110			•			•	•			•		L		•	
Teller	99778	262						•				•				•	
Tenakee Springs	99841	101	9					•	•	•	•	•	•	•		•	
Tetlin	99779	73	•			•		•				•					
Thorne Bay	99919	597	10					•		10		•	•	•	•	•	
Togiak	99678	801						•			•	•	•	•	•	•	

• Table 1: Access and Services, Selected Villages and Cities •

Community	Zip	Population[1]	On road system[2]	Car rental	Boat rental	Scheduled bus service[3]	Railroad access[3]	Scheduled air service[3]	Air taxi base[3,4]	Ferry port[3]	Boat charter service	Store[5]	Meals	Lodging	Campground	Hospital or clinic	Other
Tok	99780	1214	•	•		•		•	•			•	•	•	•	•	H
Toksook Bay	99637	515						•				•		L		•	
Trapper Creek	99683	353	•			•						•	•	•	•		
Tuluksak	99679	421						•				•		L		•	
Tuntutuliak	99680	357						•				•		L		•	
Tununak	99681	330	•					•				•		L		•	V
Twin Hills	99576	81						•				•		L		•	
Tyonek	99682	152							•		•	•	•			•	
Unalakleet	99684	784	•	•				•	•		•	•	•	•		•	
Unalaska/Dutch Hbr.	99685	4285		•	•			•	•	•	•	•	•	•		•	
Valdez	99686	4155	•	•	•	•		•	•	•	•	•	•	•	•	•	
Venetie	99781	245						•				•					
Wainwright	99782	543		•	•			•			•	•	•	•		•	V
Wales	99783	177			•			•				•		L		•	V
Wasilla	99687	5134	•			•	•		•			•	•	•	•		
White Mountain	99784	188						•			•	•		L		•	
Whittier	99693	306	9	•			•		•	•	•	•	•	•	•	•	
Willow	99688	430	•			•	•		•			•	•		•		
Wiseman	99790	19	•														
Wrangell	99929	2589	9	•				•	•	•	•	•	•	•	•	•	
Yakutat	99689	810		•	•			•	•		•	•	•	•	•	•	
Canada																	
Carcross, Y.T.		277	•			•			•	•	•	•	•	•	•	•	
Stewart, B.C.		1000	•		•	•		•	•	•	•	•	•	•	•	•	
Telegraph Creek, B.C.		300	•						•			•	•	•	•	•	
Whitehorse, Y.T.		23,475	•	•	•	•	•	•	•			•	•	•	•	•	

Table 2: Parklands—Access, Special Interests, and Recreational Use

Key

ADFG — Alaska Department of Fish and Game
ADNR — Alaska Division of Natural Resources
ADP — Alaska Division of Parks
BLM — Bureau of Land Management
M — Municipalities of St. George and St. Paul, Tanadgusix Corp., Tanaq Corp., USFW, National Marine Fisheries Service
NPS — National Park Service
USFS — U.S. Forest Service
USFW — U.S. Fish and Wildlife Service

C — Public-use cabin for rent
D — RV sanitary sewage dump station
N — Not permitted
NA — Not applicable
P — Permitted
Z — Zoned; specific areas closed or other restrictions

1 State of Alaska regulations apply wherever not specifically restricted
2 Federal Aviation Administration (FAA) regulations and restrictions apply
3 Permitted only at times with adequate snow cover
4 Includes motorized bikes, all-terrain vehicles, Hovercraft, and the like
5 Camping is permitted only in established campgrounds or campsites
6 Hunting is permitted by ADP but without the use of weapons and not within one-half mile of a developed facility or road
7 By special permit only
8 To nearby town or village
9 Access via the Alaska State ferry system
10 Access by trail or short cross-country hike from a road

		How To Get There						Special Interests						Recreational Use										
	Managed by	Automobile	Scheduled bus	Railroad	Scheduled air service	Air taxi	Ferry or scheduled boat service	Charter boat	Sightseeing tours or cruise ship	Guided wilderness trips	Canoe, kayak, or raft trips	Good for children	Good for casual visits	Camping	Fishing[1]	Hunting[1]	Trapping[1]	Firearms for self-protection	Horses	Fixed-wing[2] aircraft	Powerboats	Snowmobiles[3]	Off-road vehicles[4]	Off-road mountain bikes
Admiralty Island National Monument	USFS	9			•	•		•	•	•	•	•	•	PC	P	P	P	P	NA	P	N	P	N	P
Afognak Island State Park	ADP	•	•			•	8				•		•	P	P	P	P	P	NA	P	P	NA	N	NA
Alagnak National Wild River	NPS					•				•	•			P	P	P	P	P	NA	P	P	P	N	NA
Alaska Chilkat Bald Eagle Preserve	ADP	•			8		8	•	•			•	•	P	P	N	P	P	N	N	P	N	N	N
Alaska Maritime National Refuge	USFW				•	•		•		•			•	N	N	N	N	P	N	N	N	N	N	N
Alaska Peninsula National Refuge	USFW				•	•				•	•			P	P	P	P	P	P	P	P	P	N	N
Alatna National Wild River	NPS				•	•				•	•			P	P	N	N	P	P	P	N	P	N	NA
Aleutian Islands Subunit	USFW		•					•	•					N	N	N	N	P	N	N	N	N	N	N
Anchor R./Fritz Cr. Critical Hab. Area	ADFG	•						•				•	•	P	P	P	P	P	P	P	NA	N	N	P

Parkland	Managing Agency
Anchor River State Recreation Area	ADP
Anchor River Recreation Site	ADP
Anchorage Coastal Wildlife Refuge	ADFG
Andreafsky National Wilderness	USFW
Aniakchak National Monument	NPS
Aniakchak National Preserve	NPS
Ann Stevens–Cape Lisburne Subunit	USFW
Arctic National Wildllife Refuge	USFW
Arctic National Wilderness	USFW
Baranof Castle Hill State Historic Site	ADP
Beaver Creek Nat'l Wild and Scenic River	BLM
Becharof National Wildlife Refuge	USFW
Becharof National Wilderness	USFW
Beecher Pass State Marine Park	ADP
Bering Land Bridge Nat'l Preserve	NPS
Bering Sea Subunit	USFW
Bettles Bay State Marine Park	ADP
Big Bear/Baby Bear State Marine Park	ADP
Big Delta State Historical Park	ADP
Big Eddy State Recreation Site	ADP — (See Kenai River Special Management Area)
Big Lake North State Recreation Site	ADP
Big Lake South State Recreation Site	ADP
Bing's Landing State Recreation Site	ADP — (See Kenai River Special Management Area)
Birch Creek Nat'l Wild and Scenic River	BLM
Birch Lake State Recreation Site	ADP
Black Sands State Marine Park	ADP
Blueberry Lake State Recreation Site	ADP
Bogoslof Subunit	USFW
Bonnie Lake State Recreation Site	ADP
Boswell Bay State Marine Park	ADP
Brushkana Campground	BLM
Buskin River State Recreation Site	ADP
Caines Head State Recreation Area	ADP

	Managed by	Automobile	Scheduled bus	Railroad	Scheduled air service	Air taxi	Ferry or scheduled boat service	Charter boat	Sightseeing tours or cruise ship	Guided wilderness trips	Canoe, kayak, or raft trips	Good for children or casual visits	Camping	Fishing[1]	Hunting[1]	Trapping[1]	Firearms for self-protection	Horses	Fixed-wing[2] aircraft	Powerboats	Snowmobiles[3]	Off-road vehicles[4]	Off-road mountain bikes
		How To Get There									**Special Interests**		**Recreational Use**										
Canoe Passage State Marine Park	ADP	•				•		•		•	•		P	P	6	P	P	N	NA	P	N	N	N
Cape Krusenstern Nat'l Monument	NPS	•				•		•		•		•	N	P	N	N	P	N	P	P	P	N	N
Cape Newenham State Game Refuge	ADFG		•			•		•				•	NA	P	N	NA	P	NA	P	NA	NA	NA	NA
Captain Cook State Recreation Area	ADP	•									•	•	P	P	N	P	N	N	N	P	N	N	N
Caribou Creek Rec. Mining Area	ADNR	•									•		P	P	P	P	P	P	NA	NA	NA	NA	N
Chamisso Subunit	USFW			•		•		•					P	P	P	P	P	P	P	P	P	N	N
Chena River State Recreation Area	ADP	•										•	PC	P	N	P	N	N	N	P	N	N	N
Chena River State Recreation Site	ADP	•										•	5,D	P	N	P	P	N	N	P	N	N	N
Chilikadrotna Nat'l Wild River	NPS									•	•		P	P	N	P	P	P	P	P	P	N	NA
Chilkat Islands State Marine Park	ADP		8		8		8		•		•	•	P	P	6	P	P	N	NA	P	N	N	N
Chilkat State Park	ADP	•	•		8		8	•	•		•	•	P	P	N	P	P	N	N	P	N	N	N
Chilkat River Critical Habitat Area	ADFG	•									•	•	N	P	P	P	P	P	P	P	P	N	P
Chilkoot Lake State Recreation Site	ADP	•			8	•	8	•			•	•	5	P	N	P	P	N	NA	P	N	N	N
Chuck River Wilderness	USFS				•		•	•	•	•	•		N	P	P	P	P	NA	P	P	N	N	N
Chugach National Forest	USFS	•			•	•		•	•	•	•	•	PC	P	P	P	P	P	N	P	P	N	P
Chugach State Park	ADP	•	•	•						•	•	•	N	P	N	P	N	N	N	N	N	N	P
Ciechanski State Recreation Site	ADP	•	•										P	P	P	NA	P	P	P	NA	N	N	P
Cinder River Critical Habitat Area	ADFG	•										•	P	P	NA	P	P	P	N	N	NA	N	P
Clam Gulch Critical Habitat Area	ADFG	•									•	•	P	P	N	P	P	N	N	P	N	N	P
Clam Gulch State Recreation Area	ADP	•	•								•	•	5	P	P	P	P	P	P	NA	NA	N	N
Clearwater State Recreation Site	ADP	•									•	•	5	P	N	P	P	P	N	N	N	N	P
Copper River Delta Critical Hab. Area	ADFG	9			8	•	8	•				•	P	P	P	P	P	P	P	P	N	N	P
Coronation Island Wilderness	USFS					•		•					P	P	P	P	P	NA	P	P	N	N	N
Creamer's Field Waterfowl Refuge	ADFG	•										•	N	NA	N	N	N	P	N	NA	N	N	P

(See Kenai River Special Management Area)

Parkland	Agency
Cripple Creek Campground	BLM
Crooked Creek State Recreation Site	ADP
Dall Bay State Marine Park	ADP
Dalton Highway	BLM
Decision Point State Marine Park	ADP
Deep Creek State Recreation Area	ADP
Delta Jct. Bison Range Area	ADFG
Delta State Recreation Site	ADP
Delta Nat'l Wild, Scenic, and Rec. River	BLM
Denali National Park	NPS
Denali National Preserve	NPS
Denali National Wilderness	NPS
Denali State Park	ADP
Donnelly Creek State Recreation Site	ADP
Driftwood Bay State Marine Park	ADP
Dry Creek Recreation Site	ADP
Dude Creek Critical Habitat Area	ADFG
Eagle Beach State Recreation Area	ADP
Eagle Campground	BLM
Eagle Trail State Recreation Site	ADP
Eggegik Critical Habitat Area	ADFG
Endicott River Wilderness	USFS
Entry Cove State Marine Park	ADP
Ernie Haugen Public Use Area	ADNR
Fielding Lake State Recreation Site	ADP
Finger Lake State Recreation Site	ADP
Forrester Island Subunit	USFW
Fort Abercrombie State Historical Park	ADP
Fort Egbert National Historic Site	BLM
Fortymile Nat'l Wild, Scenic, and Rec. River	BLM
Fox River Flats Critical Habitat Area	ADFG
Funny River State Recreation Site	ADP
Funter Bay State Marine Park	ADP

(See Kenai River Special Management Area)

	Managed by	Automobile	Scheduled bus	Railroad	Scheduled air service	Air taxi	Ferry or scheduled boat service	Charter boat	Sightseeing tours or cruise ship	Guided wilderness trips	Canoe, kayak, or raft trips	Good for children or casual visits	Camping	Fishing[1]	Hunting[1]	Trapping[1]	Firearms for self-protection	Horses	Fixed-wing[2] aircraft	Powerboats	Snowmobiles[3]	Off-road vehicles[4]	Off-road mountain bikes
													Camping	**Fishing**	**Hunting**	**Trapping**	**Firearms**	**Horses**	**Fixed-wing**	**Powerboats**	**Snowmobiles**	**Off-road veh.**	**Mtn bikes**
Gates of the Arctic National Park	NPS	10			•	•				•	•		P	P	N	N	P	P	P	P	P	N	N
Gates of the Arctic National Preserve	NPS	10				•				•	•		P	P	P	N	P	P	P	P	P	N	N
Glacier Bay National Park	NPS				8	•		•	•	•	•	•	N	P	N	N	P	N	N	N	N	N	N
Glacier Bay National Preserve	NPS					•							P	P	P	P	P	P	P	P	P	N	N
Goldstream Public Use Area	ADNR	•											P	NA	P	P	P	P	NA	P	P	P	P
Goose Bay State Game Refuge	ADFG	•											P	NA	P	P	P	N	NA	N	N	N	P
Granite Bay State Marine Park	ADP					•		•			•		P	P	6	P	P	N	P	P	N	N	N
Grindall Island State Marine Park	ADP				8	•	8	•					P	P	6	P	P	NA	NA	P	NA	N	N
Gruening State Historical Site	ADP	9			8		8						P	P	6	P	P	N	N	N	N	N	N
Gulkana Nat'l Wild and Scenic River	BLM	•				•					•	•	P	P	P	P	P	P	P	N	P	N	P
Haines State Forest	ADNR	•	•		8		8					•	P	P	P	P	P	P	NA	NA	NA	P	N
Halibut Point State Recreation Site	ADP	9			8		8						N	P	N	P	P	P	P	P	N	N	P
Harding Lake State Recreation Area	ADP	•				•						•	5,D	P	P	P	P	N	NA	P	N	N	N
Hatcher Pass Public Use Area	ADNR	•			8							•	P	P	P	P	P	P	NA	NA	N	N	P
Hazy Islands Subunit	USFW												P	P	P	P	P	N	P	N	P	N	N
Homer Airport Critical Habitat Area	ADFG	•			8		8	•					NA	P	P	NA	P	N	NA	P	NA	N	P
Horseshoe Bay State Marine Park	ADP	•				•		•			•		P	P	6	P	P	N	NA	P	N	N	N
Iditarod Nat'l Historic Trail	ADP	•			•	•		•					N	N	N	P	P	N	P	N	P	N	N
Independence Mine State Park	ADP	•			8							•	N	N	N	P	P	N	N	NA	N	N	N
Innoko National Wildlife Refuge	USFW					•							N	NA	P	P	P	N	P	P	P	N	N
Innoko National Wilderness	USFW					•							P	P	P	P	P	P	P	P	P	N	N
Ivishak Nat'l Wild River	USFW							•		•			P	P	P	P	P	P	N	P	P	N	N
Izaak Walton State Recreation Site	ADP	(See Kenai River Special Management Area)			8		8	•															
Izembek National Wildlife Refuge	USFW												P	P	P	P	P	P	N	P	P	N	N

Parkland	Managing Agency
Izembek National Wilderness	USFW
Izembek State Game Refuge	ADFG
Jack Bay State Marine Park	ADP
Joe Mace Island State Marine Park	ADP
John National Wild River	NPS
Johnson Creek State Recreation Site	ADP
Johnson Lake State Recreation Area	ADP
Kachemak Bay Critical Habitat Area	ADFG
Kachemak Bay State Park	ADP
Kachemak Bay Wilderness Park	ADP
Kalgin Island Critical Habitat Area	ADFG
Kanuti National Wildlife Refuge	USFW
Karta Wilderness	USFS
Kasilof River State Recreation Site	ADP
Katmai National Park	NPS
Katmai National Preserve	NPS
Kayak Island State Marine Park	ADP
Kenai Fjords National Park	NPS
Kenai Keys State Recreation Area (See Kenai River Special Management Area)	ADP
Kenai National Wildlife Refuge	USFW
Kenai National Wilderness	USFW
Kenai River Special Mgmt. Area	ADP
Kepler–Bradley Lakes State Rec. Area	ADP
King Mountain State Recreation Site	ADP
Klondike Gold Rush National Park	NPS
Kobuk Nat'l Wild River	NPS
Kobuk Valley National Park	NPS
Kodiak National Wildlife Refuge	USFW
Kootznoowoo Wilderness	USFS
Koyukuk National Wildlife Refuge	USFW
Koyukuk National Wilderness	USFW
Kuiu Wilderness	USFS
Lake Clark National Park	NPS

	Managed by	Automobile	Scheduled bus	Railroad	Scheduled air service	Air taxi	Ferry or scheduled boat service	Charter boat	Sightseeing tours or cruise ship	Guided wilderness trips	Canoe, kayak, or raft trips	Good for children or casual visits	Camping	Fishing[1]	Hunting[1]	Trapping[1]	Firearms for self-protection	Horses	Fixed-wing[2] aircraft	Powerboats	Snowmobiles[3]	Off-road vehicles[4]	Off-road mountain bikes
								How To Get There			**Special Interests**		**Recreational Use**									
Lake Clark National Preserve	NPS				•	•		•		•	•	•	P	P	P	P	P	P	P	P	P	N	N
Lake Louise State Recreation Area	ADP	•											5	P	N	P	P	P	N	P	P	N	N
Liberty Falls State Recreation Site	ADP	•											5	P	N	P	P	P	N	N	N	N	N
Little Nelchina State Recreation Site	ADP	•	•										5	P	N	P	P	N	N	N	N	N	N
Little Susitna River Pub. Use Fac.	ADFG	•	•			•							5,D	P	N	N	P	N	NA	P	N	N	P
Little Tonsina Recreation Site	ADP	•											5	P	N	P	P	N	NA	N	N	N	N
Long Lake State Recreation Site	ADP	•	•										P	P	6	P	P	N	P	P	N	N	N
Lower Chatanika River State Rec. Area	ADP	•									•	•	P	P	N	P	P	N	N	N	N	N	N
Magoun Island State Marine Park	ADP										•	•	P	P	6	P	P	N	NA	P	N	N	N
Matanuska Glacier Recreation Site	ADP	•											P	P	6	P	P	N	N	N	N	N	N
Matanuska Valley Moose Range	ADNR	•											P	P	P	P	P	NA	NA	NA	P	P	P
Maurelle Islands Wilderness	USFS										•	•	P	P	P	P	P	P	P	P	N	N	P
McNeil River State Game Refuge	ADFG				•					•			N	P	P	P	N	NA	N	N	N	N	N
Mendenhall Wetlands State Game Refuge	ADFG	•	•						•				N	P	P	N	P	P	P	N	N	N	N
Minto Flats State Game Refuge	ADFG	•					8	•			•	•	N	P	P	P	P	P	P	P	N	N	N
Misty Fiords National Monument	USFS				•	•	•	•	•	•	•	•	PC	P	P	P	P	NA	P	P	N	N	N
Montana Creek State Recreation Site	ADP	•	•										5	P	N	P	P	P	P	N	N	N	N
Moon Lake State Recreation Site	ADP	•	•										5	P	N	P	P	P	P	P	N	N	N
Moose Creek State Recreation Site	ADP	•				•						•	5	P	N	P	P	P	P	N	N	N	N
Morgan's Landing Recreation Area	ADP	•	•						(See Kenai River Special Management Area)														
Mosquito Lake State Recreation Site	ADP	•	•										5	P	N	N	P	P	P	P	N	N	P
Mulchatna Nat'l Wild River	NPS					•							P	P	N	N	P	N	P	P	P	N	N
Nancy Lake State Recreation Area	ADP	•	•									•	PC	P	N	P	P	N	N	N	P	N	N
Nancy Lake State Recreation Site	ADP	•	•	•									5	P	N	P	P	N	N	P	N	N	N

Parkland	Agency
Nelchina Public Use Area	ADNR
Ninilchik State Recreation Area	ADP
Nilnunqua State Historic Site	ADP
(See Kenai River Special Management Area)	
Noatak National Preserve	NPS
North Fork, Koyukuk Nat'l Wild River	NPS
Nowitna National Wildlife Refuge	USFW
Nunivak Wilderness	USFW
Old Sitka State Historic Site	ADP
Oliver Inlet Marine Park	ADP
Palmer Hay Flats State Game Refuge	ADFG
Pasagshak Recreation Site	ADP
Paxson Lake Campground	BLM
Petersburg Creek–Duncan Salt Chuck Wilderness	USFS
Pilot Point Critical Habitat Area	ADFG
Pinnell Mountain Trail	BLM
Pioneer Park State Recreation Site	ADP
Pleasant/Lem./Inian Islands Wilderness	USFS
Point Bridget State Park	ADP
Porcupine Creek Recreation Site	ADP
Port Heiden Critical Habitat Area	ADFG
Port Moller Critical Habitat Area	ADFG
Portage Cove Recreation Site	ADP
Potter Section House Historic Site	ADP
Pribilof Islands	M
Quartz Lake State Recreation Area	ADP
Redoubt Bay Critical Habitat Area	ADFG
Refuge Cove State Recreation Site	ADP
Rocky Lake State Recreation Site	ADP
Russell Fiord Wilderness	USFS
St. James Bay State Marine Park	ADP
St. Lazaria Subunit	USFW
Safety Cove State Marine Park	ADP

	Managed by	Automobile	Scheduled bus	Railroad	Scheduled air service	Air taxi	Ferry or scheduled boat service	Charter boat	Sightseeing tours or cruise ship	Guided wilderness trips	Canoe, kayak, or raft trips	Good for children or casual visits	Camping	Fishing[1]	Hunting[1]	Trapping[1]	Firearms for self-protection	Horses	Fixed-wing[2] aircraft	Powerboats	Snowmobiles[3]	Off-road vehicles[4]	Off-road mountain bikes
													How To Get There / **Special Interests** / **Recreational Use**										
Salcha River State Recreation Site	ADP	•	•								•	•	P	P	N	P	P	N	N	P	P	N	N
Salmon Lake Campground	BLM	•									•	•	P	P	N	N	P	N	NA	P	P	N	P
Salmon Nat'l Wild River	NPS										•		P	P	N	N	P	P	P	P	P	N	NA
Sandspit Point State Marine Park	ADP					•		•			•		P	P	6	P	P	N	NA	P	N	N	N
Sawmill Bay State Marine Park	ADP	•				•		•			•	•	P	P	6	P	P	N	NA	P	N	N	N
Scout Lake State Recreation Site	ADP	•									•		5	P	N	P	P	N	N	N	N	N	N
Security Bay State Marine Park	ADP							•			•		P	P	6	P	P	N	NA	P	N	N	N
Selawik National Wildlife Refuge	USFW					•		•		•	•	•	P	P	P	P	P	P	P	P	P	N	N
Selawik Wilderness	USFW					•				•	•		P	P	P	P	P	P	P	P	P	N	N
Semidi Subunit	USFW								•				5	P	N	P	P	P	N	P	P	N	N
Settlers Cove State Recreation Site	ADP	9									•		P	P	6	P	P	N	NA	N	P	N	NA
Sheenjek Nat'l Wild River	USFW				8	•	8			•	•		P	P	P	P	P	P	P	P	P	N	N
Shelter Island State Marine Park	ADP							•			•		P	P	N	N	P	N	N	P	N	N	N
Shoup Bay State Marine Park	ADP					•		•			•	•	P	P	6	P	P	N	NA	P	N	N	N
Shuyak Island State Park	ADP					•		•			•	•	PC	P	P	P	P	N	NA	P	P	N	N
Simeonof Subunit	USFW				•	•							N	P	P	N	P	N	P	P	N	N	N
Sitka National Historical Park	NPS	9			8				•			•	N	P	N	N	N	N	N	N	N	N	P
Slikok Creek Recreation Area	ADP	•		(See Kenai River Special Management Area)																			
Sourdough Campground	BLM	•											P	P	N	N	P	P	NA	P	P	N	P
South Baranof Wilderness	USFS		•			•		•		•	•	•	PC	P	P	P	P	NA	P	P	N	N	N
South Esther Island State Marine Park	ADP					•		•			•		P	P	6	P	P	N	N	P	P	N	N
South Etolin Island Wilderness	USFS					•		•			•		P	P	P	P	P	NA	P	P	N	N	N
South Prince of Wales Wilderness	USFS					•					•	•	P	P	6	P	P	NA	P	P	N	N	N
Squirrel Creek State Recreation Site	ADP	•											P	P	6	P	P	N	N	N	N	N	N

Parkland	Agency
Stan Price State Wildlife Sanctuary	ADFG
Stariski State Recreation Site	ADP
Steese Nat'l Conservation Area	BLM
Stikene—LeConte Wilderness	USFS
Sullivan Island State Marine Park	ADP
Summit Lake State Recreation Site	ADP
Sunny Cove State Marine Park	ADP
Surprise Cove State Marine Park	ADP
Susitna Flats State Game Refuge	ADFG
Susitna State Recreational Rivers	ADNR
Taku Harbor State Marine Park	ADP
Tanana Valley State Forest	ADNR
Tangle Lakes Campground	BLM
Tangle River Campground	BLM
Tebenkof Bay Wilderness	USFS
Tetlin National Wildlife Refuge	USFW
Thom's Place State Marine Park	ADP
Thumb Cove State Marine Park	ADP
Tinayguk Nat'l Wild River	NPS
Tlikakila Nat'l Wild River	NPS
Togiak National Wildlife Refuge	USFW
Togiak National Wilderness	USFW
Tok River State Recreation Site	ADP
Tongass National Forest	USFS
Totem Bight State Historical Park	ADP
Tracy Arm—Fords Terror Nat'l Wild.	USFS
Trading Bay State Game Refuge	ADFG
Tugidak Island Critical Habitat Area	ADFG
Tuxedni Subunit	USFW
Unalakleet Nat'l Wild and Scenic River	BLM
Upper Chatanika River Rec. Area	ADP
Walker Fork Campground	BLM
Walrus Islands State Game Sanctuary	ADFG

Site	Managed by	Automobile	Scheduled bus	Railroad	Scheduled air service	Air taxi	Ferry or scheduled boat service	Charter boat	Sightseeing tours or cruise ship	Guided wilderness trips	Canoe, kayak, or raft trips	Good for children or casual visits	Camping	Fishing[1]	Hunting[1]	Trapping[1]	Firearms for self-protection	Horses	Fixed-wing[2] aircraft	Powerboats	Snowmobiles[3]	Off-road vehicles[4]	Off-road mountain bikes
Warren Island Wilderness	USFS					•		•			•	•	P	P	P	P	P	NA	P	P	N	N	N
West Chichagof–Yakobi Wilderness	USFS					•		•			•	•	P	P	P	P	P	NA	P	P	N	N	N
West Fork Campground	BLM	•									•	•	P	P	N	N	P	NA	NA	NA	P	N	P
White Mountains Nat'l Recreation Area	BLM	•										•	PC	P	P	NA	P	P	NA	NA	NA	N	P
Wickersham State Historic Site	ADP	• 9			•		•					•	NA	NA	NA	NA	NA	NA	NA	NA	NA	NA	N
Willow Creek State Recreation Area	ADP	•										•	P	P	6	P	P	N	N	N	N	N	N
Willow Mountain Critical Habitat Area	ADFG												P	N	P	P	P	P	P	NA	N	N	P
Wind Nat'l Wild River	USFW										•	•	P	P	P	P	P	P	P	P	P	N	NA
Wolf Lake State Recreation Site	ADP	•									•		5	P	N	P	P	N	N	N	P	N	N
Wood–Tikchik State Park	ADP				8	•		•	•		•	•	P	P	P	N	P	N	P	N	P	N	N
Woody Island State Recreation Site	ADP					•		•			•	•	P	P	P	P	P	N	NA	P	N	N	N
Worthington Glacier State Rec. Site	ADP	•										•	5	P	N	P	P	N	N	N	P	N	N
Wrangell–St. Elias Nat'l Park	NPS	•			8	•		•	•	•	•	•	P	P	N	N	P	P	P	P	P	N	N
Wrangell–St. Elias Nat'l Preserve	NPS	•			•	•		•	•		•	•	P	P	P	P	P	P	P	P	P	N	P
Yakataga State Game Refuge	ADFG				•	•							P	P	P	P	P	N	N	P	N	7	N
Yukon–Charley R. Nat'l Preserve	NPS	8				•		•			•		P	P	P	P	P	P	P	P	P	7	N
Yukon Delta National Wildlife Refuge	USFW				•	•					•		P	P	P	P	P	P	P	P	P	7	N
Yukon Flats National Wildlife Refuge	USFW					•					•	•	P	P	6	P	P	N	N	P	N	N	N
Zeigler Cove State Marine Park	ADP							•			•	•	P	P	6	P	P	N	P	P	N	N	N

334

Suggested Reading

Contact the publisher or your local library, or search the Web for the following books. A good source in Alaska is the Alaska Natural History Association, a non-profit educational organization that operates visitors' center bookstores and publishes books about Alaska's public lands. Contact them at ANHA, Mail Order Services, 605 W. Fourth Ave., Suite 105, Anchorage, Alaska 99501. Phone: (907) 271-3290 or fax (907) 271-2744.

Alaskana / History / Adventure

Chevigny, Hector. *Russian Alaska*. New York: Viking, 1965.

Ewing, Susan. *The Great Alaska Nature Factbook*. Seattle: Alaska Northwest Books, 1996.

Fredston, Jill, and Doug Fesler. *Snow Sense: A Guide to Evaluating Snow Avalanche Hazard*. 4th ed. Anchorage: Alaska Mountain Safety Center, 1994.

Freedman, Lew. *Iditarod Silver: 25 Years of the Last Great Race*. Seattle: Epicenter Press, 1997.

Gruening, Ernest, ed. *An Alaskan Reader, 1867–1967*. New York: Meredith Press, 1966.

Hirschmann, Fred (photography), and Kim Heacox (text). *Bush Pilots of Alaska*. Portland: Graphic Arts Center Publishing Company, 1989.

Hunt, William R. *Alaska: A Bicentennial History*. New York: W.W. Norton, 1976.

———. *North of 53°: The Wild Days of the Alaska–Yukon Mining Frontier, 1870–1914*. New York: Macmillan, 1974.

Kizzia, Tom. *The Wake of the Unseen Object: Among the Native Cultures of Bush Alaska*. New York: Henry Holt, 1991.

Littlepage, Dean. *Hiking Alaska*. Helena, Montana: Falcon Press Publishing Co., 1997.

Lopez, Barry. *Arctic Dreams: Imagination and Desire in a Northern Landscape*. New York: Charles Scribner's Sons, 1986.

Maschmeyer, Gloria (text), and Alissa Crandall (photography). *Along the Alaska Highway*. Seattle: Alaska Northwest Books, 1992.

McPhee, John. *Coming into the Country*. New York: Farrar, Straus & Giroux, 1985.

Muir, John. *Travels in Alaska*. Boston: Houghton Mifflin, 1979.

Naske, Claus M., and Herman E. Slotnick. *Alaska: A History of the 49th State*. 2d ed. Norman: University of Oklahoma Press, 1987.

Ritter, Harry. *Alaska's History: The People, Land, and Events of the North Country*. Seattle: Alaska Northwest Books, 1993.

Stevens, Robert W. *Alaska Aviation History*. Des Moines, Wash.: Polynyas Press, 1990.

Valencia, Kris, ed. *The Alaska Wilderness Guide*, 7th ed. Bellevue, Wash.: Vernon Publications, 1993.

Villiers, Alan. *Captain James Cook*. New York: Charles Scribner's Sons, 1967.

Birds

Armstrong, Robert. *Guide to the Birds of Alaska*, 4th ed. Seattle: Alaska Northwest Books, 1995.

Farrand, J., Jr., ed. *The Audubon Society Master Guide to Birding*. New York: Alfred A. Knopf, 1983.

Gibson, D. D. *Checklist of Alaska Birds*. Fairbanks: University of Alaska Museum, 1993.

Stromsem, N. E. *A Guide to Alaskan Seabirds*. Anchorage: Alaska Natural History Association in cooperation with the U.S. Fish and Wildlife Service, 1982.

Tobish, T. G., Jr. *Alaska Region, National Audubon Society Field Notes* (for 1994). New York: National Audubon Society.

Fish, Marine Mammals, and Wildlife

Alaska Geographic. *Alaska's Bears*. Anchorage: Alaska Geographic Society, 1993.

Alaska Sport Fishing Guide. Juneau: Alaska Department of Fish and Game.

Chadwick, Douglas. *A Beast the Color of Winter: The Mountain Goat Observed*. San Francisco: Sierra Club Books, 1983.

Hall, Cheryl, et al. *Wildlife Notebook Series*. Juneau: Alaska Department of Fish and Game, 1994.

Haley, Delphine, et. al. *Marine Mammals of Eastern North Pacific and Arctic Waters*, 2d ed. Seattle: Pacific Search Press, 1986.

Hodgson, Bryan. "Hard Harvest on the Bering Sea." *National Geographic*, October 1992, 70.

Kessler, Doyne W. *Alaska's Saltwater Fishes and Other Sea Life*. Seattle: Alaska Northwest Books, 1985.

Leatherwood, Stephen, and Randall R. Reeves. *Sierra Club Handbook of Whales and Dolphins*. San Francisco: Sierra Club Books, 1983.

Lopez, Barry Holstun. *Of Wolves and Men*. New York: Charles Scribner's Sons, 1978.

Lynch, Wayne. *Bears: Monarchs of the Northern Wilderness*. Seattle: The Mountaineers, 1993.

Matkin, Craig O. *Guide to the Killer Whales of Prince William Sound*. Valdez, Alaska: Prince William Sound Books, 1994.

Morrow, J. E. *The Freshwater Fishes of Alaska*. Seattle: Alaska Northwest Books, 1980.

National Geographic Society. *Wild Animals of North America*. Washington, D.C.: National Geographic Society, 1979.

Obee, Bruce, and Graeme Ellis. *Guardians of the Whales: The Quest to Study Whales in the Wild*. Seattle: Alaska Northwest Books, 1992.

Oceanic Society Staff. *Field Guide to the Gray Whale*. Seattle: Sasquatch Books, 1989.

Paine, Stefani. *The World of the Sea Otter*. San Francisco: Sierra Club Books, 1993.

Piper, Ernie. *Alaska Sportfishing*. Anchorage: Alaska Geographic Guides, 1997.

Riedman, Marianne. *The Pinnipeds: Seals, Sea Lions, and Walruses*. Berkeley: University of California Press, 1990.

Route, Anthony J. *Flyfishing Alaska*. Boulder, Colo.: Johnson Books; Estes Park, Colo.: Spring Creek Press, 1989.

Runtz, Michael W. P. *Moose Country: Saga of the Woodland Moose*. Minoqua, Wis.: NorthWord Press, 1991.

Smith, Dave. *Alaska's Mammals*. Seattle: Alaska Northwest Books, 1995.

———. *Backcountry Bear Basics: The Definitive Guide to Avoiding Unpleasant Encounters*. Seattle: The Mountaineers, 1997.

Sherwood, Morgan B. *Big Game in Alaska: A History of Wildlife and People*. New Haven: Yale University Press, 1981.

Sherwonit, Bill. *Alaska's Bears: Grizzlies, Black Bears, and Polar Bears*. Seattle: Alaska Northwest Books, 1998.

Stall, Chris. *Animal Tracks of Alaska*. Seattle: The Mountaineers, 1993.

Wynne, Kate. *Marine Mammals of Alaska*. Fairbanks: Alaska Sea Grant College Program, 1992.

Trees and Wild Plants

The Alaska–Yukon Wild Flowers Guide. Bothell, Wash.: Alaska Northwest Books, 1990.

Heller, Christine. *Wild, Edible, and Poisonous Plants of Alaska*. Fairbanks: Cooperative Extension Service, University of Alaska, and the U.S.D.A., 1989.

Viereck, Leslie A, and Elbert L. Little, Jr. *Alaska Trees and Shrubs*. Fairbanks: University of Alaska Press, 1986.

Schofield, Janice J. *Discovering Wild Plants: Alaska, Western Canada, The Northwest*. Bothell, Wash.: Alaska Northwest Books, 1989.

Wild Rivers

Embick, Andrew. *Fast and Cold: A Guide to Alaska Whitewater*. Valdez, Alaska: Alpine Books, 1994.

Jettmar, Karen. *The Alaska River Guide: Canoeing, Kayaking, and Rafting in the Last Frontier*, 2d ed. Seattle: Alaska Northwest Books, 1998.

Madsen, Ken, and Graham Wilson. *Rivers of the Yukon: A Paddling Guide*. Whitehorse, Yukon Territory: Primrose Publishing, 1990.

McNair, Robert E. *Basic River Canoeing*. Newington, Va.: American Canoeing Association, 1987.

Mosby, Jack, and David Dapkus. *Alaska Paddling Guide*, 3d ed. Anchorage: J&R Enterprises, 1986.

Quick, Daniel L. *The Kenai Canoe Trails*. Soldotna, Alaska: Northlite Publishing Co., 1995.

Regions

Southeast

Alaska Geographic. *Southeast Panhandle*. Anchorage: Alaska Geographic Society, 1997.

————. *Admiralty Island: Fortress of the Bears*. Anchorage: Alaska Geographic Society, 1991.

Berton, Pierre. *The Klondike Fever: The Life and Death of the Last Great Gold Rush*. New York: Alfred A. Knopf, 1958.

DuFresne, Jim. *Glacier Bay National Park: A Backcountry Guide to the Glaciers and Beyond*. Seattle: The Mountaineers, 1987.

Jettmar, Karen. *Alaska's Glacier Bay*. Seattle: Alaska Northwest Books, 1997.

Kelley, Mark, and Sherry Simpson. *Alaska's Ocean Highways: A Travel Adventure Aboard Northern Ferries*. Seattle: Epicenter Press, 1995.

O'Clair, Rita M., Robert H. Armstrong, and Richard Carstensen. *The Nature of Southeast Alaska: A Guide to Plants, Animals, and Habitats*. Seattle: Alaska Northwest Books, 1992.

Piggott, Margaret. *Discover Southeast Alaska with Pack and Paddle*. Seattle: The Mountaineers, 1990.

Southcentral / Gulf Coast

Alaska Department of Fish and Game. "Kenai Peninsula Sport and Personal Use Razor Clam Fishery." Alaska Department of Fish and Game, Division of Sport Fish, revised March 1996.

Alaska Geographic. *Kenai Peninsula*. Anchorage: Alaska Geographic Society, 1997.

Beaglehole, John Cawte. *The Life of Captain James Cook*. Stanford, Calif.: Stanford University Press, 1974.

Davidson, Art. *In the Wake of the* Exxon Valdez*: The Devastating Impact of the Alaska Oil Spill*. San Francisco: Sierra Club Books, 1990.

Simmerman, Nancy (photography), Helen Nienhueser, and John Wolfe. *55 Ways to the Wilderness of Southcentral Alaska*, 4th ed. Seattle: The Mountaineers, 1994.

Aleutian Islands and Alaska Peninsula

Alaska Geographic. *Alaska Peninsula*. Anchorage: Alaska Geographic Society, 1994.

————. *Katmai Country*. Anchorage: Alaska Geographic Society, 1989.

————. *Unalaska / Dutch Harbor*. Anchorage: Alaska Geographic Society, 1991.

————. *Volcanoes*. Anchorage: Alaska Geographic Society, 1991.

Cohen, Stan. *The Forgotten War: Pictorial History of World War II in Alaska*. Missoula, Mont.: Pictorial Histories Publishing Co., 1981.

Garfield, Brian. *The Thousand-Mile War: World War II in Alaska and the Aleutians*. Garden City, N.Y.: Doubleday and Co., 1969.

Hall, Major George L. *Sometime Again*. Seattle: Superior Publishing Co., 1945.

Lewis, Emmanuel R. *Seacoast Fortification of the United States: An Introductory History.* Washington, D.C.: Smithsonian Institution, 1970.

Rennick, Penny, ed. *The Aleutian Islands.* Anchorage: Alaska Geographic Guides, 1995.

Interior

Alaska Geographic. *Denali.* Anchorage: Alaska Geographic Society, 1995.

Beckey, Fred. *Mount McKinley: Icy Crown of North America.* Seattle: The Mountaineers, 1993.

Davidson, Art. *Minus 148°: The Winter Ascent of Mt. McKinley.* New York: W. W. Norton and Co., 1969.

Greiner, James. *Wager With the Wind: The Don Sheldon Story.* New York: Rand McNally and Co., 1974.

Moore, Terris. *Mt. McKinley: The Pioneer Climbs.* Seattle: The Mountaineers, 1981; originally published in 1967.

Murie, Adolph. *A Naturalist in Alaska.* New York: Devin-Adair Co., 1961.

Murie, Margaret E. *Two in the Far North* (1957; reprinted, Seattle: Alaska Northwest Books, 1997).

Nelson, Richard. *Hunters of the Northern Forest.* Chicago: University of Chicago Press, 1980.

———. *Make Prayers to the Raven: A Koyukon View of the Northern Forest.* Chicago: University of Chicago Press, 1983.

Sherwonit, Bill. *To the Top of Denali: Climbing Adventures on North America's Highest Peak.* Anchorage: Alaska Northwest Books, 1990.

Western / Bering Sea Coast

Alaska Geographic. *Kuskowkim.* Anchorage: Alaska Geographic Society, 1990.

———. *Lower Yukon River.* Anchorage: Alaska Geographic Society, 1990.

Matthiessen, Peter. *Oomingmak: The Expedition to the Musk ox Island in the Bering Sea.* New York: Hastings House, 1967.

Reynolds, S. H. *Pleistocene Ovibos.* New York: Johnson Reprint Corp., reprint of 1934 edition.

Arctic

Alaska Geographic. *Seward Peninsula.* Anchorage: Alaska Geographic Society, 1987.

———. *Alaska National Wildlife Refuge.* Anchorage: Alaska Geographic Society, 1993.

———. *The Brooks Range.* Anchorage: Alaska Geographic Society, 1997.

Cantin, Eugene. *Yukon Summer.* San Francisco: Chronicle Books, 1973.

Fejes, Claire. *People of the Noatak.* New York: Alfred Knopf, 1966.

Huntington, Sidney, and Jim Rearden. *Shadows on the Koyukuk.* Seattle: Alaska Northwest Books, 1998.

Kauffmann, John M. *Alaska's Brooks Range: The Ultimate Mountains.* Seattle: The Mountaineers, 1992.

Marshall, Robert. *Alaska Wilderness: Exploring the Central Brooks Range.* Berkeley: University of California Press, 1956.

———. *Arctic Village.* (1st ed., 1933) Fairbanks: University of Alaska Press, 1991.

Stuck, Hudson. *Voyages on the Yukon and Its Tributaries.* (1st ed., 1917) New York: Charles Scribner's Sons, 1975.

Hours of Daylight at Sea Level

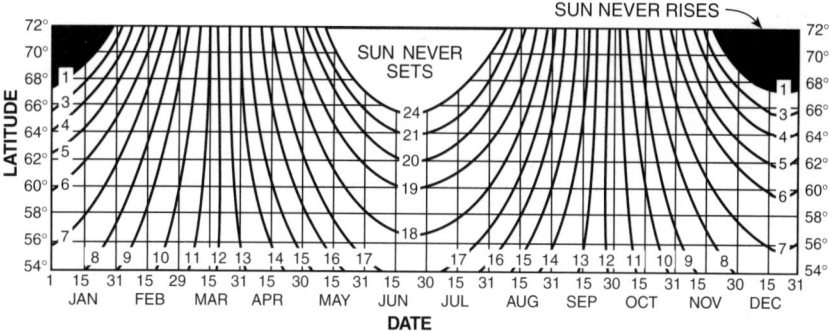

To determine the hours of daylight on any day of the year within Alaska, find the latitude of the region on a map. Follow the correspponding line on this graph to a point above the date. Read the hours from the nearest curved line, interpolating if the point falls between lines. Example: At a latitude of 62° on April 20, the sun will be above the horizon for about 15 hours.

Weather Tables

For the following weather tables, four months have been chosen as providing the most useful information: January frequently is the coldest month; April is popular for winter sports; July often is the warmest month; October is the wettest month in maritime areas. The tables also include figures for the year (annual).

Tabulated are:

- Both mean and record high and low temperatures;
- precipitation with snowfall recorded in water equivalent;
- mean snowfall, measured as it falls, storm by storm, and expressed in snow depth;
- maximum snow accumulation on the ground, expressed in snow depth;
- number of days with measurable precipitation (0.01 inch [0.025 cm] or more), known as "precipitation days."

Weather records were obtained from the Alaska State Climate Center, Environment and Natural Resources Institute (address in Information Sources, Appendix) and are available to the public.

Anchorage

		Temperatures, °F High	Low	Precip. inches	Snowfall, inches Mean	Max on grnd.	Precip. days
JAN	Mean	20	6	0.8	8	47	3
	Rec.	50	-34				
APR	Mean	42	28	0.7	7	19	2
	Rec.	65	2				
JUL	Mean	65	51	2	0	0	6
	Rec.	81	36				
OCT	Mean	41	28	2	7	13	5
	Rec.	61	-5				
ANN	Mean	42	28	15	71	47	49
	Rec.	85	-34				

Atka

		Temperatures, °F High	Low	Precip. inches	Snowfall, inches Mean	Max on grnd.	Precip. days
JAN	Mean	37	29	5	7	6	18
	Rec.	50	14				
APR	Mean	42	33	4	6	2	16
	Rec.	59	24				
JUL	Mean	53	44	4	0	0	20
	Rec.	72	37				
OCT	Mean	46	37	6	1	0	28
	Rec.	57	24				
ANN	Mean	44	36	60	61	6	246
	Rec.	77	12				

Angoon

		Temperatures, °F High	Low	Precip. inches	Snowfall, inches Mean	Max on grnd.	Precip. days
JAN	Mean	32	23	3	17	43	11
	Rec.	57	-10				
APR	Mean	47	34	2	2	29	8
	Rec.	64	20				
JUL	Mean	61	49	3	0	0	8
	Rec.	82	36				
OCT	Mean	48	39	7	0.3	2	17
	Rec.	68	23				
ANN	Mean	47	43	40	67	43	136
	Rec.	82	-10				

Barrow

		Temperatures, °F High	Low	Precip. inches	Snowfall, inches Mean	Max on grnd.	Precip. days
JAN	Mean	-8	-20	0.2	2	22	1
	Rec.	36	-53				
APR	Mean	6	-9	0.2	2	30	1
	Rec.	38	-33				
JUL	Mean	45	33	0.8	0.3	1	4
	Rec.	75	26				
OCT	Mean	19	10	0.6	6	12	3
	Rec.	43	-32				
ANN	Mean	15	4	5	25	30	25
	Rec.	76	-54				

Annette Island

		Temperatures, °F High	Low	Precip. inches	Snowfall, inches Mean	Max on grnd.	Precip. days
JAN	Mean	37	28	10	16	42	15
	Rec.	61	2				
APR	Mean	49	36	8	4	3	14
	Rec.	82	21				
JUL	Mean	64	51	5	0	0	10
	Rec.	86	40				
OCT	Mean	52	42	17	0.3	2	21
	Rec.	71	25				
ANN	Mean	51	40	115	61	42	178
	Rec.	90	1				

Bethel

		Temperatures, °F High	Low	Precip. inches	Snowfall, inches Mean	Max on grnd.	Precip. days
JAN	Mean	12	-2	0.8	7	45	3
	Rec.	48	-46				
APR	Mean	41	15	0.6	6	34	4
	Rec.	58	-31				
JUL	Mean	68	47	2	0	0	8
	Rec.	86	31				
OCT	Mean	43	24	1	4	6	5
	Rec.	65	-5				
ANN	Mean	36	21	17	51	45	63
	Rec.	86	-46				

Bettles

		Temperatures, °F High	Low	Precip. inches	Snowfall, inches Mean	Max on grnd.	Precip. days
JAN	Mean	-6	-22	0.8	11	71	3
	Rec.	42	-70				
APR	Mean	32	9	0.6	7	86	2
	Rec.	56	-25				
JUL	Mean	69	48	2	0	0	5
	Rec.	92	29				
OCT	Mean	25	12	1	11	19	5
	Rec.	53	-32				
ANN	Mean	30	12	14	77	86	48
	Rec.	92	-70				

Eagle

		Temperatures, °F High	Low	Precip. inches	Snowfall, inches Mean	Max on grnd.	Precip. days
JAN	Mean	-4	-13	0.5	8	39	2
	Rec.	47	-71				
APR	Mean	40	14	0.4	4	42	2
	Rec.	71	-37				
JUL	Mean	73	46	2	0	0	8
	Rec.	95	28				
OCT	Mean	34	17	0.9	9	14	5
	Rec.	66	-28				
ANN	Mean	36	13	11	50	42	51
	Rec.	95	-71				

Cold Bay

		Temperatures, °F High	Low	Precip. inches	Snowfall, inches Mean	Max on grnd.	Precip. days
JAN	Mean	33	24	3	9	17	9
	Rec.	50	-55				
APR	Mean	38	28	2	6	9	6
	Rec.	58	4				
JUL	Mean	55	46	2	0	0	8
	Rec.	77	36				
OCT	Mean	44	35	4	4	13	12
	Rec.	69	10				
ANN	Mean	42	33	35	55	18	106
	Rec.	77	-13				

Fairbanks

		Temperatures, °F High	Low	Precip. inches	Snowfall, inches Mean	Max on grnd.	Precip. days
JAN	Mean	-4	-21	0.6	10	40	3
	Rec.	47	-61				
APR	Mean	41	19	0.3	3	37	1
	Rec.	74	-21				
JUL	Mean	72	51	2	0	0	6
	Rec.	94	35				
OCT	Mean	32	17	0.7	10	13	3
	Rec.	65	-27				
ANN	Mean	36	16	10	65	52	40
	Rec.	96	-62				

Denali National Park

		Temperatures, °F High	Low	Precip. inches	Snowfall, inches Mean	Max on grnd.	Precip. days
JAN	Mean	11	-7	0.8	12	51	3
	Rec.	51	-51				
APR	Mean	38	16	0.6	6	43	2
	Rec.	65	-25				
JUL	Mean	66	43	3	0	0	9
	Rec.	87	23				
OCT	Mean	34	16	1	13	17	4
	Rec.	69	-24				
ANN	Mean	37	17	15	80	51	52
	Rec.	90	-52				

Fort Yukon

		Temperatures, °F High	Low	Precip. inches	Snowfall, inches Mean	Max on grnd.	Precip. days
JAN	Mean	-11	-28	0.4	7	36	4
	Rec.	40	-69				
APR	Mean	34	8	0.2	2	48	2
	Rec.	65	-41				
JUL	Mean	72	51	0.9	0	0	3
	Rec.	97	25				
OCT	Mean	28	13	0.6	7	17	5
	Rec.	61	-37				
ANN	Mean	31	10	7	44	48	42
	Rec.	97	-71				

Galbraith

		Temperatures, °F High	Temperatures, °F Low	Precip. inches	Snowfall Mean	Snowfall Max on grnd.	Precip. days
JAN	Mean	2	-7	0.4	2	13	2
	Rec.	35	-60				
APR	Mean	18	-6	0.2	2	18	1
	Rec.	50	-38				
JUL	Mean	61	40	0.9	0.5	0	4
	Rec.	76	28				
OCT	Mean	16	-3	1	9	9	4
	Rec.	47	-34				
ANN	Mean	23	3	8	48	23	30
	Rec.	82	-61				

Haines

		Temperatures, °F High	Temperatures, °F Low	Precip. inches	Snowfall Mean	Snowfall Max on grnd.	Precip. days
JAN	Mean	29	18	4	39	48	10
	Rec.	47	-10				
APR	Mean	50	34	2	0	4	5
	Rec.	74	19				
JUL	Mean	67	48	2	0	0	5
	Rec.	98	40				
OCT	Mean	48	36	10	3	19	15
	Rec.	60	10				
ANN	Mean	49	34	47	148	50	99
	Rec.	98	-14				

Galena

		Temperatures, °F High	Temperatures, °F Low	Precip. inches	Snowfall Mean	Snowfall Max on grnd.	Precip. days
JAN	Mean	-3	-20	0.7	7	32	3
	Rec.	45	-64				
APR	Mean	32	13	0.6	6	42	3
	Rec.	64	-35				
JUL	Mean	68	52	2	0	0	7
	Rec.	89	36				
OCT	Mean	29	18	1	8	16	4
	Rec.	56	-29				
ANN	Mean	32	15	13	59	42	55
	Rec.	92	-64				

Homer

		Temperatures, °F High	Temperatures, °F Low	Precip. inches	Snowfall Mean	Snowfall Max on grnd.	Precip. days
JAN	Mean	28	15	2	9	26	6
	Rec.	51	-18				
APR	Mean	42	28	1	4	23	5
	Rec.	63	-9				
JUL	Mean	61	45	2	0	0	6
	Rec.	79	34				
OCT	Mean	44	31	3	2	3	10
	Rec.	64	2				
ANN	Mean	44	30	24	58	35	80
	Rec.	80	-21				

Glacier Bay

		Temperatures, °F High	Temperatures, °F Low	Precip. inches	Snowfall Mean	Snowfall Max on grnd.	Precip. days
JAN	Mean	28	20	6	36	61	12
	Rec.	44	-11				
APR	Mean	44	33	3	3	62	9
	Rec.	59	19				
JUL	Mean	62	47	4	0	0	11
	Rec.	77	40				
OCT	Mean	46	38	12	2	9	20
	Rec.	58	19				
ANN	Mean	46	35	71	122	74	153
	Rec.	77	-11				

Juneau

		Temperatures, °F High	Temperatures, °F Low	Precip. inches	Snowfall Mean	Snowfall Max on grnd.	Precip. days
JAN	Mean	27	16	4	26	38	11
	Rec.	57	-22				
APR	Mean	47	31	3	5	33	10
	Rec.	71	6				
JUL	Mean	64	47	4	0	0	11
	Rec.	90	36				
OCT	Mean	47	36	7	2	10	18
	Rec.	61	12				
ANN	Mean	47	33	52	109	40	149
	Rec.	90	-22				

Kenai

		Temperatures, °F		Precip. inches	Snowfall, inches		Precip. days
		High	Low		Mean	Max on grnd.	
JAN	Mean	20	2	1	11	53	5
	Rec.	48	-47				
APR	Mean	41	24	1	6	35	3
	Rec.	63	-22				
JUL	Mean	62	46	2	0	0	7
	Rec.	85	32				
OCT	Mean	43	28	2	4	15	8
	Rec.	62	-11				
ANN	Mean	42	24	19	63	54	70
	Rec.	93	-48				

Kodiak

		Temperatures, °F		Precip. inches	Snowfall, inches		Precip. days
		High	Low		Mean	Max on grnd.	
JAN	Mean	34	25	5	15	21	12
	Rec.	54	-5				
APR	Mean	41	32	4	7	25	9
	Rec.	64	10				
JUL	Mean	59	49	4	0	0	10
	Rec.	82	37				
OCT	Mean	45	36	6	4	9	12
	Rec.	61	14				
ANN	Mean	42	36	57	75	35	136
	Rec.	86	-12				

Ketchikan

		Temperatures, °F		Precip. inches	Snowfall, inches		Precip. days
		High	Low		Mean	Max on grnd.	
JAN	Mean	39	29	14	14	62	16
	Rec.	62	-4				
APR	Mean	53	36	12	0.4	6	16
	Rec.	75	16				
JUL	Mean	65	50	8	0	0	12
	Rec.	88	39				
OCT	Mean	53	41	23	0.1	0	22
	Rec.	72	21				
ANN	Mean	52	39	156	41	62	193
	Rec.	90	-4				

Kotzebue

		Temperatures, °F		Precip. inches	Snowfall, inches		Precip. days
		High	Low		Mean	Max on grnd.	
JAN	Mean	4	-9	0.4	6	36	2
	Rec.	39	-47				
APR	Mean	21	3	0.3	5	53	2
	Rec.	46	-31				
JUL	Mean	59	48	1	0	0	5
	Rec.	85	30				
OCT	Mean	28	18	0.6	6	11	3
	Rec.	51	-19				
ANN	Mean	28	15	9	47	53	36
	Rec.	85	-52				

King Salmon

		Temperatures, °F		Precip. inches	Snowfall, inches		Precip. days
		High	Low		Mean	Max on grnd.	
JAN	Mean	21	6	1	6	18	4
	Rec.	53	-46				
APR	Mean	38	23	1	5	13	4
	Rec.	65	-19				
JUL	Mean	63	46	2	0	0	7
	Rec.	86	33				
OCT	Mean	40	25	2	3	10	6
	Rec.	62	-11				
ANN	Mean	41	25	19	44	19	62
	Rec.	86	-46				

Little Port Walter

		Temperatures, °F		Precip. inches	Snowfall, inches		Precip. days
		High	Low		Mean	Max on grnd.	
JAN	Mean	36	28	20	34	79	18
	Rec.	52	0				
APR	Mean	45	34	14	6	72	17
	Rec.	62	18				
JUL	Mean	61	48	9	0	0	11
	Rec.	78	37				
OCT	Mean	49	40	36	0.2	1	24
	Rec.	61	25				
ANN	Mean	48	38	224	133	117	207
	Rec.	78	0				

McCarthy

		Temperatures, °F		Precip. inches	Snowfall, inches		Precip. days
		High	Low		Mean	Max on grnd.	
JAN	Mean	-5	-23	0.6	8	42	2
	Rec.	39	-58				
APR	Mean	44	20	0.7	5	36	1
	Rec.	58	-19				
JUL	Mean	71	41	2	0	0	7
	Rec.	83	30				
OCT	Mean	38	20	3	17	18	7
	Rec.	69	-18				
ANN	Mean	39	15	17	73	50	51
	Rec.	87	-58				

North Dutch Group*

		Temperatures, °F		Precip. inches	Snowfall, inches		Precip. days
		High	Low		Mean	Max on grnd.	
JAN	Mean	33	26	10	40	56	14
	Rec.	48	4				
APR	Mean	41	32	7	11	71	13
	Rec.	53	8				
JUL	Mean	61	50	7	0	0	14
	Rec.	75	36				
OCT	Mean	44	37	17	2	4	19
	Rec.	57	26				
ANN	Mean	45	37	121	144	74	183
	Rec.	79	0				

*Near Perry Island; best represents Prince William Sound.

Moose Pass

		Temperatures, °F		Precip. inches	Snowfall, inches		Precip. days
		High	Low		Mean	Max on grnd.	
JAN	Mean	15	-4	0.8	10	32	3
	Rec.	48	-43				
APR	Mean	42	24	1	7	46	4
	Rec.	63	-8				
JUL	Mean	66	44	1	0	0	5
	Rec.	86	29				
OCT	Mean	42	27	5	5	18	10
	Rec.	66	0				
ANN	Mean	42	24	27	94	67	77
	Rec.	86	-43				

Northway

		Temperatures, °F		Precip. inches	Snowfall, inches		Precip. days
		High	Low		Mean	Max on grnd.	
JAN	Mean	-13	-30	0.3	5	52	2
	Rec.	34	-72				
APR	Mean	40	14	0.2	2	30	1
	Rec.	70	-31				
JUL	Mean	69	48	2	0	0	7
	Rec.	88	34				
OCT	Mean	29	21	0.5	6	21	2
	Rec.	58	-36				
ANN	Mean	32	11	10	31	52	38
	Rec.	91	-72				

Nome

		Temperatures, °F		Precip. inches	Snowfall, inches		Precip. days
		High	Low		Mean	Max on grnd.	
JAN	Mean	14	-2	0.9	9	57	4
	Rec.	43	-40				
APR	Mean	26	10	0.7	6	69	3
	Rec.	51	-30				
JUL	Mean	56	44	2	0	0	7
	Rec.	86	31				
OCT	Mean	34	22	1	4	9	5
	Rec.	59	-10				
ANN	Mean	32	18	16	53	74	60
	Rec.	86	-46				

Nunivak Island

		Temperatures, °F		Precip. inches	Snowfall, inches		Precip. days
		High	Low		Mean	Max on grnd.	
JAN	Mean	18	5	0.9	10	31	5
	Rec.	41	-35				
APR	Mean	29	17	0.8	3	48	4
	Rec.	48	-12				
JUL	Mean	54	43	1	0	0	7
	Rec.	76	28				
OCT	Mean	39	30	2	6	10	9
	Rec.	55	9				
ANN	Mean	35	24	15	57	48	75
	Rec.	76	-48				

Petersburg

		Temperatures, °F		Precip. inches	Snowfall, inches			Precip. days
		High	Low		Mean	Max on grnd.		
JAN	Mean	32	22	9	29	61		16
	Rec.	60	-14					
APR	Mean	48	32	7	2	37		16
	Rec.	72	10					
JUL	Mean	64	48	5	0	0		13
	Rec.	84	37					
OCT	Mean	49	38	17	0.9	8		22
	Rec.	72	12					
ANN	Mean	49	35	106	106	83		196
	Rec.	84	-14					

Sitka

		Temperatures, °F		Precip. inches	Snowfall, inches			Precip. days
		High	Low		Mean	Max on grnd.		
JAN	Mean	37	26	8	12	31		15
	Rec.	60	-8					
APR	Mean	48	33	6	3	15		13
	Rec.	79	6					
JUL	Mean	61	48	5	0	0		13
	Rec.	87	38					
OCT	Mean	52	39	15	0.3	5		22
	Rec.	70	16					
ANN	Mean	50	37	95	56	39		183
	Rec.	87	-8					

Port Alsworth

		Temperatures, °F		Precip. inches	Snowfall, inches			Precip. days
		High	Low		Mean	Max on grnd.		
JAN	Mean	22	1	0.8	14	23		3
	Rec.	54	-53					
APR	Mean	42	21	0.7	4	24		3
	Rec.	63	-18					
JUL	Mean	68	44	2	0	0		7
	Rec.	86	25					
OCT	Mean	42	25	2	2	12		6
	Rec.	66	-7					
ANN	Mean	44	22	17	68	24		54
	Rec.	86	-55					

Skagway

		Temperatures, °F		Precip. inches	Snowfall, inches			Precip. days
		High	Low		Mean	Max on grnd.		
JAN	Mean	29	19	3	9	10		8
	Rec.	50	-20					
APR	Mean	49	32	1	2	3		2
	Rec.	76	7					
JUL	Mean	67	49	1	0	0		5
	Rec.	88	35					
OCT	Mean	49	36	5	1	8		6
	Rec.	68	9					
ANN	Mean	49	34	28	36	10		54
	Rec.	92	-24					

Seward

		Temperatures, °F		Precip. inches	Snowfall, inches			Precip. days
		High	Low		Mean	Max on grnd.		
JAN	Mean	29	18	5	16	31		9
	Rec.	51	-10					
APR	Mean	44	31	4	8	37		8
	Rec.	65	-1					
JUL	Mean	63	49	3	0	0		7
	Rec.	85	36					
OCT	Mean	46	34	10	3	15		14
	Rec.	64	8					
ANN	Mean	46	33	66	87	41		117
	Rec.	85	-19					

St. Paul

		Temperatures, °F		Precip. inches	Snowfall, inches			Precip. days
		High	Low		Mean	Max on grnd.		
JAN	Mean	30	22	2	10	25		8
	Rec.	49	-14					
APR	Mean	32	23	1	6	27		6
	Rec.	45	-8					
JUL	Mean	49	42	2	0	0		8
	Rec.	63	28					
OCT	Mean	42	34	3	3	11		11
	Rec.	58	13					
ANN	Mean	38	30	23	56	32		94
	Rec.	63	-19					

Talkeetna

| | | Temperatures, °F | | Precip. inches | Snowfall, inches | | Precip. days |
		High	Low		Mean	Max on grnd.	
JAN	Mean	19	-1	2	19	97	5
	Rec.	45	-48				
APR	Mean	44	22	1	10	76	4
	Rec.	69	-37				
JUL	Mean	69	47	3	0	0	10
	Rec.	90	26				
OCT	Mean	41	24	3	10	19	8
	Rec.	68	-21				
ANN	Mean	44	22	29	115	98	80
	Rec.	91	-53				

Wrangell

| | | Temperatures, °F | | Precip. inches | Snowfall, inches | | Precip. days |
		High	Low		Mean	Max on grnd.	
JAN	Mean	34	23	7	20	38	14
	Rec.	62	-10				
APR	Mean	49	35	5	2	3	14
	Rec.	76	16				*
JUL	Mean	65	49	5	0	0	13
	Rec.	92	32				
OCT	Mean	50	38	13	0.2	3	22
	Rec.	72	18				
ANN	Mean	50	36	82	70	38	182
	Rec.	92	-10				

Wiseman*

| | | Temperatures, °F | | Precip. inches | Snowfall, inches | | Precip. days |
		High	Low		Mean	Max on grnd.	
JAN	Mean	-1	-10	0.6	13	38	7
	Rec.	35	-65				
APR	Mean	33	7	0.4	6	46	6
	Rec.	59	-39				
JUL	Mean	69	46	2	0	0	13
	Rec.	89	31				
OCT	Mean	30	14	1	15	9	7
	Rec.	56	-36				
ANN	Mean	32	12	12	85	48	95
	Rec.	89	-65				

Yakutat

| | | Temperatures, °F | | Precip. inches | Snowfall, inches | | Precip. days |
		High	Low		Mean	Max on grnd.	
JAN	Mean	28	16	9	40	83	14
	Rec.	49	-27				
APR	Mean	43	28	8	20	86	13
	Rec.	68	3				
JUL	Mean	59	47	8	0	0	13
	Rec.	84	35				
OCT	Mean	47	34	20	7	26	22
	Rec.	63	6				
ANN	Mean	45	32	133	225	100	185
	Rec.	86	-24				

*Data collected 1936–52. Records have not been kept since; these are the only figures applicable to the area.

Temperature Conversions, Fahrenheit–Celsius

General formula:
$$(°F - 32)(0.556) = °C$$
$$(°C)(1.8) + 32 = °F$$

°F	°C		°F	°C		°F	°C		°F	°C
100	38		50	10		5	-15		-45	-43
95	35		45	7		0	-18		-50	-46
90	32		40	4		-5	-21		-55	-48
85	29		35	2		-10	-23		-60	-51
80	27		32	0		-15	-26		-65	-54
75	24		30	-1		-20	-29		-70	-57
70	21		25	-4		-25	-32		-75	-59
65	18		20	-7		-30	-34		-80	-62
60	16		15	-9		-35	-37			
55	13		10	-12		-40	-40			

Index

THE MOUNTAINEERS, founded in 1906, is a nonprofit outdoor activity and conservation club, whose mission is "to explore, study, preserve, and enjoy the natural beauty of the outdoors...." Based in Seattle, Washington, the club is now the third-largest such organization in the United States, with 15,000 members and five branches throughout Washington State.

The Mountaineers sponsors both classes and year-round outdoor activities in the Pacific Northwest, which include hiking, mountain climbing, ski-touring, snowshoeing, bicycling, camping, kayaking and canoeing, nature study, sailing, and adventure travel. The club's conservation division supports environmental causes through educational activities, sponsoring legislation, and presenting informational programs. All club activities are led by skilled, experienced volunteers, who are dedicated to promoting safe and responsible enjoyment and preservation of the outdoors.

If you would like to participate in these organized outdoor activities or the club's programs, consider a membership in The Mountaineers. For information and an application, write or call The Mountaineers, Club Headquarters, 300 Third Avenue West, Seattle, Washington 98119; (206) 284-6310.

The Mountaineers Books, an active, nonprofit publishing program of the club, produces guidebooks, instructional texts, historical works, natural history guides, and works on environmental conservation. All books produced by The Mountaineers are aimed at fulfilling the club's mission.

Send or call for our catalog of more than 300 outdoor titles:

 The Mountaineers Books
1001 SW Klickitat Way, Suite 201
Seattle, WA 98134
1-800-553-4453
mbooks@mountaineers.org
www.mountaineersbooks.org

About the Author and Editor

Author Nancy Lange Simmerman arrived in Alaska in 1959 to teach chemistry at the University of Alaska in Fairbanks. She later switched from teaching to freelance photography. She has illustrated and written articles on Alaska and other outdoor subjects, and her photographs have appeared in many national and international books and magazines. For many years she was coauthor of *55 Ways to the Wilderness* (The Mountaineers) and was sole illustrator of *Alaska II* and *Southeast Alaska*, large-format pictorial books. Retired in 1991, she now lives on an island in Washington state.

Editor Tricia Brown has been publishing in the Alaska media for 20 years, during which she's received numerous awards for writing, editing, and photography. A former editor of *Alaska* magazine, she is a full-time freelance author and editor. She has written four books and edited another dozen for various regional publishers.

Other titles you may enjoy from The Mountaineers:

55 Ways to the Wilderness in Southcentral Alaska, Fourth Edition,
Helen Nienhueser & John Wolfe
An updated and revised guide to year-round hiking, skiing, and snowshoeing in southcentral Alaska.

Mount McKinley: Icy Crown of North America, *Fred Beckey*
A selective "biography" of Mount McKinley, by renowned climber and mountain historian Fred Beckey—a classic of mountaineering literature.

Discover Southeast Alaska with Pack & Paddle, Second Edition, *Margaret Piggott*
Fifty-eight hikes from Ketchikan to Skagway, plus a twelve-day paddle trip from Juneau to Angoon.

Glacier Bay National Park: A Backcountry Guide to the Glaciers and Beyond,
Jim DuFresne
The only complete backcountry-use guide to the park via foot or kayak. Includes information on the best times to go, weather, bears, fishing, wilderness camping, and route information.

High Alaska: A Historical Guide to Denali, Mount Foraker & Mount Hunter,
Jonathan Waterman
A blend of mountaineering history and route guide to these three great peaks. Includes approach information, mileage, camping, and more.

Denali's West Buttress: A Climber's Guide to Mt. McKinley's Classic Route,
Colby Coombs
A step-by-step, expert guide to Denali's West Buttress Route.

Surviving Denali: A Study of Accidents on Mt. McKinley 1910-1990,
Second Edition, *Jonathan Waterman*
A thorough analysis of the unfortunate victims of Denali, this book provides both compelling reading and invaluable advice for all climbers.

Alaska's Brooks Range: The Ultimate Mountains, *John Kauffmann*
An in-depth profile of one of the world's last unspoiled wilderness areas.